Y0-CBA-861

TEXAS REAL ESTATE LAW

TEXAS REAL ESTATE LAW

Charles J. Jacobus

Reston Publishing Company, Inc., Reston, Virginia
A Prentice-Hall Company

Library of Congress Cataloging in Publication Data

Jacobus, Charles J.
Texas real estate law.
1. Real property—Texas. 2. Vendors and purchasers—Texas. 3. Real estate business —Law and legislation—Texas. I. Title.
KFT1312.J3 346'.764'043 78-20856
ISBN 0-8359-7569-X

Reston Publishing Company, Inc.
A Prentice-Hall Company
Reston, Virginia 22090

10 9 8 7 6 5 4 3 2 1

Printed in the United States of America

CONTENTS

Preface, ix

1 INTRODUCTION TO THE BASIC PROCESSES OF REAL ESTATE LAW 1

The Role of Real Estate Law, 1; The Various Laws, 2; Historical Background of the Courts, 5; The Current Civil Court Systems, 7; *Summary*, 10.

2 ESTATES IN LAND 13

Freehold Estates, 13; Cemetery Lots, 22; Legal Estates, 23; *Summary*, 30.

3 HOW OWNERSHIP IS HELD 33

Ownership in Severalty, 33; Tenancy in Common, 34; Joint Tenancy, 35; Partnerships, 36; Corporations, 42; Ownership by Trusts, 46; *Summary*, 50.

4 FIXTURES AND EASEMENTS 51

Fixtures, 51; Trade Fixtures, 66; Easements, 66; *Summary*, 72.

5 REAL ESTATE BROKERAGE AND MANAGEMENT 75

The Texas Real Estate Commission and Licensing Requirements, 75; Actions for Commissions, 86; Duties and Obligations of Real Estate Agents, 89; Special Problem Areas, 94; The Deceptive Trade Practices—Consumer Protection Act, 100; *Summary*, 102.

6 CONTRACTS FOR THE SALE OF REAL ESTATE 105

Contracts, Generally, 105; Rules for the Construction of Contracts, 107; Earnest Money Contracts, 110; Installment Land Contracts, 142; *Summary*, 146.

7 CONVEYANCING 147

Deeds, 147; Wills, 170; Involuntary Conveyances, 172; *Summary*, 183.

8 ACKNOWLEDGEMENTS, RECORDING, AND CONSTRUCTIVE NOTICE 185

Recording and Constructive Notice, 185; Acknowledgements, 188; *Summary*, 193.

9 MORTGAGES 195

Instruments, 195; Other Types of Mortgages, 216; Assumptions and Subject To, 219; *Summary*, 223.

10 INTEREST AND FINANCE CHARGE 225

Finance Charge, 225; Interest, 226; *Summary*, 233.

11 METHODS OF TITLE ASSURANCE 235

Evidence of Title, 235; *Summary*, 247.

12 CLOSINGS 249

The Closing Process, 249; Escrows, 250; Documents for the Closing, 252; Parties to a Closing, 254; The Real Estate Settlement Procedures Act, 255; *Summary*, 259.

13 LIENS 261

Equitable Liens, 261; Statutory Liens, 262; Constitutional Liens, 269; Contractual Liens, 269; Redemption, 269; *Summary*, 270.

14 LANDLORD AND TENANT RELATIONSHIPS 271

Tenancies, 271; Statutes, 273; Lease Agreements, 281; Forcible Entry and Detainer, 286; *Summary*, 288.

15 CONDOMINIUMS AND COOPERATIVES 291

Condominiums, 291; Cooperative Housing, 303; *Summary*, 307.

16 GOVERNMENTAL REGULATION OF REAL ESTATE 309

Federal Land Use Control, 310; State Land Use Control, 316; County Regulations; 317; Municipal Land Use Control, 317; Deed Restrictions, 324; *Summary*, 326.

17 REAL ESTATE TAXATION 327

Ad Valorem Taxes, 327; Homestead Old Age Exemption, 333; Federal Income Taxation, 333; *Summary*, 343.

APPENDICES

I Texas Real Estate Licensing Act 345

II Statement of Principles by the State Bar of Texas 361

III Deceptive Trade Practices—Consumer Protection Act 369

Index and Glossary, 395

PREFACE

The primary purpose of any instructional text is to be both easy to understand and authoritative. This is not a simple matter when discussing real estate law. When made simple to understand, concepts often become so nebulous, and so many details and exceptions are overlooked, that an "easy-to-understand" text may tend to be misleading, vague, and subject to overgeneralization. It has been my experience in teaching the basic principles of real estate to find licensed sales people and brokers misconstruing a basic implication of property law because of overbroad statements they have heard or read through "easy-to-understand" instruction.

On the other hand, most people find it too frustrating and time-consuming to search through *Powell on Real Property** to understand the basics of the Texas deed of trust form. It has often been a criticism of attorneys that they are so detail conscious that they "can't see the forest for the trees" and that they tend to hinder a real estate transaction rather than seek to expedite the closing process.

This book is intended to make some headway in bridging the gap between these two extremes. I have made an attempt to cover most pertinent topics in Texas real estate law as it exists today. An in-depth study of dower and curtesy and fee tail estates and the long history of seizin and feoffments have been eliminated to narrow the broker's scope of instruction to more up-to-date applicable problems and solutions. In this same

---

*Richard R. Powell, *Powell on Real Property*, ed. Patrick J. Rohan (New York: Matthew Bender & Company., Inc., 1977). This constantly updated set of books is considered to be one of the most authoritative works on real property law.

vein, the more complex areas of securities law, federal regulations, sophisticated zoning theories, and other more complicated collateral sources of law and their effect on real estate have been omitted to avoid confusion. These areas will be left to the never-ending accumulation of litigation, legislation, and articles published for the benefit of the legal profession.

A special effort has been made, however, to utilize a certain amount of detail in the areas of real estate law that prompt the bulk of questions that occur during the day-to-day operation in the broker's office and that relate to the real estate basics that lawyers will encounter who are engaged in the business of general practice of law in the State of Texas. Legal periodicals, statutes, and cases are used freely in an effort to facilitate the steps toward more entensive research to aid the more advanced student of the law.

Acknowledgments

Special thanks to the following people for their assistance in preparing this book: Harry Baker, Suzanne Baker, Bob Goforth, Don Levi, Judy Wise, Bruce Harwood, A. J. Brune III, Horner Shelton, Keith Chunn, Jr., Kathryn Tyra, Jim Howze, and an extra thanks to Bronson Mann for his help and advice.

CHARLES J. JACOBUS

1

INTRODUCTION TO THE BASIC PROCESSES OF REAL ESTATE LAW

The Role of Real Estate Law

Brokers and lawyers will surely agree on one thing, and that is that the real estate business is becoming more and more complex. The common-law doctrines that have controlled real estate law for centuries are eroding away as a result of innumerable statutes, both at the federal and state level, which often seem to create more problems than they solve. However, this erosion is yielding some benefits in that it requires both brokers and lawyers to become more proficient and more sophisticated in keeping up with these areas of the law, and this could well force both brokers and lawyers to a more conscientious attitude in representing their various clients' interests. It has also drawn much more attention to the fact that real estate is a constantly changing subject and one that is rapidly becoming a field for true professionals.

The real estate laws have become so diversified that one can no longer think of real estate law as only one subject. Real estate law used to basically consist of brokerage negotiation, drawing legal instruments, and establishing and litigating various property rights. Only a few years ago, real estate law was just a small segment of every lawyer's practice. Today real estate involves a much broader scope of law as a result of constantly changing aspects of mortgage law; new developments in usury; changing definitions of "interest"; and modifications in agency theory. There have also been new developments in contract law, securities law, and land use planning law. In addition, there are frequent changes and supplements to landlord and tenant laws, mechanics' and materialmen's liens, and the probate, estate, and community property laws that are unique to this State.

Then to this list, one must add the never ending anathema of federal regulations.

A good example to typify this problem of diversity is a situation that arose as a result of a marketing suggestion from a real estate agent who represented a particular builder. The agent had a good idea of marketing his client's townhouses by selling them as real estate investment ''packages'' to investors across the country. It was a very elaborate scheme, well done, and would have probably been very successful; however, imagine the look on this man's face, very enthusiastic about marketing this real estate (and anticipating his commission money rolling in!), when he was told that such a marketing plan, although involving sale of real estate, violated the Securities and Exchange Acts of 1933 and 1934, and was unquestionably illegal. His particular marketing plan changed the character of these real estate parcels into ''securities,'' as defined by the Securities and Exchange Commission. Such startling discoveries are now becoming quite commonplace in a field where the interaction of various laws can further complicate the transactions of realtors and businessmen.

As we accept this premise, there is yet a deeper problem that is much more intrinsic to the real estate business; that is, a client often has two representatives, his realtor and his attorney. Now, couple this with the fact that there are at least two clients in most transactions (making a total of at least six interested parties—*all* of whom are striving to ''protect'' someone), and the result is that the problems, stories, and third-hand information (and misinformation) contribute mistrust and confusion to what is already the overregulated field of real estate law. This results in realtors versus lawyers, realtors versus realtors, lawyers versus lawyers, clients versus clients, and every other permutation and combination that can logically result from this proverbial ''can of worms.''

The Various Laws

It is interesting to note the various priorities of the laws and how they have come to interact with each other over their years of development. There are two basic sources of statutory law—one state, the other federal. In the area of real estate, state law has generally been considered controlling because of the peculiarities of the backgrounds and doctrines that various states have evolved over the years. However, we are finding in more recent times that the federal government is now taking a vital interest in protecting people from themselves and in passing voluminous amounts of federal legislation to regulate the real estate business.

Constitutions

Our basic sources of law are found in our state and federal constitutions. The U.S. Constitution is the primary source and vests in all citizens of the

United States certain inalienable rights that are considered inviolate and so basic to our system of government that no statute, ordinance, or any contractual right can waive the obligations or privileges therein contained. It is from this document that our individual freedoms and prohibition from abridging these individual freedoms are derived. For instance, discrimination on the grounds of race, color, or creed is considered patently unconstitutional. No statute, contract, or restriction upholding same will ever be enforced. Constitutional rights are, of course, the most important legal rights that one can have, and these rights can only be changed or altered by constitutional amendment.

It must also be remembered that this same Constitution also gives the federal government extraordinary powers of enforcement when it comes to federal laws or federal issues that are considered within the parameters and scope of the Constitution. In the field of real estate, one of the more important areas comes under the interstate commerce clause. For example, Congress is finding more and more ways to regulate *intrastate* real estate activities because of the far-reaching effects these have on other states by virtue of the use of the U.S. mail, telephone, or other means of *interstate* commerce. This will be discussed in greater detail in a later chapter.

Texas also has a constitution, and in this constitution are certain inalienable rights that apply to the citizens of Texas. These rights basically come from the codification and derivation of the heritage of this state and embrace a myriad of subjects, including the Texas homestead laws, certain mechanics' and materialmen's lien laws, and community property rights that exist in this state. One must remember that these rights are constitutional and cannot be waived by private contract or by subsequent statute or ordinance. The individual rights embraced by the Texas Constitution are far-reaching and in much greater detail than those of the U.S. Constitution. However, if there is a conflict between the U.S. Constitution and the Texas Constitution, one can generally consider that the U.S. Constitution would control if the issues involve a federal issue (i.e., an issue over which power has been delegated to the federal government by the Constitution) rather than a substantive state question. If the issues involved are purely state issues and do not involve powers granted to the federal government or rights reserved to individuals, the U.S. Constitution would not be involved because of the Tenth Amendment, which reserves all powers not so granted to the states respectively. If the courts determine that a federal issue exists, the U.S. Constitution would control over the Texas Constitution.

Statutes

The sources of law that affect property rights in greater detail (than what is favored in the federal or state constitutions) are those created by our legislatures, both state and federal, in their infinite wisdom. Of course, a law or a statute can be declared unconstitutional and its enforcement prohibited, which, of course, was what happened to laws on racial discrimination in the South for many years. The conflict between statutes and constitutions is often a very technical and complicated legal problem and need not be delved into at this point. However, it is clearly understood that all statutes have the force of law until declared unconstitutional by the courts. Texas state laws are codified and bound in volumes called *Vernon's Annotated Texas Statutes*, and the federal laws are likewise codified and bound in volumes called *The United States Code* and *The United States Code Annotated*. In case of a conflict between federal and state laws, federal law would control if there was a federal question involved. However, as in constitutional matters, if the issue is a particularly unique state matter of substantive law, the state statute would control, the theory being that under the Tenth Amendment to the U.S. Constitution and the derivation of local laws, the local statute is probably more pertinent to conditions as they exist in that state. In more current times, however, federal statutes seem to be getting more favoritism because of the more liberal interpretation of the federal powers given by the courts.

Ordinances and Regulations

Beyond the statutes at the state level, we generally encounter the various categories of municipal and county ordinances, as well as the rulings and regulations of the various state agencies. Those decisions made by state agencies that have quasi-judicial power (i.e., the agency can make binding decisions pursuant to the scope and powers under which that agency was created) and are generally considered to have the force of law unless there is a clear abuse of discretion on the part of that particular state agency. City and county ordinances must, of course, undergo the same constitutional scrutiny that state statutes are subject to. The local ordinances are inferior to state statutes where there is a conflict in the two laws.

Beyond the statutes at the federal level, one encounters the far more extensive rulings and regulations of federal agencies. The large number of federal regulations are a result of the fact that the federal law is often very broad, often vague, and always confusing. The particular federal agency whose duty it is to enforce the law, therefore, passes its own regulations that serve as guidelines on how that agency is going to interpret and enforce the law passed by the Congress. These regulations can be changed at the whim of the federal regulatory agency. For instance, the Internal Revenue Service can change its position on particular tax exemptions or how it will interpret a certain portion of the Internal Revenue Code. This same type of change in position can occur in all federal agencies, and each federal agency regularly publishes rules and regulations that can even expand that agency's scope of jurisdiction; and a rule or regulation can be issued to clarify a stand that the agency may have taken previously, even though the effect on the taxpayer may be entirely different. These rules and regulations issued by the federal agencies, of course, have the effect of law, subject to review by the courts. It is in this area that the federal government is gaining more and more power, which may or may not have been the purpose of the original congressional acts enacting the legislation.

Judicial Interpretation

Too often the interplay of people's emotions and interpretations of laws results in decisions being made by the final arbiter, the court system. Although sometimes unpredictable, this system is probably the best in the world. It is the basis from which precedents are set and priorities are maintained, and the courts often expose additional questions and interpretations that then become the foundation for new laws and statutes.

Historical Background of the Courts

Courts of Law

Our present court system arose from a centuries old system of an objective third party making a fair and just decision to solve a problem between two litigants. As our structure of the law developed through basic legal principles and doctrines of equity, the written aspects of a transaction were carefully and rigorously adhered to, as being important for an orderly society. Since the principles of law were fairly well settled back in the seventeenth century, when one might consider disorder as being a little more commonplace, this rigorous interpretation of law was probably a logical approach to setting up a civilized and ordered society. As a result, we fell into the situation where, if a man breached his agreement by being a day late for his mortgage payment, the mortgagee thereunder could foreclose, having the agreement strictly upheld in the courts of law. The mortgagor (who under Texas law is generally the purchaser), then, could lose his property because he was a day late in making his mortgage payment, or for some other minor breach of the contract between the parties, even though the circumstances surrounding this breach may have been beyond his control.

Courts of Equity

As our system of justice evolved, however, courts of equity were established to soften the impact of these strict legal principles. These equity courts had particular significance in the area of real estate since real estate is considered unique and money damages could not compensate for its loss. The equity courts had concurrent jurisdiction with the courts of law, which were still in existence, and would impose their jurisdiction when fairness or equity dictated that the rules in some circumstances were too strict, sometimes changing the result. For instance, if a farmer could not make his mortgage payment on the day it was due because of matters beyond his control, the court of equity could impose its jurisdiction to do what was fair and would allow him to redeem by making his payment a day late, a month late, or whatever was "reasonable" to see that equity and justice were done.

The courts of equity impose certain equitable principles. These principles such as "unjust enrichment," "unconscionability," and "irreparable harm," were used as reasons to find an equitable conclusion. They were created and construed ad infinitum (or ad nauseum, depending on your point of view) and resulted in literally hundreds of clichés, often called *equitable maxims* which were ultimately used as precedents to control later decisions. Although having no true legal effect, these maxims could also be used as grounds for the defendant and were easy to roll off the lips, so that silver-tongued orators could constantly remind the court that "he who seeks equity must do equity"; "equity does that which ought to be done"; and the all-time favorite, "he who seeks equity must have clean hands."

It was in these courts that equitable remedies such as specific performance, rescission and restitution, quantum meruit, and quasi-contractual recovery (to name a few) were imposed. These remedies, of course, differ from damages and actions in tort or contract, which arise under the law (and for which the damaged party can get money damages or recovery of his property). *Specific performance*, for instance, is generally granted where damages are not shown to be an adequate and just remedy, and can only be enforced when there is not an adequate remedy at law. *Rescission and restitution* generally arise when the breach of the contract constitutes a failure of the consideration bargained for and the nonbreaching party prefers to rescind the contract and sue for complete restitution of whatever benefits have accrued to date. *Rescission* is, of course, the voiding of the contract or agreement. *Restitution* is the restoration of the parties' original rights. In this particular equitable remedy, the parties are put back in the same condition that they were in prior to execution of the contract. *Quasi-contractual* principles generally arise when there has been something material omitted in the original contract and the court imposes its own contractual principles as if these had been bargained for and written in the contract itself. This is also the principle behind *quantum meruit*, where one party performs his part of the obligation and the breaching party refuses to pay (or perform). In this situation, the court can impose quasi-contractual remedies in order that the party performing the duties be paid the reasonable value of the performance rendered. It is interesting to note that these remedies, which are not by any means all of the equitable remedies available, are not conferred by statute or by any other type of codified jurisprudential consideration. They are remedies that have evolved over the years through the courts seeking fair and just results.

The Current Civil Court Systems

The Texas court system as it exists today, as well as the federal court system, has both legal and equitable jurisdiction merged into the same court. The distinction between the state courts, although their legal and equitable jurisdictions are similar, is not quite so simple. The jurisdictions of these courts are statutory and are maintained separate and distinct for the purposes of expediting the judicial process and facilitating access to the court system. To help simplify this explanation, we will discuss only the civil (and not the criminal) court systems. These civil court systems, for the purposes of this discussion, will be divided into two distinct and separate systems. The first is the state court system, which, in order of ascending importance, includes the justice of the peace courts and municipal courts, county courts, district courts, courts of civil appeals, and the Supreme Court of the State of Texas. The second system is the federal system, which, in order of ascending importance, includes the federal district courts, circuit courts of appeals, and the Supreme Court of the United States.

State Courts

The justice of the peace courts, small claims courts, and municipal courts have original jurisdiction for the first judicial proceeding for claims under $200; and, more important to real estate law, the justice of the peace courts have original jurisdiction in causes of action for forcible entry and detainer actions (eviction proceedings). A losing party in the lower courts can appeal his cause of action to the county court if the judgment is in excess of $20, or in other cases as provided for by statute. The county courts have no particular jurisdiction as it pertains to real estate except that of appellate jurisdiction for forcible entry and detainer cases (and probate in the less populous counties). The state district courts are probably the more important courts in the area of real estate law. The district courts by statute have original jurisdiction in civil cases of suits for the trials of title to land and for the enforcement of liens thereon, and suits for the trial of right to property levied on by virtue of any writ of execution, sequestration, or attachment. Decisions made in these courts, subject to statutory regulation for appeals, are appealed to the civil appeals courts and the Texas Supreme Court. The significance of the appellate process will be discussed later.

Federal Courts

The federal court system differs primarily in jurisdiction. Its jurisdiction basically depends either on a conflict of jurisdiction between individuals or states and an amount in excess of $10,000 in controversy, or on a question of controversy over federal law. These cases can be appealed only to one of the circuit courts of appeals (there are currently eleven). Texas is in the jurisdiction of the Fifth Circuit Court of Appeals, located in New Orleans, Louisiana. Beyond the Fifth Circuit the only avenue of appeal is to the Supreme Court of the United States. This is, of course, the highest court to which any case can be appealed.

Court Procedure

Cases can bounce from the state system to the federal system and sometimes back, depending on jurisdictional problems, amounts in controversy, and what is termed *federal questions*. It is at this point that you may very often find the demarcation between an attorney who deals primarily in real estate law and those who deal primarily in trial work. An attorney may have a particular expertise in the area of real estate law but may want a "trial attorney" or an attorney who specializes in trial work, whether it is in federal jurisdictions or state jurisdictions, to handle the case because of the technicalities involved in trial and appellate procedure. In this age of specialization for attorneys, it can be expected that there will be an increase in specialization in the field of real estate law or trial work of this type.

Interesting points about the trial procedure itself can give you some insight as to why these complexities exist, and why the details of the law are often elusive to an individual reading the statutes, a text, or reported case law. First, there are two deciding bodies, the judge and the jury. In state courts, judges are elected to their positions, must be members of the bar in courts above the justice of the peace level, and are paid a salary according to state statute. In federal courts, the judges are appointed by the president of the United States, with advice and consent of the Senate, and must pass very strict scrutiny prior to their appointment. The judge's role in the trial proceedings is to interpret the law. The jury's role is to decide the facts. There is no set rule as to when you can or cannot have a jury. The presence of a jury depends on the request of either of the parties involved.

The trial process works by putting the burden on the plaintiff (the party filing the suit) of going forward with the evidence. After the plaintiff's attorney presents his case, the defendant's attorney gets a chance to respond and put on the defendant's case; and after the defense has rested, there may be further examination of witnesses by either attorney. After the case is presented and arguments are given, the judge may render a decision. If there is a jury, the judge gives "charges" to the jury. These charges are generally prepared by the counsel for both sides under the direction of the judge. The charges that the judge reads are directions to the jury and explanations of what the Texas law is concerning the particular matter in controversy. It is the jury's job, then, to take the law and the facts as presented, and to render a decision as to which party should prevail. It puts the burden on the jury to determine which of the witnesses was telling the truth, which of the witnesses may have been stretching the truth a bit, and, ultimately, what the facts actually were. If the jury comes back with a verdict for a party that is contrary to law, then the judge can overrule the jury and enter his own ruling.

Beyond the trial stage, the only question is whether or not there is a point of law in controversy. Since the jury has decided the facts, only points of law can be appealed to the appellate court. An appeal is made only to settle a question of law or incorrect ruling that a trial court may have made. There is no jury present beyond the trial court level. The appeal might be based on a rule of evidence, procedure, substantive law, jury charge, or other more technical legal point.

The process of appeals can be a relatively complicated process in regard to exactly what it takes to appeal to which court. In the state court system, there are proceedings in which you can appeal certain matters directly to the Texas Supreme Court, but most appeals go to the courts of civil appeals first. There are other rules for appeals from the courts of civil appeals to the Texas Supreme Court. The federal courts have similar, but not the same, rules. It is not pertinent to our discussion to go into detail over these matters, but it should be emphasized that the appellate process and the infinite amount of detail that arises during litigation make any litigation very complicated and difficult to predict. It has been said that when a case goes to court, no one wins. Considering the attorneys' fees that are paid, the emotions that are dealt with, and the time consumption and overloaded dockets that litigation promotes, the amount in controversy generally has to be fairly high before litigation is worthwhile.

Keeping in mind the foregoing basic substantive and procedural aspects of the law, one can appreciate the complexities that may arise in any given legal situation, particularly if any litigation should take place. It should also be kept in mind that the impact of the law is often flexible, and most rules of law are general rules, subject to exceptions and equitable interpretation. These are the major reasons why, when asking your attorney a question, it is so difficult to get a simple answer in response. All of these alternatives, both procedural and substantive, must stay ever-present in the practitioner's "areas of concern" so that he can competently represent and advise his client.

Legal Research

One might wonder how the details of all the foregoing information become available to the attorney. It is basically through the efforts of his research in a law library. Unlike any other type of library, a law library has an almost never-ending supply of legal treatises, articles, statutes, opinions, and case law reports. Every case above the district court level in the United States is written and bound in volumes called *Reporters*, which, along with statutes, digests, and current treatises, must constantly be updated.

Texas cases are reported in the *Southwestern Reporter*. Each volume is given a separate number as it is bound (more recent cases are reported in paperback volumes). Therefore, when searching for a case, one may find it cited:

Case v. *Case*, 376 S.W.2d 941 (Tex. Civ. App.—Waco, 1936),

if it is a Texas civil appeals court decision, or

Case v. *Case*, 376 S.W.2d 941 (Tex. 1936),

if it is a Texas Supreme Court decision. Each of the foregoing examples indicates that the case is found in volume 376, page 941, of the *Southwestern Reporter*, second series. The material in parentheses refers to the court and years of decision. Statutes are normally cited as:

Tex. Rev. Civ. Stat. Ann., art. 6573a

which indicates that the statute is located in the Texas civil statutes, Article 6573a. The statutes are updated with "pocket parts" located in the back of each volume.

As the student reads the following chapters, he will find a number of citations as authority for a particular point of law. These are not intended to dazzle or baffle the reader but only to give him additional sources of information for more in-depth study.

After this cursory introduction, one will find the following chapters are in much greater detail, and concern the more substantive aspects of real property law. For the layman, it is important to recognize these problem areas and understand them as such, always keeping in mind that he should try to avoid them at all costs. Any advice, litigation, or negotiation of a client's rights should be left for the attorneys who are trained to handle such problems. It is the attorney's job to relieve real estate agents and other laypersons from shouldering this type of burden.

SUMMARY

Real estate is rapidly becoming a field for true professionals. Similarly, real estate law is becoming more and more specialized.

There are two sources of law: federal and state. Both sources have constitutional foundations. The source of law that affects property rights in greater detail is the statutes which are created by the state and federal legislatures. The city ordinances and federal regulations may apply the respective laws in even greater detail.

The modern court system is a blend of courts of law and equity. The state civil court system consists of justice of the peace courts, county courts, district courts, courts of civil appeals, and the Texas Supreme Court. The federal court system consists of the federal district court, the circuit courts of appeals, and the United States Supreme Court. Jurisdiction of the various courts can change in any given case. The rules and procedures regarding jurisdiction are defined by the various statutes and consist of substantive as well as procedural laws concerning jurisdiction, trial, and appellate procedure. Basically, the jury decides all questions of facts, while the court (the judge) decides questions of law.

2

ESTATES IN LAND

An *estate in land* has been defined as the degree, quality, nature, and extent of interest that a person has in real property. The estates in land that will be discussed in this chapter are *freehold estates* and *legal estates*. *Freehold estates* are estates that manifest some title to real property. They include estates in fee simple, life estates, fee on conditional limitations, fee on condition subsequent, and fee on condition precedent. The laterally severed estates of mineral rights and air rights will also be discussed as freehold estates. The title to freehold estates is created in the deed itself and is not to be confused with, and should be distinguished from, legal estates. *Legal estates* are created by statute and vest in the person rather than in the land itself. These legal estates will be discussed later in the chapter and consist of homestead rights and community property rights.

Not discussed under this topic will be leasehold estates (i.e., estates in which one has leasehold or tenant rights rather than legal title). Leasehold estates will be discussed in depth in Chapter 14, Landlord and Tenant Relationships.

Freehold Estates

As an introduction into the concept of freehold estates in land, there are two basic theories that need to be explained to help establish guidelines for further discussion.

Rule against Perpetuities

The first basic restriction on ownership of real property is provided for in the Texas Constitution under Article I, Section 26, and is commonly called the *Rule against Perpetuities*. This provision, quite simply set out in the constitution, reads as follows:

> **§ 26. Perpetuities and monopolies; primogeniture or entailments**
>
> Sec. 26. Perpetuities and monopolies are contrary to the genius of a free government, and shall never be allowed, nor shall the law of primogeniture or entailments ever be in force in this State.

The reasoning behind the Rule against Perpetuities is the idea that land, by its nature, is unique, and cannot be held forever by any one interest. This theory has not always been accepted. For example, there is an opposing theory in common law whereby a person could be the grantee of certain property, along with the "heirs of his body." This would enable the property to literally stay in a man's family until his bodily descendants failed. During this time in history, *primogeniture* (the right of the first male child to become legal title holder to the property upon death of the father) and *entailments* (only heirs of the individual's body could get fee title to the property) were the common practice for real proper owner, and wealthy families could effectively monopolize real estate holdings. This is not the case today. According to Article I, Section 26 of the state constitution, such conditions simply cannot exist in this state because they are "contrary to the genius of a free government." The Rule against Perpetuities, then, encourages the free transferability and conveyance of property and prohibits the monopolizing and perpetual control of certain real estate interests. It is important to remember that as we discuss real estate in Texas, this constitutional doctrine underlies all theories of ownership of real property, whether it deals with estates in land or ownership control. There have been subsequent statutes passed that further reinforce this constitutional provision, and it continues to be one of the basic underlying theories in Texas real estate law.

Title Theory versus Lien Theory

A second basic theory in Texas is that once title is conveyed, the grantee (subsequent owner) gets a true legal title. In some states it is felt that if the grantee's property is mortgaged, the owner has only an equitable title, and the lender (mortgagee) has true legal title. In those states, the borrower (mortgagor), or owner, only has a lien on the property until the mortgage is paid in full. In Texas, the theory is reversed. The homeowner, although his home is not fully paid for, has legal title to the property, and it is the lender that has a lien on the property. Therefore, Texas is called a *lien theory* state. Those states that recognize the mortgagee as legal title holder to the property are called *title theory* states.

Since Texas is a lien theory state, the owner of the property has full *legal title* to the property. Those who have any interest in the property, one that is subordinate or inferior to the owner's full legal title of the property, have what is commonly referred to as an *equity interest* or *equitable title* to that property. Those who have an equity interest in the property (there could be quite a large number) will therefore have certain rights under equitable principles in addition to whatever perfected rights they might have in law to try to enforce their rights in that property.

Types of Freehold Estates

With the foregoing fundamentals in mind, the topic of freehold estates will be somewhat easier to understand. We will explore virtually every type of freehold estate recognized in this state to give some insight into how complicated legal titles and equity interests can become.

Fee Simple Estates

A fee simple estate is one entitling the owner to:

1. The entire property;
2. With unconditional powers of disposition during his life; and
3. Title that descends to heirs and legal representatives on his death; and
4. Includes both legal and equitable title, *Field* v. *Rules*, 204 S.W.2d 1 (Tex. Civ. App.—El Paso, 1947).

This is the type of estate that most people consider when they think of a clear, unencumbered title. The four criteria referred to above indicate virtually everything that makes a title "good" for the landowner. The vast majority of real estate conveyed in this state is conveyed with fee simple title. Statutorily, an estate in fee simple in Texas is presumed unless otherwise specified in the conveyancing instrument itself.

It is important to remember that a fee simple title can be encumbered, however, in that there could be other equitable or legal interests as exceptions or reservations to the title. Although encumbered, the estate being conveyed would still be termed a fee simple estate because it had the four criteria set out above. Easements, liens, and other encumbrances on real estate do not mean that the quality of the estate one gets is less than fee simple, but they do limit the owner's use of that estate. Specific encumbrances will be discussed in detail in later chapters.

Life Estates

Estates that are less than fee simple limit the grantee's title and rights to varying degrees. A *life estate* is an estate for the life of some person, along with a second estate that is termed a *remainder interest*. The property is generally conveyed to a grantee for the term of his life, creating the life estate for the grantee's life. The remainder interest, which entitles the remainderman to possession of the property at a future date is another separate estate that takes effect in the remainderman upon the grantee's death, *Collins* v. *New*, 558 S.W.2d 108 (Tex. Civ. App.—Corpus Christi, 1977). For instance, I convey my house to my brother for his life; then upon his death it would pass to my wife (if so specified in the deed). This type of an estate creates a life estate in my brother and a remainder interest in my wife. Thus it becomes clear that there are two estates: one is the life estate, the other is the remainder interest.

No particular form of words is necessary to create a life estate. It is created by a deed or a will where the grantor manifests an intention to convey to some person the right to possess, use, or enjoy the property during the period of some person's life. It is important to understand that you can also convey the life estate interest to somebody for the life of somebody else. Life estates for the life of another person are called life estates *pur autre vie*. For instance, I could convey the life estate to my brother for the life of my great-great-grandfather. The life estate then would pass upon the death of my great-great-grandfather, and the remainder interest would go on to my wife. The life estate may be conveyed separate and apart from the remainder interest. When a life estate is conveyed, whoever purchases and takes possession of the estate under those rights does so subject to the life of the life estate grantee and the rights of the remainder interest. The interest of the life estate holder may be worth a very small amount of money, and the remainder interest may be worth a large amount of money, or vice versa. Remember that in this situation, the life estate holder has a limited legal and equitable interest, subject to the rights of the holder of the remainder interest.

As you might imagine, rights involved in a life estate situation can be fairly complicated. As discussed previously, there are basically two estates involved: one in the life tenant; the other in the remainderman (often called a *future* interest). Neither party may encumber the property if it results in waste, deterioration, or alienation of the other's rights. For instance, the life tenant, although he or she may have the right to possession of the property for his or her life, cannot unreasonably encumber, waste, or allow the property to deteriorate during his or her occupancy if it adversely affects the right of the person holding the remainder interest. The remainderman (the owner of the future interest) likewise cannot do anything that would affect the rights of the life tenant. Since the remainderman is a nonoccupant and a nontenant he has less opportunity to create waste and deterioration in the property. However, both parties have the right to hypothecate, encumber, or convey their particular interests in the real estate as long as this does not result in waste, deterioration, or alienation of any of the other's interest.

To further complicate matters, remainder interests can be of two types: (1) a vested remainder, or (2) a contingent remainder. A *vested remainder* exists if, at any moment during the continuance of the previous estate (in this case, the life estate), the remainderman is ready to come into possession whenever that life estate terminates. For instance, a vested remainder would exist if I conveyed a life estate on property. A *contingent remainder*, on the other hand, requires some sort of fulfillment of a condition before it may vest. An example of a contingent remainder interest would be a life estate to my brother with a remainder interest to go to my wife upon his death, if she is not married at that time. If she is married at that time, the future interest would not vest in her upon my brother's death, but would create a *reversionary interest* that would go to my legal heirs or to another party whose remainder interest may not be contingent. In the life estate, however, the grantor generally keeps no reversionary interest. In the common-law state, there is often a careful discrimination between a contingent remainder and what is termed a *shifting executory use* in the future interest. Texas case law appears to consider the terms basically the same.

Table 2-1 may be helpful in identifying the possible estates that may be created in freehold estates other than fee simple, as well as serving as an introduction for the following explanations on other types of estates.

TABLE 2-1

Reversionary Interest	*Current Estate*	*Future Interest*
None	Life estate	Remainderman (vested or contingent remainder)
Automatic	Fee on conditional limitation	Contingent remainder "so long as" "until" "during"
Right of reentry	Fee on condition subsequent	Contingent remainder "on the condition that" "provided however" "if"
None	Possible possession	Fee on condition precedent (ripens to fee simple)

Fee on Conditional Limitation

A *fee on conditional limitation* exists where the estate is limited to the happening of a certain event, and when such event happens, the estate is terminated and reverts back to the grantor by what is called an *eo instanti* reversion; that is, the estate automatically goes back to the grantor. This estate is also referred to as a *determinable fee*, or *fee simple defeasible*.

An example of this type of estate would be one where the estate is created by the use of a deed saying that the property will be conveyed to the grantee "so long as" intoxicating beverages are never served on the premises. Deeds creating a fee on conditional limitation generally use the words "so long as," "until," or "during," which intend to limit the type of estate that is going to be created. Upon the happening of that certain stated event, the estate automatically transfers, by operation of law, to either the grantor, by reversion, or to some third party, by executory remainder. The important thing to remember in this type of estate is that the estate is transferred *automatically* upon the happening of that certain stated conditional event.

Fee on Condition Subsequent

A *fee on condition subsequent* is very similar to a fee on conditional limitation. In fact, these two estates are so similar that there have been many judicial opinions that evidence some confusion as to what is the actual difference between the two types of estates. However, authorities generally seem to agree that the basic distinction between a fee on condition subsequent and a fee on conditional limitation lies in the fact that the fee on conditional limitation has an *automatic* reversion upon the happening of that event, but the fee on condition subsequent gives the grantor the *right* to terminate the estate by reversion, rather than the automatic reversion provided for by the fee on conditional limitation, *Field* v. *Shaw*, 535 S.W.2d 3 (Tex. Civ. App.—Amarillo, 1976). This right of reversion of the fee on condition subsequent is properly called the *right of reentry*.

An example of this type of conveyance would be one with the use of a deed that would convey the property to the grantee "on the condition that" or "provide however," or "if" the property would never be used for the sale or service of alcohol or intoxicating beverages. This type of language used in the fee on condition subsequent implies that the grantor, his heirs, or assigns would have the right to reenter the property and take it back. However, they can only get title back if they take the initiative to reenter the property within a reasonable time. It is not an automatic reversion.

Fee On Condition Precedent

A *fee on condition precedent* is a title passed by a deed such that the title will not take effect in the named grantee until a condition is performed. For instance, a conveyance may be made to a grantee with the condition being that full fee title will not vest until the grantee has built a house on the property within two years from the date of the conveyance. This would indicate a fee on condition precedent. In this case, the grantee gets a conditional title that will only be fully vested upon the construction of the home as provided for in the deed. This specifically applies when there is no other consideration shown in the deed, or no other value has changed hands except this particular condition. One generally finds this type of title when the grantor is attempting to increase the value of his property by encouraging development of the adjacent property. Using this time limitation, the grantor forces the purchaser to build something on the adjacent property to enhance the value of his own property. This type of conveyance is also often used by developers to encourage home building in a subdivision. Texas does not favor the fee-on-condition precedent. Where other conditions have to be performed or have been performed, especially when a full value has been paid, the fee on condition precedent is generally considered by courts to be a fee on condition subsequent. In the more accepted common-law usage, this type of estate is referred to as a *springing executory use*. The case law in Texas, however, does not utilize this term very freely.

Mineral Estates

Mineral interests, of course, have been a primary concern for a state like Texas where the subsurface rights have proved to be of enormous value. Subsurface rights are, by all means, a freehold estate and an interest in land; and the owner of a fee title may separate his estate on the surface from the minerals underneath and sell one type of estate (the subsurface) while reserving the other (the surface) for his own use and benefit.

Lateral Severance

It is important to understand that estates in land are generally considered to go to the center of the earth. Therefore, a separation of the mineral estate results in a *lateral severance* (separation) of the surface estate from the mineral estate. The grantor will own the surface estate, whereas a grantee of the mineral interest will own or lease the subsurface estate. Lateral severance generally provides that the grantee or lessee of the mineral estate may acquire rights to drill for oil and gas or mine certain minerals on the grantor's property, but that the grantor still owns the surface estate, subject to the rights of the mineral owner.

An interesting legal precedent has created some recent conflict in determining whether or not there is a lateral severance. In confirming a prior Texas Supreme Court case, the Texas Supreme Court in *Reed* v.

Wylie, 554 S.W.2d 169 (Tex. 1977) upheld the Texas rule that "a grant or reservation of 'minerals' or 'mineral rights' *should not be construed to include a substance that must be removed by methods that will, in effect, consume or deplete the surface estate*." The court further stated that a substance is not a mineral if substantial quantities of that substance lie so near the surface that the production will entail the stripping away and substantial destruction of the surface. This ruling has extreme importance in strip-mining coal, iron ore, and other substances that may have been presumed to be passed along with the mineral estate. If these substances are so near the surface that extraction depletes the land surface, there is no lateral severance, and the substances belong to the surface estate.

This decision, along with the controlling case, *Acker* v. *Guinn*, 464 S.W.2d 348 (Tex. 1971), probably present fact questions that will be litigated for some time to come, depending on whether the substance is mined from below the surface or strip-mined from above the land surface.

Dominant Estates

The concept of lateral severance creates a conflict of estates—between the surface owner's right to use the surface and the mineral owner's rights to enter upon that surface to extract the minerals. Under Texas law, the mineral owner has what is termed the *dominant estate*. This means that he has the right to use the surface, reasonably, to exercise his rights to extract the minerals from the subsurface, *Humble Oil and Refining Co.* v. *Williams*, 420 S.W.2d 133 (Tex. 1967). Any subsequent purchaser of the surface rights of the property would get a fee title to that property, subject to the rights of the mineral owner. This may seem at first to be a disadvantage to the surface owner. However, practically speaking, the surface owner often leases the subsurface and will receive benefit from the mining of those minerals in terms of percentage payments of the production of these minerals (called "royalties"), and perhaps even a cash "bonus" payment, in addition to the lease payments for allowing the mineral owner to mine the subsurface minerals.

In the event the surface owner does not wish to have the mineral owner on his property mining or extracting the minerals, he may reserve the sole rights to the surface estate, which may force the mineral estate owner to enter upon some adjacent property to extract the minerals through various underground drilling and excavation methods.

There has been a recent case law that indicates that this concept of the dominant estate has been eroded somewhat and must be exercised reasonably, *Getty Oil Company* v. *Jones*, 470 S.W.2d 618 (Tex. 1971). However, this case law has not yet been expanded so as to severely curtail the long-standing superior rights of the mineral owner (the dominant estate).

Realty versus Personalty

An interesting and recently litigated area of mineral estates has involved the concept of *personalty* versus *realty*. In the ownership of mineral estates, it is easy to understand that all the oil, gas, and other minerals that may be in a mineral estate are, of course, considered to be real property. Once those minerals are extracted, or the oil and gas reach the wellhead, the oil, gas, and other minerals are considered personalty rather than real property. Recently, developments that further complicate this concept have arisen from the use of underground storage of oil and gas in salt domes along the Gulf Coast area. These domes, being large underground caverns, have proved to be an effective method of storing large amounts of oil and gas beneath the surface for future use. The Texas Supreme Court has made it clear that it considers the minerals that are put *back* into the subsurface remain personalty rather than reverting back to real estate, *Humble Oil and Refining Company* v. *West*, 508 S.W.2d 812 (Tex. 1974).

Beyond the lateral severance and surface rights concepts, one steps into a deep chasm of very technical and heavily litigated oil and gas law. For the purposes of real estate law, it is most important to understand that if one acquires any property that does not include the subsurface estate and use of the surface estate has not been reserved, the owner of the surface estate may, at some future date, be surprised to find an oil company moving in its drilling equipment. This would obviously alter the rights of the person using the surface estate.

Air Rights

There is another area of lateral severance, one that involves the ownership of *air rights*. Although the concept of air rights is self-explanatory to some extent, air rights tend to be nebulous and difficult to describe. Generally, however, the concept of air rights means that the surface owner has control over his own air rights, subject to certain limitations.

The initial question of air rights came from owners of property who were adjacent to airports. It was understood that between the two private property owners (the privately owned airport and the privately owned property abutting that airport) there had to be a conflict of rights over the noise, pollution, and litter that accompanied the airplanes taking off and landing, conditions that adversely affected the adjacent property owners. This type of law found its origin in the law of nuisance, where one property owner would sue the other property owner because of the nuisance value and discomfort caused by the other property owner.

In more current times, and with municipal ownership of airports, we have found that there is a more severe problem between the concepts of private ownership versus the public welfare. In the airport situation, we find that for the good of the public there are certain ordinances that are passed prohibiting the building of structures adjacent to an airport because of both the danger to air traffic and the discomfort of the people adjacent to the airport. The municipality generally exercises its power of eminent domain to acquire adjacent property or to restrict use of the adjacent property to uses that would be nondetrimental to the public airport purposes.

Overhead Structures

Other air right concepts have involved the construction of overhead walkways, office buildings, and similar structures across streets. Such structures may create pollution hazards, carbon monoxide build-up, and other unhealthy conditions if the structure is not built properly. In these cases, of course, we have the conflict of the private ownership of the building versus the public welfare of people who have to live adjacent to or pass through the type of environment this building might create.

Solar Rights

Another concept of air rights is the right of adjacent property owners to the sun. Although this has been a very old concept, one that generally was predicated on creating "tunnels" in downtown areas, a new type of legal problem could arise because of the use of solar energy.

Cemetery Lots

One of the more unique types of estates in Texas is a cemetery lot. Since 1945 Texas state law requires that all cemeteries have a perpetual care fund for the administration and maintenance of the cemetery. The cemetery association responsible for the perpetual care has the authority to sell and convey the "exclusive right to sepulture" in the burial plots to prospective purchasers. These sales are specifically exempt from the Real Estate Licensing Act, and all of the plots are, of course, indivisible, except with the consent of the cemetery association or as provided for by law. All burial space in which the exclusive right to sepulture has been conveyed is presumed to be the separate property of the person named as grantee rather than community property. The spouse has a vested right of interment in any burial plot in which the exclusive right of sepulture has been conveyed to the other spouse.

State statutes are very specific as to how cemeteries are to be administered, how perpetual care funds are to be invested, how records are to be kept, locations of cemeteries, removals from said cemeteries, and almost every other conceivable area of property or business concerns applicable to cemeteries. After interment, the cemetery association, along with certain specified relatives, is given the power to remove any remains of the deceased person located in the cemetery.

Legal Estates

As stated previously, legal estates are estates that have been created by statute that affect the nature of degree, quality and an individual's interest in his real estate. These are not estates that attach to the real property but deal with the rights of the individuals as a result of their ownership of that real property. These legal estates exist concurrently with the states already discussed. The particular legal estates to be considered are homesteads and community property interests. Homestead rights and community property rights are vested by both constitutional and statutory laws in Texas.

Homesteads

The *homestead* in Texas is a place of residence for a family or a single adult person; it provides a secure asylum of which the family cannot be deprived. The homestead laws accomplish this protection by providing certain exemptions for the Texas homeowner against his creditors. Since a homestead is a legal estate, and not an estate in land per se, it may not be assigned or conveyed in such a manner as to vest the homestead rights in someone else. The Texas homestead laws have been so consistently upheld and liberally construed that it is important to understand some of the history behind these homestead laws before any further discussion.

History. The earliest homestead exemption law was passed as a statute on January 26, 1839. It had three basic purposes:

1. To preserve the integrity of the family as a basic element of social organization and to encourage colonization;
2. To provide the debtor with a home for his family and some means of support and to recoup economic losses so that the family would not become a burden upon the public; and
3. To retain and pioneer the feeling of freedom and a sense of independence deemed necessary to the continued existence of democratic institutions.

As a statute, the homestead exemption was subject to change by the legislature, which is not the most predictable group of lawmakers. This made the security provided by the homestead law somewhat questionable. Therefore, the homestead exemption laws first become constitutionally incorporated in 1845 to put them beyond the reach of the state legislators. Therefore, in order to change any of the homestead laws, it is now a requirement that this be done by amendment to the Texas Constitution which requires a vote of the people of the state. The legislature, by its own acts, cannot repeal, change, or modify the Texas homestead law except by passing statutes in furtherance of the basic purposes as set forth in the Texas Constitution.

To reflect on Chapter 1 of this text, it is important to remember that constitutional rights cannot be waived by mere contractual interest or by an intent of the parties. As constitutional rights, the homestead exemption is an exemption that vests in every single homeowner regardless of whatever he may have signed or agreed to after those homestead rights have been properly vested.

Criteria. Article 16, Section 50, of the Texas Constitution sets out the nature of the exemption as protection from forced sales and is set forth below:

> **§ 50. Homestead; protection from forced sale; mortgages, trust deeds and liens**
> Sec. 50. The homestead of a family shall be, and is hereby protected from forced sale, for the payment of all debts except for the purchase money thereof, or a part of such purchase money, the taxes due thereon, or for work and material used in constructing improvements thereon, and in this last case only when the work and material are contracted for in writing, with the consent of the wife given in the same manner as is required in making a sale and conveyance of the homestead; nor shall the owner, if a married man, sell the homestead without the consent of the wife, given in such manner as may be prescribed by law. No mortgage, trust deed, or other lien on the homestead shall ever be valid, except for the purchase money therefor, or improvements made thereon, as hereinbefore provided, whether such mortgage, or trust deed, or other lien, shall have been created by the husband alone, or together with his wife; and all pretended sales of the homestead involving any condition of defeasance shall be void.

Therefore, stated simply, this provision of the Texas homestead law protects the homeowner from forced sale for payment of all debts except: (1) purchase money or part thereof, (2) taxes due on the homestead (which include ad valorem taxes and all federal taxes), and (3) liens for work and material used in constructing improvements on the homestead property, *if* these liens are properly:

1. Contracted for in writing, and
2. The consent of both spouses is obtained in the same manner as is required in making the sale or conveyance of the homestead.

Clearly, neither spouse may sell or abandon the homestead without the consent of the other spouse given in such manner as may be prescribed by law. The constitutional provision also states that no encumbrance other than those provided for shall enable a forced sale of the homestead. Even the proceeds from the sale are exempt from creditors for six months after the sale of the homestead, *Simmons and Newsome Co.* v. *Malin*, 196 S.W. 281 (Tex. Civ. App.).

Once a homestead exemption has been vested in a homeowner's real property, it provides for total exemption from forced sale of the homestead. For instance, a man owning his homestead could incur $4 million in debt (even in bad faith) and default on said $4 million debt. Under the constitutional provision, his creditors could not force this man to sell his house in order to satisfy his indebtedness. This applies even if his house is owned in fee, with no encumbrances, and may be worth a substantial amount of money.

However, as you may expect, there are limitations as to exactly what can be declared as one's homestead. Article 16, Section 51, of the Texas Constitution provides for the amount and value to which a homestead exemption may apply. This provision in its entirety is set out as follows:

> **§51. Amount and value of homestead; uses**
>
> Sec. 51. The homestead, not in a town or city, shall consist of not more than two hundred acres of land, which may be in one or more parcels, with the improvements thereon; the homestead in a city, town or village, shall consist of lot, or lots, not to exceed in value Ten Thousand Dollars, at the time of their designation as the homestead, without reference to the value of any improvements thereon; provided, that the same shall be used for the purposes of a home, or as a place to exercise the calling or business of the homestead claimant, whether a single adult person, or the head of a family; provided also, that any temporary renting of the homestead shall not change the character of the same, when no other homestead has been acquired. This amendment shall become effective upon its adoption.

The provision can be most succinctly explained by defining the homestead in terms of rural and urban homestead. A *rural homestead* cannot be greater than 200 acres and must include the portion of acreage with the claimant's home on it. If the tract of land contains more than 200 acres, the owner has the option of designating which 200 acres (as long as it includes the home) constitutes the homestead. It may include more than one parcel as long as these parcels are reasonably contiguous. There has been no dollar limit put on the rural homestead. Therefore, it could reasonably be the 200 acres with the house *and* the oil well, as long as the one or more parcels are reasonably contiguous and, when combined, contain less than 200 acres. However, it must be remembered that the minerals as they reach the wellhead are personalty and are possibly subject to forced sale as

personal property, not constituting a part of the real property f
exemption.

In contrast, the *urban homestead* consists of a lot or lots w
is not greater than $10,000 *at the time of its designation* a
reference to the value of the improvements. If the homestead
nated prior to November 3, 1970, the value of the lot cann
$5,000. In addition, in the urban homestead situation, there can
business and a residence, although these may be located on sep
which can be taken together to constitute only one homestead.

Another interesting point provided for in this constitutional p
is that the homestead may be rental property. This applies to ten
may occupy said rental property as well as to homeowners w
sequently may buy a new home but keep their old home as rental p
The subject of termination of homestead rights will be discussed
this chapter.

Lots in Excess of Exemption. The next question that comes to mi
value of the low exemption provided by this constitutional provision
are a large number of homes with lots obviously costing mo
$10,000. Did these purchasers lose their homestead exemption?

Clearly, if the homestead is in excess of the allowable limit,
itor can seek to partition the homestead property, *O'Neill* v. *Mack*
Inc., 542 S.W.2d 112 (Tex. 1976). However, the creditor is not allo
benefit because of inflation, nor diminish any of the homestead cla
rights. On the forced sale, the creditor is allowed to receive o
proceeds in excess of the exemption (assuming the lot has not incre
value) that is applicable to the value of the *lot*. It does not include th
of the home. If inflation has increased the value of the lot, the credi
only receive the proceeds, *proportionately applied*, to the excess
the lot.

For instance, if the jury was to find the value of the lot at the
the homestead designation to be $25,000, the excess above the exe
at the time of the purchase is $15,000. If the total value of the *lot* a
the time of the sale is $60,000, the increased value subject to the li
the same ratio. So in this example, $10,000 is divided by $25,0
two-fifths of the lot is exempt, and three-fifths nonexempt. The
sales price, then, yields a ratio of two-fifths of $60,000; so two-fi
exempt, and three-fifths is nonexempt. The creditor, then, could
receive the proportional excess, or $36,000. The other $24,000 is still
considered exempt homestead proceeds. This assures that the family is
somewhat protected from inflation, *Hoffman* v. *Love*, 494 S.W.2d 591
(Tex. 1973).

Creation. Contrary to popular opinion and belief, creation of the homestead right is simple and requires no formal designation whatsoever. There

are no documents to sign, no oath to take, and no magic dust to sprinkle. The possession of the real estate by the owner who, whether single or with his family, resides upon it makes it the homestead of the family, both in law and in fact. If the real property is raw land (i.e., a lot in a subdivision), it is only important that the head of the family must have intended to reside there along with his family as a home, and that intention must be evidenced by some overt act of preparation. That is, there must be some other act (in addition to legal title) by the family, or the head of same, that impresses the land with the intention of establishing a home. This act can be having plans drawn, having the lot cleared, or whatever other fact may be proven to indicate that the family intended to occupy same as its homestead. Mere intent of occupying the property, by itself, is not enough to render the lot exempt pursuant to the homestead law.

Termination. The nature of the homestead exemption and the strength with which it has been applied and upheld in the State of Texas may indicate the strength to which Texas law resists termination of any homestead rights. It has been judicially determined that the only way for property to lose its homestead character is by *death, abandonment*, or *alienation*.

Death of the head of the household or homestead claimant, although terminating the claimant's homestead rights, does not necessarily terminate homestead rights altogether. In the event there is a surviving spouse, those rights pass to that surviving spouse upon the death of the original homestead claimant. The homestead rights can also pass to that claimant's heirs in the event there is an unmarried daughter or any children under legal age. In such case, regardless of the amount of indebtedness or obligations incurred on the part of the homestead claimant, his house could not be sold for any of his nonhomestead debts. In addition, the homestead rights cannot be partitioned between surviving spouse and minor children. It is in this type of situation that the homestead exemption clearly protects the family from a forced sale by creditors.

Alienation involves the sale of the house. In the event the family sells the house and buys a new home, the homestead character is terminated in the old homestead and manifests itself in the new homestead. If the family buys a new home and the old homestead is not sold, this does not necessarily terminate the old homestead, even if the old home is converted to rental property. In such a case, the creditors would have to prove abandonment of the old homestead if they were trying to force the sale of that home to satisfy the obligations.

Abandonment of a homestead has been a heavily litigated area, even in recent years. It is sufficient to say that it is not very easy to abandon a homestead. It is a question of fact for the jury to decide rather than one of law. It has been held that the acquisition of the new home is not necessarily an acquisition of a new homestead, and that an individual does not necessarily abandon a homestead by merely moving his home, *Gonzales* v. *Gonzales*, 541 S.W.2d 865 (Tex. Civ. App.—Waco, 1976). Abandonment of homestead property cannot be accomplished by mere intention. There must be a discontinuance of use, coupled with an intention *not again to use the property as a home*, to constitute abandonment. The courts put the burden of proving abandonment on the creditors, not on the homestead claimant.

Community Property Rights

The State of Texas has a very deeply ingrained Spanish heritage, which believed very firmly in the home and family unit concept. This is reflected in our homestead laws and is also reflected in certain marital property rights, which we term *community property*. Texas is one of eight states that recognize community property rights. The law in Texas basically presumes that every piece of real property acquired after marriage becomes community property, which means the property of both husband and wife. Community property rights also vest certain rights in the children in the event of the intestate death of one of the spouses. The laws were passed with the specific purpose in mind of maintaining and keeping the cohesiveness of the family unit. The community property laws become operative upon the marriage of the parties (*Powell*, supra ¶624.3 [1]).

The contrast to community property is *separate property*. Separate property is specifically designated by the Texas Constitution to be exceptions to the community property law, and those exceptions are as follows:

1. Property owned by a spouse prior to marriage, and
2. Property acquired by gift, devise, or descent during marriage.

However, any income from separate property or any offspring of said community property (i.e., cattle or other additional property that comes into being) is community property. This does not include the increase in value of separate property after marriage. For instance, if a spouse owns a home worth $60,000 at the time of the marriage and the home is worth $90,000 after the marriage, that increase in value is not community property. However, if community credit is used to secure a loan for the house, or community funds are used to maintain or improve the house, certain community property rights may accrue.

Management and Control of Community Property. No one spouse can claim all the community property because all real property that is community property is generally considered to be of joint control and cannot be conveyed without the joinder of the other spouse. There have been fairly recent statutory provisions enacted, however, that allow for a *sole control com-*

munity property, where a spouse may have the sole management, control, and disposition of real estate as if he or she were single, if the property is held in that spouse's name. This sole control community property includes, but is not limited to, revenue from separate property, personal earnings, recoveries for personal injuries, and the increase in value and revenue from all property subject to sole control and management.

Liabilities. There are different liabilities for community property depending on whether or not it is jointly controlled community property, sole control community property, or separate property of either spouse. The liabilities also change depending on whether or not the liabilities incurred are *tortious* (actions for money damages) or *contractual* (either written or oral) or whether the contract was for necessary or nonnecessary items. This text will not attempt to go into depth in the subject of marital property rights because the complex nature of those rights goes far beyond the realm of real estate law. It is more important to remember that in the marital community, any interest in real estate may be subject to joint control, and both spouses should be aware of any real estate transaction affecting presumed community property.

Common-Law Marriage. Since the marital community is the determining factor for the subject of community property, it is interesting to note what can constitute marriage in the State of Texas. A formal or ceremonial marriage, of course, presumes a legal marriage as long as the ceremonial marriage is not illegal or invalid. Texas, however, is one of the two community property states that recognize the validity of common-law marriages (*Powell*, supra, ¶624.3 [3]). It has been long upheld by statute and case law that a common-law marriage can exist if the following elements are present:

1. There is an agreement, express or implied, presently to be husband and wife;
2. The couple are living together in cohabitation as man and wife; and
3. The parties hold each other out to the public as husband and wife.

The most flexible provision of the foregoing is the first one, because the agreement between the parties need not be expressed, but can be implied if the other two elements exist. There is no authority establishing the time limit as to how long cohabitation would have to exist, and presumably it could be for a very short period of time, as long as the other two elements exist. This becomes a very complex matter in the event of an untimely death where certain heirs may have a right to community property interests. Will contests and heirship rights, as well as rights of the common-law wife, can prove to have disastrous consequences to unsuspecting family members.

Non-Operational Estates. There are certain estates which existed at common law, and still exist in some states, but are considered to be non-operational (having no effect) in the State of Texas. Even though they are not applicable, a speaking knowledge of the subject matter always helps to broaden the scope of understanding of real estate law.

Dower rights are rights a husband has in his spouse's estate upon her demise. Conversely, curtesy rights are rights that a wife has in her husband's estate when he dies. Dower and curtesy rights have varying degrees of application, depending upon jurisdiction. However, Texas concept of community property rights (discussed earlier in this chapter) as well as the laws of heirship (Prob. Code, Sec. 38, discussed in Chapter 7) preclude any rights of dower and curtesy in Texas.

The Rule in Shelley's Case is a grant of title to the grantee and his "heirs" or "the heirs of his body," in an attempt to limit the chain of title to a parcel of real estate to a particular ancestry. Although this rule is recognized in Texas, it is not looked upon with favor. Only if no other intention can be implified, and the grant is so specific that no other conclusion can be reached, will the court uphold it. The Rule in Shelley's Case (along with two other outmoded doctrines) was statutorily abolished on January 1, 1964 (*Tex. Rev. Civ. Stat. Ann., art. 1291a). Curiously, Section 3 of the Act, as passed, provides that the new statute does not apply to conveyances which took place prior to the effective date of the law. So it is presumed that the complications of the Rule of Shelley's Case will continue to arise for some time to come.*

SUMMARY

An estate in land has been defined as the degree, quality, nature, and extent of interest that a person has in real property. Freehold estates consist primarily of fee-simple estates, life estates, fee on conditional limitations, fee on condition subsequent, and fee on condition precedent. Mineral estates are freehold estates resulting primarily from *lateral severance*, a separation of the surface and subsurface estates. Texas considers the mineral estate to be the dominant estate, allowing the subsurface-mineral owner the right to cross the surface estate to extract the minerals. Air rights are another severable estate which concerns air traffic, overhead structure, and solar rights.

Cemetery lots are technically considered to be an exclusive right of sepulture.

Legal estates are rights vested in the individual by statute or constitutional provision. Homesteads are a very important legal estate in Texas and vest on the individual upon his occupancy of the property. Homestead rights provide an exemption from forced sale of the owner's principal residence except in very specific circumstances. Urban and rural homestead rights exist in Texas, and each homestead is either urban or rural but not both. A person may claim only one homestead at a time, although he may concurrently claim a business and residential urban homestead. Homesteads may only be terminated by death, abandonment, or alienation. Community property rights exist because of the marital status of the owners. There is a presumption that all property acquired during marriage is community property and subject to the joint management and control of both the husband and the wife. A concern with community property rights is the concept of common-law marriage.

3

HOW OWNERSHIP IS HELD

Ownership of real estate must be vested in a specific, identifiable legal entity. Some person, company, or organization maintains legal control over real estate and is held to be responsible for activities and obligations arising as a result of that ownership and control. A group of people, or an individual, contemplating a purchase of real estate, will want to give serious consideration as to how the ownership to that real estate should be held. This normally requires sound legal advice because the means of ownership dictates the scope of control and liabilities of that ownership—liabilities that may have far-reaching, and sometimes unexpected, legal complications.

The entities of ownership discussed in this chapter will include ownership in severalty, tenancy in common, joint tenancy, partnerships, limited partnerships, corporations, and trusts. Each type of ownership will be discussed in its purest, most basic form to simplify its unique characteristics.

Ownership in Severalty

Ownership in severalty is the easiest to understand, being simply *individual ownership*. One person is the owner. He has sole control over the use and possession of the property, and also has unlimited liability for all causes of action arising as a result of his ownership of that property.

Tenancy in Common

The ownership of real estate by multiple entities is generally for a specific purpose, or to achieve a specific, desired result. However, when there are no special circumstances to compel a different conclusion, multiple ownership in Texas is presumed to be a tenancy in common.

Tenancy in common can best be defined as an *ownership of real estate by more than one, in undivided interests*. This means there is no requirement that the fractional undivided interests be equal. The main characteristic of tenancy in common is the unity of possession (i.e., all of the co-tenants (co-owners) have the right to possession of the real estate since each interest is undivided). All of the co-tenants do not have to occupy the real estate at one time, however. A possession of one co-owner is deemed a possession by all co-owners.

Rights of Parties

Since there is a multiple ownership, there are certain obligations among the co-owners to each other. When only one of the co-owners is in possession, the relationship of the possessor and the other co-owners is generally construed to be one of landlord and tenant. However, if a co-owner receives more than his proportionate share of rights (for instance, if the property is income-producing), he owes a duty to pay the other co-owners their proportionate benefits and to give them a full accounting thereof. On the other hand, if the one co-owner's possession is clearly in disavowal of the rights of the other co-owners, this co-owner may be construed to be an adverse possessor.

Liabilities

There is no prohibition from a co-owner encumbering, selling, or leasing his respective interest as long as it does not adversely affect the rights of the other co-owners. If a co-owner chooses to be independent of the other co-owners in his financial affairs, his obligation to third-party creditors extends only to his proportionate, undivided interest in the real property. If a co-owner loses his share, the creditor becomes a tenant (owner) in common with the other co-owners. If the property is encumbered by a single mortgage incurred by all the co-owners, however, the creditors can seek collection from one or all of the co-owners, jointly or severally. In such a case, the co-owner who ultimately pays the debt has the right to reimbursement from the other co-owners.

To simplify this concept, one may want to think of ownership by tenants in common as more than one undivided ownership in severalty. Conflicts among the co-tenants (co-owners) may be resolved through an actual partition, in kind or value, of the property. Such partitioning may be a voluntary agreement or may be judicially imposed.

Joint Tenancy

Ownership by joint tenancy is often confused with ownership by tenancy in common, and an effort should be made to distinguish between the two types of ownership. *Joint tenancy* is generally defined as ownership of real estate by two or more, with the *parties having a right of survivorship*. Right of survivorship means that upon the death of one of the joint tenants, the other joint tenant(s) automatically succeeds to the decedent's interest. Normally, as tenants in common, the decedent's interest would go to his heirs and the beneficiaries of his will. This is not so if the decedent held title to his real estate as a joint tenant.

Although the primary characteristic of tenancy in common is unity of possession, joint tenancy requires four unities: time, title, interest, and possession. All of these unities must vest simultaneously, almost necessitating the use of a single conveying instrument for all grantees. That is the only sure way all four unities can vest at one time.

Creation

Texas, long steeped in the heritage of homesteads and community property rights, does not look favorably on joint tenancies because joint tenancies normally leave the joint tenants' families with no rights to the real estate. In fact, Texas even goes one step farther by statutorily abolishing joint tenancies except where created by an agreement in writing of joint owners. (V.A.T.S. Probate Code, § 46) However, in no event is such an agreement assumed from the mere fact that the property is held in joint ownership.

Since this statutory reference is the only authority for the establishment of joint tenancies in Texas, it leads one to assume that the four unities theory is not a requirement in Texas. However, this has not been judicially determined to date.

Joint tenancy between a husband and wife is called *Tenancy by the Entireties*. This means of ownership, the subject of several landmark Texas Supreme Court decisions, is not recognized in Texas. However, it has been the subject of some speculation that a husband and wife can own community property in joint tenancy in Texas. The authority for this is indirect but it involves statutory partitioning of community property (pursuant to Section 5.42 of the Family Code) and then signing a written agreement to hold said property as joint tenants. It has already been well established that a husband and wife can hold separate property as joint tenants, *Whitis* v. *Whitis*, 549 S.W.2d 54 (Tex. Civ. App.—Waco, 1977).

It would seem that a well-written will would accomplish the same end result without most of the complications and adverse case law of joint tenancies in Texas. However, creating a joint tenancy may provide the appropriate avenue to avoid will contests and lengthy probate proceedings.

Liabilities

Both joint tenancy and tenancy in common share the mutual obligations of co-ownership. That is, each of the joint tenants owes the duty of care to the other(s) not to commit waste or arbitrarily withhold economic benefits of the other(s). Each joint tenant has a liability of his fractional interest for debts. When a joint tenant conveys or loses his interest, the new owner becomes a tenant in common rather than a joint tenant, although the other joint tenants maintain their existing status. Note that the unity of time requirement, needed for the creation of a joint tenancy at common law, is not satisfied when a new co-owner receives an interest in the ownership.

Partnerships

A partnership is statutorily defined as:

> an association of two or more persons to carry on as co-owners a business for profit.

There are three basic partnership entities that will be discussed: (1) general partnerships, (2) joint ventures, and (3) limited partnerships.

General Partnerships

For general partnerships, Texas has adopted the Texas Uniform Partnership Act (*Tex. Rev. Civ. Stat. Ann.*, art. 61326), which contains a large number of statutes and sets out most of the basic guidelines within which partnership law is determined. These laws can, as in most other areas of the law, become very complicated because of the technicalities to which the statutes address themselves. Therefore, only the major components of partnerships as they pertain to real estate ownership will be discussed.

Creation. There are no specific statutory guidelines necessary for the creation of a partnership; a written or oral agreement is not necessarily essential. A partnership is normally inferred when there is a clear intention to create a partnership, and when the partners in fact have a co-ownership with the intention of sharing profits or losses on a particular business venture. Any estate in real property may be acquired in the partnership name, and any property bought by the partnership or acquired by the partnership by purchase or otherwise is considered partnership property. Once so acquired, the estate can be conveyed only in the partnership name. As a matter of form, the purchase or conveyance of partnership property generally includes the name of the partnership and then lists each of the partners individually, so that there is no mistake as to who is liable on the partnership debts or obligations.

Once it has been determined that a partnership has been created, the law tends to support the maintenance and continuity of that partnership. It is important to understand that each partner actually gets three distinct rights:

1. His rights in *specific partnership property*,
2. His *interest in the partnership*, and
3. His *right to participate in the management* of that partnership.

Of these three interests, the only one that may be considered community property (and therefore subject to a spouse's interest) is the partner's interest in the partnership. A partner's rights to specific partnership property and his right to management in the partnership are not community property but separate property and cannot be conveyed or assigned without the unanimous consent of all the members of the partnership. Similarly, a person cannot become a partner in a partnership without the consent of all the other partners.

Partnership law creates a very high duty of care and trust that each partner owes to the other partners. This relationship of trust is termed a *fiduciary* relationship. Each partner is an agent for the whole partnership and can bind the partnership to any obligations incurred in the usual course of business. For instance, where title to real property is in the partnership name, any single partner may convey title to such property by conveyance executed in the partnership name. Similarly, a single partner can incur a partnership debt or other contractual obligation without the joinder of the other partners.

Although some of these conditions may seem rather onerous, the basic reason for this regulation and total obligation of the partners revolves around the obligations and liabilities to which the partners are bound, pursuant to the provisions of the Texas Uniform Partnership Act. Since every act of the partner for carrying on in the usual way of the business of the partnership binds the partnership totally, each of the partners is liable jointly and severally; that is, the partnership is liable and each of the partners is liable individually for the entire obligation of the partnership. The partnership is bound by the partners' acts, even if they are wrongful, and even if one of the partner's acts amounts to a breach of trust between the partners.

Advantages. The advantages of a partnership are basically the pooling of resources and liabilities, so that, at least theoretically, no one partner bears the brunt of all the losses. Another advantage is that all losses to the partnership, as well as all profits, are passed through directly to each of the partners individually. Although the partnership itself is required to file a federal tax return, the payment of all taxes or deduction of all losses is proportionately applicable to the individual partner's tax return. This is in contrast to corporate or trust ownership where there are less advantageous elements of taxation. Since real estate is given special tax benefits to owners (depreciation allowances, capital gains tax treatment, tax-free exchange, and installment sale benefits), it is sometimes very important for tax purposes that these losses and deductions be able to pass to the individual purchasers rather than to an ownership entity, which provides no direct benefits to the individual's tax return.

Disadvantages. The disadvantages of a general partnership are self-explanatory. Since there is joint and several liability, one partner may be required to meet all the obligations of the partnership if the other partners choose not to fund the partnership obligations. Even though the paying partner could seek recovery from the other partners, the risk is often too high for the benefits obtained.

Joint Venture

A joint venture is a partnership, sometimes more appropriately called a *joint adventure*. This is a particular type of partnership where two or more partners jointly pursue a specified project. They are not simply in business for a profit, as is the typical definition of partnerships as a whole. Rather, they are in business for profit from a particular project. The more typical joint venture situations involve two partners, one of which is a financial partner, the other of which is a managing partner. The financial partner is generally a lending institution, insurance company, or other financially strong investment group. The managing partner is generally a very experienced developer who has had a long track record of building certain types of projects. The financial partner (company or institution) normally visualizes a chance for more profits than simply the return on its investment capital if it owns half of the project. The developer visualizes no financing worries or funding problems while the project proceeds to final completion. Both partners, of course, have mutual dependencies on each other by sharing risks, but they also have those certain areas of expertise that make those risks less. Joint ventures are usually very sophisticated transactions, although they can be as small as two realtors agreeing to work together and share a commission on a particular sale. Legally, a joint venture is governed by the same rules as partnerships generally.

Limited Partnerships

Limited partnerships have been a very effective tool for real estate ownership and investment. Such partnerships are sometimes considered the standard form of investment ownership to achieve maximum benefits for private investors. Limited partnerships have been of such long-standing acceptance that this method is considered by many professionals to be one of the more stable means of ownership, as well as one of the most beneficial. The law in this area is reasonably well settled and is generally understood by most investors. This form of ownership has been effectively utilized in very large types of investments, some of which have been syndicated using large numbers of investors and have been offered for sale by large stock brokerage firms.

Texas has adopted the Texas Uniform Limited Partnership Act (*Tex. Rev. Civ. Stat. Ann.*, art. 6132a). A limited partnership is statutorily defined as a partnership formed by two or more persons under the provisions of the Act and having as members one or more *general partners* and one or more *limited partners*. The limited partners, as such, are a separate class of partners and are not bound by the obligations of the partnerships as long as the formalities of the limited partnership agreement and applicable statutes are complied with.

Creation. The creation of a Texas limited partnership involves a certain amount of formality and structure. Two of the instruments needed to properly create a limited partnership are the *certificate of limited partnership* and the *limited partnership agreement*.

There must be a *certificate of limited partnership* filed with the secretary of state that discloses the nature of the business, the name of the partnership, the principal place of business of the partnership, who the partners are, the rights of the limited partners as to assignment, admission of additional limited partners, etc. This type of disclosure allows a private investor, or creditor, to look into the organization of the partnership and determine who the partners are before making any decisions relating to loaning money to or investing in the limited partnership. Since these disclosures are required, a lot of secrecy and questionable dealings by a limited partnership is eliminated. All of the information contained in the certificate of limited partnership is generally available by a phone call to the secretary of state's office.

The certificate of limited partnership is usually a condensation of the information and obligations contained in another instrument, the *limited partnership agreement*. This agreement, signed by all of the general and limited partners, sets out the obligations of each of the partners. The agreement typically sets out in greater detail the information contained in the certificate of limited partnership. It also specifies the obligations of each partner, events of default, dissolution procedures, and other pertinent information relating to the internal structure and operation of the limited partnership. An investor is well-advised to have his attorney review all such documentation prior to signing them.

Liabilities. One of the more attractive aspects of ownership by limited partnership is the limited liability it provides for the limited partners. The general partner in a limited partnership has all the liabilities of the partner in a general partnership, that is, joint, several, and total. The limited partners, however, are not bound by any of the obligations of the partnership, and none of the limited partner's assets are considered liable for partnership debts or liabilities. In theory, the only risk the limited partner takes is the loss of his contribution. However, it should not be overlooked that the limited partner does have the statutory liability to the partnership for the difference between his contribution as made and for any unpaid contribution that he agreed to make in the future. So where a limited partner may not be liable to third-party creditors, he may be personally liable (both by statute and by the terms of the limited partnership agreement) to his other partners for his contributions to the partnership. Limited partners, because of the nature of their contribution, are sometimes given preferential returns on their contribution. However, they cannot get a return on their investment until all of the obligations of the partnership have been met. The limited partnership's interest is generally assignable, subject to the restrictions in the limited partnership agreement and the certificate of limited partnership.

Advantages. The advantages of limited partnership are self-explanatory once the basic provisions of the law concerning limited partnerships are understood. The main advantage, of course, is the limited liabilities of the limited partners as far as business obligations of the partnership are concerned. As stated previously, the limited partner's liability to a third party is limited to his contribution to the partnership and the obligations for additional contribution, but he may also have a personal liability to the other partners for his contributions.

Tax benefits are, of course, an additional advantage to limited partnerships. Partnerships, as stated previously, are taxed as a partnership; but the profits are normally passed through to the individual partners, who get the benefits of whatever tax savings, investment credit, or depreciation benefits accrue to the partnership. Therefore, at least in theory, the limited partner gets all the benefits of tax-sheltered real estate investments with virtually no liability except for his contribution to the partnership.

Disadvantages. The one main disadvantage to a limited partnership is that there is total reliance by the limited partners on the expertise and management capabilities of the general partner. Although the general partner enjoys joint, several, and total liability, one normally expects that the general partner selected will be one of prudent and capable past experience. There have been recent attempts to make the general partner a corporation, thereby limiting the liability of the general partner as well as that of the limited partners. Although this is not in itself illegal, it should be understood that there are certain tax consequences that may arise as a result of this type of organization. The Internal Revenue Service sometimes feels that if the general partner is a corporation, the limited partners are, in effect, shareholders rather than limited partners. The Internal Revenue Service, then, would look on the partnership as a corporation that would be taxed as a corporation rather than as a limited partnership. The guidelines and criteria for the Internal Revenue Service can sometimes be very technical, and one's accountant should always be consulted when considering this type of investment.

A second disadvantage revolves around the Securities and Exchange Commission. Limited partnerships, being investments, are normally considered securities and must be filed either with the Texas State Securities Board or with the federal Securities and Exchange Commission. This requirement to file is always a requirement unless the limited partnership falls under one of two basic exemptions provided by the Securities and Exchange Act or under the one single exemption provided by the Texas State Securities Board. The scope of these exemptions will be discussed in Chapter 16 on Governmental Regulation of Real Estate.

A third disadvantage is that in filing a certificate of limited partnership, there is a certain amount of disclosure of personal business that an individual may not want the public to know. There are times when a private investor may prefer not to have his interest known to the public when making real estate investments. If this is the case, limited partnerships may not be the most effective tool of investment.

In addition to the required disclosures, there are certain costs involved in forming limited partnerships. To file the certificate of limited partnership with the secretary of state, the law provides that you must pay ½ of 1% of the amount of cash contributed by each limited partner, as well as of his additional contributions. This may involve a substantial amount of money. However, the statute puts cash limits of a $100 minimum and a maximum of $2500 to file the certificate of limited partnership.

The last disadvantage to be discussed is one important to all investors and realtors anticipating this type of investment. This disadvantage is one of control. It is statutorily provided that only general partners are allowed to take part in the control of the business. If any limited partner assumes the position of taking control of the business or taking part in any significant management of the partnership, he will become a general partner and be liable as a general partner. This principle applies even though the limited partner may assume such control in good faith and in the best interest of the partnership. Therefore, when a client or investor is interested in taking part in the business of the limited partnership, he may be well-advised to keep his involvement to a minimum or he may be construed as a general partner.

Corporations

Corporations as an ownership entity are probably affected by more statutory provisions than any other type of ownership entity in Texas. Corporations are rather complicated in nature, and it is important that the basics of the corporate structure be understood before further legal aspects of corporation ownership and control of real estate are discussed.

There are three basic classes of individuals involved in the organization of all corporations: officers, directors, and shareholders.

Shareholders are, in fact, the owners of the corporation. A corporation normally raises its money for capital and initial ownership costs by selling shares to the shareholders. The shareholders, after advancing the money for the corporation's initial costs, ultimately control the corporation through the corporation's bylaws and voting of their shares at the annual shareholders' meeting. At the annual shareholders' meeting, the shareholders elect the board of directors. The business and affairs of the corporation are managed by the board of directors, who are not required by law to be residents of the state, or even shareholders of the corporation. The officers of the corporation are elected by the board of directors. The officers and agents of the corporation (including employees) have the authority to perform the duties of the management of the corporation on a day-to-day basis and as may be determined by the board of directors. The corporation may then return the shareholders' investments through payment of dividends, normally paid quarterly. The following chart (Figure 3-1) may serve to diagram these functions more clearly.

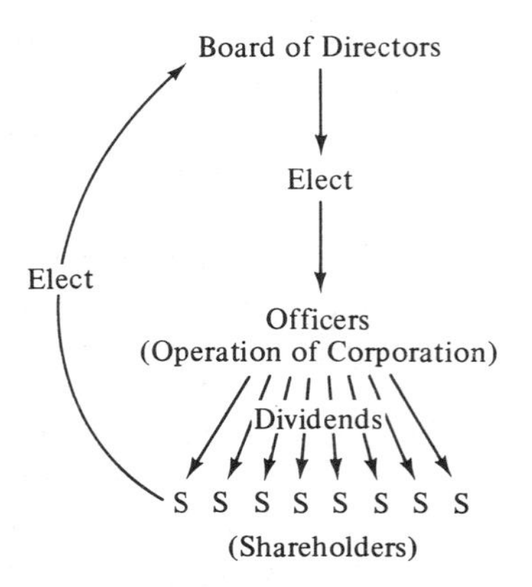

FIGURE 3-1. Corporate organization.

Creation

A corporation is created upon filing of the charter with the office of the secretary of state. There is a statutory filing fee, which is currently $100. The corporation's charter, though fairly general, requires certain disclosures similar to those of a limited partnership certificate. The corporation must have a certain amount of capital funds, which must be at least $1000, in services performed, money, or assets. The charter also requires disclosure of the incorporators and of the first officers and directors, as well as of the number of shares authorized to be distributed. After the corporation has been formed, the only requirement to maintain the corporate entity is to pay its corporate franchise tax each year.

Although creation of a corporation may appear to be deceptively simple, it is important to realize that this normally requires the services of an attorney who is experienced in corporation law. There are additional statutory requirements for shareholders' and directors' meetings, minutes to be kept, bylaws, and other ancillary documents and functions required by law but which are not part of the simple filing of the corporate charter. These additional requirements, along with others involving corporate ownership (particularly in the field of real estate), require the expertise of individuals well-versed in the area of corporate law as well as real estate law.

Corporate Real Estate

Since all aspects of corporations are so carefully controlled by statute, it is only logical that the ownership and management of corporate real estate also are controlled by statute. Corporations are given the specific power to purchase and acquire real property, as well as the specific power to sell same. However, there is a significant difference between selling property and assets of a corporation in the regular course of business, and the sale of all, or substantially all, of the corporation's assets. Sales in the regular course of business (a real estate developer, for instance) can effect the conveyance of real estate simply by the signature of the president, vice president, or attorney-in-fact of the corporation. A deed conveying a corporation's real property is normally accompanied by a resolution of the board of directors authorizing said sale, but the conveyance may be achieved without the resolution. If the sale of the real estate consists of substantially all of the assets of said corporation, however, ratification by four-fifths of the shareholders is required before such conveyance can be made.

There are some specific miscellaneous provisions pertaining to corporate ownership of real estate that are not contained in the Texas Business Corporation Act, but rather in the Texas Miscellaneous Corporation Laws Act, particularly in Part 4 of said act. Briefly stated, the Texas Miscellaneous Corporation Laws Act provides that no private corporation may purchase any land unless such land is necessary to enable the corporation to do business in this state or to secure a debt in due course of business (for instance, buying secure land at a foreclosure sale to protect its interest). Any land owned by a corporation that is not primarily held so as to enable it (the corporation) to do business in this state may not be held for any longer than 15 years. The act further states that no private corporation whose main purpose as stated in this chapter is the acquisition and ownership of real estate shall be permitted to acquire land within this state by purchase, lease, or otherwise. There is a blanket exception, however, to land that is located inside any incorporated city limits.

The first reaction of most students to the foregoing statutory provisions is logically confusion and doubt. The reason for this statute, and all fifty states have such statutes, is to keep corporate ownership of real estate from becoming a monopoly. Corporations, by the terms of their charters, are generally perpetual in nature. Article 1, Section 26, of the Texas Constitution provides that real estate owned in perpetuity is contrary to the genius of a free government. Therefore, corporate ownership of property can be considered to be "contrary to the genius of a free government." Since corporations have become such an important factor in ownership of real estate in recent years, this statute has, of course, created a number of problems in other states. To date, these statutory provisions against ownership of real estate by a corporation have not been enforced. They must be enforced by the attorney general, rather than by a private party, because it is considered in the best interest of the state that the statutory provision be enforced. The law was first passed in 1898 when people were concerned about corporations owning entire states, which would be contrary to the interest of the people who live in that state. Some of the case law in this area in states other than Texas has witnessed some very interesting cases that have upheld the validity of such a law. It is conceivable that the law could be enforced in Texas at some later date.

Corporate Liability

The primary purpose for which any group of people incorporates is for the protection and insulation from any liability of the shareholders and individuals organizing the corporation. There is absolutely no personal liability whatsoever for individuals working in the corporation to third parties dealing with the corporation. Individuals can guarantee a corporate note or a corporate liability, or an officer can sign individually for the corporation and be personally liable. As a general rule, shareholders, officers, and directors are totally insulated from any liability whatsoever. The liability of the assets of the corporation is the only exposure.

Advantages of Corporate Ownership

The primary advantage of corporate ownership consists of the insulation from liabilities of all individuals concerned. As long as all the corporate debts, liabilities, and obligations are incurred through the corporate name, and without fraud or material misrepresentation, there is no personal liability on the part of the shareholders, officers, or directors of the corporation.

Another distinct advantage to corporate ownership, and a major reason for the use of family corporations, is for estate planning purposes. The U.S. Congress and the Internal Revenue Service have constantly provided for better pension and retirement plans for those utilizing the corporate entity of ownership. As in other tax benefits, this has proved to be an incentive for many unincorporated entities to incorporate to effect a greater tax savings.

Disadvantages of Corporate Ownership

It has often been stated that the corporate ownership of real estate is not a desirable form of ownership because of the technical problems that result through the corporate tax laws and the structures of organization within the corporation itself.

One of the biggest drawbacks of corporate ownership is the problem of double taxation. Income from real estate, profits from tax-free exchanges, capital gains benefits, and depreciation benefits—all normally considered attributable to real estate tax-shelter techniques, are benefits accrued on behalf of the corporation, not on behalf of the shareholders. Therefore, the corporation gets the extra tax benefits and tax shelter, not the shareholders. To further complicate matters, all income of the corporation is taxed twice if it is distributed to the shareholders. To explain, the corporation is taxed once on its real estate income. Then, if there are any excess profits to be distributed to the shareholders, these profits are distributed in the form of dividends, which are taxed a second time and are reflected on the shareholder's individual income tax. Therefore, as a tax shelter, corporations are generally not considered the best form of ownership for real estate purposes.

Further problems in corporate ownership result from the technical requirements of state law pertaining to corporate ownership, to distribution of securities, and to disclosure to shareholders, as well as the requirements of other statutes pertaining to shareholders' and directors' obligations that are peculiar to corporate law.

A third difficulty of corporate ownership, particularly if the corporation is a large one, involves the infrastructure of the corporation itself. For example, it is not always clear who has the authority to negotiate contracts, attend closings, and sign papers on behalf of the corporation. There has been further concern over the fact that it takes too much time for a corporation to operate from the initial negotiations between parties to the final ratification by shareholders and directors, plus the never-ending complications that "committees" create in the corporate process. There have been a number of theories that contend that corporations per se, as owners and managers of real estate, can never operate as fast as individuals or partnerships, and, therefore, they are not one of the better methods of owning, acquiring and developing real estate. These theories are based on the assumption that decisions cannot be made quickly enough to satisfy the real estate market. It should be pointed out, however, that there are a number of extremely large corporations that own, operate, and develop real estate very profitably because of the corporation's strength and stability, qualities that generally are not affected by the cyclical tendencies normally incident to the real estate industry as a whole.

Subchapter S Corporations

There has been some attempt at making corporate ownership of real estate more attractive to investors. For example, Subchapter S of the Internal Revenue Code permits certain small business corporations to be exempt from federal taxation. This was specifically enacted to allow certain small businesses to enjoy the advantages of corporate ownership without being subject to the disadvantage of double taxation. In the Subchapter S corporation, the tax benefits are shifted to the shareholders individually. The Subchapter S corporation itself is not subject to federal taxation generally. Its income is taxable as prorated to its shareholders, whether this income is distributed to them or not. Although this may seem an answer to one of the bigger problems of corporate ownership, it should be pointed out that there are a number of very restrictive requirements put on Subchapter S corporations. For instance, the corporation cannot initially have more than ten shareholders, all of whom must be residents of the state in which the corporation is chartered. Also, the vast majority of its income (80%) must be from active involvement in real estate, rather than passive income such as rents, dividends, interest, and annuities. Therefore, in electing Subchapter S status on the part of the corporation, it is very important that there should be unanimity among the shareholders, and there should also be competent legal advice to help the corporation avoid some of the peculiar pitfalls of the application of corporate statutes, as well as to help it to cope with the unique requirements of the Internal Revenue Service as they apply to Subchapter S corporations.

Ownership By Trusts

In Texas, there are three major types of trust ownership. These include (1) *testamentary* or *inter vivos trusts*, (2) *land trusts*, and (3) *real estate in-*

vestment trusts. As in corporate ownership, it is fairly important that we understand the basics of how a trust form of ownership operates before going into each of the individual types of trusts. Trusts generally have a *trustor*, sometimes called a *settlor*, who establishes the trust. Ownership and control of the trust are held by the *trustee*, who holds the trust in name only for the true owners, the *beneficiaries* of the trust. Normally, once a trust has been established by the trustor, it is irrevocable and title stays in the name of the trustee until the assets of the trust (called the *corpus*) are ultimately distributed to the beneficiaries. The income from the trust can be distributed to the beneficiaries at varying intervals depending on the trust instrument. Trusts per se do not pay taxes if the income is distributed to the beneficiaries. The income is taxed as it is distributed to the beneficiaries. When the corpus of the trust and other undistributed income vest in the beneficiaries, however, it should be understood that the entire amount is taxed at that time, and this tax can be quite substantial. Figure 3-2 may help assist in explaining how the trust form of ownership generally operates.

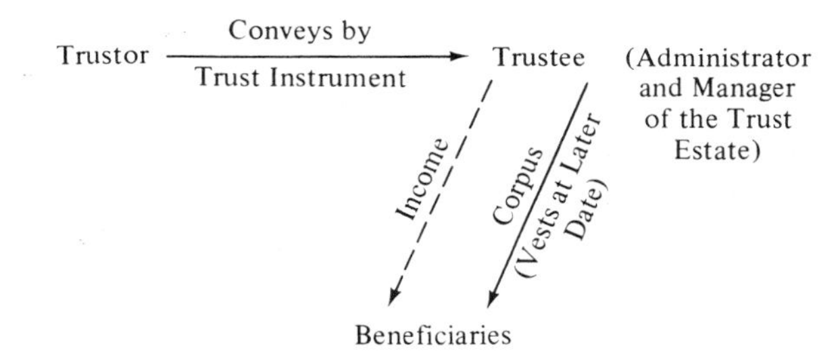

FIGURE 3-2. Trust organization.

According to the Texas Trust Act, the trustee individually is not liable for debts or obligations of the trust. The only liability is to the assets of the trust. The trustee has a fiduciary obligation to administer the trust properly; otherwise he can be held personally liable to the beneficiaries for not protecting the beneficiaries' respective interests. As in corporate ownership, however, when a third party deals with a person who operates as a trustee, such party is bound by law to understand that the trustee is not individually liable under most circumstances.

Testamentary and Inter Vivos *Trusts*

Testamentary and *inter vivos* trusts are normally trusts set up for the benefit of the beneficiaries for estate purposes of the trustor. The Rule against Perpetuities dictates that the period that the trust may exist is limited to approximately 21 years after the death of the trustor at the time the trust was created, plus any actual period of gestation (this period of time is typically 21 years, plus 9 months after the death of the trustor). If the beneficiaries are children or grandchildren of the trustor, it is generally very functional for the trustor to set up his estate in a trust so that it will not be taxed, and the income and benefits of that trust will be managed professionally by a bank trust department or by some other responsible entity. The corpus of the estate will vest in the settlor's grandchildren (probably at a lower tax rate, depending on their incomes when it vests), and will provide for their well-being, expenses, and usual standard of living.

As previously discussed, real estate held by a trustee in this capacity is subject to very high fiduciary obligations between the trustee and beneficiaries. The only personal liability involved is that of the trustee to the beneficiaries, and not to third-party creditors. If a trustee has mismanaged the assets or acted in bad faith, the beneficiaries have a cause of action against the trustee. Real estate conveyed, sold, mortgaged, or encumbered on the part of the trustee, therefore, must be done only in good faith and in the exercise of sound business judgment. The trustee binds the assets of the trust for whatever obligations may be incurred.

Land Trusts

A second type of trust that has been emerging in Texas in recent years has been what we are now calling the *land trust*. This type of trust has been called an Illinois Land Trust, and sometimes a Massachusetts Business Trust. Texas is now developing its own brand of this trust, which is becoming a common means of ownership in Texas. This type of ownership is normally created by an individual or promoter who buys land for a venture for management or speculative holding purposes for a group of individual investors. The theory behind this is that the management, handling, and ownership will vest in only one person, who will be the trustee, for the benefit of the investors, who are the beneficiaries. The same fiduciary capacity exists between the trustee and beneficiaries, and the trustee generally recognizes having a duty of full disclosure for aspects of the transaction and in keeping the beneficiaries fully informed. There has been very little litigation in this area with the exception of one case, *Spiritas* v. *Robinowitz*, 544 S.W.2d 710 (Tex. Civ. App.—Dallas, 1976).

For the purposes of this discussion, it is most important to say that in a land trust of this type, there must be a very carefully and adequately drawn trust instrument identifying all the beneficiaries and carefully defining the powers and obligations of both beneficiaries and trustee. If this is not done correctly, the trustee may be held personally liable, although the beneficiaries may be insulated from most types of liability. This type of trust is a very functional, expedient, and simple way of owning and controlling real estate, but it must be understood that the laws affecting the liabilities of the parties are not well settled and may be subject to a wide variety of interpretations by the Texas courts. This type of ownership does maintain the secrecy of all the beneficiaries (often called beneficial owners); it requires no initial cost to form this kind of entity; and it has been used countless times without any adverse consequences. However, before this type of ownership is utilized, it is very important to get very competent legal counsel to assure the maximum protection for everyone's interest.

Real Estate Investment Trusts

The real estate investment trust was specifically provided for by federal statute in the form of an amendment to the Internal Revenue Code. The new provision enables the ownership and development of large real estate interests by a trust for the benefit of large numbers of investors while maintaining the tax benefits of real estate ownership for each investor. In these cases, the promoter or developer is the trustor, and the assets of the trust are the investors' cash. The trust is generally administered by a board of trustees (who are professional real estate consultants), and the beneficiaries are, of course, the investors.

Real estate investment trusts for a number of years prospered very heavily on the real estate investment market and sold shares as over-the-counter stocks or were registered on the New York Stock Exchange or American Stock Exchange. This form of real estate ownership encouraged the small investor to invest small amounts of money in very large projects; but unlike other investments on the stock market, the small investor could enjoy all the tax shelter benefits of real estate ownership in addition to the income from the project. In theory, this turned out to be one of the true booms in the real estate industry because it provided a large amount of capital and equity dollars to buy and develop projects from private sources (i.e., small individual investors). However, in the early to middle 1970s, there were a number of mismanagement, overextension, and negligence problems that arose as a result of this boom in real estate investment. This caused a decline in real estate investment trusts. Other reasons for the decline are unusually complicated because they involve not only the technicalities of real estate law but also technicalities pursuant to stock exchange registration, disclosures required by the Securities and Exchange Commission, and certain theories of economics and finance. However, the basic premises under which real estate investment trusts were originally formed are still good, and these trusts will probably become strong once again, perhaps under a little more strict federal regulation. Any real estate investment trust formed in Texas must additionally comply with Article 6138A, which is the Texas Real Estate Investment Trust Act, as far as the formation and managing of said trust. These requirements, coupled with the additional requirements of the Internal Revenue Service and the Securities and Exchange Commission, make this a relatively complicated method of real estate ownership. However, its effectiveness should not be underestimated.

SUMMARY

Anyone contemplating the purchase of real estate will want to give serious consideration to how the ownership of that real estate should be held. Ownership in severalty is individual ownership. Ownership by more than one person normally involves a tenancy in common, joint tenancy, and partnerships. Partnerships are classified further as general partnerships, joint ventures, or limited partnerships.

Ownership in severalty can also include two other forms of ownership: corporate and trust. Ownership in these are controlled and regulated by both state and federal statutes.

Each type of ownership has its own advantages and disadvantages. Determination of an owner's rights and considerations of any ownership entity require sound legal advice.

4

FIXTURES AND EASEMENTS

Fixtures and easements each have one common characteristic which enables them to be discussed in the same chapter. That characteristic is that they each involve rights that a third party may have in an owner's real estate. Fixtures involve the rights that a materialman, supplier, seller, or purchaser may have in certain appliances or appurtenances to one's real estate. Easements, on the other hand, involve the rights of a third party to access across an individual's real estate.

Fixtures

There is a large number of different laws applicable to the concept of fixtures making the exact meaning of the term "fixture," as used in every case, difficult to define. A fixture has been defined by case law as an article of personalty that has been attached to the real estate so that it becomes real estate, *Ruby* v. *Cambridge Mutual Fire Ins. Co.*, 358 S.W.2d 945 (Tex. Civ. App.—Dallas, 1962). Statutorily, it has been determined that goods are "fixtures" when they become so related to particular real estate that an interest in them arises under the real estate law of the state in which the real estate is situated, *Texas Business and Commerce Code*, Section 9.313.

Realty to Personalty—Personalty to Realty

The difficulty in the determination of fixtures results from the change in the nature of articles that are to become fixtures. For instance, a light fixture is very clearly an item of personalty (properly called *chattel*) that one may buy at a store that sells lights. However, once the fixture has been bolted into the ceiling and has been established as a part of the particular decor of a dining room, one might expect that it will become part of the real estate. Similar problems occur with drapes, certain types of shelving, carpeting, and many other objects that can be affixed to real estate in one form or another. On the other hand, there is an equal difficulty in determining the characteristics of items that are real estate and then become personalty. There are interesting applications of this concept in the oil and gas law, where the minerals are considered part of the real estate, but once they reach the wellhead or are extracted from the ground, they are considered personalty, to be sold by the owners as a nonreal estate item. Similarly, it is easy to envision a house being destroyed and several items of realty being converted for personal use and sold at auctions, garage sales, and even lumber and brick yards.

This problem can be further complicated by the fact that the conveyancing instruments utilized for realty and personalty are entirely different. Real estate is normally conveyed by the use of a deed, will, or other conveyancing instrument; whereas items of personalty (legally termed *chattel*) are normally transferred by an instrument called a *bill of sale*. A copy of a bill of sale is shown in Figure 4-1.

To add more confusion, it should also be mentioned that additional complications can arise in fixtures depending on who is claiming an interest in those fixtures. Once it has been determined that an item is a fixture, real estate law applies, along with certain mechanics' and materialmen's liens statutes and certain laws relating to mortgages. If an item is not a fixture, the Uniform Commercial Code applies to rights of parties, and the real estate law does not. A party may also qualify to claim an interest in the item both as an item of realty and as an item of personalty. Therefore, the law of fixtures must include certain applications of mortgage law, real estate liens, and fixture filing provisions of the Texas Business and Commerce Code. It is through the interrelationships of these three areas of the law that one can determine who has the right to a particular item, after it has been determined whether or not that item is a fixture.

Now that total confusion has set in, it is important to discuss the determination of a fixture and then attempt to untangle the problem of priorities once the concept of fixture is fully understood.

Determination of a Fixture

In most real estate sales the key concern in the determination of a fixture generally involves a fact situation where a prospective purchaser is buying real estate, normally a home, and this purchaser expects certain items to remain with the real estate because he considers them to be fixtures. To

NOTICE Prepared by the State Bar of Texas for use by Lawyers only.
To select the proper form, fill in blank spaces, strike out form provisions or insert special terms constitutes the practice of law. No "standard form" can meet all requirements.

BILL OF SALE

THE STATE OF TEXAS
COUNTY OF HARRIS } KNOW ALL MEN BY THESE PRESENTS:

THAT CAVEAT VENDOR, INC.

of the County of Harris and State aforesaid, for and in consideration of the sum of TEN AND NO/100THS-- DOLLARS,

to it in hand paid by BUYER BEWARE

the receipt of which is hereby acknowledged, have Bargained, Sold and Delivered, and by these presents do Bargain, Sell and Deliver, unto the said BUYER BEWARE

of the County of Harris and State of Texas

all of the following described personal property in Harris County, Texas, to-wit:

1. One High Performance Central Air Conditioning Unit, Model No. 694, Serial No. SE3469R739.

2. Deluxe Woodburner One Freestanding Stove, Model No. 3, Serial No. WRS86543.

And it does ~~do~~ hereby bind itself, its successors/ and assigns ~~xxxxxxxxxxxxxxxxxxxxxxx~~ to forever Warrant and Defend the title to the aforesaid property unto the said BUYER BEWARE, his heirs and assigns, against the lawful claim or claims of any and all persons whomsoever.

EXECUTED this 32nd day of February , A. D. 19 78 .

Witnesses at request of Grantor:

.... CAVEAT VENDOR, INC.

.... BY: ....
Dewey Cheatham, President

FIGURE 4-1. Bill of sale.

(Acknowledgment)

THE STATE OF TEXAS }
COUNTY OF }

Before me, the undersigned authority, on this day personally appeared

known to me to be the person........ whose name.................. subscribed to the foregoing instrument, and acknowledged to me that...... he...... executed the same for the purposes and consideration therein expressed.

Given under my hand and seal of office on this the day of , A. D. 19

....
Notary Public in and for County, Texas.

(Acknowledgment)

THE STATE OF TEXAS }
COUNTY OF }

Before me, the undersigned authority, on this day personally appeared

known to me to be the person .... whose name.................. subscribed to the foregoing instrument, and acknowledged to me that...... he ......executed the same for the purposes and consideration therein expressed.

Given under my hand and seal of office on this the day of , A. D. 19

....
Notary Public in and for County, Texas.

BILL OF SALE

TO

PREPARED IN THE LAW OFFICE OF:

PLEASE RETURN TO:

(Corporate acknowledgment)

THE STATE OF TEXAS }
COUNTY OF HARRIS }

Before me, the undersigned authority, on this day personally appeared DEWEY CHEATHAM, President of CAVEAT VENDOR, INC., a corporation, known to me to be the person whose name is subscribed to the foregoing instrument, and acknowledged to me that he executed the same for the purposes and consideration therein expressed, in the capacity therein stated and as the act and deed of said corporation.

Given under my hand and seal of office on this the 32nd day of February , A. D. 19 78 .

....
Notary Public in and for Harris County, Texas.

FIGURE 4-1 (*continued*).

make the situation more interesting, however, we may also have a homeowner, who, having installed a fixture, fully expects to remove it and take it with him to his new residence. It is at this point that we set the stage (a stage found in many home sales) to determine whether an item is a fixture. Inevitably, the criteria revolve around the fact situations as they occur, and the facts seem to differ in every case.

Mode of Annexation. The first method of determining whether or not an item is a fixture is by the manner in which the article is attached to the real estate, *First National Bank* v. *Whirlpool*, 517 S.W.2d 262 (Tex. 1974). It is easy to see that wallpaper, for instance, is attached to the real estate in such a manner that it is certainly meant to stay with the property as the property is sold. The same is generally true of shelves that have been built into the wall of the house. At the opposite end of the spectrum, however, we have pictures, hanging plants, swag lamps, and furniture. The questionable areas, of course, in this particular method can be quite large. Light bulbs, for instance, are certainly attached to the real estate but are easily removable, as are drapes, light switch plates, carpeting, and light fixtures that have been attached to the ceiling.

Adaptation. A second method for determining whether or not an article is a fixture depends on the character of the article and its adaptation to the real estate. It is certainly easy to determine that a lamp or freestanding stove would not have to be used in just one place; they could readily be removed and be used in another residence. However, these examples should be contrasted with custom-made drapes, custom-built bookcases, and even movable, matching kitchen counters, which have been made for a particular home. All of these items can easily be seen to be movable but probably would not have an equally effective use in another home.

Therefore, adaptation, combined with (the mode of annexation of the article), forms the basis for the third method, which is the intention of the parties.

Intention. The intention of the parties is, of course, the ultimate fact situation—What did each of the parties, the home purchaser and the homeowner, really intend to transfer when their earnest money contract was signed? The question of intention is inferable from the acts of the parties and the nature of the article, and incorporates the first two methods—the mode of annexation and the adaptation to real estate—because it is all of these particular factors that come into the minds of the purchaser and seller as they enter into their negotiations, *McConnell* v. *Frost*, 45 S.W.2d 777 (Tex. Civ. App.—Waco, 1932).

In utilizing the above three criteria, preference is given to the question of intention in deciding what constitutes a fixture. The question of intent is not a question of law but of fact, as created by the conduct of the parties. The intent should be clearly expressed in the earnest money contract. There can never be enough emphasis given to the duty of care a real estate agent must utilize in representing either party in a contractual negotiation.

Other Determinations

When one steps out of the realm of the real estate purchaser and homeowner negotiating a contract, the determination of fixtures becomes very important to vendors (sellers of the merchandise), mechanics and materialmen (sellers and installers of the merchandise), and the holder of the mortgage on the house to which that item has become attached. These people are not interested in the subsequent purchase of a house but have a very important interest in those fixtures as they are installed in the house if the fixtures are not paid for. For example, take the situation of a homeowner purchasing a central air-conditioning unit. The seller of the air-conditioning unit has an interest in that chattel even before it becomes attached to the real estate, and he maintains his interest after it becomes attached as a fixture (until it has been paid for). The man who installs it may have an interest in that fixture if his labor was performed in installing it (and he has not been paid), and the mortgage company is interested in that fixture because it materially affects the value of the lender's lien interest in the real estate.

Therefore, it is important to realize that another determinative test is frequently employed in the event of conflicting interests in a fixture, that is, whether or not the fixture may be removed from the real estate without material injury to the building [*First National Bank* v. *Whirlpool, supra; Texas Business and Commerce Code*, Section 9.313(a)]. If it can be so removed, it will not ordinarily be considered a fixture and may be subject to prior claims of materialmen, suppliers, and vendors of that particular fixture. Therefore, even if the home purchaser and homeowner fully agree on an item being a fixture, the purchaser may be subsequently surprised when a prior existing security interest in that fixture may have priority interest in his new home.

Security Interests

To help explain the conflict in the fixture that may be created, it must be understood that when personalty (chattel) is purchased on credit, the seller of that item may protect his interest in it by recording his lien interest in that chattel pursuant to the statutes contained in the Texas Business Commerce Code. These liens are commonly called UCC liens (named after the Uniform Commercial Code) and "chattel mortgage" liens. For instance, if a homeowner purchased a new central air-conditioning unit and did not pay cash for same, the seller of that unit may wish to reflect that he still has an interest in the air-conditioning unit because it has not been fully paid for. As the item is purchased, the purchaser would sign a promissory note for payment, a security agreement (a copy of which is shown in Figure 4-2), and two financing statements (the financing statements are commonly called *UCC-1 forms*).* The seller would record his interest in that chattel by filing the financing statements or security agreement in two places: (1) in the UCC lien records in the county clerk's office in the county of the purchaser's residence, and (2) in the office of the secretary of state. When a UCC lien has been properly recorded, it is considered to be "perfected," and the public is legally on notice of that vendor's interest in the air-conditioning unit. A copy of a UCC-1 Financing Statement is shown in Figure 4-3. A subsequent purchaser, for his own protection, is supposed to search the records of the county and determine that no such liens exist against the real estate he is about to purchase.

When it is anticipated that the collateral will be affixed to real estate, there are additional provisions for filing the UCC liens in the fixture records of the county in which the real estate is located, as well as in the office of the secretary of state of the State of Texas. This type of lien is also referred to as a *UCC lien*, and its recordation is termed a *fixture filing*. A copy of a UCC-1 Financing Statement for fixtures is shown in Figure 4-4. It has long been determined in Texas law that a perfected security interest in fixtures has a priority over the conflicting interest of an encumbrance or owner of the real estate where the security interest is:

1. A purchase money interest; or
2. The fixture filing is perfected before the interest of the encumbrance or owner is of record; or
3. The fixture is readily removable factory or office machines; or
4. The lien is prior in time to any other conflicting security interest.

The legal ramifications of chattel mortgages and fixture filings can be rather far-reaching. However, it is very important that all real estate agents understand the complications and conflicts that can arise if a UCC lien is of record in the county courthouse affecting a property that the agent may be attempting to sell or list.

Once a chattel mortgage is perfected, it is released by the use of a UCC-3 form for termination of a security agreement. A copy of a UCC-3 form is shown in Figure 4-5.

The conflicts of mechanics' and materialmen's liens and mortgagees' liens have special applications to other areas of real estate law and will be discussed in greater detail in later chapters.

*UCC stands for Uniform Commercial Code.

NOTICE Prepared by the State Bar of Texas for use by Lawyers only.
To select the proper form, fill in blank spaces, strike out form provisions or insert special terms constitutes the practice of law. No "standard form" can meet all requirements.

PROMISSORY NOTE

$ 9,400.00 Houston , Texas, February 32, 1978

For value received, I, We, or either of us, as principals, promise to pay to the order of CAVEAT VENDOR, INC., a Texas corporation, in the City of Houston , Harris County, Texas, the sum of NINE THOUSAND FOUR HUNDRED AND NO/100THS-----------------Dollars ($9,400.00), in legal and lawful money of the United States of America, with interest thereon from date hereof until maturity at the rate of eighteen per cent (18%) per annum; the interest payable monthly as it accrues; matured unpaid principal and interest shall bear interest at the rate of ten per cent (10%) per annum from date of maturity until paid.

This note is due and payable as follows, to-wit:

On or before the 32nd day of February, 1979.

It is expressly provided that upon default in the punctual payment of this note or any part thereof, principal or interest, as the same shall become due and payable, the entire indebtedness evidenced hereby shall be matured, at the option of the holder. In the event this Note, or any part hereof, is collected through Probate, Bankruptcy or other judicial proceedings by an attorney or is placed in the hands of an attorney for collection after maturity, then the undersigned agree and promise to pay a reasonable attorney's fee for collection, which in no event shall be less than ten per cent (10%) of the principal and interest then owing.

Each maker, surety and endorser of this Note expressly waives all notices, demands for payment, presentations for payment, notices of intention to accelerate the maturity, protest and notice of protest, as to this note and as to each, every and all installments hereof, and each consents that the payee or other holder of this Note may at any time, and from time to time, upon request of or by agreement with any of us, extend the date of maturity hereof or change the time or method of payments without notice to any of the other makers, sureties or endorsers, who shall remain bound for the payment hereof.

Address 4736 Madison
Houston, Texas

BUYER BEWARE

PROMISSORY NOTE

TO

PREPARED IN THE LAW OFFICE OF:

FIGURE 4-2. Promissory note.

Prepared by the State Bar of Texas for use by Lawyers only. 8-73-5M
To select the proper form, fill in blank spaces, strike out form provisions or insert special terms constitutes the practice of law. No "standard form" can meet all requirements.

SECURITY AGREEMENT

(CONSUMER GOODS, EQUIPMENT AND FARM PRODUCTS)

THE STATE OF TEXAS
COUNTY OF HARRIS } KNOW ALL MEN BY THESE PRESENTS:

That BUYER BEWARE

whose address is 4736 Madison (No. and Street) Houston (City)
Harris County, Texas (State) hereinafter called "Debtor" (whether one or more),
hereby GRANTS to CAVEAT VENDOR, INC.

whose address is 3737 Arnold (No. and Street) Houston (City)
Harris County, Texas (State) hereinafter called "Secured Party"
(whether one or more), a security interest in the following described personal property now located and situated
at 4736 Madison (No. and Street) Houston (City) Harris County, Texas,
together with all additions and accessions thereto (in the event such property be livestock, then together with the increase, if any, therefrom), and proceeds thereof (the inclusion of such proceeds does not authorize Debtor to sell, dispose of or otherwise use the Collateral in any manner not authorized by this agreement), all hereinafter called the "Collateral", to-wit:

1. One High Performance Air Conditioning Unit, Model No. 694, Serial No. SE3469R739.

2. Deluxe Woodburner One Freestanding Stove, Model No. 3, Serial No. QRS86543.

FIGURE 4-2 (*continued*).

which Collateral is of the following classification (s):

[X] Consumer Goods
[ ] Equipment (Farm Use)
[ ] Equipment (Business Use)
[ ] Farm Products

and which Collateral is to be wholly or partly affixed to real estate or other goods, a description of which real estate or other goods is as follows: (if not to be so affixed, insert the word "None"):

Lot 6, Block 37, Section 4, High Cloud Subdivision, Harris County, Texas.

This security interest is to secure the payment of an indebtedness owing by Debtor to Secured Party and evidenced by that one certain promissory note, dated February 32, 1978 in the original principal sum of NINE THOUSAND FOUR HUNDRED AND NO/100THS------------------Dollars ($ 9,400.00) executed by Debtor, payable to the order of Secured Party as follows:

On or before the 32nd day of February, 1979.

and bearing interest as therein stipulated, providing for acceleration of maturity and for attorney's fees; and to secure all renewals and extensions of all or any part of said indebtedness hereby secured.

Debtor warrants, covenants, represents and agrees as follows:

(1) That Debtor is the full owner of said Collateral and has authority to grant this security interest therein; that no Financing Statement is on file covering the Collateral or its proceeds; and except for the security interest granted hereby, there is no lien or encumbrance in or on the Collateral, unless otherwise expressly stated herein.

(2) That Debtor's residence is the address shown at the beginning hereof, and Debtor will immediately notify Secured Party in writing of any change of such residence.

(3) That the Collateral will not be sold, transferred, rented, leased, pledged, made subject to a security agreement, or removed from its present location above named without the written consent of Secured Party and that the Collateral will not be misused or abused, wasted or allowed to deteriorate, except for ordinary wear and tear from its intended use. The Collateral shall remain in Debtor's possession or control at all times at Debtor's risk of loss.

(4) That the Collateral will be used primarily for the classification of use above stated, and for no other use without the written consent of Secured Party. The Collateral will not be affixed to any real estate or other goods so as to become a fixture on real estate or accession to other goods, unless such real estate or other goods be described hereinabove; if said Collateral is to be so affixed, Debtor will upon demand of Secured Party furnish written consent or consents to the security interest hereby created or disclaimer or disclaimers signed by all persons having an interest in the real estate or other goods.

(5) That Debtor will sign and execute, upon request of Secured Party, any Financing Statement or other document or procure any document, and pay all connected costs, necessary to protect the security interest granted hereby against the rights or interests of third persons.

(6) That Debtor will protect the title and possession of the Collateral and will pay promptly, when due and before becoming delinquent, all taxes and assessments now existing or hereafter levied or assessed against said Collateral or any part thereof, and will keep said Collateral insured, if insurable, to the extent of the original amount of the indebtedness hereby secured or to the full insurable value of said Collateral, whichever is the lesser, against loss or damage by fire, windstorm and theft and any other hazard or hazards as may be reasonably required from time to time by Secured Party, in such form and with such insurance company or companies as may be approved by Secured Party and will deliver to Secured Party the policies of such insurance, having attached thereto such mortgage indemnity clause as Secured Party shall direct, and will deliver renewals of such policies to Secured Party at least ten (10) days before any such insurance policies expire; any sums which may become due under any such policy, or policies, may be applied by Secured Party, at his option, to reduce said indebtedness, whether due or not, or Secured Party may permit Debtor to use said sums to repair or replace all Collateral damaged or destroyed and covered by such insurance.

FIGURE 4-2 (*continued*).

In the event Debtor shall fail to keep said Collateral in good repair and condition, or to pay promptly when due all taxes and assessments, as aforesaid, or to preserve the prior security interest hereby granted in said Collateral, or to keep said Collateral insured, as aforesaid, or to deliver the policy or policies of insurance or the renewal thereof to Secured Party, as aforesaid, then Secured Party may, at his option, but without being required to do so, make such repairs, pay such taxes and assessments, remove any prior liens or security interests and prosecute or defend any suits in relation to the prior security interest of this agreement in said Collateral, or insure and keep insured said Collateral in an amount not to exceed that above stipulated; that any sum which may be so paid out by Secured Party and all sums paid for insurance premiums, as aforesaid, including the costs, expenses and attorney's fees paid in any suit affecting said Collateral when necessary to protect the security interest hereof shall bear interest from the dates of such payments at ten (10%) per cent per annum and shall be paid by Debtor to Secured Party upon demand, at the same place at which the above described note or notes are payable and shall be a part of the indebtedness hereby secured and recoverable as such in all respects.

Debtor shall be in default under this Security Agreement upon the happening of any of the following events or conditions (herein called an "Event of Default"):

(1) Debtor's failure to pay when due, or declared due, the indebtedness hereby secured, or any installment thereof, principal or interest;

(2) Debtor's default in the punctual performance of any of the obligations, covenants, terms or provisions contained herein or in the note or notes hereby secured;

(3) If any warranty, covenant or representation made herein by Debtor proves to have been false in any material respect when so made;

(4) Debtor's dissolution, termination of existence, insolvency or business failure, or Debtor making an assignment for the benefit of creditors or the commission of an act of bankruptcy, or the institution of voluntary or involuntary bankruptcy proceedings, or the taking over of the Collateral or any part thereof by a Receiver for Debtor or the placing of same in the custody of any court or an officer or appointee thereof;

(5) Loss, theft, substantial damage, destruction, sale, abandonment or encumbrance of or to the Collateral or any part thereof.

Upon the occurrence of an Event of Default, and at any time thereafter, Secured Party may elect, Debtor hereby expressly waiving notice, demand and presentment, to declare the entire indebtedness hereby secured immediately due and payable.

In the event of default in the payment of said indebtedness when due or declared due, Secured Party, without waiving any rights and remedies of a Secured Party under the Uniform Commercial Code of Texas, shall have the right to require Debtor to assemble the Collateral and make it available to Secured Party at a place to be designated by Secured Party which is reasonably convenient to both Parties, and the right to take immediate possession of any and all of the Collateral and for this purpose shall have the right to enter upon the premises where said Collateral may be located and remove the same or may leave the same where it is then located, and sell the Collateral or such part thereof as Secured Party may elect (without exhausting the power to sell the remainder or any part thereof at Public Sale as herein provided or at Public or Private Sale as provided in the Uniform Commercial Code of Texas) at Public Sale to the highest bidder for cash at the Courthouse door of the County hereinabove stated where the Collateral is now located, after having first given notice of the time, place and terms of such Public Sale by posting a written or printed notice (which notice shall also show the then location of the Collateral to be sold) of said sale at the Courthouse door of said County, at least ten days before the day of sale and after sending reasonable notice to Debtor and to such other person or persons legally entitled thereto under the Uniform Commercial Code of Texas, of the time and place of the Public Sale; the Collateral to be sold may be sold as an entirety or in such parcels as Secured Party may elect and it shall not be necessary for Secured Party to have actual possession of the Collateral or to have it present when the sale is made, but full and perfect title shall pass wheresoever said Collateral may then be, and Secured Party thus selling said Collateral shall deliver to the purchaser thereof a Bill of Sale or Transfer therefor, binding Debtor to warrant and forever defend the title to such Collateral, and out of the proceeds of the sale pay the reasonable expenses of retaking, holding, preparing for sale, selling and the like, reasonable attorney's fees and legal expenses so incurred by Secured Party, and the balance remaining shall thereupon be applied toward the payment of the amount then owing on the indebtedness hereby secured, including principal, interest and attorney's fees as provided herein and in said Note, rendering the balance, if any, and surplus, if any, to the person or persons legally entitled thereto under the Uniform Commercial Code of Texas, but if there be any deficiency, Debtor shall remain liable therefor. Secured Party shall have the right to purchase at such Public Sale, being the highest bidder. The recitals in the Bill of Sale or Transfer to the purchaser at such sale shall be prima facie evidence of the truth of the matters therein stated and all prerequisites to said sale required hereunder and under the Uniform Commerical Code of Texas shall be presumed to have been performed.

Secured Party, in addition to the rights and remedies provided for in the preceding paragraph, shall have all the rights and remedies of a Secured Party under the Uniform Commercial Code of Texas and Secured Party shall be entitled to avail himself of all such other rights and remedies as may now or hereafter exist at law or in equity for the collection of said indebtedness and the enforcement of the covenants herein and the foreclosure of the security interest created hereby and the resort to any remedy provided hereunder or provided by the Uniform Commercial Code of Texas, or by any other law of Texas, shall not prevent the concurrent or subsequent employment of any other appropriate remedy or remedies.

FIGURE 4-2 (*continued*).

The requirement of reasonable notice to Debtor of the time and place of any Public Sale of the Collateral or of the time after which any Private Sale, or any other intended disposition thereof is to be made, shall be met if such notice is mailed, postage prepaid, to Debtor at the address of Debtor designated at the beginning of this Security Agreement, at least five days before the date of any Public Sale or at least five days before the time after which any Private Sale or other disposition is to be made.

Secured Party may remedy any default, without waiving same, or may waive any default without waiving any prior or subsequent default.

The security interest herein granted shall not be affected by nor affect any other security taken for the indebtedness hereby secured, or any part thereof; and any extensions may be made of the indebtedness and this security interest and any releases may be executed of the Collateral, or any part thereof, herein conveyed without affecting the priority of this security interest or the validity thereof with reference to any third person, and the holder of said indebtedness shall not be limited by any election of remedies if he chooses to foreclose this security interest by suit. The right to sell under the terms hereof shall also exist cumulative with said suit; and one method so resorted to shall not bar the other, but both may be exercised at the same or different times, nor shall one be a defense to the other.

The pronouns used in this agreement are in the masculine gender but shall be construed as feminine or neuter as occasion may require. "Secured Party" and "Debtor" as used in this agreement include, shall bind and shall inure to the benefit of the respective heirs, executors or administrators, successors, representatives, receivers, trustees or assigns of such parties. If there be more than one Debtor, their obligations shall be joint and several.

The law governing this secured transaction shall be the Uniform Commercial Code of Texas and other applicable laws of the State of Texas. All terms used herein which are defined in the Uniform Commercial Code of Texas shall have the same meaning herein as in said Code.

EXECUTED THIS ....32nd.................. day of ....February.............................., A. D. 1978...

CAVEAT VENDOR, INC. .... BUYER BEWARE ....

BY:

....

Secured Party — Debtor

Dewey Cheatham, President

FIGURE 4-2 (*continued*).

Uniform Commercial Code—FINANCING STATEMENT—Form UCC-1 (Rev. 6-19-75)

"Litho Snap" * * * Lithographed by Hart Graphics, Austin, Texas * * *

Filing Fee $3.00 IMPORTANT—Read instructions on back before filling out form

This Financing Statement is presented to a Filing Officer for filing pursuant to the Uniform Commercial Code

1. Debtor(s) Name and Mailing Address: (Do not abbreviate)	2. Secured Party(ies) Name and Address:	3. For Filing Officer (Date, Time, Number and Filing Office):
BUYER BEWARE 4736 Madison Houston, Texas	CAVEAT VENDOR, INC. 3737 Arnold Houston, Texas	

4. This Financing Statement covers the following types (or items) of property. (WARNING: If collateral is crops, fixtures, timber or minerals, read instructions on back.)

One (1) Deluxe Woodburner One Freestanding Stove, Model No. 3, Serial No. QRS86543.

5. Name and Address of Assignee of Secured Party: (Use this space to describe collateral, if needed)

Check only if applicable

☐ This Financing Statement is to be filed for record in the real estate records.

Number of additional sheets presented ________

☐ Products of collateral are also covered.

6. This Statement is signed by the Secured Party instead of the Debtor to perfect a security interest in collateral

(Please check appropriate box)

☐ already subject to a security interest in another jurisdiction when it was brought into this state, or when the debtor's location was changed to this state, or

☐ already subject to a financing statement filed in another county.

☐ which is proceeds of the original collateral described above in which a security interest was perfected, or

☐ as to which the filing has lapsed, or

☐ acquired after a change of name, identity or corporate structure of the debtor.

Use whichever signature line is applicable.

By Buyer Beware Signature(s) of Debtor(s)

By ________________ Signature(s) of Secured Party(ies)

(1) Filing Officer Copy—Numerical

STANDARD FORM—FORM UCC-1 (REV. 6-19-75) APPROVED BY THE SECRETARY OF STATE OF TEXAS—FORM 15-1549—HART GRAPHICS, P. O. BOX 968, AUSTIN, TEXAS 78767

INSTRUCTIONS

1. PLEASE TYPE this form. Do not write in Box 3.
2. If collateral is CROPS, state in Box 4, "The above described crops are growing or are to be grown on: (Describe Real Estate concerned)."
3. If collateral is or will become FIXTURES, or is TIMBER, or is MINERALS OR THE LIKE (INCLUDING OIL AND GAS) or ACCOUNTS THAT WILL BE FINANCED AT THE WELLHEAD OR MINEHEAD, CHECK ☑. "This Financing Statement is to be filed for record in the Real Estate records, in box 4" and State if applicable, "The above goods are, or are to become fixtures on: ________________", or where appropriate substitute either, "The above timber is standing on: ________________", or, "The above minerals or the like (including oil and gas) or accounts will be financed at the wellhead or minehead of the well or mine located on ________________". Describe real estate concerned sufficient as if it were contained in a mortgage of real estate to give constructive notice of the mortgage under the law of this State. If the debtor does not have an interest of record in the realty, give the name of a record owner of the real estate concerned. FEE FOR THIS TYPE FILING IS $6.00. IF ANY OTHER FORM IS USED, THE FEE IS $9.00.
4. If the space provided for any item on the form is inadequate, the item should be continued on additional sheets, preferably 7⅜" x 5". Please do not staple or tape additional sheets directly on item 4 of this form.
5. FILING FEE for this standard form is $3.00 (except a filing under instruction 3 above). If any other form is used, the fee is $6.00.
6. Remove Secured Party and Debtor copies, and send other 3 copies with interleaved carbon paper still intact to the filing officer.
7. Fold only above or below TAB card for mailing. DO NOT bend TAB card.
8. At the time of original filing, the filing officer will return second copy as an acknowledgment. If acknowledgment copy is to be returned to other than the Secured Party or Assignee, please enclose a self-addressed envelope.

FIGURE 4-3.

Uniform Commercial Code—FINANCING STATEMENT—Form UCC-1 (Rev. 6-19-75)

"Litho Snap" * * * Lithographed by Hart Graphics, Austin, Texas * * *

Filing Fee $3.00 IMPORTANT—Read instructions on back before filling out form

This Financing Statement is presented to a Filing Officer for filing pursuant to the Uniform Commercial Code

3. For Filing Officer (Date, Time, Number and Filing Office):

1. Debtor(s) Name and Mailing Address: (Do not abbreviate)

BUYER BEWARE
4736 Madison
Houston, Texas

2. Secured Party(ies) Name and Address:

CAVEAT VENDOR, INC.
3737 Arnold
Houston, Texas

4. This Financing Statement covers the following types (or items) of property. (WARNING: If collateral is crops, fixtures, timber or minerals, read instructions on back.)

One (1) High Performance Air Conditioning Unit, Model No. 694, Serial No. SE3469R739.

The above goods are, or are to become, fixtures on March 1, 1978.

5. Name and Address of Assignee of Secured Party: (Use this space to describe collateral, if needed)

Check only if applicable
☒ This Financing Statement is to be filed for record in the real estate records.

Number of additional sheets presented ________
☐ Products of collateral are also covered.

6. This Statement is signed by the Secured Party instead of the Debtor to perfect a security interest in collateral
(Please check appropriate box)
☐ already subject to a security interest in another jurisdiction when it was brought into this state, or when the debtor's location was changed to this state, or
☐ already subject to a financing statement filed in another county.
☐ which is proceeds of the original collateral described above in which a security interest was perfected, or
☐ as to which the filing has lapsed, or
☐ acquired after a change of name, identity or corporate structure of the debtor.

CAVEAT VENDOR, INC.

Use whichever signature line is applicable.

By Buyer Beware Signature(s) of Debtor(s)

By Dewey Cheatham, President Signature(s) of Secured Party(ies)

(1) Filing Officer Copy—Numerical

STANDARD FORM—FORM UCC-1 (REV. 6-19-75) APPROVED BY THE SECRETARY OF STATE OF TEXAS—FORM 15-1548—HART GRAPHICS, P. O. BOX 968, AUSTIN, TEXAS 78767

INSTRUCTIONS

1. PLEASE TYPE this form. Do not write in Box 3.
2. If collateral is CROPS, state in Box 4, "The above described crops are growing or are to be grown on: (Describe Real Estate concerned)."
3. If collateral is or will become FIXTURES, or is TIMBER, or is MINERALS OR THE LIKE (INCLUDING OIL AND GAS) or ACCOUNTS THAT WILL BE FINANCED AT THE WELLHEAD OR MINEHEAD, CHECK ☑. "This Financing Statement is to be filed for record in the Real Estate records, in box 4" and State if applicable, "The above goods are, or are to become fixtures on: ______________", or where appropriate substitute either, "The above timber is standing on: ______________", or, "The above minerals or the like (including oil and gas) or accounts will be financed at the well-head or minehead of the well or mine located on ______________". Describe real estate concerned sufficient as if it were contained in a mortgage of real estate to give constructive notice of the mortgage under the law of this State. If the debtor does not have an interest of record in the realty, give the name of a record owner of the real estate concerned. FEE FOR THIS TYPE FILING IS $6.00. IF ANY OTHER FORM IS USED, THE FEE IS $9.00.
4. If the space provided for any item on the form is inadequate, the item should be continued on additional sheets, preferably 7⅜" x 5". Please do not staple or tape additional sheets directly on item 4 of this form.
5. FILING FEE for this standard form is $3.00 (except a filing under instruction 3 above). If any other form is used, the fee is $6.00.
6. Remove Secured Party and Debtor copies, and send other 3 copies with interleaved carbon paper still intact to the filing officer.
7. Fold only above or below TAB card for mailing. DO NOT bend TAB card.
8. At the time of original filing, the filing officer will return second copy as an acknowledgment. If acknowledgment copy is to be returned to other than the Secured Party or Assignee, please enclose a self-addressed envelope.

FIGURE 4-4.

Uniform Commercial Code—FINANCING STATEMENT CHANGE—Form UCC-3 (Rev. 6-19-75)

"Litho Snap" * * * Lithographed by Hart Graphics, Austin, Texas * * *

Filing Fee $3.00 IMPORTANT—Read instructions on back before filling out form

This Statement is presented to a Filing Officer for filing pursuant to the Uniform Commercial Code

1. Debtor(s) Name and Mailing Address: (Do not abbreviate)	2. Secured Party(ies) Name and Address:	3. For Filing Officer (Date, Time and Filing Office):
BUYER BEWARE 4736 Madison Houston, Texas	CAVEAT VENDOR, INC. 3737 Arnold Houston, Texas	

4. This statement refers to original Financing Statement No. ______ Date Filed February 32, 1978

Check if applicable ☒ This Financing Statement Change is to be filed for record in the real estate records.

5. A. Continuation ☐	B. Assignment ☐	C. Termination ☒	D. Partial Release ☐	E. Amendment ☐
The original Financing Statement is still effective.	The Secured Party of record has assigned his interest in the following collateral to:	The Secured Party of record no longer claims a security interest under the Financing Statement	The Secured Party of record releases the following collateral:	The Financing Statement is amended as set forth below:

6.

CAVEAT VENDOR, INC.

By ______ Signature(s) of Debtor(s)

By ______ Signature(s) of Secured Party(ies)

Dewey Cheatham, President

(1) Filing Officer Copy—Numerical

STANDARD FORM—FORM UCC-3 (REV. 6-19-75)—APPROVED BY THE SECRETARY OF STATE OF TEXAS—FORM 13-1336—HART GRAPHICS, P. O. BOX 968, AUSTIN, TEXAS 78767

INSTRUCTIONS

1. PLEASE TYPE this form. Do not write in Box 3.
2. Boxes 1 and 2 should read identical to boxes 1 and 2 of the original filed financing statement. All changes should be noted in box 6.
3. Fold only above or below TAB card copy for mailing. DO NOT bend TAB card.
4. This form must be signed by the Secured Party of record. An amendment should also be signed by the Debtor.
5. If the space provided for any item is inadequate, the item should be continued on additional sheets, preferably 7⅝" x 5". Please do not staple or tape additional sheets directly on item 6 of this form.
6. If this statement refers to an original financing statement which covers collateral which is or will become FIXTURES or is TIMBER, or is MINERALS OR THE LIKE (INCLUDING OIL AND GAS) or ACCOUNTS THAT WILL BE FINANCED AT THE WELLHEAD OR MINEHEAD, check the box in item 4. The filing fee for this type filing is $6.00 for this standard form. If any other form is used, the fee is $9.00.
7. FILING FEE for this standard form is $3.00 (except a filing under instruction 6 above). If any other form is used, the filing fee is $6.00.
8. Remove Secured Party and Debtor copies, and send other 3 copies with the interleaved carbon paper still intact to the filing officer.
9. At the time of filing, the filing officer will return second copy as an acknowledgment. If acknowledgment copy is to be returned to other than the Secured Party or Assignee, enclose a self-addressed envelope.

FIGURE 4-5.

Trade Fixtures

There is a special class of fixtures that are termed *trade fixtures*, which refer to articles that enable a tenant to carry on his business for trade. One normally finds the concept of trade fixtures in landlord-tenant situations where the tenant installs certain fixtures for his own use and benefit and for his own specific business purposes.

With few exceptions, the concept of trade fixtures is well settled in Texas law. The parties' rights are usually set out in a lease or other contractual obligation between the parties. The general rule is that all trade fixtures are ordinarily removable during or at the expiration of the tenant's term of occupancy, provided they can be removed without material or permanent injury to the building. Unless otherwise specified in the contract, the fixtures must be removed within a reasonable time after the termination of the tenant's occupancy. "Reasonable," as in other cases, is a question of fact for the jury to decide. In the event the tenant does fail to remove the trade fixtures within a reasonable period of time, he forfeits his rights to those improvements, and they will become the property of the landlord.

Although this concept may seem to be simple and hardly worthy of explanation, one must remember that even when the rights are set up by terms of a written agreement between the parties, conflicts may arise and can create difficult situations. In at least one Texas case, "fixtures and floor coverings" were judged to include permanent floor coverings and various built-in items that could not be removed without material damage to the premises, *Haverfield Company* v. *Siegel*, 366 S.W.2d 790 (Tex. Civ. App.—San Antonio, 1963). There are always exceptions!

Easements

An easement is generally defined as the right acquired by one person to the use of the land of another for a special purpose. If you would like to dazzle your friends with your brilliance, you may choose to describe easements as "incorporeal hereditaments" because they are, in fact, incorporeal (intangible) rights that may be inherited. Each easement carries with it the right to reasonable use, but only reasonable use, such that it is necessary, convenient, and as little burden to the owner of that real estate as possible, *Exxon Corp.* v. *Schutzmaier*, 537 S.W.2d 282 (Tex. Civ. App.—Beaumont, 1976). An easement right carries with it only user privilege and not any privilege of ownership. A mere easement can *never* be transposed into fee simple title or a feasible claim of title to the real estate, *Reiter* v. *Coastal States*, 382 S.W.2d 243 (Tex. 1964).

Appurtenant versus In Gross

Easements are generally categorized into two types: (1) an easement appurtenant and (2) an easement in gross. An *easement appurtenant* is an easement created for the benefit of another tract of land. There must be two different owners involved, one being the owner of the estate over which the easement crosses; this is called the *servient estate*. The other owner owns the property that the easement serves; this is called the *dominant estate*. Figure 4-6 illustrates how the appurtenant easement concept can be applied. Because of the nature of an appurtenant easement (it benefits a particular piece of property), an appurtenant easement is considered to be a covenant running with the land; that is, the right to use that easement passes along with the title to the dominant estate, *Hidalgo* v. *Maverick*, 349 S.W.2d 768 (Tex. Civ. App.—San Antonio, 1961).

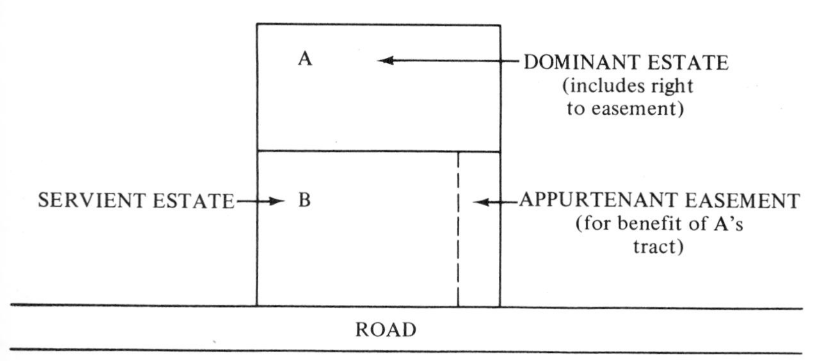

FIGURE 4-6. Estates created by an appurtenant easement.

An *easement in gross*, on the other hand, is an easement that does not normally benefit any particular piece of property but benefits only the individual owner for their particular use. Such easement cannot be sold and normally terminates with the dissolution of the entity that has the right to use that easement. This type of easement is generally a right-of-way easement for power companies, gas transmission companies, flood-control authorities, and other governmental and quasi-governmental authorities. It should be emphasized that if the court is in the position of determining whether or not an easement is an easement in gross or an easement appurtenant, the court will generally attempt to find that it is an easement appurtenant since easements in gross are not favored under Texas law. An easement in gross is generally in writing and is agreed to by all the parties; it is often acquired by eminent domain proceedings by some condemning authority.

Creation

Creation of an easement can be either express or implied, written or oral. Easements are normally created in one of six ways: (1) by express grant, (2) by express reservation, (3) by implication, (4) by prescription, (5) by reference to a plat, or (6) by estoppel. We will discuss each of these methods individually.

Easement by Express Grant. If an express easement is made by an agreement between the parties (easement by express grant), it has to follow the normal formalities of any real estate instrument and be in writing, properly subscribed by the party to be charged, with adequate legal description, acknowledged (if it is to be recorded), and properly delivered. This is, by all means, the simplest and most direct method of creating an easement: the intent of the parties is obviously clear, the use is properly set out, and includes termination and other pertinent terms requested by the respective parties. If recorded, the instrument can meet all the requirements of constructive notice for the parties' own protection, as well as for the protection of third parties.

Easement by Express Reservation. An easement created by express reservation in a deed is also an express easement. However, the details and terms of an easement created in this manner are often left out because the use of an easement reserved in a conveyance by a deed is usually appurtenant and necessary for either the property being conveyed or for the real estate contiguous thereto. For instance, property owner *A* may be willing to sell his frontage to property owner *B* but will reserve an easement to himself for access to the remainder of his property. The property over which the easement crosses still vests fee title unto the grantee but reserves the right to reasonable use to the grantor. Note that this is usually not an exception to title but rather a property right reserved out of the conveyance passed by the deed. A more detailed discussion of exceptions and reservations in deeds will be discussed in Chapter 7, Conveyancing.

Easement by Implication. An easement by implication is one that is not in writing. It is one that is imposed by a court in the form of an equitable remedy to provide access to a landlocked parcel of real estate. This is normally an easement that has been in continuous use for some time but was not created by any agreement in writing between the parties affected. However, before a court will impose such an easement by implication, certain criteria must be met to justify the court's intervention:

1. The prior use of the easement must be apparent and obvious by the party seeking to enforce his easement right.
2. The prior use must also have been reasonably continuous. This

does not mean that the party must have used it every day, but he must have used it often enough to establish a certain continuity of use.

3. The use of that easement must be reasonably necessary to a fair and enjoyable use of the dominant estate.
4. There must have originally been a unity of ownership of the dominant and servient estates immediately prior to the easement being created, *Westbrook* v. *Wright*, 477 S.W.2d 663 (Tex. Civ. App.—Houston, 1972).

The typical fact situation surrounding an easement by implication is where two owners have an oral agreement for the use of an easement to a landlocked parcel of real estate that was originally owned by one of the two parties. When the oral agreement is breached, the aggrieved party petitions the court for intervention.

Easement by Prescription. An easement by prescription is one that has been obtained and is held by a claimant against the wishes of the landowner. It is very similar and analogous to obtaining title to property by adverse possession. However, one should remember that adverse possession and easement by prescription are entirely different concepts. An easement, as stated previously, never ripens into fee simple ownership, but adverse possession does. The requirements to create an easement by prescription are understandably a little more difficult than those required to create an easement by implication. A claimant's right to this easement is generally imposed by a court, as is the case in an easement by implication. The requirements for an easement by prescription are as follows:

1. The use of the easement must be adverse, open, notorious, and hostile to the interest of the landowner over which the easement passes. This does not mean that the claimant must have used the easement under artillery fire or carrying a sack of grenades, but the landowner must have been clearly against the creation and use of said easement; and
2. The use of the easement must be exclusive to the claimant and not to the public; and
3. The use of the easement must have been uninterrupted and continuous for a period of at least ten years, *Davis* v. *Carriker*, 536 S.W.2d 246 (Tex. Civ. App.—Amarillo, 1976), *Exxon* v. *Schutzmaier, supra*.

Easement by Reference to a Plat. An easement can be created by reference to an existing subdivision plat. It is quite common for subdivision developers, when laying out a subdivision, to record that subdivision's plat in the county in which the subdivision is located. The legal descriptions to a given lot, block, and section can then be made by reference to the plat rather than by the more complicated metes and bounds system. It logically follows that as the developer changes the legal description to a piece of property by filing a subdivision plat, he may also create easements for water mains, gas distribution lines, road rights-of-way, and other types of easements that are necessary for the use and benefit of that subdivision. Easements are similarly created by governmental and quasi-governmental authorities through the promulgation of official city, county, and state maps that delineate flood-way areas, flood-control districts, power lines, and major utility distribution systems.

Easement by Estoppel. "Estoppel" is a rather elusive legal concept that alludes to a claim made as an affirmative defense to a cause of action when the defendant has been induced into doing an act by the plaintiff. This concept is sometimes called *promissory estoppel*. An easement by estoppel normally occurs where a party, by oral agreement, has granted a right to an easement in his land upon which the other party has relied in good faith and has expended money—money that would be lost if the right to use and enjoy that easement is revoked by the promissor. Since the owner of the dominant estate relied on the servient tenant's promise for using that easement, equity normally prohibits the owner of the servient estate from preventing the dominant owner's use of that easement. The only requirements for creating an easement by estoppel are that:

1. The representation must have been communicated to the promisee or owner of the dominant estate; and
2. The representation must have been believed by that promisee; and
3. There must have been a reliance on such promise to the detriment of the dominant estate owner (*Exxon Corp.* v. *Schutzmaier, supra*).

The nature of an easement by estoppel is one that is imposed by equity because of the bad faith evidenced by the promisor in granting an easement and then attempting to take it back after the promisee has relied on his promise. The strong equitable nature of this particular type of easement is such that the same strict and conclusive rules of law as an easement by implication, which has many of the same characteristics, do not apply. As in the case of all other easements, generally, the use of this easement can only be reasonable use that is necessary and convenient and of as little burden to the servient estate as possible.

Termination

If it has been determined that an easement has been properly created and is in existence, even if it is an oral easement created by implication, estoppel, or by prescription, the termination of that easement, as in the termination of most other property rights, has certain requirements that must be met before that termination becomes effective. The methods of terminating an easement are release, merger, failure of purpose, and abandonment.

Release. As an easement can be created by an express reservation or express grant, it can also be released by express agreement of termination between the parties involved. The same care in drawing the instrument for creating the easement should also be taken in the termination of that easement. There may be rights created that could be overlooked when the release is drawn, and such an oversight may inadvertently create a cloud on the title.

Merger. Merger is accomplished when the owner of the dominant estate purchases the servient estate or vice versa and therefore owns fee simple title to the entire property and no longer has any use for the easement. Figure 4-7 will help to illustrate this matter more clearly. Note that prop-

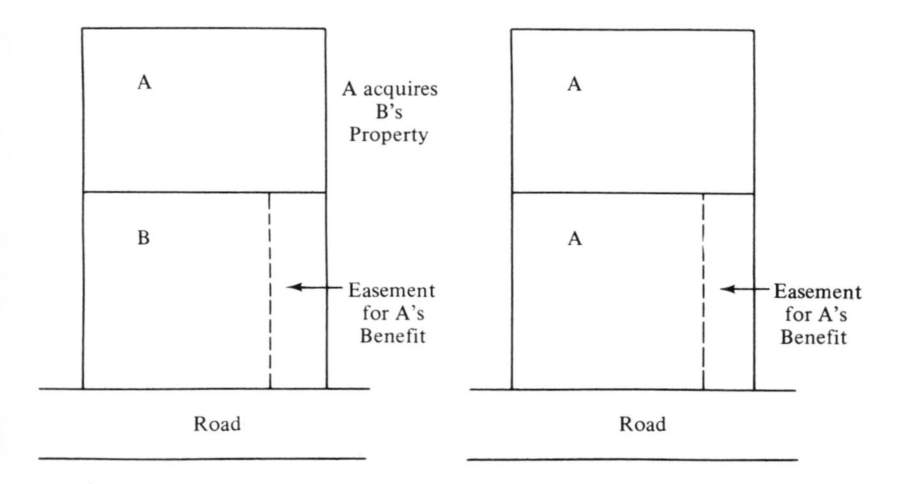

FIGURE 4-7.

erty owner A has the dominant estate and property owner B has the servient estate that is encumbered by the easement. Recall that the easement is a right that vests in the dominant estate. Although property owner B still owns the land encumbered by the easement, it logically follows that when property owner A acquires property owner B's interest to the fee title to the property, the rights in the easement and his rights to the fee title of the real estate merge, and the easement terminates.

Failure of Purpose. Easements are normally created for a particular purpose, whether express or implied. It is within this purpose that guidelines are established for reasonable use. When the purpose for an easement fails, so does the easement. An illustration of this would be a road that was created to cross property because there was no other access to the dominant estate. When a new road is constructed along public right-of-way that provides other access to the dominant estate such that the easement is no longer needed, it may be reasonably assumed that the servient owner may terminate the easement for failure of purpose. It is interesting to note that due to the failure of purpose doctrine, it is, at least theoretically, possible to have a perpetual easement. For instance, consider an easement for flood-control drainage or public street access. Once the easement has been created by a third party or governmental authority, the doctrines of merger and release will probably never be satisfied, and one would have to rely on the failure of purpose doctrine for a party to effectively terminate the easement. Without some change in condition, these easements would effectively last forever.

Abandonment. An easement can be terminated by abandonment. However, as in the terminations of all other real estate rights, abandonment is difficult to prove and is not an easy method of termination. There must be proof of an intent of the party using the easement to abandon that easement before it can be properly terminated. This abandonment must be proved by the person attempting to terminate the easement rights, and must be established by clear and satisfactory evidence. Mere nonuse, by itself, does not constitute abandonment, *Peterson* v. *Greenway Parks*, 408 S.W.2d 261 (Tex. Civ. App.—Dallas, 1966). It is not difficult to see that the burden of proof in a situation constituting abandonment requires much more effort than the failure of purpose or merger doctrines that can be proved without such intent.

SUMMARY

The determination of the fixture is made by considering the mode of attachment, the adaptation of that fixture, and the intention of the parties to the agreement. Another determination involves the rights of the vendor or seller of the fixture and whether or not the fixture can be removed without material injury to the premises. This last determination is normally construed in accordance with the Texas Business and Commerce Code, which deals with security interests of the buyer versus those of the seller of the fixture. An exception to the general classification of fixtures is trade fixtures. An owner of a trade fixture normally retains title to that fixture, regardless of how it is attached to the realty.

An easement is the right acquired by the owner of one parcel of land to the use of someone else's land for a special purpose. An easement right carries with it only user privilege and not any privilege of ownership. Easements are further classified into appurtenant easements and easements in gross. An appurtenant easement is one which benefits an adjoining piece of property. An easement in gross does not normally benefit any particular piece of property. It benefits only the individual user for his particular use. An easement may be created in writing, verbally, or through the actions and conduct of the parties. Easements can be terminated by express release, merger, failure of purpose, or abandonment.

5

REAL ESTATE BROKERAGE AND MANAGEMENT

Real estate brokers and real estate brokerage have been regulated by law in Texas since 1939. The Texas Real Estate Licensing Act (the "Act") was significantly revised, effective May 19, 1975. This revision upgraded the educational requirements for brokers and specifically set out certain duties of care a real estate licensee has toward the public, as well as to his client. Certain provisions of the Texas Real Estate Licensing Act will be reproduced in their entirety throughout this chapter. The provisions of the entire Texas Real Estate Licensing Act are reproduced in the Appendix for reference purposes. The act must be read thoroughly and be understood in detail since all brokers and salespersons are regulated by it. Ignorance of the law is no excuse for violations of it.

The Texas Real Estate Commission and Licensing Requirements

The Real Estate Licensing Act is administered through the Texas Real Estate Commission, which is a body composed of six members appointed by the governor with the advice and consent of two-thirds of the senate present. The commission administers all rules and regulations that govern the procedure, for the institution, conduct, and determination of all causes and proceedings before the commission. The rules that the commission administers additionally promulgate the canons of professional ethics and conduct for real estate licensees, to which the commission expects all licensees to adhere.

To be eligible for a real estate license, an individual must be a citizen of the United States, or a lawfully admitted alien, be at least 18 years of age, and be a legal resident of Texas for at least six months immediately preceding the filing of the application. He must also satisfy the commission as to his honesty, trustworthiness, integrity, and competency. Competency is established by an examination prepared by the commission. The educational requirements established by the act are as follows:

As of January 1, 1977, an applicant for a real estate brokerage license must furnish evidence of successful completion of 12 semester hours of real estate or related courses accepted by the Real Estate Commission, with the following scheduled increases:

On or After	January 1, 1979	January 1, 1981	January 1, 1983	January 1, 1985
Semester Hours That Must Be Completed	15	36	48	60

As of January 1, 1977, an applicant for real estate salesman license must furnish evidence of successful completion of six semester hours of real estate or related courses accepted by the Commission, with the following scheduled increases:

On or After	January 1, 1979	January 1, 1981	January 1, 1983
Semester Hours That Must Be Completed	12	21	36

Beginning January 1, 1985, the Commission will accept applications for a brokerage license only.

In enforcing the rules and regulations, the commission inspects and credits educational programs and establishes standards for accreditation of such programs conducted in the state. To facilitate enforcement of the new standards, Section 8 of the Real Estate Licensing Act also establishes procedural requirements for filing complaints against a particular licensee and establishes a recovery fund to assure an aggrieved party that money for damages will be available in the event he is successful in pursuing a cause of action against a licensee.

Brokers and Salesmen

The act requires licensure for a person to perform certain functions applicable to real estate transactions. It is specifically unlawful for a person to hold himself out or engage in the business of brokerage without being licensed by the Texas Real Estate Commission. It is also unlawful for any salesman to conduct any acts or attempts to act as a real estate agent unless he is associated with a Texas real estate broker, and the salesman cannot accept compensation from any person other than that broker. The definitions of *broker* and *salesman* are the key to how closely the commission can regulate the industry. Sections 2(2) through 2(4) of the act define real estate broker and real estate salesman as follows:

(2) "Real estate broker" means a person who, for another person and for a fee, commission, or other valuable consideration, or with the intention or in the expectation or on the promise of receiving or collecting a fee, commission, or other valuable consideration from another person:

(A) sells, exchanges, purchases, rents, or leases real estate;

(B) offers to sell, exchange, purchase, rent, or lease real estate;

(C) negotiates or attempts to negotiate the listing, sale, exchange, purchase, rental, or leasing of real estate;

(D) lists or offers or attempts or agrees to list real estate for sale, rental, lease, exchange, or trade;

(E) appraises or offers or attempts or agrees to appraise real estate;

(F) auctions, or offers or attempts or agrees to auction, real estate;

(G) buys or sells or offers to buy or sell, or otherwise deals in options on real estate;

(H) aids, attempts, or offers to aid in locating or obtaining for purchase, rent, or lease any real estate;

(I) procures or assists in the procuring of prospects for the purpose of effecting the sale, exchange, lease, or rental of real estate; or

(J) procures or assists in the procuring of properties for the purpose of effecting the sale, exchange, lease, or rental of real estate.

(3) "Broker" also includes a person employed by or on behalf of the owner or owners of lots or other parcels of real estate, at a salary, fee, commission, or any other valuable consideration, to sell the real estate or any part thereof, in lots or parcels or other disposition thereof. It also includes a person who engages in the business of charging an advance fee or contracting for collection of a fee in connection with a contract whereby he undertakes primarily to promote the sale of real estate either through its listing in a publication issued primarily for such purpose, or for referral of information concerning the real estate to brokers, or both.

(4) "Real estate salesman" means a person associated with a Texas-licensed real estate broker for the purposes of performing acts or transactions comprehended by the definition of "real estate broker" as defined in this Act.

Real estate is defined by the act as a leasehold, as well as any other interest or estate in land, whether corporeal, incorporeal, freehold, or nonfreehold, and whether the real estate is situated in this state or elsewhere.

A *person* as defined by the act means an individual, a partnership, or a corporation; this person may hold a broker's or salesman's license. However, there is some indication under Section 6(c) of the act that the corporation must have an officer to act for it who must be qualified as a real estate broker, which may indicate that a corporation, technically, could not be a salesman. There are no provisions in the act for the licensing of a partnership. There has been some case law, however, that indicates that if the partners are brokers, the partnership may seek and obtain a real estate commission, *Kaufhold* v. *Curtis and Ewing*, 557 S.W.2d 334 (Tex. Civ. App.—Houston, 1977).

Considering the foregoing definitions, the commission can actually regulate every phase of the real estate industry, unless the individual performing the functions of a licensee is exempt from the application of the act.

Section 3 of the act provides for circumstances by which real estate transactions can be consummated by an unlicensed (exempt) person. These circumstances are very strictly construed, however, and include the following:

(a) an attorney at law licensed in this state or in any other state;
(b) an attorney in fact under a duly-executed power of attorney authorizing the consummation of a real estate transaction;
(c) a public official in the conduct of his official duties;
(d) a person acting officially as a receiver, trustee, administrator, executor, or guardian;
(e) a person acting under a court order or under the authority of a will or a written trust instrument;
(f) a salesperson employed by an owner in the sale of structures and land on which said structures are situated, provided such structures are erected by the owner in the due course of his business;
(g) an on-site manager of an apartment complex;
(h) transactions involving the sale, lease, or transfer of any mineral or mining interest in real property;
(i) an owner or his employees in renting or leasing his own real estate whether improved or unimproved;
(j) transactions involving the sale, lease, or transfer of cemetery lots.

The act provides that a nonexempt person acting as a real estate broker or salesman without obtaining a license is guilty of a misdemeanor and shall be punishable by a fine not less than $100 nor more than $500 or by imprisonment in the county jail for a term not to exceed one year, or both. If the violations are made by a corporation, they shall be punishable by a fine of not less than $1000 nor more than $2000. There are increased fines for second and subsequent offenses.

If the person received money, or the equivalent thereof, or profited by the consequence of his violation, he shall additionally be liable for damages. The amounts are limited to not less than the amount so received, nor more than three times the sum received, as may be determined by the court [*Tex. Rev. Civ. Stat. Ann.*, art. 6573a, Sec. 19(b)].

Licensee's Employment

The act specifically states under Section 20(b) that an action may not be brought in a court in this state for the recovery of a commission for the sale or purchase of real estate unless the agreement on which the action is brought, *or some memorandum thereof*, is in writing and is signed by the party to be charged. As in all other real estate contracts, the listing agreement must be sufficient to enforce performance. A listing agreement, or memorandum thereof, is normally considered to be specific enough when:

1. It is in writing and is signed by the person to be charged with the commission;
2. It promises a definite commission will be paid, or refers to a written commission schedule;
3. It specifies the name of the broker to whom the commission is to be paid; and
4. It must, either itself or by reference to some other existing writing, identify with reasonable certainty the land to be conveyed, *Knights* v. *Hicks*, 505 S.W.2d 638 (Tex. Civ. App.—Amarillo, 1974).

If the written agreement does not contain the required information, it must refer to an existing agreement or form from which the information can be obtained. If there is no listing agreement, or memorandum thereof, an obligation to pay the broker's commission contained in the earnest money contract may be specific enough to enforce payment, *Maloney* v. *Strain*, 410 S.W.2d 650 (Tex. Civ. App.—Eastland, 1966).

Although not a legal requirement of enforceability, the listing agreement should also contain a definite termination date. Section 15 (4)(G) of the Real Estate License Act specifies that failure to specify a definite termination date in the listing contract proves grounds for license revocation or suspension.

Types of Listing Agreements

Most real estate brokers prefer to use standard-form listing agreements supplied by the local board of realtors to keep their rights more clearly specified and defined. Standard listing agreements are generally considered to be of five types: (1) the exclusive right to sell, (2) the exclusive agency to sell, (3) the open listing, (4) the net listing, and (5) the multiple listing. Copies of some of these standard forms of listing agreements are shown in Figure 5-1.

EXCLUSIVE RIGHT TO SELL
LISTING AGREEMENT

, a real estate broker duly licensed under the Texas Real Estate Licensing Act, hereinafter called Agent, and I.M. SELLER and wife, MAY B. SELLER, the legal owner of the property described below, hereinafter called Owner, hereby agree as follows:

1. Owner hereby grants to Agent the sole and exclusive right to sell the property described below for ninety (90) days from this date and thereafter until Owner shall give Agent written notice of termination.

   Property Description: Lot 1, Block 1, Shakey Acres Subdivision, Harris County, Texas, as shown of record at Volume 7, Page 3 of the Map Records of Harris County, Texas.

2. Agent agrees to employ concentrated and diligent effort to procure a buyer for the property at a price of $80,000, payable in cash at closing, or at such other price and terms as are acceptable to owner.

3. In the event that a ready, willing, and able buyer is obtained during the term of this agreement, whether such sale is made by Agent, by Owner, or by any other person, Owner agrees and promises to pay Agent a commission of seven percent (7%) of the sales price.

4. Owner agrees to:

   a. Grant possession of the property to buyer on funding of buyer's loan, or upon closing, whichever is later, and,

   b. Allow Agent to place a "for sale" sign in Owner's yard, and

   c. Furnish to the buyer, at Owner's expense, title insurance policy to the purchaser, and

   d. Execute and deliver a general warranty deed at the closing of the sale, to the purchaser of the property.

EXECUTED by the parties hereto this 32nd day of January, 1994.

AGENT:

MANNY LISTER & ASSOCIATES, INC.,
Real Estate Agents

by: ______________________
Manny Lister, President

OWNER:
I. M. SELLER and wife, MAY B. SELLER

____
I. M. Seller

____
May B. Seller

FIGURE 5-1.

OPEN LISTING

LISTING AGREEMENT

_____, a real estate broker duly licensed under the Texas Real Estate Licensing Act, hereinafter called Agent, and I. M. SELLER and wife, MAY B. SELLER, the legal owner of the property described below, hereinafter called Owner, hereby agree as follows:

1. Owner hereby employs and appoints Agent to sell the property described herein for a period of ninety (90) days and thereafter until Owner shall give Agent written notice of termination.

   Property Description: Lot 1, Block 1, Shakey Acres Subdivision, Harris County, Texas, as shown of record at Volume 7, Page 3 of the Map Records of Harris County, Texas.

2. Agent agress to employ concentrated and diligent effort to procure a buyer for the property at a price of $80,000, payable in cash at closing, or at such other price and terms as are acceptable to Owner.

3. In the event that the property is sold during the term of this agreement and such sale be made by Agent, or by any person acting through or for Agent, Owner agrees and promises to pay Agent a commission of seven percent (7%) of the sales price.

4. Owner agrees to:

   a. Grant possession of the property to buyer on funding of buyer's loan, or upon closing, whichever is later, and

   b. Allow Agent to place a "for sale" sign in Owner's yard, and

   c. Furnish to the buyer, at Owner's expense title insurance policy to the purchaser, and

   d. Execute and deliver a general warranty deed at the closing of the sale, to the purchaser of the property.

EXECUTED by the parties hereto this 32nd day of January, 1994.

AGENT:

MANNY LISTER & ASSOCIATES, INC.,
Real Estate Agents

by: ____________________
Manny Lister, President

OWNER:
I. M. SELLER and wife, MAY B. SELLER

____
I. M. Seller

____
May B. Seller

FIGURE 5-1 (*continued*).

CDC • CONTROL DATA HOUSTON

MULTIPLE LISTING SERVICE

EXCLUSIVE RIGHT TO SELL LISTING AGREEMENT

________________, Texas (Date) ________________________, 19

PRICES AND TERMS. In consideration of services to be performed by the undersigned Realtor, the undersigned Owner, or legal agent, herein called Owner, does hereby appoint the undersigned Realtor exclusive agent and grant to Realtor the irrevocable and exclusive right to sell, for a term commencing on the date hereof and expiring at 5:00 P.M. on the ________ day of ________________________, 19______, at a price of $________________ on the terms of ________________________________ or any price and/or terms that Owner may accept, the following property with all improvements and fixtures thereon:

PROPERTY DESCRIPTION. Lot ________________ Block ________________, Addition ________________

otherwise known as ________________________________ County, Texas. ________________

M.L.S. FILING. Realtor is a participant of the Multiple Listing Service of the Houston Board of Realtors and Realtor binds himself that he will file this listing with said service within four (4) days after Owner signs same.

COMMISSION. Owner agrees to pay Realtor a commission of ____________% of the sale price (1) if there is a sale, exchange or disposition of said property during the term of this agreement or any extension thereof, whether made by Realtor, by Owner, or by anyone else, at the price and on the terms stated herein, or at any other price and terms accepted by Owner, or (2) upon Realtor individually or in cooperation with another real estate broker finding a buyer during the term of this agreement or any extension thereof who is ready, willing and able to purchase said property at the price and on the terms stated herein or at any other price and terms acceptable to Owner.

NAME RESERVATION. If within ____________ days following the expiration of this contract, a sale, exchange, or disposition of the above property is made, directly or indirectly, to any person with whom Realtor or any cooperating broker has had negotiations for such sale, exchange, or disposition during the exclusive listing term, Owner agrees to pay Realtor said commission, provided, however, that: Realtor shall register with Owner on a single piece of paper, a written list of the names of such persons, either by mail (return receipt requested) postmarked at least three (3) days prior to expiration of listing or by wire or hand delivery prior to final expiration of listing. If upon expiration of this listing, the property is relisted with another broker, the provisions of this paragraph will not be effective during the term of such relisting and extensions, if any.

PAYMENT OF COMMISSION. Any such commission or fee shall be payable in Harris County, Texas, not later than the time of closing of the sale.

TITLE INSURANCE AND DEED. Owner does hereby certify and represent that Owner has fee simple title to the property and all improvements and fixtures thereon and the legal capacity to convey such property. The Owner agrees to furnish, at his expense, a title insurance policy to the purchaser, and to deliver a properly executed General Warranty Deed, conveying title to purchaser.

SIGNS. During the continuance of this agreement, Owner agrees to refer to Realtor all inquiries he may receive; he authorizes Realtor to place a "For Sale" sign on said property, and to place a "Multiple Listing" sign thereon, and will permit Realtor to enter said property at reasonable times to show it to prospective buyers.

LIMITATION OF LIABILITY. Realtor does not assume any responsibility for and Owner will not hold Realtor liable for loss of personal or real property due to vandalism, theft, freezing water pipes, or any other damage or loss whatever. Owner is advised to notify his insurance company and request a "Vacancy Clause" to cover above property in the event said property is to be vacated.

FAIR HOUSING. This property will be shown and made available for sale to all persons without regard to race, color, religion, national origin or sex.

PROPERTY DEFECTS. Owner certifies and represents that the property has no known latent structural defects or any other defects, except the following: ________________________________

(The Texas Real Estate License Act, Section 15 (4) (A) states "Latent structural defects and any other defects do not refer to trivial or insignificant defects but refer to those defects that would be a significant factor to a reasonable and prudent purchaser in making a decision to purchase.")

LEGAL FEES. In the event it becomes necessary for Realtor to initiate legal proceedings of any nature in order to secure payment of the real estate commission provided for in this Agreement, in addition to all other sums to which Realtor may be entitled, such Realtor shall be entitled to recover all costs of suit and a reasonable attorney's fee.

ENTIRE AGREEMENT. All parties hereto affirm that this contract contains the entire agreement and no other contract has been entered into as a condition of this listing. Owner acknowledges receipt of a copy of this Listing Agreement. This is a legal document. If not understood, seek competent advice.

________________________ Realtor ________________________ Owner

By ________________________ ________________________ Owner

Address of Realtor ________ Telephone No. ________ Address of Owner ________ Telephone No. ________

FIGURE 5-1 (*continued*).

(AGENT REMARKS—NOT TO BE DISPATCHED TO PARTICIPANTS.)

IMPORTANT: Use designations shown below as indicated:

UTILITY ROOM – show size
PATIO – show size
FLOORS – show type:
C - carpet H - hardwood
V - vinyl T - terrazzo
P - parquet
FIREPLACE – W - woodburning
M - mock
CORNER – If yes, name the street

DRAPERIES – Y for yes, N for no
DATE – (in financial information portion) show month and year (i.e. 11/74)
OVEN, RANGE AND DRYER – E - electric G - gas
FENCE – show type (chain link, redwood, etc.)
TOT. ANN. TAX – include city, state and county

GARAGE – 1A - 1-car attached
2A - 2-car attached
1D - 1-car detached
2D - 2-car detached
1A-CP - 1-car attached carport
2A-CP - 2-car attached carport
1D-CP - 1-car detached carport
2D-CP - 2-car detached carport
3A/D - 3 car or more, etc.

HOUSTON

No representations or warranties, either expressed or implied, are made as to the accuracy of the information herein.

MLS #			
Address			
Subdivision			
City			
Price			
BR	Bath	Gar	Den
Stry	Age	VAC	LB
Lot Size			Corner ☐

		FLR		DEP				
Extr.	LR		x		Heat		Date 1st	P/I
Style	DR		x		Cent A/C	YES ☐ NO ☐	Date 2nd	P/I
Roof	Den		x		A/C Units		Escrow	
Fndtn	Kit		x		Fire Pl	Ex Fan	Tot Monthly	
Sdwlk. C/G	Brk		x		D/W	Dsp	1st With	
Swr Stms	BR		x		Oven	Range	Loan #	Int.
St Sur	BR		x		Wsh C	Dry C	Type	Mat
Patio	BR		x		Util Rm		2nd With	Int.
Pool	BR		x		Water District		Tot. Ann. Tax	
Fence			x		Possn.		Ann. Maint. Fee	

Terms:

Sch. Elm. Jr. Hi. Sr. Hi. Other

Owner Phone

Legal:

Remarks:

Realtor Ph. N/Ph.

Realtor # TC SR Key Map Area Top Side

(Box 1) 1 2 3 4 5 6 7 8 9 (Box 2) 1 2 3 4 5 6 7 (Features) 11 12 13 14 15 16 17 18 19 20 21 22 23 24

TYPE OF PROPERTY
BOX 1

1. 1 Story
2. 1½ Story or more
3. Townhouse/Condominium 1 Story
4. Townhouse/Condominium 1½ Story or more
5. Residential Land
6. Duplex - Triplex - 4-Plex
7. Apartments 5 to 12 Units
8. Mobile Home & Lot
9. Property for Lease (Use Lease Box 2)

BOX 2

1. Colonial
2. Contemporary - Modern
3. French
4. Old English
5. Ranch
6. Spanish/Mediterranean
7. Traditional
8. Styles not Listed Above

LEASE PROPERTY
BOX 2
(Use only if item 9 BOX 1 circled - for Lease Property only).

1. Resid. - 1 Story
2. Resid. - 1½ Story or more
3. Townhouse/Condominium 1 Story
4. Townhouse/Condominium 1½ Story or more
5. Apartment(s)
6. Duplex through - 4-plex
7. Mobile Home

FEATURES:

11. Brick
12. 2-Car or more garage
13. More than one bath
14. One living area
15. Formal Living room
16. One Acre or more or Horses
17. Separate Dining room
18. Central Air Conditioning
19. Fireplace (Wood-Burning)
20. Kitchen Built-ins (Range, Oven or more)
21. FHA or VA Financing
22. Detached Garage
23. Unrestricted Usage
24. On Site Pool

M.L.S. OFFICE COPY

REV.: (8-76) 4000

FIGURE 5-1 (*continued*).

EXCLUSIVE AGENCY TO SELL

LISTING AGREEMENT

, a real estate broker duly licensed under the Texas Real Estate Licensing Act, hereinafter called Agent, and I. M. SELLER and wife, MAY B. SELLER, the legal owner of the property described below, hereinafter called Owner, hereby agree as follows:

1. Owner hereby employs and appoints Agent as the sole and exclusive agent to sell the property described below for a period of ninety (90) days and thereafter until Owner shall give Agent written notice of termination.

   Property Description: Lot 1, Block 1, Shakey Acres Subdivision, Harris County, Texas, as shown of record at Volume 7, Page 3 of the Map Records of Harris County, Texas.

2. Agent agrees to employ concentrated and diligent effort to procure a buyer for the property at a price of $80,000, payable in cash at closing, or at such other price and terms as are acceptable to Owner.

3. In the event that the property is sold during the term of this agreement and such sale be made by Agent, or by any other person except Owner, Owner agrees and promises to pay Agent a commission of seven percent (7%) of the sales price.

4. Owner agrees to:

   a. Grant possession of the property to buyer on funding of buyer's loan, or upon closing, whichever is later, and

   b. Allow Agent to place a "for sale" sign in Owner's yard, and

   c. Furnish to the buyer, at Owner's expense, title insurance policy to the purchaser, and

   d. Execute and deliver a general warranty deed at the closing of the sale, to the purchaser of the property.

EXECUTED by the parties hereto this 32nd day of January, 1994.

AGENT:

MANNY LISTER & ASSOCIATES, INC.,
Real Estate Agents

by:________________________
Manny Lister, President

OWNER:

I. M. SELLER and wife, MAY B. SELLER

____
I. M. Seller

____
May B. Seller

FIGURE 5-1 (*continued*).

Exclusive Right to Sell. In the exclusive right to sell listing, the property owner agrees to employ the real estate broker to sell the property and, in addition, he (the property owner) is prohibited from selling the property himself without paying the broker a commission. Thus the broker is entitled to his commission if the owner or anybody else makes a sale of the real estate during the term of the listing agreement even though the broker may have had nothing to do with the sale, *Wade* v. *Austin*, 524 S.W.2d 79 (Tex. Civ. App.—Texarkana, 1975). It gives the broker complete protection against "back door" dealings by others in the profession, or by the owner himself.

Exclusive Agency to Sell. Under the exclusive agency to sell agreement, the owner employs the broker to sell the property, and if so sold, the broker is entitled to a commission. This is true even if the property is sold through another broker's efforts. However, in contrast to the exclusive right to sell agreement, in this situation the owner reserves the right to sell the house himself and does not have to pay the commission to the broker.

Open Agency Listing. An open agency listing merely gives the broker the right to sell the property, and if the broker sells the property, he is entitled to his commission. Such an agreement is effective in enforcing the payment of a commission, but serious conflicts may arise as to whether or not the broker under an open listing agreement is truly the "procuring cause" of finding the purchaser. The open agency listing agreement clearly allows the owner to give other open agency agreements to other brokers, and the facts surrounding any particular transaction can create quite a lengthy dispute between brokers. The widespread use of the multiple listing service by realtors normally precludes the use of open listings. The exposure to several brokers, although originally obtained for the owner's benefit, also protects the listing broker from potential conflicts.

Net Listing. A net listing agreement can technically be used in any listing agreement. The term *net listing* refers to the payment of commission rather than to the broker's rights to sell the property. In a net listing agreement the commission is not specified, but, rather, is referred to in terms of the owner's net profit to be made out of the sale of the real estate. For instance, an owner may require that a broker sell the property for whatever price will net $35,000 for the owner. The broker, then, is free to sell the property for whatever price the open market may bring, knowing that out of his sales price, the first $35,000 will go to the owner; the remaining monies will go to closing costs; and if any additional monies are still available, the funds will go to the broker as his commission. Although a net listing can be lucrative, most brokers prefer to rely on a percentage of the sales price for the purposes of convenience and to avoid any conflicts of interest of the property owner. One can see that if a broker walks away from a closing with more money than the property owner, there may be some question as to how well the property owner was represented in the sale.

Multiple Listing. A multiple listing is a listing that is normally an exclusive right to sell taken by a broker who is a member of an association of brokers. The brokers use their association as a means of providing all member brokers a right to find an interested client. Usually the commissions earned on such listings are split by an agreement between cooperating brokers.

Actions for Commissions

In most written agreements, each party promises to perform an obligation. These are called *bilateral contracts*. A listing agreement, on the other hand, is termed a *unilateral contract* because only one party promises to perform, the owner. The owner promises to pay the broker a commission to sell certain property, for a certain price, and within a certain period of time. The broker, in effect, makes no promises and incurs no obligations other than to use his best efforts to market the property. Therefore, the contract is considered completed and the contractual obligations fulfilled when the broker performs his part of the agreement and produces a ready, willing, and able buyer to purchase the property according to the terms of the listing agreement. The broker completes his half of the contract by performance rather than by satisfying promises contained in the listing agreement.

A broker's right to a commission is conditioned on five factors. First, Section 20(a) of the Texas Real Estate Licensing Act specifically requires that any person bringing an action for a commission must be a duly licensed real estate broker or salesman at the time the alleged services are commenced.

Second, Section 20(b) of the act requires that the agreement for the payment of the commission must be in writing. This requirement is satisfied if there is a listing agreement or if the promise to pay the commission is set out in the earnest money contract.

The third requirement is set out in Section 20(c) of the Real Estate Licensing Act. The broker must advise the purchaser, in writing, that the purchaser should have the abstract covering the real estate examined by an attorney, or obtain a policy of title insurance, *Jones* v. *Del Anderson and Associates*, 539 S.W.2d 348 (Tex. 1976).

The fourth requirement applies to the terms of the listing agreement. If the broker has an exclusive right to sell listing agreement and *produces a ready, willing, and able buyer*, he is entitled to his commission if the first three requirements are met.

The fifth requirement, occurring when using listing agreements other than the exclusive right to sell, requires the broker to be the *procuring cause* of the sale. If the broker has an exclusive right to sell, the owner is bound to pay the commission, pursuant to the terms of the listing agreement. In the exclusive agency listing agreement, if a purchaser deals with the owner directly, the seller would not be obligated to pay a commission. In the open listing situation, when a ready, willing, and able buyer is produced, there may be some question as to who is the procuring cause of the sale. It is only in this situation that the procuring cause requirement normally becomes important.

Once all the foregoing requirements have been met, the broker is entitled to his commission. There have been a number of cases in which the seller has refused to pay the commission because the sale was not consummated. It must be emphasized that the closing of the sale, by itself, is *not* the determinative factor as to whether or not the broker is entitled to a commission. If the seller backs out, he clearly has breached the terms of the listing agreement, and the commission must be paid. If the sale has not been consummated through no fault of the broker, the broker is still entitled to his commission. Even if the commission is contingent upon the consummation of the sale, as provided in many earnest money contracts, the agent can maintain successfully an action for the commission if the seller chooses to back out, on the grounds that the production of a ready, willing, and able buyer consummated the terms of that listing agreement upon signing the earnest money contract, *Duckworth* v. *Field*, 516 F.2d 952 (5th Cir. 1975). There has been additional authority that even if the purchaser backs out of the agreement and the seller chooses not to enforce specific performance, the broker still may maintain a successful cause of action to obtain his commission, *Davidson* v. *Suber*, 553 S.W.2d 430 (Tex. Civ. App.—Austin, 1977). In most cases, if a broker is required to sue the seller, he is also entitled to the attorneys' fees incurred.

Except for filing suit to recover commissions pursuant to the terms of the listing agreement, the broker is rather limited as to how else he can protect his interest. There has been some question in the past as to whether or not a realtor may file a lien against the real estate while maintaining an action for his commission. It must be emphasized that the realtor has no interest in the real estate at all. He only has an interest in consummating the sale of that real estate. Therefore, he is not entitled to cloud the title to real estate, nor attempt to put a lien on that real estate, nor in any other way slander the title of an owner's parcel of real estate if he (the broker) is only maintaining an action for his brokerage commission. If title to an owner's real estate becomes clouded as a result of a broker's intentional act, the broker may be liable for significant damages.

Duties and Obligations of Real Estate Agents

Agency Relationships

The duties and obligations of a real estate agent and the property owner (or seller) are those of agent and principal. There is a difference, however, in the agency relationship between a broker and seller (or buyer) and the relationship between a broker and his salesperson, sometimes called a *subagent*. The agency relationship between the employing homeowner (or home purchaser) and his broker is one termed a *special agency*. A special agency indicates an agent employed for a particular purpose and without the power to bind his principal. A *general agency*, on the other hand, carries with it the implication that the agent has the power to bind his principal. The relationship between the employing broker and his sales agent is more properly construed to be a general agency.

Duties to the Principal

The relationship between agent and principal is commonly termed a *fiduciary* relationship. When the agent acts in the capacity of a fiduciary, there is a duty of trust and honest business dealing, which he owes to his principal. There will probably be communications between the principal and agent that could not be disclosed to third parties without breaching that fiduciary relationship. An example of this would be a principal who chooses to list his house for a $76,000 sales price but informs the broker that he would probably take $74,000 from a qualified purchaser who offers good terms. The agent is, of course, under a fiduciary capacity not to disclose anything that would be adverse to the interest of his principal.

Performance. Generally, it has been held by Texas courts that a real estate broker, as an agent, owes the duty to his principal of *performance, loyalty, reasonable care*, and an *accounting* for all monies received with regard to the transaction.

Performance, of course, indicates that the broker will use his best efforts and diligence to market the property on behalf of his principal and to obey the principal's instructions as to asking price, condition of the property, and marketing practices. The recently revised Texas Real Estate Licensing Act specifically speaks to these obligations of performance under Section 15, which provides for license revocation if it has been determined that the broker or salesman has been guilty of:

(1) making a false promise of a character likely to influence, persuade, or induce any person to enter into a contract or agreement when the licensee could not or did not intend to keep such promise [Section 15(4)(B)]; or

(2) soliciting, selling, or offering for sale real property under a scheme or program that constitutes a lottery or deceptive practice [Section 15(4)(I)]; or

(3) acting in the dual capacity of broker and undisclosed principal in a transaction [Section 15(4)(J)]; or

(4) placing a sign on real property offering it for sale, lease, or rent without the written consent of the owner or his authorized agent [Section 15(4)(L)]; or

(5) negotiating or attempting to negotiate the sale, exchange, lease, or rental of real property with an owner or lessor, knowing that the owner or lessor had a written outstanding contract, granting exclusive agency in connection with the property to another real estate broker [Section 15(4)(N)]; or

(6) offering real property for sale or for lease without the knowledge and consent of the owner or his authorized agent, or on terms other than those authorized by the owner or his authorized agent [Section 15(4)(O)]; or

(7) publishing, or causing to be published, an advertisement including, but not limited to, advertising by newspaper, radio, television, or display which is misleading, or which is likely to deceive the public, or which in any manner tends to create a misleading impression, or which fails to identify the person causing the advertisement to be published as a licensed real estate broker or agent [Section 15(4)(P)]; or

(8) establishing an association, by employment or otherwise, with an unlicensed person who is expected or required to act as a real estate licensee, or aiding or abetting or conspiring with a person to circumvent the requirements of this Act [Section 15(4)(S)]; or

(9) conduct which constitutes dishonest dealings, bad faith, or untrustworthiness [Section 15(4)(V)]; or

(10) acting negligently or incompetently in performing an act for which a person is required to hold a real estate license [Section 15(4)(W)].

Loyalty. The duty of *loyalty* is a very touchy subject for real estate agents. It is common practice for a broker to feel that he acts on behalf of both the buyer and the seller in a transaction. There is even some case law that reflects that this may be done properly, but only with the full knowledge and consent of both principals (the buyer and the seller). In most circumstances, however, it is a near impossibility to represent both the buyer and the seller. This situation is analogous to a couple going to one lawyer for a divorce and asking that lawyer to represent both the husband and the wife. It simply cannot be done because no one can represent a client to the very best interest when he represents two opponents. For instance, how can a broker represent a seller to get the highest price for the house when he is also representing a purchaser trying to get the best buy for the same house?

Loyalty also implies the broker's duty not to advance his own interest in profit to the detriment of his principal. This may occur when an agent finds a particularly good buy on a house that the seller is willing to sell, and, knowing that it is below market value, the broker purchases that house for himself without advising his principal of the true value. The Texas Real Estate Licensing Act has statutorily provided for license revocation for disloyalty under Section 15(3), if the licensee has been found guilty of any of the following actions:

(1) the licensee, when selling, trading, or renting real property in his own name, engaged in misrepresentation or dishonest or fraudulent action [Section 15(3)]; or
(2) making a false promise of a character likely to influence, persuade, or induce any person to enter into a contract or agreement when the licensee could not or did not intend to keep such promise [Section 15(4)(B)]; or
(3) failing to make clear, to all parties to a transaction, which party he is acting for, or receiving compensation from more than one party except with the full knowledge and consent of all parties [Section 15(4)(D)]; or
(4) accepting, receiving, or charging an undisclosed commission, rebate, or direct profit on expenditures made for a principal [Section 15(4)(H)]; or
(5) acting in the dual capacity of broker and undisclosed principal in a transaction [Section 15(4)(J)]; or
(6) failing or refusing on demand to produce a document, book, or record in his possession concerning a real estate transaction conducted by him for inspection by the Real Estate Commission or its authorized personnel or representative [Section 15(4)(AA)]; or
(7) failing without just cause to surrender to the rightful owner, on demand, a document or instrument coming into his possession [Section 15(4)(CC)].

Reasonable Care. The duty of *reasonable care* generally implies competence and expertise on the part of the broker. He has a duty to disclose knowledge and material facts concerning the property and cannot become a party to any fraud or misrepresentation likely to affect the sound judgment of the principal. In procuring a purchaser, the broker obviously has a duty to discover whether or not that purchaser is financially able to pursue the transaction. The broker should also disclose any material changes in property values so that his principal may stay fully informed at all times. The broker further has a duty to make sure that all material facts of a transaction are disclosed to his principal. However, the broker may not give legal interpretations of the documents involved in a transaction. To give legal interpretations of an instrument is practicing law without a license and is specifically prohibited under Section 16 of the Texas Real Estate Licensing Act.

There are other provisions in the Texas Real Estate Licensing Act that provide for license revocation if the duty of reasonable care has been breached, including the following:

(1) making a material misrepresentation, or failing to disclose to a potential purchaser any latent structural defect or any other defect known to the broker or salesman. Latent structural defects and other defects do not refer to trivial or insignificant defects but refer to those defects that would be a significant factor to a reasonable and prudent purchaser in making a decision to purchase [Section 15(4)(A)]; or

(2) pursuing a continued and flagrant course of misrepresentation or making of false promises through agents, salesmen, advertising, or otherwise [Section 15(4)(C)]; or

(3) having knowingly withheld from or inserted in a statement of account or invoice, a statement that made it inaccurate in a material particular [Section 15(4)(Q)]; or

(4) failing or refusing on demand to furnish copies of a document pertaining to a transaction dealing with real estate to a person whose signature is affixed to the document [Section 15(4)(T)].

Accounting. The duty of *accounting* is provided for generally in requiring that any money accepted as earnest money must be placed in a proper escrow account within a reasonable amount of time [Section 15(4)(E)]. This duty of accounting would also apply to failure to report undisclosed commissions or failure to disclose the true purchase price of the seller's property. This type of conduct, of course, represents the severest type of fraud and misrepresentation. These subjects are discussed in almost every provision of the Texas Real Estate Licensing Act.

The areas that deal specifically with escrow and accounting for funds are set out in the following sections, which prohibit:

(1) accepting, receiving, or charging an undisclosed commission, rebate, or direct profit on expenditures made for a principal [Section 15(4)(H)]; or

(2) failing within a reasonable time to deposit money received as escrow agent in a real estate transaction, either in trust with a title company authorized to do business in this state, or in a custodial, trust, or escrow account maintained for that purpose in a banking institution authorized to do business in this state [Section 15(4)(Y)]; or

(3) disbursing money deposited in a custodial, trust, or escrow account, as provided in Subsection (Y) before the transaction concerned has been consummated or finally otherwise terminated [Section 15(4)(Z)].

Duties to Third Parties

Even though the broker is supposed to act on his principal's behalf and only in the best interest of his principal, he does have a duty of care to third persons of utilizing fair and honest business practices. The agent cannot be a part of any fraud on behalf of his principal, and if a case arises where the principal asks the agent to lie or misrepresent certain material defects, the broker should terminate his listing agreement and refuse to engage in any such acts on behalf of his principal. A broker is, of course, liable to third parties for misrepresentations and particularly for failure to disclose certain material defects that may affect the buyer's good judgment and sound business practice. The Texas Real Estate Licensing Act specifically speaks to this, again under Section 15, under the following prohibitions:

(1) making a material misrepresentation, or failing to disclose to a potential purchaser any latent structural defect or any other defect known to the broker or salesman. Latent structural defects and other defects do not refer to trivial or insignificant defects but refer to those defects that would be a significant factor to a reasonable and prudent purchaser in making a decision to purchase [Section 15(4)(A)]; or

(2) making a false promise of a character likely to influence, persuade, or induce any person to enter into a contract or agreement when the licensee could not or did not intend to keep such promise [Section 15(4)(B)]; or

(3) pursuing a continued and flagrant course of misrepresentation or making of false promises through agents, salesmen, advertising, or otherwise [Section 15(4)(C)]; or

(4) soliciting, selling, or offering for sale real property under a scheme or program that constitutes a lottery or deceptive practice [Section 15(4)(I)]; or

(5) guaranteeing, authorizing, or permitting a person to guarantee that future profits will result from a resale of real property [Section 15(4)(K)]; or

(6) negotiating or attempting to negotiate the sale, exchange, lease, or rental of real property with an owner or lessor, knowing that the owner had a written outstanding contract, granting exclusive agency in connection with the property to another real estate broker [Section 15(4)(N)]; or

(7) publishing, or causing to be published an advertisement including, but not limited to, advertising by newspaper, radio, television, or display which is misleading, or which is likely to deceive the public, or which in any manner tends to create a misleading impression, or which fails to identify the person causing the advertisement to be published as a licensed real estate broker or agent [Section 15(4)(P)]; or

(8) failing to advise a purchaser in writing before the closing of a transaction that the purchaser should either have the abstract

covering the real estate which is the subject of the contract examined by an attorney of the purchaser's own selection, or be furnished with or obtain a policy of title insurance [Section 15(4)(U)]; or

(9) failing or refusing on demand to produce a document, book, or record in his possession concerning a real estate transaction conducted by him for inspection by the Real Estate Commission or its authorized personnel or representative [Section 15(4)(AA)]; or

(10) failing without just cause to surrender to the rightful owner, on demand, a document or instrument coming into his possession [Section 15(4)(CC)].

There is a further exposure and liability of brokers since they are in the business of transacting real estate. If they deal with a potential home purchaser, as a consumer, the broker may become liable for any misrepresentations under the Deceptive Trade Practices—Consumer Protection Act, as provided under the Texas Business and Commerce Code. This is a very strongly worded statute that prohibits any misrepresentation constituting dishonest or bad faith business dealings when dealing with consumers. It has been recently held by the Texas Supreme Court that anyone found to have violated this act by using false or misleading advertisement or misrepresentations is liable for three times the actual damages suffered by the aggrieved party, *Woods* v. *Littleton*, 554 S.W.2d 662 (Tex. 1977). The broker additionally may be liable for attorneys' fees, court costs, return of his commission, and a rescission of the transaction (which may also involve liability of the broker to his principal).

It is also important to point out that Article 2226 of the Texas Revised Civil Statutes now clearly provides that if an individual fails to pay for any services performed, pursuant to any contract, express or implied, he may maintain an action not only for damages but also for attorneys' fees. Any misrepresentation as a manager of real estate while an agent, whether disclosed or undisclosed, may also bring that misrepresentation under the Deceptive Trade Practices—Consumer Protection Act, discussed earlier in this chapter. The passage of this act has unquestionably done more for the protection of consumers and third parties than any other act in the history of the state. A copy of the Deceptive Trade Practices—Consumer Protection Act is in the Appendix for reference. It is suggested that this be very carefully read to help understand the scope of a broker's liability when dealing with consumers. Remember, ignorance of the law is no excuse.

Management Responsibilities

Different problems arise if a broker is acting as a manager of real estate, rather than simply as a broker in a sales transaction. His duties to owners and third parties in this situation relate to service contracts for services to be performed on a particular project, as well as to properly maintaining the property such that no one suffers any injury caused by the broker's negligence in maintaining the property. The problem of management liability may occur when the property management company, or broker, does not want to become obligated for the payment of the expenses of a project. On the other hand, the vendors and suppliers who must perform the services must know who they should pursue in the event they are not paid. The fundamentals of principal and agent again apply, and the liabilities can be summarized as follows:

1. Where an agent (the broker) acts on behalf of a principal who is known to the service company performing the work, and the agent is acting within the scope of his authority, the principal is liable, and the agent will not ordinarily be personally liable to the third party. If the agent exercises *ostensible* (apparent) authority that he does not have, and the third party reasonably relied on such representation, an agency will be presumed, and the principal is still liable rather than the agent. The principal may also *ratify* an agent's acts after they have been performed (even if they were wrongfully performed by the agent) and become liable for the agent's acts. However, if the agent was not acting within his scope of authority, the principal has a cause of action against the agent to recover whatever losses may have been incurred.
2. If the broker discloses the fact that he is an agent, but does not disclose the identity of the principal, the broker will generally be considered personally liable on the agreement. This logically follows that the third party is advancing services only on the agent's good name and promise to pay, even though the third party knows that the broker is acting only as an agent. A third party performing services should not expect to be paid by a principal when he does not know who that principal is or anything about that principal's ability to pay. If the third party subsequently discovers the identity of the principal, both the principal and the agent may be liable to that third party.
3. It follows then, that if the principal is undisclosed, and the agency is also undisclosed, the agent has ostensible authority and is liable to third parties for all acts that he performs, as if they were the principal's.

Special Problem Areas

There are certain problem areas unique to the real estate brokerage business that deserve special discussion in order to make a real estate agent more aware of these problems and, hopefully, to help him avoid them.

Securities

There has been a lot of emphasis on investment real estate in recent years. Real estate has special tax benefits that many other investment opportunities do not share. For example, the investments generally take the form of syndication interests (usually limited partnerships or land trusts) or ownership of rental housing such as resort condominiums (which can be readily rented by a project manager when not in use by the owner). In these cases, the broker may be selling real estate *interests*, from which the owner expects a *profit* through the *efforts of a third party*. This, by definition, *SEC* v. *Howey*, 328 U.S. 293 (1946), is considered to be a security rather than a parcel of real estate. In the event the interest sold is in fact deemed a security, the broker may find he cannot maintain an action for a commission on the sale unless he has a securities broker's license, *Sunshine* v. *Mid-Smith Construction*, 496 S.W.2d 708 (Tex. Civ. App.—Dallas, 1973). After all, a stockbroker cannot maintain an action for a commission on a real estate sale unless he is licensed. The converse is true of a real estate broker.

Truth-in-Lending

The Board of Governors of the Federal Reserve Board has passed a series of regulations known as *Regulation Z*, to implement enforcement of the Federal Truth-in-Lending Act (T-i-L Act). The T-i-L Act, simply explained, requires the lending institution (in the business of loaning money) to make a full disclosure of all costs of a loan to a consumer. Although the first impression of the T-i-L Act makes very good sense, it does provide a pitfall for an unwary broker. In at least one case, *Eby* v. *Reb Realty*, 495 F.2d 646 (9th Cir.—1974), a broker who personally financed five real property sales (typical in many real estate sales situations) was found to be "in the business of making loans." The broker, never realizing he should make a full disclosure as required by Regulation Z, was found in violation of the T-i-L Act, and was subjected to severe penalties.

Employees versus Independent Contractors

When a real estate broker hires sales personnel to represent his brokerage company in seeking listings and negotiating real estate transactions, something that is far too often overlooked is whether or not that sales agent should be classified as an independent contractor or as an employee.

The broker normally assumes that the sales agent will be an independent contractor because there are a number of advantages, from the broker's point of view, favoring independent contractor status of the sales personnel. These advantages generally include a smaller amount of paperwork and fewer records to maintain on behalf of the broker; no office hours are required to be kept; and the sales personnel are more motivated to sell if they work on a commission basis only. There also are tax savings to the firm because there are no social security and unemployment taxes to be paid by the firm, and the system tends to promote more professionalism and advantages for more experienced sales agents. The independent contractor status basically provides for a more professional, harder working, motivated sales agent because there is no limit to his potential income, and there are fewer controls on the individual's time and effort.

If classified as an employee, on the other hand, the individual sales person may not be as well motivated since the basic check amount is the same every month regardless of whether or not any results are achieved. Furthermore, the employing broker's overhead remains relatively constant but quite high. Accounting and bookkeeping become more expensive because of the larger amount of paperwork and office records required; and there are added costs of social security taxes and unemployment benefits; as well as other requirements by the federal government that apply to employees generally.

In 1976, the Internal Revenue Service set forth guidelines as to how it would look at a broker-salesman relationship to determine whether or not a sales agent would be classified as an independent contractor or as an employee. Revenue Ruling 76-136 sets out the guidelines to determine when the sales personnel are *not* employees (see below). These guidelines were based on the facts set forth in a landmark case styled, *Dimmitt-Rickhoff-Bayer Real Estate Co.* v. *Finnegan,* 179 F.2d 882 (8th Cir. 1950).

1. The sales personnel should be remunerated solely by commission on their sales of real estate, and the companies cannot give them advances against their commissions. However, the company can make facilities and offices available to sales people and can furnish them with the necessary forms and stationery.
2. The broker may furnish a manual for policies and procedures, but it may be advisory only, and the sales personnel cannot be required to follow the policies and procedures as criteria for their own employment.
3. The sales personnel should not be required to work a set number of hours.
4. The salesman should pay his own expenses, such as his own license fees, transportation expenses, association memberships, business entertainment expenses, and the like.
5. There should not be mandatory sales meetings or requirements to participate in any training programs.
6. Sales persons should not be allowed to participate in any group insurance or retirement programs of the broker companies.

Although all of these factors are important, no one single factor is controlling; nor are these factors exclusive. The relationship is to be ascertained by an overall view of the entire situation. The result in each case must be governed by the special facts and circumstances surrounding each fact situation, *Illinois Tri-Seal Products, Inc.* v. *United States*, 353 F.2d 216 (U.S. Ct. Claims 1965).

Revenue Ruling 76-137 sets out the guidelines for real estate sales people as employees with the company. This ruling, along with Revenue Ruling 76-136, distinguishes very clearly between employee status and independent contractor status. The distinction generally is based on the scope of control the broker has over the sales personnel, as well as on how the sales personnel consider themselves in the broker-salesman relationship. Basically, the guidelines are the antithesis of Revenue Ruling 76-136, and are generally set out as follows (for designation of employee status):

1. If they [the sales people] are sponsored and the registration fees are paid for by the broker.
2. If the broker makes available office furniture, stenographic help, and telephone service, as well as stationery and business cards.
3. If there are company rules and policies that must govern how transactions are negotiated, and if there is an attempt to control the salesperson's actions on a day-to-day basis.
4. If the company has the right to discharge salespersons for any violation of instructions, or if it sets up quotas and minimum sales requirements for the sales agents.
5. If the sales agents generally consider themselves as part of a team, all of whom are governed by the sale rules and regulations, rather than having individualistic rules between the independent contractor and the broker.
6. If the brokerage company's plan for dividing commissions between sales people depends on rotation of outside referrals and required time in the office by certain agents.
7. If there is guaranteed minimum monthly compensation.

The IRS regulations (for Ruling 76-137) do not preclude having monthly sales agents' meetings, but the requirement of mandatory attendance may make a difference in the eyes of the Internal Revenue Service as to whether the sales person is classified as an independent contractor or as an employee. Educational facilities or review classes for sales agents who make frequent errors may still be offered by the broker as long as attendance is not required for the independent contractor. It is probably a good idea if the broker also reminds these sales agents (independent contractors) of their obligations to pay quarterly income taxes, to file their Schedule C of the federal income tax form along with Form 1040, and to pay the self-employment tax. It should be emphasized that no single criterion (and all of the criteria of the revenue rulings are not discussed here) is controlling, but very great care should be taken to generate the proper emphasis on the independent contractor status if the broker wishes to maintain this type of broker-salesman relationship. It appears that less emphasis on teamwork and more emphasis on individualism should be the rule.

Brokers versus Lawyers

Saying that there is a conflict between brokers and lawyers in Texas has got to be the understatement of the century. Both represent clients. Furthermore, they often represent the same client, and conflicts in this type of situation are inevitable. In an attempt to resolve certain conflicts, the State Bar of Texas and the Texas Real Estate Commission have produced a Statement of Principles in an effort to help define the lawyers' and brokers' roles in a real estate transaction. A copy of this Statement of Principles is located in the Appendix for reference purposes. The Statement of Principles basically sets out that it is the broker's obligation to negotiate the transaction and to be well-informed about the marketplace in order to give good advice to his client's business judgment. The lawyer, on the other hand, is to use his best efforts to proceed diligently to the conclusion of the transaction and to prepare the required documents. The principles specifically state that the lawyer "shall not give his opinion of the physical condition or the market value of the real estate involved in the transaction, unless expressly employed by the principal to perform that function."

It should be emphasized that this is only a "Statement of Principles," and it does not have the binding force of law. Unfortunately, you will find brokers who attempt to give legal advice, and you will find lawyers who attempt to give advice to their clients on the fair market value of real estate. You will also find attorneys who attempt to split the commission on the sale of a piece of property. (A split commission is generally more than legal fees.)

On the other hand, you will find that there are many brokers who are more than happy to give their clients all types of legal advice concerning the interpretation of legal instruments, although this is specifically prohibited under the Texas Real Estate Licensing Act. But it should also be pointed out that the broker's ability to "fill in the blanks" of an earnest money contract is specifically approved through the use of the Texas Real Estate Commission and State Bar promulgated contract forms, which are prescribed for brokers' use. Prior to the promulgation of the forms sanctioned by the commission and the state bar, the use of any form by a real estate broker was considered suspect, and possibly in violation of the

Texas Real Estate Licensing Act (Attorney General's Opinion Number M-1256, November 1, 1972).

The relationship between a professional broker and a professional lawyer should be complementary, and neither profession should make even the slightest attempt to downgrade the other while working together, before working together, or after working together. Unfortunately, there will be lawyers and brokers who are "unprincipled." It will take the efforts of both parties, and the understanding of both parties, to help keep these conflicts at a minimum.

Anti-Trust Laws

Anti-trust laws may seem to have a limited impact on the individual licensee, however they create an increasing concern for brokers, Realtor boards, and Multiple Listing Services.

There are several common names for the anti-trust statutes and their subsequent amendments. The two that have the most far reaching impact on real estate are the Sherman Anti-Trust Act (15 U.S.C.A. § 1 *et seq*) and the Clayton Anti-Trust Act (15 U.S.C.A. § 12 *et seq*). The provisions of these Acts are enforced by the Federal Trade Commission and the Department of Justice. The basic theory of anti-trust laws is that monopolies and dominance in any industry is against the public interest and free flow of goods and services through interstate commerce.

Pertinent provisions of the Sherman Anti-Trust Act prohibit unreasonable restraint of trade and monopolies. This Act was "specifically intended to prohibit independent businesses from becoming 'associates' in a common plan which is bound to reduce their competitor's opportunity . . ." This has recently been interpreted by the Supreme Court of Pennsylvania as prohibiting a Board of Realtors from excluding a licensee from MLS memberships, even for cause, *Collins* v. *Main Line Board of Realtors*, 304 A.2d 493 (Sup. Ct. of Pennsylvania—1973). While the Pennsylvania case is a fairly complicated one, its primary holding is well reasoned, and the U.S. Supreme Court declined to hear an appeal.

The Clayton Act is not as broad in scope as the Sherman Act and seeks to reach certain specified practices which have been held by courts to be outside the scope of the Sherman Act, but which Congress considered to adversely affect free competition. It specifically deals with price discrimination, acquisition and mergers, and exclusive dealing arrangements. The Clayton Act was passed to complement the Sherman Act, although both can be violated at the same time.

One of the key areas of concern for real estate licensees has been "price fixing," which is generally defined as the setting of prices by an industry at an artificial level. Price fixing, whether good or evil, express or implied is illegal *per se*. In theory, prices must be set by competitors only, and not by any agreement between or among competitors. Recently, Realtors in Maryland were found by the Federal District Court to be in criminal violation of the Clayton Anti-Trust Act of "fixing" their fees at 7% of the gross sales price of the real estate. Similar actions have been filed in other states, including Texas. However, none of these cases have been decided on appeal, so no negative decisions on Realtor's "price fixing" has been precedent setting—yet.

As in all areas of the law, particularly those involving very sophisticated federal laws, arguments on both sides of the issues are very good. The public needs to be protected against restraints in trade and price fixing in order to increase competition and to prevent conspiracy. However, suggested fee schedules are not uncommon in other businesses, and, as all licensees know, there are very few businesses as competitive as the real estate business. It is probably fair to say, again, that the decisions yet to be made in this area will be determined largely by the facts of each case, and how the respective federal laws apply to those facts.

The Deceptive Trade Practices—Consumer Protection Act

In an ordinary real estate transaction one might find that there is only one licensee and the two parties (consumers) attempting to negotiate the terms of a real estate transaction. In such transactions, when all fails and someone feels damaged, the only professional available to accept the blame is the real estate licensee. He is often the only person in the transaction who is deemed knowledgeable enough to have prevented foreseen difficulties or misunderstandings. Recent Texas court rulings seem to indicate that the trend toward suing licensees may be warranted for misrepresentation as to encumbrances; *Stone* v. *Lawyers Title Ins. Corp.* 554 S.W.2d 183 (Tex. 1977); *Ingalls* v. *Rice* 511 S.W.2d 78 (Tex. Civ. App.—Houston 1974), terms of agreements; *Newsom* v. *Starkey* 541 S.W.2d 468 (Tex. Civ. App.—Dallas 1976); and slandering title; *Walker* v. *Ruggles* 540 S.W.2d 470 (Tex. Civ. App.—Houston, 1976). The rise of "consumerism" in recent years has formed another trend which exaggerates the liability of licensees, the Deceptive Trade Practices—Consumer Protection Act (Tex. Business and Commerce Code, Section 17.41, et seq.). A copy of this statute is reproduced in the Appendix for reference purposes.

This statute, originally enacted in 1973, was made specifically applicable to real estate by an amendment made effective September 1, 1975. The statute declares "false, misleading or deceptive acts or practices" (which can include almost anything deceptive) in the conduct of any trade or commerce to be unlawful. Coincidentally, the new Real Estate Licensing Act (made effective May 20, 1975) provided grounds for revoking or suspending real estate license if the licensee has been guilty of schemes or programs that constitute deceptive practices. The application of the statutes to real estate licensees appears to be quite clear. The Deceptive Trade Practices—Consumer Protection Act *(DTP-CPA)* is to be liberally construed to protect consumers, and such has been the practices of Texas courts in recent years.

A "consumer," as defined by the *DTP-CPA* (see appendix) may maintain an action if he has been adversely affected by any of the following:

1. the use or employment by any person of an act or practice declared to be unlawful by Section 17.46 of this subchapter;
2. breach of an express or implied warranty;
3. any unconscionable action or course of action by any person; or
4. the use or employment by any person of an act or practice in violation of Article 21.21, Texas Insurance Code, as amended, or rules or regulations issued by the State Board of Insurance under Article 21.21, Texas Insurance Code, as amended.

If he wins, he *may* obtain as remedies:

1. three times the amount of actual damages plus court costs and attorneys' fees reasonable in relation to the amount of work expended;
2. an order enjoining such acts or failure to act;
3. orders necessary to restore to any party to the suit any money or property, real or personal, which may have been acquired in violation of this subchapter; and
4. any other relief which the court deems proper, including the appointment of a receiver or the revocation of a license or certificate authorizing a person to engage in business in this state if the judgment has not been satisfied within three months of the date of the final judgment. *The court may not revoke or suspend a license to do business in this state or appoint a receiver to take over the affairs of a person who has failed to satisfy a judgment if the person is a licensee of or regulated by a state agency which has statutory authority to revoke or suspend a license or to appoint a receiver or trustee.* [emphasis added]

In a recent landmark decision, the Texas Supreme Court construed the treble damage provision (number 1 above) to be mandatory if the consumer requests that remedy, *Woods* v. *Littleton*, 554 S.W.2d 662 (Tex. 1977).

Section 17.50 A of the *DTP-CPA* limits the treble damage provision to only actual damage, reasonable attorneys' fees, and court costs where the defendant:

1. proves the action complained of resulted from a bona fide error notwithstanding the use of reasonable procedures adopted to avoid the error; or
2. proves that he had no written notice of the consumer's complaint before suit was filed, or that within 30 days after he was given written notice he tendered to the consumer (a) the cash value of the consideration received from the consumer or the cash value of the benefit promised, whichever is greater, and (b) the expenses, including attorney's fees, if any, reasonably incurred by the consumer in asserting his claim against the defendant; or
3. in the case of a suit under Section 17.50(a)(2) [breach of an express or implied warranty], defendant proves he was not given a reasonable opportunity to cure the defects or malfunctions before suit was filed. Tex. Laws 1977, ch. 216, § 6, at 604.

Note that in Section 17.50 A, the burden of proof is on the defendant, not the plaintiff.

Since the *DTP-CPA* is a relatively new statute, a lot of law is yet to be decided concerning real estate licensees. However, the results are fairly predictable.

SUMMARY

Recent revisions in the Texas Real Estate Licensing Act have upgraded the educational requirements for brokers and salesmen. The Texas Real Estate Commission administers all rules and regulations that govern the procedure for institution, conduct, and determination of all causes and proceedings before the Real Estate Commission. Licensing requirements are specific and strictly adhered to. The definitions of "broker" and "salesman" are very broad and meant to be all inclusive in order to effect a more comprehensive regulation of the real estate industry.

Brokers and salesmen are employed through listing agreements, which must be in writing in order for the broker to maintain *an action in court* for a commission.

In addition to the specific statutory requirements that concern the duties and obligations of a real estate licensee, the laws of principal and agent apply to the broker in his normal employment relationship. As an agent, the real estate licensee has certain duties to the principal as well as to third parties. The laws of agency are of particular application in management responsibilities when a licensee may be transacting business on behalf of his principal.

There are special problem areas in real estate brokerage which have become increasingly important over the past few years. These include securities law, truth-in-lending laws, the employment status of sales personnel, relationships between brokers and lawyers, and application of federal anti-trust laws.

6

CONTRACTS FOR THE SALE OF REAL ESTATE

The law of contracts is one of the most complex areas of the law to study. A complete discussion of the law of contracts would require many volumes for a thorough study and explanation. Contracts normally used in real estate include listing agreements, earnest money contracts, installment land contracts, leases, easement agreements, deeds, mortgages, security agreements, liens, construction contracts, and partnership agreements. For the purposes of this chapter, the discussions of contract law will be centered around the creation and construction of contracts generally, earnest money contracts, and installment land contracts.

Contracts, Generally

It is important that some of the fundamental elements of contracts be understood before discussing the specific requirements and peculiarities of real estate contracts. A contract can be most simply defined as a deliberate or voluntary engagement between competent parties, made on a sufficient legal consideration, to do or not to do a particular act or thing. Contracts may be oral or express, although in matters involving real estate, Texas law requires that some contracts be in writing in order to be enforceable. The Texas statute applied to this theory is Section 26.01 of the Texas Business and Commerce Code, more commonly called the *Statute of Frauds*.

Creation

Creating a contract, in its simplest form, requires an *offer*, an *acceptance*, and *consideration* for the promises therein contained. Encompassing all three requirements is the general requirement of mutual assent between the parties. There must have been facts existing that created a "meeting of the minds."

Offer

An *offer* is a proposal by one competent party to another competent party manifesting an intention to enter into a valid contract. In considering whether or not an offer was effective, it must be determined that the offering party was indeed *competent* (he was not a minor, insane, or deceased), and that he had the *present intent* of making a final proposal, such that, upon acceptance, it would create a binding contract. The offer must have been made to a *specific, identifiable person* (the offeree). The offer must also be *specific enough* that the two parties can determine, without mistake, what *obligations* are to be performed, that is, whether the subject matter, price, time of performance, and other obligations are both legal and sufficiently identified so that there is no mistake or misunderstanding to prevent a true "meeting of the minds."

Acceptance

In determining whether or not there was an effective *acceptance* of the contract, the points generally considered are those of *intent*, the *manner* of acceptance, the *timeliness* of the acceptance, and whether or not that acceptance was *unconditional*.

Intent, also one of the main criteria for an effective offer, speaks to the intent of the parties' bargain. Did the person accepting the contract intend, by his words and conduct, to create a contractual relationship by accepting the offer?

The *manner of acceptance* is also important. There must not have been any jest, qualification, or proposed change in the offeree's mind or in the manner in which he accepted the offer. The offeree must also have been the party to whom the offer was made, and not someone who simply may have overheard the offer being made.

The concept of *timeliness* alludes to the time in which the contract is to be performed. The offeree must have accepted the offer within a reasonable period of time, and before the offer was revoked, either by act or by operation of law. If the contract is unilateral (as in a listing agreement), the offeree must have performed his part of the contract within a reasonable period of time in order to make it enforceable against the offeror.

To effect a proper acceptance, there also must be an *unqualified, unconditional acceptance* of the offer communicated to the offeree. Any acceptance that is not an acceptance of the whole offer becomes a conditional acceptance, and a conditional acceptance becomes a *counter offer*. Therefore, the contract is not completed until the offeror has accepted the counter offer to complete the agreement.

Consideration

Once a proper offer and a proper acceptance have been made in an effort to complete the contract, the only remaining requirement is what is termed *consideration*. Consideration is often thought of as the money or goods exchanged between the parties. However, consideration can best be defined as the obligation that each party makes to the other in order to make the contract enforceable. In most cases, money or promises are mutually exchanged, and each party suffers a detriment (that is, each party promises to give something away). In the typical earnest money contract situation, the seller offers to give up his house, and the purchaser offers to give up his money. In the seller-broker relationship, the seller offers to give up his money, and the broker incurs the obligation to perform; and, as may be recalled from the previous chapter, when the broker has performed, the contract has been completed. In performing, the broker has suffered the detriment of spending his time and labor in advertising, marketing, and selling the real estate.

Sufficiency of consideration is not, by itself, a controlling factor in whether or not a contract is enforceable. The court will generally strive to find consideration if in fact both parties have suffered a legal detriment and have bound themselves to perform on a legal obligation. The old law school adage is that a "mere peppercorn" can be enough to support legal consideration. However, in more practical use, even though legal consideration may be a "mere peppercorn," the courts often look to more equitable relief and require that consideration be adequate enough to have the contract performed without giving the other party undue advantage or being unjustly enriched.

Rules for the Construction of Contracts

Once it has been determined that a legal contract has been formed, the court will make every effort not to strike down the contract unless it was illegal or was made under fraud, duress, or mistake. The underlying theory is that if two parties care enough to make a binding contract, and each performs to some extent on that contract, there must have been sufficient intent to warrant enforcement of that contract. As an introduction into contracts, it is helpful to understand some basic "rules of thumb" that courts generally use in interpreting and construing the intent of contracts.

Validity

Contracts are always construed in favor of upholding the contract. Forfeitures of contracts are not favored in the law, and if given an equal choice, the court will always choose to uphold the contract rather than strike it down. If there are two contracts that seem to conflict, the court will attempt to construe them so that each will be permitted to stand.

Four Corners Doctrine

Another standard construction of contracts is called the *Four Corners Doctrine*. This doctrine states that the instrument must be read in its entirety. No particular provision may be lifted out of context and be construed on its own merits. When you are reading each provision in the contract, every other provision of that contract must be kept in mind also, so that no inequitable constructions will be made on a clause or paragraph contrary to the intent of the rest of that contract.

Interlineations, "Fill-in-the-Blanks"

All interlineations (writing between the lines) of contracts are deemed part of that contract and stand on an equal footing with the remainder of the contract. The same is true of addendums or other instruments that are incorporated by reference in the contract, or attached to the back thereof. There is a difficult problem of proof when there are interlineations and addendums. Good practice suggests that when an interlineation, addendum, or an incorporation by reference is made, said interlineation should be initialed by all parties to the contract. In addition, all addendums, or documents incorporated by reference, should be indicated on the face of the contract. Addendums to the document should also be initialed, indicating that all parties to the contract knew which documents were being incorporated.

Against Maker

When a contract is unclear or ambiguous, and both possible interpretations stand on an equal footing, the court will construe the instrument most strictly against the party who drafted it and is responsible for the language used. This does not mean the court chooses to penalize the person who drew the contract, but merely that in a case of reasonable doubt as to interpretation, the equities will be construed against the drafter of the contract.

Parol Evidence Rule

In construing a contract, as well as in courtroom proceedings, one of the critically important factors in determining interpretations of contractual instruments is what is termed the *parol evidence rule*. Very simply explained, the parol evidence rule stands for the theory that when an agreement has been reduced to writing, parol evidence (oral or additional writings) is not admissible to add to or vary the promises contained in the original instrument. However, the contract must be clear and certain as to its terms, and not ambiguous in order for the parol evidence to apply.

This rule is critically important when drafting earnest money contracts. There is very often underlying intent in areas of financing, fixtures, and repairs, which can be agreed to orally and with the best of intentions. However, when one party fails to perform on an implied or oral agreement (even though the agreement may have been considered an important part of the earnest money contract), the court will not allow this evidence to be introduced so that it can construe the terms of the earnest money contract if it is otherwise unambiguous. In other words, a person can say whatever he wishes, but if it is not in the contract, he will have a very difficult time of proof and enforcement.

Printed versus Typed

When a contract uses a printed form contract, and there are typed provisions put into that contract that conflict with a statement in the form of the contract, the typed provisions will control over the printed provisions since it was the language of the parties used and should carry more weight than that of the printed form. The same is true of a handwritten provision versus a typed or printed provision in a contract. The changes usually imply the intent of the parties, possibly done as a last-minute change, to give more effect to prior provisions in the contract, or to clarify same.

Effective Date

The standard rule for the effective date of the contract is *not* when the contract is delivered (this is true of deeds and leases, but not of contracts generally). The contract takes effect when it is dated or when both parties have signed it.

The foregoing general rules are by no means conclusive, as each fact situation can, of course, impose its own equities and variations. Inevitably, conflicts will arise, and even the foregoing general rules can conflict in many situations. In a recent case, the court had to construe a conflict between the foregoing general rules when a real estate broker used a form contract on which he typed special provisions. The court had to decide which rule should be applied—the rule that says that typed matter controls over printed matter, or the rule that says the contract should be construed against the author (the broker). In this particular case, the court held that the rule should be applied that typed matter controls over printed matter instead of the rule of construction against the author, *Innes* v. *Webb*, 538 S.W.2d 237 (Tex. Civ. App.—Corpus Christi, 1976). Unfortunately, this type of problem with earnest money contracts comes up far too often, and great care should be taken to help avoid such situations.

Earnest Money Contracts

Now that there has been a preliminary introduction into contracts, it may be a little easier to comprehend the requirements of a contract for the sale of real estate, more commonly called the *earnest money contract*.

The earnest money contract is by far the most important instrument that a real estate agent comes into contact with in the general day-to-day business of his real estate practice. Earnest money contracts are, of course, binding obligations; they normally involve substantial amounts of money and very often control the biggest investment a family makes in its lifetime. It simply cannot be overemphasized how important this document is.

Even though the earnest money contract has such important legal significance, the drafting of these instruments is usually done by real estate agents and is seldom left to the expertise of attorneys. Attorneys are specifically trained in the field of drafting contracts, and there has been some objection to this practice by real estate agents. An attorney general's opinion drafted November 1, 1972, stated clearly that:

> The drawing up or supplying of any preliminary or earnest money contract form and the filling in of the blanks for the parties by a real estate dealer may reasonably be deemed suspect and possibly in violation of Section 17 [now Section 16] of Article 6573a under the existing state court decisions in this field.

However, the attorney general's opinion went on to say that the use of the Texas Real Estate Commission's standard form would not constitute a violation of the Licensing Act or constitute the illegal practice of law. The Standard Assumption of Loan contract forms have been promulgated; other forms are under active consideration at this time. It can be emphasized that the Texas Real Estate Commission, in conjunction with the

State Bar of Texas, has been seeking to follow the attorney general's opinion to facilitate some of the more basic real estate transactions that the real estate broker and sales agent must face on a day-to-day basis. In light of the foregoing facts, it can reasonably be ascertained that using the commission-promulgated form is clearly sanctioned, and such use is not a violation of the law. However, stepping beyond the commission's standard form may still be suspect, and this form of practicing law may be in violation of the newly revised Texas Real Estate Licensing Act.

Copies of the commission-promulgated Assumption of Loan Earnest Money Contract forms, and some of the other forms under consideration, are included in this chapter in Figures 6-1 through 6-6. Effective April 2, 1979 real estate licensees will be required to use, when appropriate, one of the six standard contract forms in real estate transactions. For a more in-depth discussion of these forms, please see Harwood and Jacobus, *Texas Real Estate, An Introduction to the Profession.**

Requirements of Earnest Money Contracts

Oral Contracts. If you recall the discussion at the beginning of this chapter, you will remember that there was a general requirement that all contracts affecting the transfer of real estate must be in writing, in order to comply with the Statute of Frauds. We will depart from this basic underlying theory just enough to prove that there are exceptions to every rule. There *is* such a thing as an *oral earnest money contract* (horror of horrors!). There are basically three requirements to enforce an oral earnest money contract, and these all must exist simultaneously, *Hooks* v. *Bridgewater*, 229 S.W.2d 1114 (Tex. 1921):

1. There must be payment of the consideration, whether it be in money or services; and
2. The possession of the subject property must be taken by the purchaser; and
3. The purchaser must have made payment and valuable improvements on the property with the seller's consent.

Payment of the consideration in full (no. 1 above) is not required if the other requirements are met, *Cheatwood* v. *De Los Santos*, 561 S.W.2d 273 (Tex. Civ. App.—Eastland, 1978). While the reader is scratching his head in bewilderment, we will attempt to explain a fact situation under which an oral earnest money contract could be enforced:

*Bruce Harwood and Charles J. Jacobus, *Texas Real Estate, An Introduction to the Profession*, Reston Publishing Company, Inc., Reston, Virginia, 1978.

ASSUMPTION OF LOAN - RESIDENTIAL EARNEST MONEY CONTRACT

PROMULGATED BY TEXAS REAL ESTATE COMMISSION

1. PARTIES: ____________ (Seller) agrees to sell and convey to ____________ (Buyer) and Buyer agrees to buy from Seller the following property situated in ____________ County, Texas, known as ____________ (Address).

2. PROPERTY: Lot ____________ Block ________, ____________ ____________ Addition, City of ____________, or as described on attached exhibit, together with the following fixtures, if any: curtain and drapery rods, venetian blinds, window shades, screens and shutters, awnings, wall-to-wall carpeting, mirrors fixed in place, attic fans, permanently installed heating and air conditioning units and equipment, lighting and plumbing fixtures, TV antennas, mail boxes, water softeners, shrubbery and other property attached to the Property and owned by Seller. All property sold by this contract is called "Property."

3. CONTRACT SALES PRICE:

A. The Exact ☐ Approximate ☐ Cash down payment ....$________

B. Buyer's assumption of the unpaid balance of a promissory note, payable to Noteholder, with present monthly installments of $________, including principal, interest and escrow deposit, with Buyer's first payment due ____________, the unpaid principal balance of which (allowing for an agreed $100 variance) is ....$________

C. Any balance of Sales Price to be evidenced by a second lien note payable to [check (1) or (2) below]:

☐ (1) Seller, bearing interest at the rate of ______% per annum, either in

☐ lump sum on or before ____________ or

☐ principal and interest installments of $________, or more per ________, with first installment payment on ____________.

☐ (2) Third Party in principal and interest installments not in excess of $________ per month;

and in the Exact ☐ Approximate ☐ (check "Approximate" only if A. above and D. below are "Exact") amount of ....$________

D. The Exact ☐ Approximate ☐ total Sales Price of (Sum of A., B. and C. above) $________

4. EARNEST MONEY: $________ of the cash down payment is herewith tendered and is to be deposited as Earnest Money with ____________ as Escrow Agent, upon execution of the contract by both parties. Additional Earnest Money, if any, shall be deposited with the Escrow Agent on or before the ________ day of ____________, 197____, in the amount of $________.

5. SPECIAL PROVISIONS:

(Set forth above terms and conditions of a factual nature applicable to this sale, e.g., personal property included in sale, prior purchase or sale of other property, lessee's surrender of possession, and the like.)

6. REPRESENTATIONS: Seller represents that at the time of closing there will be no Title I liens, unrecorded liens or Uniform Commercial Code liens against any of the Property, that loan(s) will be without default, and escrow account will not be deficient. If above representations are untrue or if Noteholder raises the existing interest rate above ____% or requires Buyer to pay an assumption fee in excess of $____________, then this contract may, at Buyer's option, be declared null and void and Earnest Money shall be returned without delay. Representations shall survive closing.

7. TITLE: Seller at Seller's expense shall furnish either:

☐ A. Owner's Policy of Title Insurance (the Title Policy) issued by ______________________ ______________________ in the amount of the Sales Price dated at or after closing, OR,

☐ B. Complete Abstract of Title certified by ______________________ to current date.

NOTICE TO BUYER: If neither an Abstract of Title nor a Policy of Title Insurance is provided for herein, then AS REQUIRED BY LAW, Broker hereby advises YOU that YOU should have an abstract covering the real estate which YOU are hereby buying examined by an attorney of YOUR own selection, or that YOU should be furnished with or obtain a Policy of Title Insurance.

8. PROPERTY CONDITION (Check "A" or "B"):

☐ A. Buyer accepts the Property in its present condition, subject only to the following exceptions: ____________ ______________________________________

☐ B. Buyer requires inspections and repairs as provided by the attached addendum.

Buyer acknowledges that Broker and sales associates have no responsibility or liability for the repair or replacement of the Property or related equipment or fixtures.

9. PRORATION: Taxes, insurance, rents, interest and maintenance fees, if any, SHALL ☐ SHALL NOT ☐ be prorated to the date of closing. If these are not prorated, all funds held in escrow for payment of taxes, maintenance fees and insurance shall be transferred to the account of Buyer by Seller without cost to Buyer.

10. BROKER'S FEE: ______________________, as Real Estate Broker ("Broker") has negotiated this sale and Seller agrees to pay Broker in ______________ County, Texas, a fee in cash in the amount of ______________ of the total Sales Price at closing or upon Seller's default when completion of sale is prevented through fault of Seller.

11. CLOSING: The closing of the sale shall be on or before ______________ or within 7 days after objections to title have been cured, whichever date is later.

12. POSSESSION: The Property shall be delivered to Buyer on ______________________ in its present condition, ordinary wear and tear excepted, unless otherwise specified herein.

TREC NO. 1-0

FIGURE 6-1.

13. ASSUMPTION APPROVAL: If Noteholder requires approval of Buyer, or can accelerate note upon assumption, or both, then approval of Buyer and waiver of right of acceleration in writing by Noteholder prior to closing shall be required, otherwise this contract may, at Buyer's option, be declared null and void and Earnest Money shall be returned without delay. Buyer will use every reasonable effort to obtain such approval and waiver.
14. TITLE APPROVAL: If Abstract of Title is furnished, Seller shall deliver same to Buyer within 20 days from the date of application therefor. Buyer or Buyer's attorney shall have 20 days from date of Buyer's receipt of Abstract to examine and deliver a copy of the written report thereon to Seller, stating any objections to title made by Buyer, and only objections thereto so stated shall be considered. If Owner's Policy of Title Insurance is furnished, Seller shall have 20 days from the date of application therefor to secure assurance that Title Insurance may be issued. In either instance, if title objections are disclosed, Seller shall have 30 days to cure the same. Exceptions permitted to the Deed and zoning ordinances shall not be valid objections to title.

    The Title Policy (form prescribed by State Board of Insurance of the State of Texas) shall guarantee Buyer's title to be good and indefeasible subject only to the following:
    A. Restrictive covenants affecting the Property.
    B. Any discrepancies, conflicts, or shortages in area or boundary lines, or any encroachments, or any overlapping of improvements.
    C. All taxes for the current and subsequent years.
    D. Any existing building and zoning ordinances.
    E. Rights of parties in possession.
    F. Any liens which are recited as part of the consideration for the Property being purchased.

    Seller agrees to furnish at Seller's expense tax certificates showing no delinquent taxes, and a general Warranty Deed conveying title subject only to liens created or assumed as a part of the consideration, taxes for the current year, usual restrictive covenants and utility easements common to any regularly platted subdivision where Property is located and any other reservations or exceptions acceptable to Buyer. Each note herein provided shall be secured by a Vendor's and Deed of Trust lien. A Vendor's lien shall be retained and a Deed of Trust to Secure Assumption required, which liens shall be automatically released on execution and delivery of a release by Noteholder. Unless otherwise mutually agreed, the Deed, Notes and Deeds of Trust shall be upon forms currently published by the State Bar of Texas, or those required by any lending institution or governmental agency providing funds, guaranties or insurance for financing.
15. LOSS: If any part of Property is damaged or destroyed by fire or other casualty loss, Seller shall restore the same to its previous condition as soon as reasonably possible, but in any event within 30 days after the herein recited period of time for closing (and the closing date shall be extended accordingly); and if Seller is unable to do so, Buyer may cancel and terminate this Contract, whereupon all Earnest Money shall be returned to Buyer, and Broker shall not be entitled to any fee.
16. DEFAULT: If Buyer fails to comply herewith, Seller may either enforce specific performance or receive the Earnest Money as liquidated damages, one-half of which (but not exceeding the amount of the Broker's fee recited herein) shall be paid by Seller to Broker in full payment for Broker's services. If Seller is unable, through no fault of his own, to obtain abstract or title information from the Title Company or to make any repairs required herein, within the time herein specified, Buyer may, at his option, extend the time or terminate the contract, and receive the Earnest Money back as the sole remedy. If Seller fails to comply herewith for any other reason, Buyer may demand the Earnest Money, thereby releasing Seller from this contract, or Buyer may either enforce specific performance hereof or seek such other relief as may be provided by law. If completion of sale is prevented by Buyer's default, and Seller elects to enforce specific performance, the Broker's Fee is payable only if and when Seller collects judgment for such default by suit, compromise, settlement or otherwise, and after first deducting the expenses of collection, and then only in an amount equal to one-half of that portion collected, but not exceeding the amount of Broker's fee.

17. ESCROW: Funds are deposited with Escrow Agent with the understanding that Escrow Agent (i) does not assume or have any liability for performance or nonperformance of any party (ii) has the right to require the receipt, release and authorization in writing of all parties before paying the deposit to any party and (iii) is not liable for interest or other charge on the funds held. Any excess of Earnest Money over the amount required for down payment shall be applied against Buyer's closing costs.
18. EXPENSES OF SALE: Preparing and recording Deed of Trust to Secure Assumption and one-half of Escrow Fees shall be Seller's expense. All other costs and expenses incurred in connection with this contract which are not recited herein to be the obligation of Seller, shall be the obligation of Buyer. Unless otherwise paid, before Buyer shall be entitled to return of Earnest Money, any such costs and expenses shall be deducted therefrom and paid to the creditors entitled thereto.
19. THIRD PARTY FINANCING: If financing by third party is provided herein, Buyer shall have 15 days to obtain the same, and failure to secure the same after reasonable effort shall render this contract null and void, and the Earnest Money returned without delay.
20. EXTENDED CLOSING: If necessary to comply with REAL ESTATE SETTLEMENT PROCEDURES ACT of 1974, closing shall be extended daily up to 30 days.
21. AGREEMENT OF PARTIES: This contract contains the entire agreement of the parties and cannot be changed except by their written consent.
22. CONSULT YOUR ATTORNEY: This is a legally binding contract. READ IT CAREFULLY. If you do not understand the effect of any part, consult your attorney BEFORE signing. The Broker cannot give you legal advice - only factual and business details concerning this land and its improvements. If desired, attorneys to represent parties may be designated below, and, so employment may be accepted, Broker shall promptly deliver a copy of this contract to such attorneys.

Seller's Atty: ______________ Buyer's Atty: ______________

EXECUTED in multiple copies effective the ______ day of ______________ 197____ (Broker fill in date after last party signs).

Receipt of $______________ Earnest Money is acknowledged in the form of ______________

Escrow Agent ______ Date	Seller
By______________	Seller
Broker ______ License No.	Seller's Address ______ Tel.
By______________	Buyer
Broker ______ License No.	Buyer
By______________	Buyer's Address ______ Tel.

The form of this contract has been approved by the Texas Real Estate Commission and the State Bar of Texas. No representation is made as to the legal validity or adequacy of any provision in any specific transaction. It is not suitable for complex transactions and extensive riders or additions are not to be used. (9-75) TREC No. 1-0.

FIGURE 6-1 (*continued*).

ADDENDUM TO EARNEST MONEY CONTRACT
BETWEEN THE UNDERSIGNED PARTIES

DATED ________________

CHECK APPLICABLE BOXES:

☐ A. TERMITES: Seller agrees at his expense to furnish Buyer with a letter of current date from a licensed exterminator stating there is no visible evidence of active termites or other wood destroying insects or damage from same in need of repair to the improvements on the Property. Said letter shall guarantee the improvements free of infestation for a period of 90 days.

☐ B. INSPECTIONS BY BUYER, REPAIRS BY SELLER: Buyer, at Buyer's option and expense, shall have 10 days from the effective date of the contract to have the structure, foundation, roof, dishwasher, disposal, trash compactor, range, oven exhaust fan, heating and air conditioning system, plumbing (including well and septic tank) system, electrical system, swimming pool and ______________________________ ______________________________ inspected by specialists of Buyer's choice and shall give Seller written notice of required repairs to any of the above items which are not performing the function for which intended or which are in need of immediate repair. Failure to do so shall be deemed a waiver of Buyer's inspection and repair rights and Buyer agrees to accept Property in its present condition. Seller shall cause the repairs to be made without delay and prior to closing. Any inspections or repairs shall be by trained and qualified parties who are licensed or bonded whenever such license or bond is required by law or by a manufacturer-approved service person in the event of equipment items.

REPAIR EXPENSES: Seller's repair expenses from A and B shall not exceed $________________. If such repairs exceed such amount and Seller refuses to pay the balance of the cost, Buyer may pay the additional cost or accept the Property with the above limited repairs, and this sale shall be closed as scheduled, or Buyer may declare this contract null and void and the Earnest Money returned, less any inspection expenses to be paid to third parties. If Seller fails to commence immediately and complete the agreed repairs, Buyer may make the repairs and Seller shall be liable up to the amount specified, and the same paid from the proceeds of the sale.

If Broker and sales associates are requested to recommend inspectors or repairmen, Broker and sales associates are not liable for the results and have no responsibility for the performance of any firms making inspections or repairs pursuant to this contract.

______________________________ ______________________________
SELLER BUYER

SELLER BUYER

PROMULGATED BY TEXAS REAL ESTATE COMMISSION

The form of this contract has been approved by the Texas Real Estate Commission and the State Bar of Texas. No representation is made as to the legal validity or adequacy of any provision in any specific transaction. It is not suitable for complex transactions and extensive riders or additions are not to be used. (9-75) TREC No. 2-0.

FIGURE 6-1 *(continued)*.

VA GUARANTEED LOAN — RESIDENTIAL EARNEST MONEY CONTRACT (RESALE)

1. PARTIES: ______________________________ (Seller) agrees to sell and convey to ______________________________ (Buyer) and Buyer agrees to buy from Seller the following property situated in ______________________ County, Texas, known as ______________________________ (Address).

2. PROPERTY: Lot ______________, Block ______________, ______________ ______________ Addition, City of ______________________, or as described on attached exhibit, together with the following fixtures, if any: curtain rods, drapery rods, venetian blinds, window shades, screens and shutters, awnings, wall-to-wall carpeting, mirrors fixed in place, attic fans, permanently installed heating and air conditioning units and equipment, lighting and plumbing fixtures, TV antennas, mail boxes, water softeners, shrubbery and other property owned by Seller and attached to the above described real property. All property sold by this contract is called "Property".

3. CONTRACT SALES PRICE:
   - A. Cash down payment payable at closing . . . . $ ______________
   - B. Note described in 4 below (the Note) in the amount of . . . . $ ______________
   - C. Sales Price payable to Seller on Loan funding after closing (Sum of A and B) . . . . $ ______________

4. FINANCING CONDITIONS: This contract is subject to approval for Buyer of a VA loan (the Loan) of not less than the amount of the Note, amortizable monthly for not less than __________ years, with interest at maximum rate allowable at time of Loan funding. Buyer shall apply for the Loan within __________ days from the effective date of this contract and shall make every reasonable effort to obtain approval. If the Loan has not been approved by the Closing Date, this contract shall terminate and the Earnest Money shall be refunded to Buyer without delay. VA NOTICE TO BUYER: "It is expressly agreed that, notwithstanding any other provisions of this contract, the Buyer shall not incur any penalty by forfeiture of earnest money or otherwise or be obligated to complete the purchase of the Property described herein, if the contract purchase price or cost exceeds the reasonable value of the Property established by the Veterans Administration. The Buyer shall, however, have the privilege and option of proceeding with the consummation of this contract without regard to the amount of the reasonable value established by the Veterans Administration." Buyer agrees that should Buyer elect to complete the purchase at an amount in excess of the reasonable value established by VA, Buyer shall pay such excess amount in cash from a source which Buyer agrees to disclose to the VA and which Buyer represents will not be from borrowed funds except as approved by VA. If VA reasonable value of the Property is less than the Sales Price (3C above), Seller may reduce the Sales Price to an amount equal to the VA reasonable value and both parties agree to close the sale at such lower Sales Price with appropriate adjustments to 3A and 3B above.

5. EARNEST MONEY: $__________ is herewith tendered and is to be deposited as Earnest Money with ______________________________, as Escrow Agent, upon execution of the contract by both parties. Additional Earnest Money, if any, shall be deposited with the Escrow Agent on or before ______________, 19 _____, in the amount of $__________

6. TITLE: Seller at Seller's expense shall furnish either:
   - ☐ A. Owner's Policy of Title Insurance (the Title Policy) issued by ______________________________ in the amount of the Sales Price and dated at or after closing: OR
   - ☐ B. Complete Abstract of Title (the Abstract) certified by ______________________________ to current date.

   NOTICE TO BUYER: AS REQUIRED BY LAW, Broker advises that YOU should have the Abstract covering the Property examined by an attorney of YOUR selection, or YOU should be furnished with or obtain a Title Policy.

7. **PROPERTY CONDITION** (Check "A" or "B"):
   ☐ **A.** **Buyer accepts the Property in its present condition, subject only to VA required repairs and** ______________________
   ____

   ☐ **B.** **Buyer requires inspections and repairs required by the Property Condition Addendum (the Addendum) and those required by VA. Upon Seller's receipt of all loan approvals and inspection reports Seller shall commence and complete prior to closing all required repairs at Seller's expense.**

   All inspections, reports and repairs required of Seller by this contract and the Addendum shall not exceed $__________. If Seller fails to complete such requirements, Buyer may do so and Seller shall be liable up to the amount specified and the same paid from the proceeds of the sale. Broker and sales associates have no responsibility or liability for repair or replacement of any of the Property.

8. **BROKER'S FEE:** ______________________________ **Listing Broker (_____%) and** ______________________ ______________________ **Co-Broker (_____%), as Real Estate Broker (the Broker), has negotiated this sale and Seller agrees to pay Broker in** ______________________ **County, Texas, on consummation of this sale or on Seller's default (unless otherwise provided herein) a total cash fee of** ______________ **of the total Sales Price, which Escrow Agent may pay from the sale proceeds.**

9. CLOSING: The closing of the sale (the Closing Date) shall be on or before ______________, 19 _____, or within 7 days after objections to title have been cured, whichever date is later; however, if necessary to complete loan requirements, the Closing Date shall be extended daily up to 15 days.

10. POSSESSION: The possession of the Property shall be delivered to Buyer on ______________________ in its present or required improved condition, ordinary wear and tear excepted. Any possession by Buyer prior to or by Seller after Closing Date shall establish a landlord-tenant at sufferance relationship between the parties.

11. SPECIAL PROVISIONS:

(Insert terms and conditions of a factual nature applicable to this sale, e.g., prior purchase or sale of other property, lessee's surrender of possession, and the like.).

FIGURE 6-2.

12. SALES EXPENSES TO BE PAID IN CASH AT OR PRIOR TO CLOSING:

A. Loan appraisal fees shall be paid by ______________________________.

B. Seller's Expenses:

(1) Seller's Loan discount points not exceeding ______________________________

(2) VA required repairs and any other inspections, reports and repairs required of Seller herein, and in the Addendum.

(3) Releases of existing loans, including prepayment penalties and recordation: escrow fee; tax statements; preparation of Deed, Note and Deed of Trust; expenses VA prohibits Buyer to pay, (e.g., copies of restrictions, photos, excess cost of survey of Property); other expenses stipulated to be paid by Seller under other provisions of this contract.

C. Buyer's Expenses: Expenses incident to Loan (e.g., credit reports; recording fees; Mortgagee's Title Policy; Loan origination fee; that portion of survey cost Buyer can pay by VA regulation; Loan related inspection fees; premiums for 1 year's hazard insurance and any flood insurance; required reserve deposits for insurance premiums, ad valorem taxes and special assessments; interest from date of disbursement to 1 month prior to date of first monthly payment on the Note); premiums on non-required insurance; expenses stipulated to be paid by Buyer under other provisions of this contract.

D. If any sales expenses exceed the maximum amount herein stipulated to be paid by either party, such party may terminate this contract unless the other party agrees to pay such excess. In no event shall Buyer pay charges and fees other than those expressly permitted by VA Regulations.

13. PRORATIONS: Insurance (at Buyer's option), taxes and any rents and maintenance fees shall be prorated to the Closing Date.

14. TITLE APPROVAL: If Abstract is furnished, Seller shall deliver same to Buyer within 20 days from the effective date hereof. Buyer shall have 20 days from date of receipt of Abstract to deliver a copy of the title opinion to Seller, stating any objections to title, and only objections so stated shall be considered. If Title Policy is furnished, the Title Policy shall guarantee Buyer's title to be good and indefeasible subject only to (i) restrictive covenants affecting the Property (ii) any discrepancies, conflicts or shortages in area or boundary lines or any encroachments, or any overlapping of improvements (iii) all taxes for the current and subsequent years (iv) any existing building and zoning ordinances (v) rights of parties in possession (vi) any liens created as security for the sale and consideration and (vii) any reservations or exceptions contained in the Deed. In either instance, if title objections are disclosed, Seller shall have 30 days to cure the same. Exceptions permitted in the Deed and zoning ordinances shall not be valid objections to title. Seller shall furnish at Seller's expense tax statements showing no delinquent taxes and a General Warranty Deed conveying title subject only to liens securing debt created as part of the consideration, taxes for the current year, usual restrictive covenants and utility easements common to any regularly platted subdivision where Property is located and any other reservations or exceptions acceptable to Buyer. The note shall be secured by Vendor's and Deed of Trust liens. In case of dispute as to the form of Deed, such shall be upon a form prepared by the State Bar of Texas.

15. CASUALTY LOSS: If any part of Property is damaged or destroyed by fire or other casualty loss, Seller shall restore the same to its previous condition as soon as reasonably possible, but in any event by Closing Date; and if Seller is unable to do so without fault, this contract shall terminate and Earnest Money shall be refunded with no Broker's fee due.

16. DEFAULT: A. If Buyer fails to comply herewith, Seller may either enforce specific performance or terminate this contract and receive the Earnest Money as liquidated damages, one-half of which (but not exceeding the herein recited Broker's fee) shall be paid by Seller to Broker in full payment for Broker's services. If Seller is unable without fault to deliver Abstract or Title Policy or to make any non-casualty repairs required herein within the time herein specified, Buyer may either terminate this contract and receive the Earnest Money as the sole remedy, and no Broker's fee shall be earned, or extend the time up to 30 days. If Seller fails to comply herewith for any other reason, Buyer may (i) terminate this contract and receive the Earnest Money, thereby releasing Seller from this contract (ii) enforce specific performance hereof or (iii) seek such other relief as may be provided by law. If completion of sale is prevented by Buyer's default, and Seller elects to enforce specific performance, the Broker's fee is payable only if and when Seller collects damages for such default by suit, compromise, settlement or otherwise, and after first deducting the expenses of collection, and then only in an amount equal to one-half of that portion collected, but not exceeding the amount of Broker's fee.

B. Any signatory to this contract who is the prevailing party in any legal proceeding against any other signatory brought under or with relation to this contract shall be additionally entitled to recover court costs and reasonable attorney fees from the non-prevailing party.

17. ESCROW: Earnest Money is deposited with Escrow Agent with the understanding that Escrow Agent (i) does not assume or have any liability for performance or nonperformance of any party (ii) has the right to require the receipt, release and authorization in writing of all parties before paying the deposit to any party and (iii) is not liable for interest or other charge on the funds held. If any party unreasonably fails to agree in writing to an appropriate release of Earnest Money, then such party shall be liable to the other parties to the extent provided in paragraph 16B. At closing, Earnest Money shall be applied to any cash down payment required, next to Buyer's closing costs and any excess refunded to Buyer. Before Buyer shall be entitled to refund of Earnest Money, any actual and VA allowable expenses incurred or paid on Buyer's behalf shall be deducted therefrom and paid to the creditors entitled thereto.

18. REPRESENTATIONS: Seller represents that there will be no Title I liens, unrecorded liens or Uniform Commercial Code liens against any of the Property on Closing Date. If any representation above is untrue this contract may be terminated by Buyer and the Earnest Money shall be refunded without delay. Representations shall survive closing.

19. AGREEMENT OF PARTIES: This contract contains the entire agreement of the parties and cannot be changed except by their written consent

20. CONSULT YOUR ATTORNEY: This is intended to be a legally binding contract. READ IT CAREFULLY. If you do not understand the effect of any part, consult your attorney BEFORE signing. The Broker cannot give you legal advice — only factual and business details concerning land and improvements. Attorneys to represent parties may be designated below, and, so employment may be accepted, Broker shall promptly deliver a copy of this contract to such attorneys.

Seller's Atty: ______________________ Buyer's Atty: ______________________

EXECUTED in multiple originals effective the _____ day of ______________, 19 _____ **(BROKER FILL IN DATE AFTER LAST PARTY SIGNS).**

______________________	______________________
Listing Broker License No.	Seller
By ______________________	______________________
	Seller
______________________	______________________
Co-Broker License No.	Seller's Address Tel.
By ______________________	______________________
	Buyer
Receipt of $ __________ Earnest Money is acknowledged in the form	______________________
	Buyer
of ______________________	______________________
	Buyer's Address Tel.
______________________	
Escrow Agent Date	
By ______________________	

2/6/78

FIGURE 6-2 (*continued*).

CONVENTIONAL LOAN — RESIDENTIAL EARNEST MONEY CONTRACT (RESALE)

1. PARTIES: ______________________________ (Seller) agrees to sell and convey to ______________________________ (Buyer) and Buyer agrees to buy from Seller the following property situated in ______________ County, Texas, known as ______________________________ (Address).

2. PROPERTY: Lot ______________, Block ______________, ______________ ______________ Addition, City of ______________, or as described on attached exhibit, together with the following fixtures, if any: curtain rods, drapery rods, venetian blinds, window shades, screens and shutters, awnings, wall-to-wall carpeting, mirrors fixed in place, attic fans, permanently installed heating and air conditioning units and equipment, lighting and plumbing fixtures, TV antennas, mail boxes, water softeners, shrubbery and other property owned by Seller and attached to the above described real property. All property sold by this contract is called "Property".

3. CONTRACT SALES PRICE:
   A. Cash down payment payable at closing .... $ ________
   B. Note described in 4 below (the Note) in the amount of .... $ ________
   C. Any balance of Sales Price to be evidenced by a second lien note (the Second Note) payable to [check (1) or (2) below]:
      ☐ (1) Seller, bearing interest at the rate of ________ % per annum, in
         ☐ lump sum on or before ______________
         ☐ principal and interest installments of $________, or more per ________,
         with first installment payable on ______________
      ☐ (2) Third Party in principal and interest installments not in excess of $ ________ per month
      in the principal amount of .... $ ________
   D. Sales Price payable to Seller on Loan funding after closing (Sum of A, B & C) .... $ ________

4. FINANCING CONDITIONS: This contract is subject to approval for Buyer of a ☐ Conventional or ☐ Conventional private mortgage insured third party loan (the Loan) of not less than the amount of the Note, amortizable monthly for not less than ________ years, with interest not to exceed ________ percent per annum, and approval of any third party Second Note. Buyer shall apply for all financing within ________ days from the effective date of this contract and shall make every reasonable effort to obtain approval. If all financing cannot be approved within ________ days from effective date of this contract, this contract shall terminate and Earnest Money shall be refunded to Buyer without delay.

5. EARNEST MONEY: $________ is herewith tendered and is to be deposited as Earnest Money with ______________ ______________, as Escrow Agent, upon execution of the contract by both parties. Additional Earnest Money, if any, shall be deposited with the Escrow Agent on or before ______________, 19 ____, in the amount of $________.

6. TITLE: Seller at Seller's expense shall furnish either:
   ☐ A. Owner's Policy of Title Insurance (the Title Policy) issued by ________________
   in the amount of the Sales Price and dated at or after closing: OR
   ☐ B. Complete Abstract of Title (the Abstract) certified by ________________ to current date.

   NOTICE TO BUYER: AS REQUIRED BY LAW, Broker advises that YOU should have the Abstract covering the Property examined by an attorney of YOUR selection, or YOU should be furnished with or obtain a Title Policy.

7. PROPERTY CONDITION (Check "A" or "B"):
   ☐ A. Buyer accepts the Property in its present condition, subject only to lender required repairs and ________________
   ________________.
   ☐ B. Buyer requires inspections and repairs required by the Property Condition Addendum (the Addendum) and any lender.

   Upon Seller's receipt of all loan approvals and inspection reports Seller shall commence and complete prior to closing all required repairs at Seller's expense.

   All inspections, reports and repairs required of Seller by this contract and the Addendum shall not exceed $________. If Seller fails to complete such requirements, Buyer may do so and Seller shall be liable up to the amount specified and the same paid from the proceeds of the sale. Broker and sales associates have no responsibility or liability for repair or replacement of any of the Property.

8. BROKER'S FEE: ________________ Listing Broker (____%) and ________________ Co-Broker (____%), as Real Estate Broker (the Broker), has negotiated this sale and Seller agrees to pay Broker in ________________ County, Texas, on consummation of this sale or on Seller's default (unless otherwise provided herein) a total cash fee of ________ of the total Sales Price, which Escrow Agent may pay from the sale proceeds.

9. CLOSING: The closing of the sale (the Closing Date) shall be on or before ________________, 19 ____, or within 7 days after objections to title have been cured, whichever date is later; however, if necessary to complete loan requirements, the Closing Date shall be extended daily up to 15 days.

10. POSSESSION: The possession of the Property shall be delivered to Buyer on ________________ in its present or required improved condition, ordinary wear and tear excepted. Any possession by Buyer prior to or by Seller after Closing Date shall establish a landlord-tenant at sufferance relationship between the parties.

11. SPECIAL PROVISIONS:

(Insert terms and conditions of a factual nature applicable to this sale, e.g., personal property included in sale [curtains, draperies, valances, etc.], prior purchase or sale of other property, lessee's surrender of possession, and the like.)

FIGURE 6-3.

12. SALES EXPENSES TO BE PAID IN CASH AT OR PRIOR TO CLOSING:

A. Seller's Expenses:

(1) Any inspections, reports and repairs required of Seller herein, and in the Addendum.

(2) All cost of releasing existing loans and recording the releases; tax statements; 1/2 of any escrow fee; preparation of Deed; copies of restrictions and easements; other expenses stipulated to be paid by Seller under other provisions of this contract.

B. Buyer's Expenses: All expenses incident to any loan (e.g., preparation of Note, Deed of Trust and other loan documents, recording fees, Mortgagee's Title Policy, credit reports); 1/2 of any escrow fee; one year premium for hazard insurance unless insurance is prorated; and expenses stipulated to be paid by Buyer under other provisions of this contract.

C. If any sales expenses exceed the maximum amount herein stipulated to be paid by either party, such party may terminate this contract unless the other party agrees to pay such excess.

13. PRORATIONS: Insurance (at Buyer's option), taxes and any rents and maintenance fees, shall be prorated to the Closing Date.

14. TITLE APPROVAL: If Abstract is furnished, Seller shall deliver same to buyer within 20 days from the effective date hereof. Buyer shall have 20 days from date of receipt of Abstract to deliver a copy of the title opinion to Seller, stating any objections to title, and only objections so stated shall be considered. If Title Policy is furnished, the Title Policy shall guarantee Buyer's title to be good and indefeasible subject only to (i) restrictive covenants affecting the Property (ii) any discrepancies, conflicts or shortages in area or boundary lines or any encroachments, or any overlapping of improvements (iii) all taxes for the current and subsequent years (iv) any existing building and zoning ordinances (v) rights of parties in possesion (vi) any liens created as security for the sale consideration and (vii) any reservations or exceptions contained in the Deed. In either instance, if title objections are disclosed, Seller shall have 30 days to cure the same. Exceptions permitted in the Deed and zoning ordinances shall not be valid objections to title. Seller shall furnish at Seller's expense tax statements showing no delinquent taxes and a General Warranty Deed conveying title subject only to liens securing debt created as part of the consideration, taxes for the current year, usual restrictive covenants and utility easements common to any regularly platted subdivision where Property is located and any other reservations or exceptions acceptable to Buyer. The note shall be secured by Vendor's and Deed of Trust liens. In case of dispute as to the form of Deed, Deed of Trust or Note, such shall be upon a form prepared by the State Bar of Texas.

15. CASUALTY LOSS: If any part of Property is damaged or destroyed by fire or other casualty loss, Seller shall restore the same to its previous condition as soon as reasonably possible, but in any event by Closing Date; and if Seller is unable to do so without fault, this contract shall terminate and Earnest Money shall be refunded with no Broker's fee due.

16. DEFAULT: A. If Buyer fails to comply herewith, Seller may either enforce specific performance or terminate this contract and receive the Earnest Money as liquidated damages, one-half of which (but not exceeding the herein recited Broker's fee) shall be paid by Seller to Broker in full payment for Broker's services. If Seller is unable without fault to deliver Abstract or Title Policy or to make any non-casualty repairs required herein within the time herein specified, Buyer may either terminate this contract and receive the Earnest Money as the sole remedy, and no Broker's fee shall be earned, or extend the time up to 30 days. If Seller fails to comply herewith for any other reason, Buyer may (i) terminate this contract and receive the Earnest Money, thereby releasing Seller from this contract (ii) enforce specific performance hereof or (iii) seek such other relief as may be provided by law. If completion of sale is prevented by Buyer's default, and Seller elects to enforce specific performance, the Broker's fee is payable only if and when Seller collects damages for such default by suit, compromise, settlement or otherwise, and after first deducting the expenses of collection, and then only in an amount equal to one-half of that portion collected, but not exceeding the amount of Broker's fee.

B. Any signatory to this contract who is the prevailing party in any legal proceeding against any other signatory brought under or with relation to this contract shall be additionally entitled to recover court costs and reasonable attorney fees from the non-prevailing party.

17. ESCROW: Earnest Money is deposited with Escrow Agent with the understanding that Escrow Agent (i) does not assume or have any liability for performance or nonperformance of any party (ii) has the right to require the receipt, release and authorization in writing of all parties before paying the deposit to any party and (iii) is not liable for interest or other charge on the funds held. If any party unreasonably fails to agree in writing to an appropriate release of Earnest Money, then such party shall be liable to the other parties to the extent provided in paragraph 16B. At closing, Earnest Money shall be applied to any cash down payment required, next to Buyer's closing costs and any excess refunded to Buyer. Before Buyer shall be entitled to refund of Earnest Money, any actual expenses incurred or paid on Buyer's behalf shall be deducted therefrom and paid to the creditors entitled thereto.

18. REPRESENTATIONS: Seller represents that there will be no Title I liens, unrecorded liens or Uniform Commercial Code liens against any of the Property on Closing Date. If any representation above is untrue this contract may be terminated by Buyer and the Earnest Money shall be refunded without delay. Representations shall survive closing.

19. AGREEMENT OF PARTIES: This contract contains the entire agreement of the parties and cannot be changed except by their written consent.

20. CONSULT YOUR ATTORNEY: This is intended to be a legally binding contract. READ IT CAREFULLY. If you do not understand the effect of any part, consult your attorney BEFORE signing. The Broker cannot give you legal advice — only factual and business details concerning land and improvements. Attorneys to represent parties may be designated below, and, so employment may be accepted, Broker shall promptly deliver a copy of this contract to such attorneys.

Seller's Atty: ______________________ Buyer's Atty: ______________________

EXECUTED in multiple originals effective the _____ day of ______________, 19 _____. **(BROKER FILL IN DATE AFTER LAST PARTY SIGNS).**

____
Listing Broker License No.

By ______________________________

____
Co-Broker License No.

By ______________________________

Receipt of $ _______ Earnest Money is acknowledged in the form

of ______________________________

____
Escrow Agent Date

By ______________________________

____
Seller

____
Seller

____
Seller's Address Tel.

____
Buyer

____
Buyer

____
Buyer's Address Tel.

2/8/78

FIGURE 6-3 (*continued*).

FHA INSURED LOAN — RESIDENTIAL EARNEST MONEY CONTRACT (RESALE)

1. **PARTIES:** ______________________________ (Seller) agrees to sell and convey to ______________________________ (Buyer) and Buyer agrees to buy from Seller the following property situated in ______________________ County, Texas, known as ______________________________ (Address).

2. **PROPERTY:** Lot ______________, Block ________, ______________ ____________ Addition, City of ______________, or as described on attached exhibit, together with the following fixtures, if any: curtain rods, drapery rods, venetian blinds, window shades, screens and shutters, awnings, wall-to-wall carpeting, mirrors fixed in place, attic fans, permanently installed heating and air conditioning units and equipment, lighting and plumbing fixtures, TV antennas, mail boxes, water softeners, shrubbery and other property owned by Seller and attached to the above described real property. All property sold by this contract is called "Property".

3. **CONTRACT SALES PRICE:**
   - A. Cash down payment payable at closing . . . . $__________
   - B. Amount of Note (the Note) described in 4-A below . . . . $__________
   - C. Sales Price payable to Seller on Loan funding after closing (Sum of A plus B) . . . . $__________

4. **FINANCING CONDITIONS:**
   - A. This contract is subject to approval for Buyer of a Section ______________ FHA Insured Loan (the Loan) of not less than the amount of the Note, amortizable monthly for not less than ________ years, with interest at maximum rate allowable at time of loan funding. Buyer shall apply for the Loan within ________ days from the effective date of this contract and shall make every reasonable effort to obtain approval of the Loan. If the loan has not been approved by the Closing Date, this contract shall terminate and Earnest Money shall be refunded to Buyer without delay.
   - B. As required by HUD-FHA regulation, if FHA valuation is unknown, "It is expressly agreed that, notwithstanding any other provisions of this contract, the Purchaser (Buyer) shall not be obligated to complete the purchase of the Property described herein or to incur any penalty by forfeiture of Earnest Money deposits or otherwise unless the Seller has delivered to the Purchaser (Buyer) a written statement issued by the Federal Housing Commissioner setting forth the appraised value of the Property (exclusive of closing costs) of not less than $__________, which statement Seller hereby agrees to deliver to the Purchaser (Buyer) promptly after such appraised value statement is made available to the Seller. The Purchaser (Buyer) shall, however, have the privilege and option of proceeding with this consummation of this contract without regard to the amount of the appraised valuation made by the Federal Housing Commissioner."

5. **EARNEST MONEY:** $________ is herewith tendered and is to be deposited as Earnest Money with ______________ ______________________, as Escrow Agent, upon execution of the contract by both parties. Additional Earnest Money, if any, shall be deposited with the Escrow Agent on or before ______________, 19 ____, in the amount of $________.

6. **TITLE:** Seller at Seller's expense shall furnish either:
   - ☐ A. Owner's Policy of Title Insurance (the Title Policy) issued by ______________________ in the amount of the Sales Price and dated at or after closing: OR
   - ☐ B. Complete Abstract of Title (the Abstract) certified by ______________________ to current date.

   NOTICE TO BUYER: AS REQUIRED BY LAW, Broker advises that YOU should have the Abstract covering the Property examined by an attorney of YOUR selection, or YOU should be furnished with or obtain a Title Policy.

7. **PROPERTY CONDITION** (Check "A" or "B"):
☐ A. Buyer accepts the Property in its present condition, subject only to FHA required repairs and ______________________________
____.

☐ **B. Buyer requires inspections and repairs required by the Property Condition Addendum (the Addendum) and those required by FHA. Upon Seller's receipt of all loan approvals and inspection reports Seller shall commence and complete prior to closing all required repairs at Seller's expense.**

All inspections, reports and repairs required of Seller by this contract and the Addendum shall not exceed $__________. If Seller fails to complete such requirements, Buyer may do so and Seller shall be liable up to the amount specified and the same paid from the proceeds of the sale. Broker and sales associates have no responsibility or liability for repair or replacement of any of the Property.

8. BROKER'S FEE: ______________________________ Listing Broker (_____%) and ______________________________ Co-Broker (_____%), as Real Estate Broker (the Broker), has negotiated this sale and Seller agrees to pay Broker in ______________________________ County, Texas, on consummation of this sale or on Seller's default (unless otherwise provided herein) a total cash fee of ______________ of the total Sales Price, which Escrow Agent may pay from the sale proceeds.

9. CLOSING: The closing of the sale (the Closing Date) shall be on or before ____________________, 19 _____, or within 7 days after objections to title have been cured, whichever date is later; however, if necessary to complete loan requirements, the Closing Date shall be extended daily up to 15 days.

10. POSSESSION: The possession of the Property shall be delivered to Buyer on ______________________________ in its present or required improved condition, ordinary wear and tear excepted. Any possession by Buyer prior to or by Seller after Closing Date shall establish a landlord-tenant at sufferance relationship between the parties.

11. SPECIAL PROVISIONS:

(Insert terms and conditions of a factual nature applicable to this sale, e.g., prior purchase or sale of other property, lessee's surrender of possession, and the like.)

FIGURE 6-4.

12. SALES EXPENSES TO BE PAID IN CASH AT OR PRIOR TO CLOSING:

A. Loan appraisal fee (FHA application fee) shall be paid by ______

B. Seller's Expenses:

(1) Seller's Loan discount points not exceeding ______.

(2) FHA required repairs and any other inspections, reports and repairs required of Seller herein, and in the Addendum.

(3) Expenses incident to Loan (e.g., preparation of Loan documents, survey, recording fees, copies of restrictions and easements, amortization schedule, Mortgagee's Title Policy, Loan origination fee, credit reports, photographs).

(4) Releases of existing loans, including prepayment penalties and recordation; tax statements; preparation of Deed; escrow fee; and other expenses stipulated to be paid by Seller under other provisions of this contract.

C. Buyer's Expenses: All prepaid items required by applicable HUD-FHA or other regulations (e.g., required premiums for flood and hazard insurance; required reserve deposits for FHA and other insurance, ad valorem taxes and special assessments); interest on the Note from date of disbursement to one month prior to date of first monthly payment; expenses stipulated to be paid by Buyer under other provisions of this contract.

D. If any sales expenses exceed the maximum amount herein stipulated to be paid by either party, such party may terminate this Contract unless other party agrees to pay such excess. In no event shall Buyer pay charges and fees other than those expressly permitted by FHA regulation.

13. PRORATIONS: Insurance (at Buyer's option), taxes, and any rents and maintenance fees shall be prorated to the Closing Date.

14. TITLE APPROVAL: If Abstract is furnished, Seller shall deliver same to Buyer within 20 days from the effective date hereof. Buyer shall have 20 days from date of receipt of Abstract to deliver a copy of the title opinion to Seller, stating any objections to title, and only objections so stated shall be considered. If Title Policy is furnished, the Title Policy shall guarantee Buyer's title to be good and indefeasible subject only to (i) restrictive covenants affecting the Property (ii) any discrepancies, conflicts or shortages in area or boundary lines or any encroachments, or any overlapping of improvements (iii) all taxes for the current and subsequent years (iv) any existing building and zoning ordinances (v) rights of properties in possession (vi) any liens created as security for the sale consideration and (vii) any reservations or exceptions contained in the Deed. In either instance, if title objections are disclosed, Seller shall have 30 days to cure the same. Exceptions permitted in the Deed and zoning ordinances shall not be valid objections to title. Seller shall furnish at Seller's expense tax statements showing no delinquent taxes and a General Warranty Deed conveying title subject only to liens securing debt created as part of the consideration, taxes for the current year, usual restrictive covenants and utility easements common to any regularly platted subdivision where Property is located and any other reservations or exceptions acceptable to Buyer. The note shall be secured by Vendor's and Deed of Trust liens. In case of dispute as to the form of Deed, such shall be upon a form prepared by the State Bar of Texas.

15. CASUALTY LOSS: If any part of Property is damaged or destroyed by fire or other casualty loss, Seller shall restore the same to its previous condition as soon as reasonably possible, but in any event by Closing Date; and if Seller is unable to do so without fault, this contract shall terminate and Earnest Money shall be refunded with no Broker's fee due.

16. DEFAULT: A. If Buyer fails to comply herewith, Seller may either enforce specific performance or terminate this contract and receive the Earnest Money as liquidated damages, one-half of which (but not exceeding the herein recited Broker's fee) shall be paid by Seller to Broker in full payment for Broker's services. If Seller is unable without fault to deliver Abstract or Title Policy or to make any non-casualty repairs required herein within the time herein specified, Buyer may either terminate this contract and receive the Earnest Money as the sole remedy, and no Broker's fee shall be earned, or extend the time up to 30 days. If Seller fails to comply herewith for any other reason, Buyer may (i) terminate this contract and receive the Earnest Money, thereby releasing Seller from this contract (ii) enforce specific performance hereof or (iii) seek such other relief as may be provided by law. If completion of sale is prevented by Buyer's default, and Seller elects to enforce specific performance, the Broker's fee is payable only if and when Seller collects damages for such default by suit, compromise, settlement or otherwise, and after first deducting the expenses of collection, and then only in an amount equal to one-half of that portion collected, but not exceeding the amount of Broker's fee.

B. Any signatory to this contract who is the prevailing party in any legal proceeding against any other signatory brought under or with relation to this contract shall be additionally entitled to recover court costs and reasonable attorney fees from the non-prevailing party.

17. ESCROW: Earnest Money is deposited with Escrow Agent with the understanding that Escrow Agent (i) does not assume or have any liability for performance or nonperformance of any party (ii) has the right to require the receipt, release and authorization in writing of all parties before paying the deposit to any party and (iii) is not liable for interest or other charge on the funds held. If any party unreasonably fails to agree in writing to an appropriate release of Earnest Money, then such party shall be liable to the other parties to the extent provided in paragraph 16B. At Closing, Earnest Money shall be applied to any cash down payment required, next to Buyer's closing costs and any excess refunded to Buyer. Before Buyer shall be entitled to refund of Earnest Money, any actual and FHA allowable expenses incurred or paid on Buyer's behalf shall be deducted therefrom and paid to the creditors entitled thereto.

18. REPRESENTATIONS: Seller represents that there will be no Title I liens, unrecorded liens or Uniform Commercial Code liens against any of the Property on Closing Date. If any representation above is untrue this contract may be terminated by Buyer and the Earnest Money shall be refunded without delay. Representations shall survive closing.

19. AGREEMENT OF PARTIES: This contract contains the entire agreement of the parties and cannot be changed except by their written consent.

20. CONSULT YOUR ATTORNEY: This is intended to be a legally binding contract. READ IT CAREFULLY. If you do not understand the effect of any part, consult your attorney BEFORE signing. The Broker cannot give you legal advice — only factual and business details concerning land and improvements. Attorneys to represent parties may be designated below, and, so employment may be accepted, Broker shall promptly deliver a copy of this contract to such attorneys.

Seller's Atty: ______________________ Buyer's Atty: ______________________

EXECUTED in multiple originals effective the _____ day of ______________, 19 _____. **(BROKER FILL IN DATE AFTER LAST PARTY SIGNS).**

______________________	______________________
Listing Broker License No.	Seller
By ______________________	______________________
	Seller
______________________	______________________
Co-Broker License No.	**Seller's Address** **Tel.**
By ______________________	______________________
	Buyer
Receipt of $ ________ Earnest Money is acknowledged in the form	______________________
of ______________________	Buyer
______________________	______________________
Escrow Agent **Date**	**Buyer's Address** **Tel.**
By ______________________	

2/8/78

FIGURE 6-4 *(continued)*.

ALL CASH OR OWNER FINANCED — RESIDENTIAL EARNEST MONEY CONTRACT (RESALE)

1. PARTIES: ______________________________ (Seller) agrees to sell and convey to ______________________________ (Buyer) and Buyer agrees to buy from Seller the following property situated in ______________ County, Texas, known as ______________________________ (Address).

2. PROPERTY: Lot ______________, Block ________, ______________ ______________ Addition, City of ______________, or as described on attached exhibit, together with the following fixtures, if any: curtain rods, drapery rods, venetian blinds, window shades, screens and shutters, awnings, wall-to-wall carpeting, mirrors fixed in place, attic fans, permanently installed heating and air conditioning units and equipment, lighting and plumbing fixtures, TV antennas, mail boxes, water softeners, shrubbery and other property owned by Seller and attached to the above described real property. All property sold by this contract is called "Property".

3. CONTRACT SALES PRICE:
   A. Cash payment payable at closing . . . . $ __________
   B. Note described in 4 B below (the Note) . . . . $ __________
   C. Sales Price payable to Seller (Sum of A and B) . . . . $ __________

4. FINANCING CONDITIONS:
   [ ] A. This is an all cash sale; no financing is involved.
   [ ] B. The Note in the principal sum shown in 3 B above, dated as of the Closing Date, to be executed and delivered by Buyer and payable to the order of Seller, bearing interest at the rate of __________ percent per annum from date thereof until maturity, matured unpaid principal and interest to bear interest at the rate of 10% per annum, principal and interest to be due and payable
      [ ] (1) In ______________ installments of $__________ or more each, beginning on or before ______________ after date of the Note, and (Check Box a or b)
         [ ] a. continuing regularly and at the same intervals thereafter until fully paid.
         [ ] b. continuing regularly and at the same intervals thereafter until ______________, 19 ______, when the entire balance of principal and accrued interest shall be due and payable.
      [ ] (2) In a lump sum on or before ______________ after date of the Note,
   [ ] C. This contract is subject to Buyer furnishing Seller evidence that Buyer has a history of good credit.

5. EARNEST MONEY: $__________ is herewith tendered and is to be deposited as Earnest Money with ______________ ______________________________, as Escrow Agent, upon execution of the contract by both parties. Additional Earnest Money, if any, shall be deposited with the Escrow Agent on or before ______________, 19 ______, in the amount of $__________

6. TITLE: Seller at Seller's expense shall furnish either:
   [ ] A. Owner's Policy of Title Insurance (the Title Policy) issued by ______________________________ in the amount of the Sales Price and dated at or after closing: OR
   [ ] B. Complete Abstract of Title (the Abstract) certified by ______________________________ to current date.

NOTICE TO BUYER: AS REQUIRED BY LAW, Broker advises that YOU should have the Abstract covering the Property examined by an attorney of YOUR selection, or YOU should be furnished with or obtain a Title Policy.

7. PROPERTY CONDITION (Check "A" or "B"):
   [ ] A. Buyer accepts the Property in its present condition, subject only to ____________________
   ____

   [ ] B. Buyer requires inspections and repairs required by the Property Condition Addendum (the Addendum). Seller shall commence and complete prior to closing all required repairs at Seller's expense.

   All inspections, reports and repairs required of Seller by this contract and the Addendum shall not exceed $__________. If Seller fails to complete such requirements, Buyer may do so and Seller shall be liable up to the amount specified and the same paid from the proceeds of the sale. Broker and sales associates have no responsibility or liability for repair or replacement of any of the Property.

8. **BROKER'S FEE:** ____________________ **Listing Broker (_____%) and** ____________________ **Co-Broker (_____%), as Real Estate Broker (the Broker), has negotiated this sale and Seller agrees to pay Broker in** ____________________ **County, Texas, on consummation of this sale or on Seller's default (unless otherwise provided herein) a total cash fee of** __________ **of the total Sales Price, which Escrow Agent may pay from the sale proceeds.**

9. CLOSING: The closing of the sale (the Closing Date) shall be on or before ____________________, 19 _____, **or within 7 days after objections** to title have been cured, whichever date is later.

10. POSSESSION: The possession of the Property shall be delivered to Buyer on ____________________ in its present or required improved condition, ordinary wear and tear excepted. Any possession by Buyer prior to or by Seller after Closing Date shall establish a landlord-tenant at sufferance relationship between the parties.

11. SPECIAL PROVISIONS:

(Insert terms and conditions of a factual nature applicable to this sale, e.g., personal property included in **sale [curtains, draperies, valances, etc.]**, prior purchase or sale of other property, lessee's surrender of possession, and the like.)

FIGURE 6-5.

12. **SALES EXPENSES TO BE PAID IN CASH AT OR PRIOR TO CLOSING:**

A. Loan appraisal fees shall be paid by ______________________

B. Seller's Expenses:

(1) Seller's loan discount points not exceeding ______________________.

(2) Lender required repairs and any other inspections, reports and repairs required of Seller herein and in the Addendum.

(3) Prepayment penalties on any existing loans, plus cost of releasing such loans and recording releases; tax statements; 1/2 of any escrow fee; preparation of Deed; other expenses stipulated to be paid by Seller under other provisions of this contract.

C. Buyer's Expenses:

(1) Fees for loans (e.g., any private mortgage insurance premiums; loan and mortgage application, origination and commitment fees; Buyer's loan discount points) not exceeding $______________________.

(2) Expenses incident to loan(s) (e.g., preparation of any Note, Deed of Trust and other loan documents, survey, recording fees, copies of restrictions and easements, Mortgagee's Title Policies, credit reports, photos); 1/2 of any escrow fee; any required premiums for flood and hazard insurance; any required reserve deposits for insurance premiums, ad valorem taxes and special assessments; interest on all monthly installment payment notes from date of disbursements to 1 month prior to dates of first monthly payments; expenses stipulated to be paid by Buyer under other provisions of this contract.

D. If any sales expenses exceed the maximum amount herein stipulated to be paid by either party, such party may terminate this contract unless the other party agrees to pay such excess.

13. PRORATIONS: Insurance (at Buyer's option), taxes and any rents and maintenance fees shall be prorated to the Closing Date.

14. TITLE APPROVAL: If Abstract is furnished, Seller shall deliver same to Buyer within 20 days from the effective date hereof. Buyer shall have 20 days from date of receipt of Abstract to deliver a copy of the title opinion to Seller, stating any objections to title, and only objections so stated shall be considered. If Title Policy is furnished, the Title Policy shall guarantee Buyer's title to be good and indefeasible subject only to (i) restrictive covenants affecting the Property (ii) any discrepancies, conflicts or shortages in area or boundary lines or any encroachments, or any overlapping of improvements (iii) all taxes for the current and subsequent years (iv) any existing building and zoning ordinances (v) rights of parties in possession (vi) any liens created as security for the sale consideration and (vii) any reservations or exceptions contained in the Deed. In either instance, if title objections are disclosed, Seller shall have 30 days to cure the same. Exceptions permitted in the Deed and zoning ordinances shall not be valid objections to title. Seller shall furnish at Seller's expense tax statements showing no delinquent taxes and a General Warranty Deed conveying title subject only to liens securing debt created as part of the consideration, taxes for the current year, usual restrictive covenants and utility easements common to any regularly platted subdivision where Property is located and any other reservations or exceptions acceptable to Buyer. Each note herein provided shall be secured by Vendor's and Deed of Trust liens. In case of dispute as to the form of Deed, Note(s) or Deed(s) of Trust, such shall be upon a form prepared by the State Bar of Texas.

15. CASUALTY LOSS: If any part of Property is damaged or destroyed by fire or other casualty loss, Seller shall restore the same to its previous condition as soon as reasonably possible, but in any event by Closing Date; and if Seller is unable to do so without fault, this contract shall terminate and Earnest Money shall be refunded with no Broker's fee due.

16. DEFAULT: A. If Buyer fails to comply herewith, Seller may either enforce specific performance or terminate this contract and receive the Earnest Money as liquidated damages, one-half of which (but not exceeding the herein recited Broker's fee) shall be paid by Seller to Broker in full payment for Broker's services. If Seller is unable without fault to deliver Abstract or Title Policy or to make any non-casualty repairs required herein within the time herein specified, Buyer may either terminate this contract and receive the Earnest Money as the sole remedy, and no Broker's fee shall be earned, or extend the time up to 30 days. If Seller fails to comply herewith for any other reason, Buyer may (i) terminate this contract and receive the Earnest Money, thereby releasing Seller from this contract (ii) enforce specific performance hereof or (iii) seek such other relief as may be provided by law. If completion of sale is prevented by Buyer's default, and Seller elects to enforce specific performance, the Broker's fee is payable only if and when Seller collects damages for such default by suit, compromise, settlement or otherwise, and after first deducting the expenses of collection, and then only in an amount equal to one-half of that portion collected, but not exceeding the amount of Broker's fee.

B. Any signatory to this contract who is the prevailing party in any legal proceeding against any other signatory brought under or with relation to this contract shall be additionally entitled to recover court costs and reasonable attorney fees from the non-prevailing party.

17. ESCROW: Earnest Money is deposited with Escrow Agent with the understanding that Escrow Agent (i) does not assume or have any liability for performance or nonperformance of any party (ii) has the right to require the receipt, release and authorization in writing of all parties before paying the deposit to any party and (iii) is not liable for interest or other charge on the funds held. If any party unreasonably fails to agree in writing to an appropriate release of Earnest Money, then such party shall be liable to the other parties to the extent provided in paragraph 16B. At closing, Earnest Money shall be applied to any cash down payment required, next to Buyer's closing costs and any excess refunded to Buyer.

    Before Buyer shall be entitled to refund of Earnest Money, any actual expenses incurred or paid on Buyer's behalf shall be deducted therefrom and paid to the creditors entitled thereto.

18. REPRESENTATIONS: Seller represents that unless securing payment of the Note there will be no Title I liens, unrecorded liens or Uniform Commercial Code liens against any of the Property on Closing Date. If any representation above is untrue this contract may be terminated by Buyer and the Earnest Money shall be refunded without delay. Representations shall survive closing.

19. AGREEMENT OF PARTIES: This contract contains the entire agreement of the parties and cannot be changed except by their written consent.

20. CONSULT YOUR ATTORNEY: This is intended to be a legally binding contract. READ IT CAREFULLY. If you do not understand the effect of any part, consult your attorney BEFORE signing. The Broker cannot give you legal advice — only factual and business details concerning land and improvements. Attorneys to represent parties may be designated below, and, so employment may be accepted, Broker shall promptly deliver a copy of this contract to such attorneys.

Seller's Atty: ______________________ Buyer's Atty: ______________________

EXECUTED in multiple originals effective the _____ day of ______________, 19 _____ **(BROKER FILL IN DATE AFTER LAST PARTY SIGNS).**

______________________ **Listing Broker** License No.	______________________ Seller
By ______________________	______________________ Seller
______________________ **Co-Broker** License No.	______________________ Seller's Address Tel.
By ______________________	______________________ Buyer
Receipt of $ __________ Earnest Money is acknowledged in the form	______________________ Buyer
of ______________________	______________________ Buyer's Address Tel.
______________________ **Escrow Agent** Date	
By ______________________	

2/8/78

FIGURE 6-5 *(continued)*.

CAUTION: NOT TO BE USED WITH THE TREC PROMULGATED RESIDENTIAL ASSUMPTION EARNEST MONEY CONTRACT.

PROPERTY CONDITION ADDENDUM

ADDENDUM TO EARNEST MONEY CONTRACT BETWEEN THE UNDERSIGNED PARTIES CONCERNING THE PROPERTY AT ______________________________
(Street Address and City)

CHECK APPLICABLE BOXES:

☐ A. TERMITES: Seller, at Seller's expense, shall furnish to Buyer at or prior to closing a written report by a Structural Pest Control Business Licensee, dated within 30 days before Closing Date and stating that there is no visible evidence of active termites or visible damage to the improvements from the same in need of repair. Such report shall not cover fences, trees and shrubs.

☐ B. CONDITION OF PROPERTY:
Buyer shall have the right at Buyer's expense (i) within __________ days from the effective date of this contract to have any of the STRUCTURAL items indicated below, and (ii) within __________ days from the effective date of this contract to have any of the EQUIPMENT AND SYSTEMS items indicated below, inspected by inspectors of Buyer's choice and to give Seller within such time periods a written report of required repairs to any of the items checked below which are not performing the function for which intended or which are in need of immediate repair. Failure to do so shall be deemed a waiver of Buyer's inspection and repair rights and Buyer agrees to accept Property in its present condition.

ITEMS THAT BUYER MAY REQUIRE TO BE INSPECTED (check applicable boxes):

STRUCTURAL:
☐ foundation, ☐ roof, ☐ load bearing walls, ☐ floors, ☐ ceilings, ☐ basement, ☐ water penetration

☐ and ______________________________
____
____

EQUIPMENT AND SYSTEMS:

☐ plumbing system (including any water heaters, wells and septic system), ☐ central heating and air conditioning, ☐ electrical system, ☐ heating and cooling units in the walls, floors, ceilings, roof or windows, ☐ any built-in range, oven, dishwasher, disposer, kitchen exhaust fan, trash compactor, ☐ swimming pool and related mechanical equipment, ☐ sprinkler systems

☐ and ______________________________

____

____

Repairs required by inspections and reports shall be at Seller's expense.

☐ C. Seller shall make the following repairs in addition to those required above: ______________________________

____

____

All inspections shall be by trained and qualified persons who regularly provide such service and all repairs shall be by trained and qualified persons who are, whenever possible, manufacturer-approved service persons or are licensed or bonded whenever such license or bond is required by law. For these purposes and for reinspections after repairs have been completed, Seller shall permit access to the Property at any reasonable time.

☐ D. Where gas supplier, regulations or ordinances require inspection on transfer of gas service, Seller consents to transfer of gas service to Buyer's name within 7 days prior to closing. Seller shall arrange and pay at closing for any repairs necessary if gas leak is discovered. Buyer's failure to request such transfer in time to complete the inspection prior to closing shall release the Seller of liability for repair of gas leaks.

Broker and sales associates shall not be liable or responsible for any inspections or repairs pursuant to this contract and Addendum. Seller's liability for Addendum expenses is limited by paragraph 7 of this contract.

______________________ ______________________
Seller Buyer

______________________ ______________________
Seller Buyer

The form of this Addendum has been approved by the Texas Real Estate Commission and the State Bar of Texas for use only with similarly approved and promulgated forms of contracts. No representation is made as to the legal validity or adequacy of any provision in any specific transaction. (Rev. 5-78) TREC No. 2-0

2/6/78

FIGURE 6-6.

> Vendee agrees to pay vendor $10,000 as full purchase price for vendor's house. Vendee moves in, takes possession of that house, and then constructs some valuable improvement to that property with the vendor's consent. Vendor subsequently tries to renounce the sale and get his property back. Since there was nothing in writing to enforce the conveyance by deed or other acceptable means of property transfer, the court will seek to uphold an oral earnest money contract that vendee can specifically enforce.

Although the above situation may seem rather bizarre, it must be remembered that there are a lot of people who buy real estate not knowing that they are supposed to have a deed or earnest money contract, or any other evidence of title. Most experienced real estate practitioners would probably not be involved in a situation of this type. It is important only to realize that oral earnest money contracts can exist, but under very strict guidelines. No reasonable real estate agent, attorney, or well-informed client should ever rely on an oral earnest money contract, except as a last resort.

Express Contracts. Express contracts are, of course, written contracts. As our discussion comes back into more identifiable current business practices, it should be pointed out that earnest money contracts, as in all other real estate instruments, have specific and basic requirements that must be satisfied before such contracts will be considered to be enforceable in the State of Texas. These requirements are as follows:

1. *There must be a written instrument* (the only exception is the one noted above); and
2. *The instrument must be signed by the party to be charged*. This means that the person against whom the instrument is being enforced must have signed the contract; for instance, if *A* and *B* contract to sell real estate, and only *A* has signed the contract, it can reasonably be assumed that *B* could enforce the contract against *A*, but *A* could not enforce the contract against *B* until *B* signs the contract. With one signature on the contract, it is now a standing offer, which *B* can accept at any time by simply signing his name (provided that this was within the guidelines of acceptances described above); and
3. *There must be evidence of an intent to convey an interest in the real estate at sometime in the future*. This requirement generally meets the consideration guidelines in that one party offers to give up his money while the other party offers to convey his interest in some real estate at a future date; and
4. *There must be an identifiable grantor and grantee*. The grantor

and grantee must, of course, be identifiable and be competent as described earlier.

5. *The subject matter to be conveyed must be identifiable*. This, of course, is the requirement of a proper legal description so that there can be no mistake as to which property is the subject matter of the contract.

Once these formalities have been met, the contract is considered specific enough to be enforceable in a court of law.

Provisions of Earnest Money Contracts

As real estate agents know, most earnest money contracts go into much greater depth than the foregoing requirements, and a much more in-depth discussion of each of these requirements is necessary to clarify and understand the need for each of these provisions.

Legal Description. Legal sufficiency of the description of the property is essential to any contract that relates to real estate. The legal description must be contained in the instrument itself, or it may refer to another instrument from which the data to describe the property may be obtained with reasonable certainty. It is not necessary that the property be described beyond all reasonable doubt, but it must be described with reasonable certainty so that a person familiar with the locality can identify the property, *Foster* v. *Bullard*, 496 S.W.2d 724 (Tex. Civ. App.—Austin, 1973). A recital of ownership may be sufficient, or a map attached to the contract may be used as long as the map contains the necessary descriptive information.

Generally, if a metes and bounds description is required, the foregoing rules will be sufficient. In most residential situations a lot and block number in a specific, recorded, and identifiable subdivision within a county will be sufficient, *Riebe* v. *Foale*, 508 S.W.2d 175 (Tex. Civ. App.—Corpus Christi, 1974). Of course, a street address, by itself, is not sufficiently specific to be enforceable.

The real estate agent must remember to have adequate descriptions of any items of personalty that are to be included in the sale of the property, and he should also note a requirement for a bill of sale to be executed by the seller.

Financial Considerations. When an earnest money contract is contingent upon the buyer securing a loan, the buyer impliedly promises to make application for the loan and to diligently pursue obtaining the loan. If the buyer fails to exercise this diligence, or causes a cancellation of his loan, he may not recover his earnest money because of his failure to obtain that loan, *Williford* v. *Walker*, 499 S.W.2d 190 (Tex. Civ. App.—Corpus Christi, 1973).

However, if the sale is other than one for cash, it probably involves an assumption of seller financing. When such is the case, it is very important that all the terms of the purchase price are clearly set out. These requirements would usually include the down payment, the terms of the note (to be assumed or to be newly incurred), and the identification of the type of mortgage to be utilized.

For the purchaser, these requirements help to operate as a full disclosure of the indebtedness charged against the property. The seller is also assured that the purchaser is capable of completing the sale, because he (the purchaser) is fully appraised of all obligations he is about to undertake.

Title Matters. Section 20(c) of the Real Estate Licensing Act requires certain title matters to be disclosed before the real estate agent can maintain an action for a commission. Therefore, from an agent's point of view, this is a critical inclusion in the earnest money contract, *Jones* v. *Del Anderson and Associates*, 539 S.W.2d 348 (Tex. 1977).

Beyond this concern, ''title'' means much more than a title policy or mere ownership of the property. It encompasses all matters that affect the title and use of the subject property. There are frequent considerations of reservations of mineral rights, restrictions on land use, homestead rights, leasehold interests, liens, and boundary disputes. Most contracts require a title policy guaranteeing good and indefeasible title, and making all encumbrances (beyond the standard exceptions) subject to the purchaser's approval. If no exceptions are specified in the contract, it may be interpreted to mean a title policy with no exceptions, *Suiter* v. *Gregory*, 279 S.W.2d 902 (Tex. Civ. App.—Galveston, 1955). A survey is usually a necessity to assure proper title, and it is required by most title insurance companies. Most earnest money contracts require the seller to cure all title defects to the purchaser's satisfaction prior to closing the sale.

If a title company is to be used, the normal procedure is for the seller to purchase the title policy (it is his certification that the title is good), but it is usually the purchaser's prerogative as to which title company to use. The purchaser is the one who is having the title insured. Therefore, he should be careful to select a title company that he knows is solvent, reputable, and accommodating to his needs.

Earnest Money. There is no legal requirement for earnest money in a contract. However, it is often customary to put in a certain amount of earnest money, both to enforce consideration and to assure the seller that the purchaser is, in fact, serious about buying the property. Provisions in most earnest money contracts provide that in the event that a purchaser does not perform, the earnest money should go to the seller as liquidated damages. The amount of escrow deposited, or even the requirement of escrow deposited, is normally not a legal matter but rather one of negotiation between the parties.

When the earnest money is deposited, the title company normally serves as the escrow agent. However, other parties may perform this function if it is acceptable to the parties. One party's attorney, a broker, or a financial institution can serve this same function, particularly when the closing is not to take place at a title company.

Another consideration concerning the earnest money provision of the contract may involve the type of earnest money to be used. Earnest money deposits other than cash often include a letter of credit, a certificate of deposit, a check or bank draft, and sometimes a promissory note, made due and payable upon the date of closing.

Normally, if the seller defaults, the earnest money is returned to the purchaser. However, a significant factor concerning the deposit of earnest money involves the escrow agent's obligation to protect the earnest money and the interests of the parties involved. Regardless of the facts surrounding a default in an earnest money contract, most escrow agents are very reluctant to release the earnest money to either party without the other party's written consent. No matter how blatant or obvious the breach of the contract may be, one will seldom find that an escrow agent will readily forward the earnest money to either party unless he (the escrow agent) is adequately protected by some other agreement, affidavit, bond, or other assurance. It is all too often that a purchaser simply backs out of a sale but will not sign a written consent to allow the earnest money to be forwarded to the seller. When this happens, there is very little available to the seller as a remedy except at the courthouse.

Representations. There are often representations in earnest money contracts that the property is in good condition. These representations are sometimes supported by a further representation that the seller will complete the repair of certain items in the house, or building, or whatever might be the subject of the sale. It should be noted that there are distinct differences between a representation and a warranty. A representation may hinder the closing or create certain verbal adversities, whereas a warranty generally gives the purchaser a certain damage claim, *Fant* v. *Howell*, 547 S.W.2d 261 (Tex. 1977).

Although the number of representations or warranties that could be contained in earnest money contracts are as vast as the imagination could conceive, great care should be taken by the agent to see that both parties have their representations very clearly stated. There should be specific provisions made for remedies in the event one of the representations is not true, or is not performed as required by the contract.

Representations and covenants are often omitted altogether by granting the purchaser a right of inspection prior to the closing.*

Closing. *Closing* is the term normally given to the process of consummating the sale of real estate. Provisions pertaining to a closing generally specify the date, any automatic extensions if needed, and an absolute date by which the closing must take place or the contract becomes voidable at the option of either party. Specific provisions provided for under closing conditions normally include right to possession of the real estate (which usually is not given until the seller has received all of his funds), and requirements for the documentation needed at the closing (usually including the deed, mortgage procedures, assignments, bills of sale, and application of escrow funds). There may be additional provisions for surveys, delivery of title policy, and allocation of expenses to be borne by each party. The expenses include the attorneys' fees, brokerage fees, survey fees, inspection fees, proration of taxes, utilities and insurance, and recording and escrow fees.

Time Is of the Essence. Unless a contract clearly indicates that time is of the essence, it will not be construed to be so, *Helsley* v. *Anderson*, 519 S.W.2d 130 (Tex. Civ. App.—Dallas, 1975). However, in an option contract, time is always of the essence, *Tabor* v. *Ragle*, 526 S.W.2d 670 (Tex. Civ. App.—Ft. Worth, 1975), although the stipulated time limit may be extended by agreement of the parties.

Assignment. Unless otherwise provided for, contracts for the sale of real property are assignable. However, when the sale is to be made on credit or other condition of performance by one of the parties, the contract is normally not considered to be assignable unless made specifically assignable by its terms, *Farrell* v. *Evans*, 517 S.W.2d 585 (Tex. Civ. App.—Houston, 1974).

Although the foregoing is not intended to be an exhaustive review of all the provisions that may be contained in contracts, it must be remembered that each contract stands on its own and must be read very carefully to determine the rights of the parties involved. Whenever a party signs a contract, he is deemed by law to have read and understood all the provisions. It is always wise to have a party's attorney review his contract. This puts the burden of interpretation and reliance on the attorney, and not on the broker, who may be liable for misrepresentations, as well as being

---

*The Real Estate Commission and the State Bar of Texas, in an effort to alleviate some of these anticipated problems, have promulgated the *Property Condition Addendum* to be used in conjunction with the similarly promulgated earnest money contracts. A copy of this form is shown in Figure 6-6.

prohibited (by statute) from the practice of law. If a broker's client relied on certain representations or promises made by the real estate broker or sales agent (conditions that were not met by the broker), said agent may further be liable for deceptive trade practices.

Contingencies. Purchasers often desire to tie up the seller's property for a "free look" by putting unreasonable or frivolous contingencies in the contract for sale. These contingencies may be solely at the purchaser's option, such that the purchaser has no obligation at all. For instance, the purchaser may make his contract:

> . . . contingent upon the approval of purchaser's attorney. In the event said approval is not obtained, this contract shall become null and void, at the purchaser's option.

This type of contingency contains no time for performance, does not name the attorney, and gives no rights at all to the seller.

Such contingencies are not only vague and ambiguous but they may also be complicated by unexpected legal problems. If there is a contingency, the law generally imposes a standard of reasonable diligence on the purchaser, regardless of the terms of the contract. If the terms are too one-sided, the court may even refuse to enforce them because of a lack of mutuality and be construed to be an option to purchase, not a contract for sale. So when trying for the "free look," it is not always as simple as it may seem.

Default and Remedies. In the event of material default of the terms of an earnest money contract, there are remedies provided for the purchaser and the seller, respectively. In the event of the purchaser's default, the remedies are normally that the seller retain the earnest money as *liquidated damages* (a stated predetermined sum of money awarded to the seller for holding his property off the market for the requisite period of time) and a liability for damages. There may be an additional provision that the liquidated damages be divided between the seller and the listing broker. In the event the seller chooses to default, the purchaser is normally limited to an action for damages and a return of his earnest money.

A remedy that both parties may seek to enforce is one called *specific performance*. Although this provision is often deleted in a contract—which probably limits a party's action to one for money damages, *Brewer* v. *Meyers*, 545 S.W.2d 235 (Tex. Civ. App.—Tyler, 1976)—one may find that the remedy of specific performance has not been deleted but may be interpreted in favor of only one party. In seeking the remedy of specific performance, it must be remembered that it is an equitable remedy, and the party seeking specific performance must have acted in good faith and not himself committed a material breach of the contract. Specific performance is not an easy remedy to pursue because there are a number of requirements that must be met before specific performance can be decreed. The essential terms of the contract must be expressed with reasonable certainty, *Smith* v. *Hughes*, 540 S.W.2d 485 (Tex. Civ. App.—Houston, 1976); adequate damages must be virtually impossible to ascertain; and the default must result in irreparable harm and hardship to the party seeking specific performance, *Cowman* v. *Allen Monuments, Inc.*, 500 S.W.2d 223 (Tex. Civ. App.—Texarkana, 1973). However, some courts have seen fit to pursue this remedy because of the traditionally "unique" nature of real estate.

The Merger Doctrine

It is a well-understood point of law that the earnest money contract is a contract for sale and performs precisely that function. Most contracts for sale contain a provision that the written contract must embody the entire agreement of the parties and that there is no other oral or written agreement between the parties. This provision is commonly called a *merger provision*; it is enforced by excluding parol evidence, unless the intention of the parties indicates otherwise, *Humber* v. *Morton*, 426 S.W.2d 554 (Tex. 1968). Once the sale has been closed and the deed has been transferred, the earnest money contract has no force or effect whatsoever on either party, because the purpose of the contract (the sale) has been fulfilled.

One may often find that an earnest money contract has certain representations and warranties that are intentionally specified to extend beyond the closing (properly termed *survive the closing*). However, unless these provisions are carefully drawn and unless the parties understand the intention to survive the closing, such provisions will not so survive. Upon closing, it is normally determined that the terms of the earnest money contract are merged into the deed, or other instrument executed at the closing, and any cause of action for representation or warranties must be on the basis of the deed, rather than on the basis of the earnest money contract.

Installment Land Contracts

An installment land contract is a contract for the sale of real estate that extends over a long period of time. It is called an executory contract, because the terms of the contract are not to be completed in the near future—this contrasts with an *executed* contract. It is also called a *contract for deed*, and it is precisely that. It is a contract entered into between the buyer and seller to deliver a deed at some future date. This contract may last as long as ten years or longer, depending on the terms. An installment land contract has been likened to a marital agreement in that the parties have just entered into an agreement that may produce adverse results that they had not anticipated at the time they made the deal. There is very little difference between a vendor-buyer relationship under an installment land contract situation and a landlord-tenant relationship except that the purchaser (unlike the lessee) expects to gain title to the property at some future date. All of the purchaser's rights to the property are defined by that contract, just as a lessee's rights are defined by a lease.

Disadvantages

There are several major pitfalls for the buyer in an installment land contract. First of all, there is usually no escrow required for the deed instrument. Second, there is normally no warranty that the seller can deliver a free and clear title. Third, there is very seldom any provision for a title insurance policy. Fourth, in the event of default by the buyer, the seller merely tears up the contract for sale, and there is no recordable interest that the purchaser can use to protect himself. Fifth, if the seller dies, becomes mentally incompetent, goes bankrupt, moves back to Indiana, neglects to pay his income tax, fails to keep up the payments on the mortgage governing the property, suffers an adverse judgment, refuses to pay off creditors, or transfers his interest to a six-year-old Indian boy in Broken Bow, Oklahoma—it may cause real legal complications for the installment land purchaser.

An exhaustive review of installment land sales contracts is covered in Warren, "California Installment Land Sales Contracts," *U.C.L.A. Law Review*, Volume 9 (1962), 608. An even more exhaustive review of installment land sales contracts in Texas is covered by John Mixon, "Installment Lands Contracts, A Study of Low-Income Transactions, with Proposals for Reform and a New Program to Provide Home Ownership in the Inner City," *Houston Law Review*, Volume 7 (1970), 523.

Default and Remedies

In the event the installment land contract is breached by the purchaser, the remedies of a vendor generally include rescission, eviction, suit for price, damages for the breach, and possibly suit for specific performance; but his most useful remedy is that of simple forfeiture by the purchaser. If the seller can declare the installment land contract forfeited, he can simply remove the tenant purchaser and sell the house to someone else. Although it is true that the purchaser under an installment land contract does get a certain identifiable equity interest in the property (the right to purchase same), most installment land contracts provide that the contract itself is not recordable, and therefore it is difficult for the purchaser to record his interest to protect himself and to put third parties on notice, as required by the Texas Recording Act. In such a case, the purchaser may want to assign his interest in the contract to a friendly party, and record the assignment, or he may do some work on the house and record a mechanic's and materialman's lien in order to be sure that his interest is properly reflected into the records of real property.

In an effort to remedy the difficult situations often created by installment land contracts, the Texas legislature passed Article 1301b, Texas Revised Civil Statutes, which provides for certain advance notice before the seller in an installment land contract can force forfeiture and acceleration. The statute is relatively short and simple and reads as follows:

Art. 1301b. Forfeiture and acceleration under executory contract for conveyance; notice; avoidance

Section 1. A forfeiture of the interest and the acceleration of the indebtedness of a purchaser in default under an executory contract for conveyance of real property used or to be used as the purchaser's residence may be enforced only after notice of seller's intentions to enforce the forfeiture and acceleration has been given to the purchaser and only after the expiration of the periods provided below:

(a) When the purchaser has paid less than 10% of the purchase price, 15 days from the date notice is given.

(b) When the purchaser has paid 10% but less than 20% of the purchase price, 30 days from the date notice is given.

(c) When the purchaser has paid 20%, or more, of the purchase price, 60 days from the date notice is given.

(d) Notice must be by mail or other writing. If by mail, it must be registered or certified and shall be considered given at the time mailed to his residence or place of business, and notification by other writing shall be considered given at the time delivered to the purchaser at his residence or place of business.

(e) Such notice shall be conspicuously set out; shall be printed in 10 point bold face type or upper case typewritten letters; and shall include the following:

NOTICE

YOU ARE LATE IN MAKING YOUR PAYMENT UNDER THE CONTRACT TO BUY YOUR HOME. UNLESS YOU MAKE THE PAYMENT BY ___*(date)*___ THE SELLER HAS THE RIGHT TO TAKE POSSESSION OF YOUR HOME AND TO KEEP ALL PAYMENTS YOU HAVE MADE TO DATE.

Sec. 2. A purchaser in default under an executory contract for the conveyance of real property used or to be used as the purchaser's residence, may at any time prior to expiration of the period provided for in Section 1, avoid the forfeiture of his interest and the acceleration of his indebtedness by complying with the terms of the contract up to the date of compliance notwithstanding any agreement to the contrary.

The Texas courts have been very liberal in construing this act, both on the part of the vendor and on the part of the purchaser. *Wentworth* v. *Medellin*, 529 S.W.2d 125 (Tex. Civ. App.—San Antonio, 1975), indicated that as far as the vendor's rights were concerned, substantial compliance with the statute was enough to warrant enforcement. However, in the interest of the purchaser, there have been several recent cases that provide for the protection of the purchaser. *De Leon* v. *Aldrete*, 398 S.W.2d 160 (Tex. Civ. App.—San Antonio, 1965), forced a vendor who exercised his right of forfeiture to make restitution under the principles of equity and to reimburse some funds that the purchaser had expended on the residence. In a more significant decision, Texas courts have held that Article 1301b, although it became effective in 1969, applies to all contracts entered into before 1969, as long as they are still in effect after passage of the statute, *Pratt* v. *Story*, 530 S.W.2d 325 (Tex. Civ. App.—Tyler, 1975). There may also be prohibitions against forfeiture and acceleration of an installment land contract if the vendor has made a practice of accepting late payments in the past, and if no installments were delinquent at the time the vendor attempted to effect forfeiture, *Jordan* v. *Crockett*, 511 S.W.2d 618 (Tex. Civ. App.—Austin, 1974).

Of course, the horrors of installment land contracts are supported by a number of stories and fact situations, such as the following:

1. A property owner purchased a lot from a resort subdivision developer on an installment land contract. He subsequently paid the full price for the lot and received a deed subject to the underlying indebtedness that the developer incurred to develop the subdivision. When the developer defaulted on his mortgage, the lender foreclosed. The property owner, even though he paid the full price for his lot, lost all of his interest in the property because of the underlying and prior indebtedness incurred by his vendor.
2. A lot purchaser purchased a lot in a subdivision with a very low down payment and very low monthly payments. After calculating the price of his lot and the amount of his monthly payments, he determined that his monthly payments were not even enough to pay the interest and debt service on the lot. He, in effect, could pay his installments the rest of his life and never acquire the lot. One must remember that he signed a contract for this purchase, and all the construction and basic elements of interpretation of that contract must be complied with.
3. Since the installment land contract is normally unrecordable, there have been repeated situations where a developer has sold the same lot to several different people. None of the subsequent purchasers are on notice, nor under a duty to be on notice, because of the requirements of the recording act.

Unfortunately, the installment land contract has been a very useful tool for the unscrupulous land developer. However, installment land contracts, by themselves, are not necessarily bad if the vendor is acting in good faith. They are a very common tool for financing low-income housing, and, if properly used, are probably the best means of such financing. The mortgage aspects of installment land contracts will be discussed in greater detail in Chapter 9, Mortgages.

SUMMARY

The law of contracts is one of the most complex areas of the law to study. The fundamental elements of the contract consist of the offer, acceptance, and consideration. There are standard rules of construction for contracts which, while not controlling, usually give guidance as to how the contract will be interpreted by the courts.

Earnest money contracts have particular application to real estate transactions. They may be oral or expressed and, in each case, have very specific requirements in order to be valid and enforceable. At closing, it is said that the earnest money contract "merges" into the deed and other instruments because the purpose of that contract "sale" has been accomplished.

Installment land contracts are also known as contracts for deed. They are contracts for the sale of real estate that normally extend over a period of years. There are many disadvantages to an installment land contract, and they have often been abused by unscrupulous land developers. There have been statutory provisions enacted in Texas which provide additional rights for purchasers under installment land contracts in the event of default. Installment land contracts are not all bad, however, and have been used to effect a convenient method of financing for low-income housing.

7

CONVEYANCING

For centuries there has been a legal and practical method by which an owner can convey his interest in real estate; and he can have it conveyed in his absence, or even without his consent. It was obviously apparent from the initial concepts of individual real estate ownership that something had to evidence title, and something had to transfer that title, short of armed combat. The scope of this chapter is to study these means of conveyance. The types of conveyances discussed will be divided into two categories: (1) *voluntary conveyances*, which encompass deeds and wills (wills are a voluntary means of conveyance, although the means to effect that conveyance may not be so voluntary); and (2) *involuntary conveyances*, which include adverse possession, condemnation, foreclosure, intestacy (death of the owner leaving no will), tax sales, and escheat.

Deeds

A deed is a written instrument by which a landowner transfers the ownership of his land. The quality of title that the landowner (grantor) conveys to the purchaser (grantee) is controlled by the type of deed utilized, by the warranties included, and by the restrictions and exceptions to the title contained in that deed.

Types of Deeds

Before getting into the legal requirements, details, and interpretations of deeds, one should be familiar with the different types of deeds in order to establish the proper basis for more in-depth discussion. The types of deeds to be discussed, in their descending order of warranty, are: general warranty deeds, special warranty deeds, trustee's deeds, court-ordered deeds, deeds of bargain and sale, and quitclaim deeds. Copies of these various deed forms and notations as to their various clauses are included in Figures 7-1 through 7-5 for your reference.

General Warranty Deeds. The general warranty deed is the most widely used deed in this state, and by both statute and case law, assures the highest warranty the law recognizes. A general warranty deed is shown in Figure 7-1. Statutorily, since the general warranty deed uses the words *grant* or *convey*, the law implies that the grantee gets two warranties. One of these warranties is called the *covenant of seizin*. This means that the grantor has not conveyed the same estate previously, has good title to the property, and will indemnify the grantor against any claims due to failure of title, *Davis* v. *Andrews*, 361 S.W.2d 419 (Tex. Civ. App.—Dallas, 1962). The second warranty is the *covenant against encumbrances*. This covenant warrants that there are no other encumbrances affecting the property other than those shown in the deed, if any. This covenant implies that the grantor will indemnify the grantee from claims arising from any third party seeking to establish an interest in the real estate. It also imposes a duty on the grantor to discharge all liens and encumbrances incurred prior to the conveyance, *Triplett* v. *Shield*, 406 S.W.2d 941 (Tex. Civ. App.—Eastland, 1966).

In addition, when using the general warranty deed, the grantor warrants not only that the title is free of these encumbrances, but also he is well seized of the premises and that this covenant is through his entire chain of title. To help soften the impact of this warranty, there are certain adverse possession statutes (to be discussed later in this chapter) that maintain that the title cannot be litigated after somebody has been in possession of the property for a certain period of years. Since title can be perfected by adverse possession, title is not necessarily guaranteed back to the original land grant. This is discussed in more depth in the discussion of "Chain of Title" in Chapter 8.

Special Warranty Deeds. A special warranty deed has basically the same language as the general warranty deed, as shown in Figure 7-2. The only difference is that in the *habendum* and warranty clause of the special warranty deed, the warranty extends only to the previous grantor; that is, the grantor does not warrant any chain of title beyond himself. The grantor's warranty is to warrant the title against all claimants to the title that was acquired, "by or through me," *Owen* v. *Yocum*, 341 S.W.2d 709 (Tex. Civ. App.—Ft. Worth, 1960). Note the difference in the habendum and warranty paragraph in the special warranty deed in Figure 7-2, as compared to that of the general warranty deed in Figure 7-1. Special warranty deeds have a particularly useful application for trustees in bank trust departments, in major corporations, and in governmental entities. These entities are generally owners who have held the property for a particular use, that use has expired, and they now wish to sell it to a new owner. In the event title fails, and the title company (if one is used) balks at paying the claim, these entities do not want to be bound by whatever discrepancies in the title may have plagued the property prior to their purchase of it. However, they are willing to say that the warranties of title passed by and through them are good; and that they have not clouded or encumbered title to that property. It does not necessarily mean a lesser quality of deed, but the warranties are not as good as a general warranty since the grantee effectively waives his rights against the grantor as to any encumbrances existing prior to the grantor's ownership. There is always a risk that discrepancies may materialize at some future date because of a deficiency in title caused by an owner prior to the immediate grantor.

Trustee's Deeds. A trustee's deed is generally thought of, in this state, as a foreclosure deed. A trustee's deed is shown in Figure 7-3. The trustee's warranty binds the owner because the trustee is generally liable only in his representative capacity, and recovery is only against the trust assets, whatever they may be. The trustee normally operates as a pure nominee (legal title holder) for another person or persons, whom we term *beneficial owners*, and acts only on their behalf. The title is, of course, perfectly valid, and it contains all the covenants of general warranty, which bind the previous owner, not the trustee. Title is also passed subject to any encumbrances superior to those of the beneficial owner. The only risk to the grantee, generally, is whether or not the trustee is acting in the proper capacity.

Court-Ordered Deeds. A court-ordered deed or sheriff's deed is a deed given pursuant to a court order or a forced sale by execution (that is, a creditor is probably selling a property because of a debt owed to him by the property owner), and the title, of course, in this case has a good warranty. However, the court does not want to take the obligation of generally warranting title to the property. Therefore, conveyance exists of only the right, title, interest, and claim that the defendant in execution had in the property sold. A sheriff's deed is substantially the same as the trustee's deed.

Bargain and Sale Deeds. The deed of bargain and sale contains no warranties at all; however, it has a particular value in that it does purport to convey property. Therefore, the After-Acquired Title Doctrine (discussed later in this chapter) does apply to bargain and sale deeds even though there are no warranties on the part of the grantor. The grantor in a bargain and sale deed conveys whatever interest that grantor has in the land, but is not

Prepared by the State Bar of Texas for use by Lawyers only.
To select the proper form, fill in blank spaces, strike out form provisions or insert special terms constitutes the practice of law. No "standard form" can meet all requirements.

WARRANTY DEED

THE STATE OF TEXAS
COUNTY OF HARRIS } KNOW ALL MEN BY THESE PRESENTS:

That I. M. Seller and wife, Happy Seller

of the County of Harris and State of Texas for and in consideration of the sum of TEN AND NO/100---------------($10.00)------------------DOLLARS and other valuable consideration to the undersigned paid by the grantee herein named, the receipt of which is hereby acknowledged,

have GRANTED, SOLD AND CONVEYED, and by these presents do GRANT, SELL AND CONVEY unto

N. Debted and wife May B. Debted

of the County of Harris and State of Texas , all of the following described real property in Harris County, Texas, to-wit:

Lot 1, Block 1, Shakey Acres Subdivision,
Harris County, Texas, as shown of record
at Volume 7, Page 3, of the Map Records
of Harris County, Texas,

TO HAVE AND TO HOLD the above described premises, together with all and singular the rights and appurtenances thereto in anywise belonging, unto the said grantee s , their heirs and assigns forever; and we do hereby bind ourselves, our heirs, executors and administrators to WARRANT AND FOREVER DEFEND all and singular the said premises unto the said grantee s, their heirs and assigns, against every person whomsoever lawfully claiming or to claim the same or any part thereof.

EXECUTED this 30th day of February , A. D. 1994

I. M. Seller

Happy Seller

FIGURE 7-1. General warranty deed.

(Acknowledgment)

THE STATE OF TEXAS }
COUNTY OF }

Before me, the undersigned authority, on this day personally appeared

known to me to be the person........ whose name................ subscribed to the foregoing instrument, and acknowledged to me that....... he ..... executed the same for the purposes and consideration therein expressed.

Given under my hand and seal of office on this the day of , A. D. 19

....
Notary Public in and for County, Texas.

(Acknowledgment)

THE STATE OF TEXAS }
COUNTY OF }

Before me, the undersigned authority, on this day personally appeared

known to me to be the person .... whose name.................. subscribed to the foregoing instrument, and acknowledged to me that....... he ....executed the same for the purposes and consideration therein expressed.

Given under my hand and seal of office on this the day of , A. D. 19

....
Notary Public in and for County, Texas.

WARRANTY DEED

TO

PREPARED IN THE LAW OFFICE OF:

PLEASE RETURN TO:

(Corporate acknowledgment)

THE STATE OF TEXAS }
COUNTY OF }

Before me, the undersigned authority, on this day personally appeared

of

a corporation, known to me to be the person whose name is subscribed to the foregoing instrument, and acknowledged to me that he executed the same for the purposes and consideration therein expressed, in the capacity therein stated and as the act and deed of said corporation.

Given under my hand and seal of office on this the day of , A. D. 19

Notary Public in and for County, Texas.

FIGURE 7-1 (*continued*).

NOTICE Prepared by the State Bar of Texas for use by Lawyers only.
To select the proper form, fill in blank spaces, strike out form provisions or insert special terms constitutes the practice of law. No "standard form" can meet all requirements.

SPECIAL
WARRANTY DEED

THE STATE OF TEXAS
COUNTY OF HARRIS } KNOW ALL MEN BY THESE PRESENTS:

That I. M. Seller and wife, Happy Seller

of the County of Harris and State of Texas for and in consideration of the sum of TEN AND NO/100----------------($10.00)---------------- DOLLARS and other valuable consideration to the undersigned paid by the grantee herein named, the receipt of which is hereby acknowledged,

have GRANTED, SOLD AND CONVEYED, and by these presents do GRANT, SELL AND CONVEY unto

N. Debted and wife May B. Debted

of the County of Harris and State of Texas , all of the following described real property in Harris County, Texas, to-wit:

Lot 1, Block 1, Shakey Acres Subdivision,
Harris County, Texas, as shown of record
at Volume 7, Page 3, of the Map Records
of Harris County, Texas,

TO HAVE AND TO HOLD the above described premises, together with all and singular the rights and appurtenances thereto in anywise belonging, unto the said grantees, their heirs and assigns forever; and we do hereby bind ourselves, our heirs, executors and administrators to WARRANT AND FOREVER DEFEND all and singular the said premises unto the said grantees, their heirs and assigns, against every person whomsoever lawfully claiming or to claim the same or any part thereof, by, through, or under us, but not otherwise.

EXECUTED this 30th day of February, A. D. 1994

I. M. Seller

Happy Seller

FIGURE 7-2. Special warranty deed.

(Acknowledgment)

THE STATE OF TEXAS }
COUNTY OF HARRIS }

Before me, the undersigned authority, on this day personally appeared

known to me to be the person......... whose name.............. subscribed to the foregoing instrument, and acknowledged to me that....... he ..... executed the same for the purposes and consideration therein expressed.

Given under my hand and seal of office on this the day of , A. D. 19

....
Notary Public in and for County, Texas.

(Acknowledgment)

THE STATE OF TEXAS }
COUNTY OF }

Before me, the undersigned authority, on this day personally appeared

known to me to be the person .... whose name.............. subscribed to the foregoing instrument, and acknowledged to me that....... he ....executed the same for the purposes and consideration therein expressed.

Given under my hand and seal of office on this the day of , A. D. 19

....
Notary Public in and for County, Texas.

WARRANTY DEED

TO

PREPARED IN THE LAW OFFICE OF:

PLEASE RETURN TO:

(Corporate acknowledgment)

THE STATE OF TEXAS }
COUNTY OF }

Before me, the undersigned authority, on this day personally appeared ,
of ,
a corporation, known to me to be the person whose name is subscribed to the foregoing instrument, and acknowledged to me that he executed the same for the purposes and consideration therein expressed, in the capacity therein stated and as the act and deed of said corporation.

Given under my hand and seal of office on this the day of , A. D. 19

Notary Public in and for County, Texas.

FIGURE 7-2 (*continued*).

TRUSTEE'S DEED
(With Affidavit Attached)

THE STATE OF TEXAS *
KNOW ALL MEN BY THESE PRESENTS:
COUNTY OF HARRIS *

WHEREAS, by a certain Deed of Trust dated February 30, 1994, recorded under Clerk's File No. Q107636, and File Code No. 530-67-6108 of the official Public Records of Real Property of Harris County, Texas, N. Debted and wife May B. Debted, as grantors, conveyed to the undersigned, as Trustee, certain property hereinafter described, for the purpose of securing and enforcing payment of a certain note described in said Deed of Trust, of even date therewith and in the original principal sum of $50,000.00; and

WHEREAS, Friendly Lender Savings and Loan Association, the holder of said note and Deed of Trust, requested the undersigned, as Trustee, to enforce the trust, the said grantors having made default in the payment of said note when due and therebeing due thereon the principal sum of $50,000.00, plus interest and attorney's fees as provided in said note; and

WHEREAS, I, as Trustee, did on the 4th day of April, 1994, after having posted written notice of the time, place and terms of a public sale of the hereinafter described property, which written notice was posted at the courthouse door of Harris County, Texas, the county in which said real estate is situated, and which said notice was posted for at least twenty-one (21) days preceding the date of the sale, sell the hereinafter described property at public vendue, at the courthouse door of Harris County, Texas, to Friendly Lender Savings and Loan Association, he being the highest bidder, for the sum of $1,000.00; and

WHEREAS, from the affidavit hereto attached and made a part hereof, it appears that the beneficiary (holder of the indebtedness above described) served

FIGURE 7-3. A trustee's deed.

notice of such Trustee's Sale by certified mail at least twenty-one (21) days preceding the date of sale on each debtor obligated to pay such indebtedness according to the records of beneficiary and as required by law; and

WHEREAS, all prerequisites required by law and/or by said Deed of Trust have been duly satisfied by the beneficiary therein and by said Trustee:

NOW, THEREFORE, in consideration of the premises and of the payment to me of the sum of $1,000.00, by the said Friendly Lender Savings and Loan Association, I, as Trustee, by virtue of the authority conferred upon me in said Deed of Trust, have GRANTED, SOLD AND CONVEYED, and by these presents do GRANT, SELL AND CONVEY, unto the said Friendly Lender Savings and Loan Association its successors and assigns, all of the following described property situated in Harris County, Texas:

Lot 1, Block 1, Shakey Acres Subdivision,
Harris County, Texas, as shown of record
of Volume 7, Page 3 of the Map Records
of Harris County, Texas.

TO HAVE AND TO HOLD the above described premises and property, together with the rights, privileges and appurtenances thereto belonging, unto the said Friendly Lender Savings and Loan Association, its successors and assigns, forever; and I, as said Trustee, do hereby bind the said N. Debted and wife, May B. Debted, their heirs, executors and administrators, to warrant and forever defend the said premises unto the said Friendly Lender Savings and Loan Association, its successors and assigns forever, against the claim or claims of all persons claiming or to claim the same or any part thereof.

EXECUTED this 42nd day of April, 1994.

____
Charles J. Jacobus, Trustee

FIGURE 7-3 (*continued*).

giving any warranty of title. A bargain and sale deed is shown in Figure 7-4. Note the absence of warranty in the habendum clause in the bargain and sale deed, as well as the absence of the words *grant* or *convey* (which, statutorily, you will recall, reflect the two general warranties).

Quitclaim Deeds. The quitclaim deed is a deed by which the grantor quitclaims unto the grantee all of his rights, title, and interests in the property. A quitclaim deed is shown in Figure 7-5. Note that the grantor does not claim to have any interest in that particular piece of property, but is saying that if he does have any interest in that property, he conveys it to the grantee by virtue of the quitclaim deed.

Quitclaim deeds have a valuable use in clearing up clouds on title. A title company or abstractor, in searching the chain of title to a property, may determine that some heir or some grantee in the chain of title may have some interest in that property as the result of a previous transaction. Often, however, this heir, or possible title holder, does not know that he has any interest (and maybe he does not actually have any). Therefore, to clear up this cloud on the title, the title company will request that this "possible heir" execute a quitclaim deed, which contains no warranties whatsoever and is not binding as to any warranties on the grantor. The individual with the outstanding interest, then, can convey the interest, if there is any, but without worry that anybody will hold him to any type of warranty as to the title that is being conveyed. An interesting thing about quitclaim deeds is that since they make no warranty at all (you will notice the words *grant* or *convey* are also not used in the quitclaim deed), one can literally give a quitclaim deed to anything. For instance, one can quitclaim the Brooklyn Bridge to convey whatever right, title, and interest one had, if any, in the Brooklyn Bridge to the grantee. It is a perfectly valid deed, and if the grantee is willing to pay consideration for it, the grantee obtains whatever right, title, and interest that the grantor happens to have in the Brooklyn Bridge (which, of course, is nothing beyond what the normal taxpayer has).

It is important to understand, however, that if a person conveys his house to somebody by virtue of a quitclaim deed (or by any of the other kinds of deeds described herein), whatever right, title, and interest he has in his house are certainly conveyed along with that deed. The only difference is the warranty of the grantor. Therefore, a quitclaim deed can pass good title if the grantor has good title at the time of the conveyance.

Requirements of a Deed

Although it is not particularly beneficial for the average nonlaw student to go into the details of requirements and legal technicalities of a deed, it is important that the average real estate professional be familiar with enough

DEED

STATE OF TEXAS)
)
COUNTY OF HARRIS)

KNOW ALL MEN BY THESE PRESENTS:

THAT WE, I. M. SELLER and wife, MAY B. SELLER, of the County of Harris and State of Texas, for and in consideration of the sum of TEN AND NO/100 DOLLARS ($10.00) and other good and valuable consideration in hand paid by the grantees herein named, the receipt and sufficiency of which is hereby acknowledged, have bargained, sold, and by these presents do bargain and sell unto WILL B. DEBTED and wife, N. DEBTED, of the County of Harris and State of Texas, the following described real property situated in Harris County, Texas, to wit:

Lot 1, Block 1, Shakey Acres Subdivision,
Harris County, Texas, as shown of record
at Volume 7, Page 3 of the Map Records of
Harris County, Texas.

TO HAVE AND TO HOLD the above described property and premises unto the said Grantees, their heirs and assigns forever, so that neither we nor our heirs, legal representatives or assigns shall at any time hereafter have, claim or deemed any right or title to the aforesaid property, premises or appurtenances or any part thereof.

EXECUTED this 30th day of February, 1994.

____
I. M. Seller

____
May B. Seller

FIGURE 7-4. A bargain and sale deed.

NOTICE Prepared by the State Bar of Texas for use by Lawyers Only.
To select the proper form, fill in blank spaces, strike out form provisions or insert special terms constitutes the practice of law. No "standard form" can meet all requirements.

QUITCLAIM DEED

THE STATE OF TEXAS
COUNTY OF HARRIS } KNOW ALL MEN BY THESE PRESENTS:

That I. M. Seller and wife, Happy Seller

of the County of Harris, State of Texas, for and in consideration of the sum of TEN AND NO/100-------------($10.00)-------------------DOLLARS in hand paid by the grantee herein named, the receipt of which is hereby acknowledged, have QUITCLAIMED, and by these presents do QUITCLAIM unto N. Debted and wife, May B. Debted .... of the County of Harris, State of Texas, all of their right, title and interest in and to the following described real property situated in Harris County, Texas, to-wit:

Lot 1, Block 1, Shakey Acres Subdivision,
Harris County, Texas, as shown of record
at Volume 7, Page 3, of the Map Records
of Harris County, Texas,

TO HAVE AND TO HOLD all of our **right, title and interest in and to the above described property and premises unto the said grantee** s, their **heirs and assigns forever, so that neither** we **nor** our **heirs, legal representatives or assigns shall have, claim or demand any right or title to the aforesaid property, premises or appurtenances or any part thereof.**

EXECUTED this 30th **day of** February **, A. D. 19** 94 **.**

....
I. M. Seller

....
Happy Seller

....

FIGURE 7-5. A quitclaim deed.

(Acknowledgment)

THE STATE OF TEXAS }
COUNTY OF }

Before me, the undersigned authority, on this day personally appeared

known to me to be the person ... whose name ...... subscribed to the foregoing instrument, and acknowledged to me that he executed the same for the purposes and consideration therein expressed.

Given under my hand and seal of office on this the day of , A. D. 19

....

Notary Public in and for County, Texas.

(Acknowledgment)

THE STATE OF TEXAS }
COUNTY OF }

Before me, the undersigned authority, on this day personally appeared

known to me to be the person ... whose name ...... subscribed to the foregoing instrument, and acknowledged to me that he ... executed the same for the purposes and consideration therein expressed.

Given under my hand and seal of office on this the day of , A. D. 19

....

Notary Public in and for County, Texas.

QUITCLAIM DEED

TO

PREPARED IN THE LAW OFFICE OF:

PLEASE RETURN TO:

(Acknowledgment)

THE STATE OF TEXAS }
COUNTY OF }

Before me, the undersigned authority, on this day personally appeared

known to me to be the person whose name subscribed to the foregoing instrument, and acknowledged to me that he executed the same for the purposes and consideration therein expressed.

Given under my hand and seal of office on this the day of , A. D. 19

Notary Public in and for County, Texas.

FIGURE 7-5 *(continued)*.

of the details of these instruments to be able to glibly discuss them with his attorneys or the clients' attorneys in a professional manner.

The statutory requirements for a deed are very simple. The deed must be in writing, be subscribed to, and be properly delivered (*Tex. Rev. Civ. Stat. Ann.*, art. 1288). *Delivered* is a key word. If the deed is not properly delivered, it is not a valid conveyance.

In general, case law has held that a deed by its nature is a contract, and it must have all the essential elements of a contract before it can be supported either in law or in equity. If you refer back to Chapter 6, you will recall that there are certain provisional requirements for the enforcement of an earnest money contract since it deals with real estate and also has to satisfy the Statute of Frauds in order to be upheld. It follows then, that since a deed is also a contract, and one that purports to transfer an interest in real estate, then, like an earnest money contract, it also should have specific requirements above and beyond the normal contract requirements required in most nonreal estate situations.

In a recent Texas case, the court, in determining the existence of a valid deed, stated that:

> [i]f from the whole instrument, the *grantor* and *grantee* can be ascertained and there are *operative words of grant showing intent to grant title and sufficiently describing the land* and it is *signed and acknowledged* by the grantor, it is a deed [emphasis supplied], *Brown* v. *Byrd*, 512 S.W.2d 753 (Tex. Civ. App.—Tyler, 1974).

Now let us compare this statement with the same requirements for earnest money contracts. The requirements for an earnest money contract are as follows:

1. It must be a written instrument;
2. It must be signed by the party to be charged;
3. There must be operative words of grant showing intent to convey an interest at sometime in the future;
4. The grantor and grantee must be identifiable;
5. The subject matter to be conveyed must be identifiable.

You will note the only difference between the two instruments as far as the legal requirements are concerned is that the deed must show a *present* intent to convey; whereas the earnest money contract has a *future* intent to convey. Aside from this, the legal requirements of two instruments are basically the same. This similarity also serves to reinforce the Doctrine of Merger discussed in the previous chapter. The change in time of the intent to convey, along with the statutorily required delivery, logically merges the terms of the earnest money contract into the deed.

Therefore, the legal requirements of a deed can be summarized as:

1. It must be a written instrument (to satisfy the Statute of Frauds); and
2. It must be signed by the party to be charged (the grantor); and
3. There must be operative words of grant showing a present intent to convey; and
4. The grantor and grantee must be identifiable (legal entities); and
5. The subject matter to be conveyed must be identifiable (sufficient legal description); and
6. It must be delivered (*Tex. Rev. Civ. Stat. Ann.*, art. 1288).

Of course, the terminology, format, and net effect of the two instruments are entirely different. There has been a considerable amount of discussion as to why a real estate licensee, for instance, can fill in the blanks of an earnest money contract but cannot fill in the blanks of a deed. One must remember that there is a certain finality in a properly executed and delivered deed. If there is a mistake in the deed, the mistake can only be corrected by subsequent correction deed or by subsequent trips to the courthouse to try to get the deed reformed. If there is a mistake in an earnest money contract, on the other hand, it can often be renegotiated, changed, or rescinded with considerably less effort or legal formality.

To keep these statutory and case law requirements from appearing too simple, one must realize that each of these requirements, of course, has further requirements. It is not so simple to determine who an identifiable grantor or grantee may be, what constitutes delivery, and so forth. So to make these matters more clear, we will attempt to discuss each of these requirements to help determine how any given fact situation may affect each of these requirements.

Requirements of Grantor and Grantee. The *grantor* is, of course, the owner and seller of the property. The grantor must have sufficient mental capacity to reasonably understand the transaction, or else the deed is voidable. The name of the grantor must appear on the document, but it is not necessary that it appear on the body of the deed. The name of the grantor could be just a signature, but it must be somewhere on the instrument, and the grantor must be identifiable. Texas community property laws present an additional concern. It is a generally accepted practice to put the marital status of the grantor into the deed so that the grantee will be on notice of any conflicts of community property laws that may arise as a result of a husband conveying his property without the joinder of his wife, or vice versa. A more complete discussion of how the community property laws affect this is discussed in Chapter 2, Estates in Land.

A deed must also have an identifiable *grantee*; if it does not, it is void. Not voidable, but void. If the instrument does not purport to convey property to any particular grantee, it simply is not a conveyance. The grantee, of course, must be a legal entity. This does not preclude, of course, the deed being put into the hands of an agent for delivery at a later date. For instance, it can be left with any third-party escrow agent with the provision that it is to be delivered to "the first person who donates $5000 to my church," or with some other such contingency. Providing it was properly delivered to the agent, such a conveyance would be considered valid. An interesting note is that the grantee must be alive; a dead man cannot be a grantee. If the grantee dies before the deed is delivered, the conveyance is void.

Intent to Grant Title. Intent to grant title can generally be construed from the consideration recited and the words of conveyance. Consideration is a requirement for contracts generally, and is properly considered as a part of the intent to convey. However, consideration occupies a peculiar position in regard to the deed as a contract in that it is *not* necessary to effect the conveyance of real estate. Therefore, intent to convey title does not necessarily mean consideration, but would include consideration if any is given. For instance, "$1 or $10," "love and affection," "support and maintenance," are consideration and can effect the conveyance of property. This type of conveyance, supported without valuable consideration, is generally used to transfer property to a loved one, heir, or other situation where a gift or donation suffices for sufficient intent and consideration.

However, none of the foregoing is considered "valuable consideration" in a legal sense. "Ten Dollars and other good and valuable consideration" may not be enough in a true legal sense, *Crane* v. *Glenney*, 352 S.W.2d 773 (Tex. Civ. App.—Houston, 1961), because to effect a valid contract in the true legal sense, there must be true mutuality. If a conveyance is contested by a third party, it has been held that the consideration, at law, must be substantially equal to value; however, the inadequacy of price must be extreme to obtain relief in equity unless coupled with concealment or misrepresentation.

Legal Description. The deed must have an adequate legal description. There are a lot of "gray areas" surrounding what is considered an adequate legal description. The general maxim is that the property must be sufficiently described so that it is distinct from any other property, and so that it can be reasonably ascertained exactly which property is being conveyed. If the description of the real property is so indefinite that it cannot be identified with some certainty, the deed is void, *Young* v. *Gharis*, 170 S.W. 796 (Tex. Civ. App.—Dallas, 1914).

Signature of Grantor. The deed, of course, as discussed before, must be signed by the party to be charged (the grantor), and by the party's spouse if it is community property or homestead property. The grantee is not generally a signatory party to the deed. The grantee's possession of the deed, constituting acceptance of delivery, is enough to hold the grantee to any responsibilities or liabilities expressed in that deed.

Delivery. To be effective as a valid conveyance, a deed must be properly delivered and be accepted by the grantee. In the actual delivery of a deed, intention of the parties is the primary factor, and this is a fact question for the jury to decide. If a deed has been recorded, it is prima facie evidence that proper delivery has been effected. The more serious delivery problems arise when there is a grantee who refuses delivery or there is a partial delivery of the deed to several grantees. In addition, there may be a fact question as to whether or not a delivery to a third person as agent for the grantee is a proper delivery, or whether the agent can operate in that fiduciary capacity. The particular facts involved play a key role in determining the question of delivery, and the questions of law generally hinge on these facts.

Acknowledgment. An acknowledgment is not necessary for the valid conveyance of real estate and is necessary only for recording. Even if a valid deed is not acknowledged, it is still good and binding between the parties, *Haile* v. *Holtzclaw*, 414 S.W.2d 916 (Tex. 1967), although it does not constitute public notice and may not be good in enforcing rights against third parties who may acquire rights in the same property.

After Acquired Title Doctrine

To give proper effect to certain conveyances, the courts have developed an equitable doctrine that is termed the *After Acquired Title Doctrine*. This doctrine basically sets out that if the grantor conveys the property to the grantee, when, in fact, the grantor did not have title to same, title would be conveyed whenever the grantor subsequently obtained title. The theory is that the grantor is estopped from claiming a title that he has assumed to convey.

For instance, grantor *A* conveys a property to grantee *B* by general warranty deed. Grantor *A*, at the time of conveyance and delivery of the deed, does not have title to the mineral rights of the property; however, he has every expectation of obtaining same. Although there are a number of fact questions involved in a problem like this, the After Acquired Title Doctrine stands for the principle that when grantor *A* does acquire the mineral rights, the conveyance will be valid to the first grantee *B* because of the grantor's initial conveyance. Note that the After Acquired Title Doctrine does *not* apply to quitclaim deeds because quitclaim deeds do not purport to convey title to real estate; however, the doctrine does presumably apply to bargain and sale deeds. It is for purposes of this After Acquired Title Doctrine that a bargain and sale deed is often used instead of a quitclaim deed. If there is a question of grantor's title in a bargain and sale deed, it may be later clarified by the After Acquired Title Doctrine concept. The same is not true of a quitclaim deed.

The After Acquired Title Doctrine also is very effective in eliminating problems of fraudulent conveyance. If a grantor induced the grantee to enter into a transaction and conveyed the property to grantee while the property was still under contract to the grantor, the law would not allow the grantor to obtain title to the property adverse to the present grantee's interest.

Exceptions and Reservations in Deeds

You may recall that, if an estate is not expressly limited, Texas law presumes fee simple title. Exceptions and reservations are limitations on the title being passed from the grantor to the grantee. These two types of limitations are significantly different. *Exceptions* are deficiencies in the existing title as part of the grant, which are excepted at the time of the conveyance; that is, they are deficiencies in the title that the grantor has at the time of conveyance. Exceptions would include easements, mineral rights held by third parties, rights-of-way, deed restrictions, or other encumbrances on the grantor's property. They would be excepted from the legal title conveyed because they are not part of the fee title that the grantor holds.

A *reservation*, on the other hand, is a paragraph in a deed creating or reserving an interest to the grantor out of the title being conveyed. Reservations might be mineral rights reserved to the seller. For instance, the grantor would convey the surface of some property but reserve the mineral rights to himself. Often an easement may be reserved to the grantor, by selling the frontage but reserving an easement for the grantor's benefit across the property being conveyed in the grantor's deed. All exceptions and reservations are part of the deed and are enforced under purely contractual principles.

Wills

The conveyance of property by virtue of a will is a voluntary conveyance in that the person conveying the property by will (the "testator") does purport to convey his property to a definite grantee. In the strict application to real estate law, I do not think conveyance by wills needs to be discussed in any great depth, especially as the vast majority of the law involved in this area is best considered in other works on probate law and estate planning. However, it is important to understand the bases of wills as these pertain to certain real estate interests.

Types of Wills

Texas law basically recognizes three types of wills:

1. A *witnessed will*, which, by statute, must:
   (a) Be in writing;
   (b) Be signed by the testator or by another person for him by his direction and in his presence; and
   (c) Be attested by two or more creditable witnesses above the age of 14 years.

   This is generally what we consider as a formal will, drawn by a lawyer, with the formality, self-proving affidavit, and other more particular requirements and details that competent estate-planning attorneys utilize in performing their services for their clients.
2. A *holographic will* is a will written wholly in the handwriting of the testator. It does not require any subscribing witnesses, may also have a self-proving affidavit, and is by all means a valid, binding will.
3. A *nuncupative will* is an oral will that must be made at the time of the last sickness of the deceased, at his home or where he has resided for ten days or more next preceding the date of such will. If the value of any property distributed under a nuncupative will exceeds $30, it must be proved by three creditable witnesses that the testator called upon a person to take notice or bear testimony that this was his will. A nuncupative will may dispose of personal property only.

Conveyance by Will

Once it has been conclusively established that a will exists, the most pertinent point that needs to be made is that encompassed by Section 37 of the Probate Code of the Texas Revised Civil Statutes, which states quite succinctly:

> When a person dies, leaving a lawful will, *all of his estate* devised or bequeathed by such will, and all powers of appointment granted in such will, *shall vest immediately* in the devisees or legatees of such estate

> and the donees of such power; and all the estate of such person, not devised or bequeathed, shall vest immediately in his heirs at law; *subject, however, to the payments of the debts of the testator or intestate, except such as exempted by law* [emphasis supplied].

Therefore, unless there is a contest of the will or other probate complications, the estate of the deceased passes immediately, subject to the settling of the affairs of that estate. It is particularly important for a realtor to acknowledge the fact that complications may exist in the estate of the deceased and to be sure that listing agreements, contracts, and all other legal instruments pertinent to any real estate involved in this estate are signed by all heirs at law or beneficiaries of the will, to protect both the real estate agent and the purchaser in any subsequent transaction. When an estate is involved, it is very important that the realtor rely heavily on the activities of the decedent's lawyers to assure himself of proper compliance with any legal technicalities that may be pertinent.

Involuntary Conveyances

Involuntary conveyances are generally categorized as those conveyances over which the grantor has little or no control. The conveyance is generally controlled by statute (as in eminent domain, escheat, and intestacy), but the discretion of third parties is sometimes an important factor in matters concerning tax sales and foreclosures.

Eminent Domain

By enactment of eminent domain statutes, legislators have established an expeditious procedure whereby possession of property may quickly be taken for its application to *public use*. Eminent domain is exercised through a legal process called *condemnation*. The condemnation procedures are in the interest of the general public and do not require the balancing of the relative interests of the parties involved. There must, of course, be *just compensation*, and there are eminent domain statutes that provide for the proper procedure for awarding these damages in the event that just compensation cannot be reached by agreement between the parties.

The power of eminent domain vests in the state, county, or political subdivision of a county; or in a city or town; or in the U.S. government; or in irrigation districts, water improvement districts, or water power control districts created by authority of law; or in any other corporation or entity who has been granted the right of eminent domain by the state, *Benat* v. *Dallas County*, 266 S.W. 539 (Tex. Civ. App.—Dallas, 1924). It can readily be ascertained that there are a number of different organizations that can exercise their power of eminent domain; these basically include any sort of entity that has been granted that authority by state law, including privately owned authorities such as gas companies, electric companies, and utility districts that are not owned by nor under direct control of state or governmental agencies.

The compensation rights of the grantor under eminent domain proceedings are basically founded in the Fifth and Fourteenth Amendments to the Constitution of the United States. The Fifth Amendment states that no one can be denied the right to his property without due process of law. Therefore, if required by the property owner, the condemning authority must go to the court to secure the condemnation if an agreed compensation cannot be reached between the parties. The Fifth Amendment is applied to the individual states by virtue of the Fourteenth Amendment. Therefore, the basis for the just compensation requirement is not something that can be changed by legislative enactment, judicial order, or executive decision. Although the constitutional interpretations may vary from time to time, changes in these rights can only be properly made by an amendment to the U.S. Constitution.

Texas has a specific set of statutes that deal with these eminent domain rights as they apply in this state.

It is important to understand that the fact situation surrounding the eminent domain proceeding, and the skill of the appraisers and the attorneys involved, weigh very heavily on how the compensation provisions of the eminent domain proceeding will be determined. There is generally no question as to whether or not an entity has the power of eminent domain. But, as in all other court proceedings, there is some flexibility as to how the facts are introduced and how the values are presented to influence the decision, so as to determine "just compensation."

Adverse Possession

Adverse possession is statutorily defined as:

> An actual and visible appropriation of the land, commenced and continued under a claim of right inconsistent with and hostile to the claim of another.

This means basically that somebody can enter upon the property of another, establish his claim of right to that property, and if the true owner is not diligent enough in trying to effect removal of this adverse claim to his property, the adverse claimant's right to that property can ripen into full legal title against the interest of the true owner.

Texas has provisions for 3-, 5-, 10-, and 25-year statutes of limitations under which an adverse claimant can gain title of the property adversely to the true owner. The 3-year statute of limitation is as follows:

Art. 5507. Three years' possession

Suits to recover real estate, as against a person in peaceable and adverse possession thereof under *title* or *color of title* [emphasis supplied], shall be instituted within three years next after the cause of action accrued, and not afterward.

Title refers to a regular chain of transfers from or under the sovereignty of the soil, and *color of title* is meant as a consecutive chain of such transfers down to the person in possession. This chain of transfers might even be "irregular" (that is, one or more of the documents of title may not be duly registered), but "irregular" does not include any documents obtained that may have been obtained through fraudulent or dishonest means. Therefore, under the 3-year adverse possession statute, if the party has taken possession of the property under some color of title or some chain of title, the owner of the real estate cannot institute suit to dispossess him of that property after 3 years after the cause of action accrued. The cause of action is presumed to have accrued upon entry of the adverse claimant to the property, *Hickman* v. *Ferguson*, 164 S.W. 1085 (Tex. Civ. App.—Austin, 1914).

The 5-year adverse possession statute is set out as follows:

Art. 5509. [5674] [3342] [3193] Five years' possession

Every suit to recover real estate as against a person having peaceable and adverse possession thereof, cultivating, using or enjoying the same, and paying taxes thereon, if any, and claiming under a deed or deeds duly registered, shall be instituted within five years next after cause of action shall have accrued, and not afterward. This article shall not apply to one in possession of land, who deraigns title through a forged deed. And no one claiming under a forged deed, or deed executed under a forged power of attorney shall be allowed the benefits of this article.

Notice that the 5-year possession statute does not require a title or color of title requirement as the 3-year possession statute does. It requires only the cultivating, using or enjoying of the property, paying taxes on it, and claiming under a deed. However, as in all other cases, a void deed or one obtained through fraudulent or dishonest practices is not allowed the benefits of the 5-year adverse possession statute.

The 10-year adverse possession statute is set out as follows:

Art. 5510. [5675–5676] [3343] Ten years' possession

Any person who has the right of action for the recovery of lands, tenements or hereditaments against another having peaceable and adverse possession thereof, cultivating, using or enjoying the same, shall institute his suit therefor within ten years next after his cause of action shall have accrued, and not afterward. The peaceable and adverse possession contemplated in this article, as against the person having right of action, shall be construed to embrace not more than one hundred and sixty acres, including the improvements or the number of acres actually enclosed, should the same exceed one hundred and sixty acres; but when such possession is taken and held under some written memorandum of title, other than a deed, which fixes the boundaries of the possessor's claim and is duly registered, such peaceable possession shall be construed to be co-extensive with the boundaries specified in such instrument.

The burden of proof in the 10-year adverse possession statute is considerably less than even that of the 5-year statute. Again, the adverse possessor must only be cultivating, using, or enjoying the real estate. However, the real estate cannot exceed 160 acres unless it has been actually enclosed by a fence or some other barricade that would manifest the adverse possessor's claim to that property that is in excess of 160 acres.

The same claim to an amount of property in excess of 160 acres can also be held to ripen into full title when a written *memorandum of title* (other than a deed) is recorded. The adverse possessor's claim of the property shall be presumed to be coextensive with the boundary.

Therefore, the requirements under the 10-year adverse possession statute really require very little effort other than occupying, cultivating, and enjoying the premises. If the adverse possessor wants more than 160 acres, his right to the excess acreage is presumed if it is actually enclosed by a fence, or a written memorandum of title duly recorded reflects such excess acreage.

The 25-year adverse possession statute is set out as follows:

Art. 5519. [5684a] [3352] Action barred in twenty-five years

No person who has a right of action for the recovery of real estate shall be permitted to maintain an action therefor against any person having peaceable and adverse possession of such real estate for a period of twenty-five years prior to the filing of such action, under claim of right, in good faith, under a deed or deeds, or any instrument or instruments, purporting to convey the same, which deed or deeds or instrument or instruments purporting to convey the same have been recorded in the deed records of the county in which the real estate or a part thereof is situated; and one so holding and claiming such real estate under such claim of title and possession shall be held to have a good marketable title thereto, and on proof of the above facts shall be held to have established title by limitation to such real estate regardless of minority, insanity or other disability in the adverse claimant, or any person under whom such adverse claimant claims, existing at the time of the accrual of the cause of action, or at any time thereafter. Such peaceable and adverse possession need not be continued in the same person, but when held by different persons successively there must be a privity of estate

> between them. The adverse possession of any part of such real estate shall extend to and be held to include all of the property described in such deed or instrument conveying or purporting to convey, under which entry was made upon such land or any part thereof, and by instrument purporting to convey shall be meant any instrument in the form of a deed or which contains language showing an intention to convey even though such instrument, for want of proper execution or for other cause is void on its face or in fact.

The 25-year statute of limitation is logically the one that requires the least burden of proof on the part of the adverse possessor. Note that the only thing required to ripen adverse possession after 25 years is any instrument (or instruments) purporting to convey the property to the adverse possessor that has been recorded in the deed records of the county in which the real estate is situated. Such title can even vest unto the adverse possessor's successors as long as there is a privity of estate between them, that is, some sort of conveyance reflected to the successor.

There are a number of questions that come up as to the time of recordation of the deed and conflicting interests between various deed holders. The law in Texas is that title given by adverse possession of the property is equivalent to that of constructive notice, *Bell* v. *Smith*, 532 S.W.2d 680 (Tex. Civ. App.—Ft. Worth, 1976), so that actual possession of the property is enough to put the purchaser or true owner on constructive notice that said adverse possessor may have a claim. There is no requirement that the adverse possessor be openly defiant.

Although the adverse possession statutes specify hostile claim, the adverse possessor need not sit with a rifle, gun, or other military paraphernalia to try to establish the adverse claim. The mere fact that the claim is against the wishes of the landowners is enough to determine that the possession is hostile. All Texas real estate agents who have grown up in the shadow of the great Texas land barons should now understand why it was so necessary to ride the range on a regular basis. If the owners of land did not keep their property properly fenced and remove the poachers on a regular basis, they would be forever fighting claims of adverse possession.

In more modern times, it can be understood that the title companies, on examining title to a piece of property back to the sovereign, can generally rely on a 3-year adverse possession statute in the event there is a claim at a later date concerning title discrepancies to any given piece of real estate on which they have insured title.

Intestate Succession

When a person dies leaving no will, it is said that he has died *intestate*. Therefore, all of his property passes purely by operation of statutory law.

The specific statute that controls how the property is distributed is as follows:

§ 38. Persons Who Take Upon Intestacy

(a) Intestate Leaving No Husband or Wife. Where any person, having title to any estate, real, personal or mixed, shall die intestate, leaving no husband or wife, it shall descend and pass in parcenary to his kindred, male and female, in the following course:

1. To his children and their descendants.
2. If there be no children nor their descendants, then to his father and mother, in equal portions. But if only the father or mother survive the intestate, then his estate shall be divided into two equal portions, one of which shall pass to such survivor, and the other half shall pass to the brothers and sisters of the deceased, and to their descendants; but if there be none such, then the whole estate shall be inherited by the surviving father or mother.
3. If there be neither father nor mother, then the whole of such estate shall pass to the brothers and sisters of the intestate, and to their descendants.
4. If there be none of the kindred aforesaid, then the inheritance shall be divided into two moieties, one of which shall go to the paternal and the other to the maternal kindred, in the following course: To the grandfather and grandmother in equal portions, but if only one of these be living, then the estate shall be divided into two equal parts, one of which shall go to such survivor, and the other shall go to the descendant or descendants of such deceased grandfather or grandmother. If there be no such descendants, then the whole estate shall be inherited by the surviving grandfather or grandmother. If there be no surviving grandfather or grandmother, then the whole of such estate shall go to their descendants, and so on without end, passing in like manner to the nearest lineal ancestors and their descendants.

(b) Intestate Leaving Husband or Wife. Where any person having title to any estate, real, personal or mixed, other than a community estate, shall die intestate as to such estate, and shall leave a surviving husband or wife, such estate of such intestate shall descend and pass as follows:

1. If the deceased have a child or children, or their descendants, the surviving husband or wife shall take one-third of the personal estate, and the balance of such personal estate shall go to the child or children of the deceased and their descendants. The surviving husband or wife shall also be entitled to an estate for life, in one-third of the land of the intestate, with remainder to the child or children of the intestate and their descendants.
2. If the deceased have no child or children, or their descendants, then the surviving husband or wife shall be entitled to all the personal estate, and to one-half of the lands of the intestate, with-

> out remainder to any person, and the other half shall pass and be inherited according to the rules of descent and distribution; provided, however, that if the deceased has neither surviving father nor mother nor surviving brothers or sisters, or their descendants, then the surviving husband or wife shall be entitled to the whole of the estate of such intestate.
>
> Constitutional provisions. Const. art. 3, § 56, provides, in part, that the Legislature shall not, except as otherwise provided in this Constitution, pass any local or special law changing the law of descent or succession.

When someone dies intestate, the heirs of the decedent must take the affirmative approach to have the estate of the decedent probated and to have a final determination as to how the estate is to be divided. The court normally appoints an *administrator* or *administratrix* (intestate succession, the will appoints an *executor* or *executrix*) to oversee the proper distribution of the decedent's estate. Without going into a great amount of detail, it is only important to realize that the estate of the decedent is generally split amongst his heirs, depending on whether or not he had a wife and/or children, and whether or not that property was separate or community property. There is very little chance that all of the property will go to one individual if the decedent dies intestate, unless it is community property and the decedent has no children. The distribution of intestate succession is graphically shown in Figure 7-6.

Beyond these few initial facts, it is obviously wise for anybody interested in acquiring real estate through the estate of an intestate decedent to be absolutely sure that all the legal aspects are properly taken care of through the courts before taking any action.

Foreclosure

The Texas standard deed of trust form (to be discussed in greater detail in Chapter 9), used in the great majority of mortgage transactions, contains a "power of sale" clause. Although this mortgage instrument has consistently been held to be a contractual obligation between the parties, and not under authority of the state, the procedure for the foreclosure proceedings is codified under Texas Revised Civil Statutes, article 3810. Generally, all sales conferred by any deed of trust or other contractual lien shall be made:

1. At the door of the county courthouse;
2. In the county in which the land is located;
3. At public vendue between 10:00 A.M. and 4:00 P.M. of the first Tuesday of any month;
4. After proper notice has been posted at said courthouse door, and notice of sale has been mailed by certified mail to each debtor at least 21 days preceding the date of sale.

Surviving Spouse with Child or Children

Separate Property

$\frac{2}{3}$ Equally Divided Among Children

$\frac{1}{3}$ to Wife or Husband for Life

Community Property

$\frac{1}{2}$ Equally Divided Among Children

$\frac{1}{2}$ to Wife or Husband

Surviving Spouse with no Children

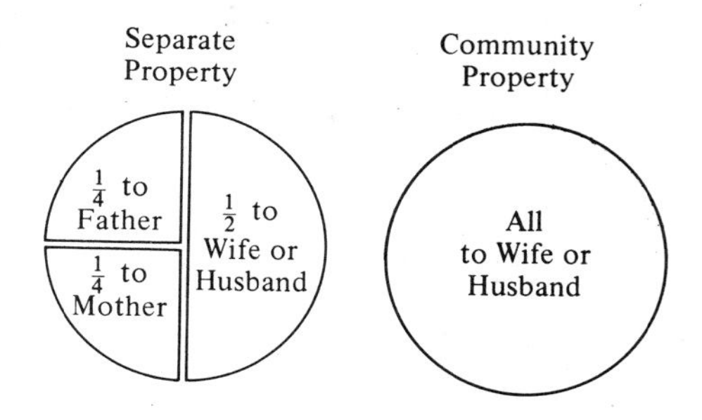

Unmarried, Father and Mother Surviving, No Children

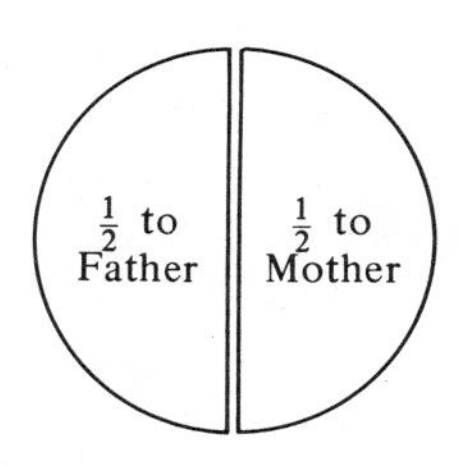

Unmarried, Father or Mother Surviving and Brothers and Sisters Surviving

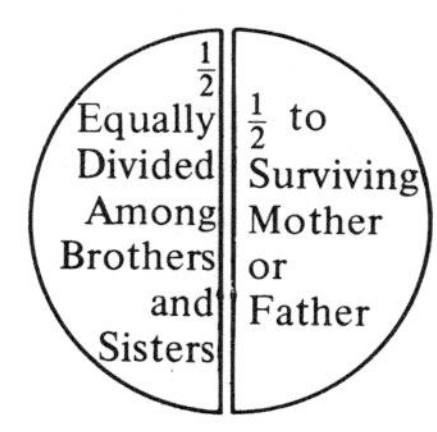

FIGURE 7-6. Distribution of intestate succession.

In practice, the holder of the note (mortgage lender) acts through a trustee, who literally holds a public auction between 10:00 A.M. and 4:00 P.M. on the first Tuesday of the month, after proper notice has been posted. Anyone can bid for and buy the real estate providing the purchaser has enough *cash* to buy the property at the auction. The purchaser, by means of a trustee's deed, buys whatever interest the lien holder has in the real estate. The lien holder, through his trustee, can sell the property for whatever price he deems sufficient.

Once the sale has been made and the trustee's deed has been delivered, the new purchaser succeeds to the lien holder's rights. Conceivably, the lien holder can then sell the property for $10 and take a judgment against the debtor for the deficiency (the difference between the amount owed and the foreclosure sale price received for the property). This procedure can, of course, lead to abuses when a valuable parcel of real estate can be sold for a grossly inadequate price to a nominee of the lien holder, leaving the debtor liable for a personal judgment for the difference. However, providing there is no irregularity in the sale, the deed of trust foreclosure sale will not be avoided merely because of inadequacy of price. The mortgagee can purchase the property at the sale so long as the sale is conducted fairly and in accordance with the terms of the deed of trust. If there are any excess funds, they are forwarded to the borrower after the expenses of the sale have been paid.

There are always additional questions of presentment, payment acceleration of all the payments, and other technical legal aspects of the sale, abuse of which can set aside the foreclosure sale. It is well-advised, however, to take foreclosure proceedings seriously. They are seldom set aside. The law clearly seems to favor the mortgagee in a foreclosure. It must be remembered that if the rights of the debtor or the mortgagee have to be balanced, the mortgagee often has more interest in the land than the debtor, and in order to encourage real estate loans, the lender needs to be protected. Without this type of protection, mortgagees might prefer to place their lendable sources of cash into other types of investments.

Tax Sales

The only sale of real property for taxes in Texas is for ad valorem taxes pursuant to state law. There are no federal ad valorem taxes, and tax sales of real property for other than state ad valorem taxes are not going to be considered here. It is sufficient to say only that the federal government can sell virtually anything to recover their tax debt.

It is generally understood that all property in this state is liable for taxes. That is, if ad valorem taxes have not been paid, the owner's property, whether real or personal, may be levied against to satisfy all delinquent taxes. Sales of real property for delinquent taxes of any type are specifically provided for in this state by statute. There are exceptions to this rule—one is the sacred cow of Texas, the homestead. Statutorily, the homestead cannot be sold for taxes other than the taxes due on such homestead (*Tex. Rev. Civ. Stat. Ann.*, art. 7279). The other exception is the elderly. If the homeowner is older than 65 years of age, no sale can take place while that person still owns the house (*Tex. Rev. Civ. Stat. Ann.*, art. 7329a).

As in most other involuntary sales of real estate, the property must be properly advertised. In the case of tax sales, the advertisement for the sale must occur for three consecutive weeks in some newspaper published in the county where the land is to be sold. The advertisement must state the time, place, and terms of sale; and, like the foreclosure sale, it must be held at public outcry at the courthouse door, between legal hours on the first Tuesday of the month.

To effect the sale, then, a tax deed is used. The tax deed provides for conveyance of all the rights and interest the former owner had at the time when the assessment was made. The deed also specifically provides for the redemption period and penalties specified in Article 7345a, *Texas Revised Civil Statutes, et seq.*. A copy of a tax deed is shown in Figure 7-7.

TAX DEED

THE STATE OF TEXAS ⌶
⌶ KNOW ALL MEN BY THESE PRESENTS
COUNTY OF ____________________ ⌶

THAT WHEREAS, by virtue of an Order of Sale issued by the Clerk of the District Court in and for ______________________ County, dated ______________________, on a certain Judgment rendered in said Court on ______________________, in a certain suit No. ______________ styled ____ ______________________________________ I, ______________________ Sheriff of said County, did upon ______________________, levy upon and advertise the said premises as described in said Order of Sale, by giving public notice of the time and place of said sale by an advertisement in the English Language, published once a week for three consecutive weeks preceding such sale, the first publication appearing not less than twenty days immediately preceding the day of sale, beginning on the __________day of ____________ A.D. 19 ______, in the ______________________________ a newspaper published in the County of ______________________________, stating in said advertisement the authority by virtue of which said sale was to be made, the time of levy, the time and place of sale, a brief description of the property to be sold, the number of acres, the original survey, its locality in the County, and the name by which the land is generally known, and by delivering a similar notice to each of the above named defendants, and on the first Tuesday in ____________________, 19 ______, within the hours prescribed by law, sold said hereinafter described land or lots at public vendue, at the Courthouse door of said County, at which sale the premises hereinafter described were struck off to:

for the sum of

(he, she, they) being the highest bidder(s) therefore, and that being the highest bid for the same,

NOW, THEREFORE, in consideration of the premises aforesaid, and of the payment of the said sum of

the receipt of which is hereby acknowledged, I, __________________________, Sheriff as aforesaid, have Granted, Sold and Conveyed, and by these presents do Grant, Sell and Convey unto the said

all of the estate, right, title and interest which the defendants in such suit had on the date said Judgment was rendered or at any time afterwards, in and to the following described land and premises, as described in the Order of Sale, viz:

FIGURE 7-7. Tax deed.

TO HAVE AND TO HOLD the above described premises, subject, however, to the defendant's right to redeem the same in the manner prescribed by law within two years from the date of recordation of this deed, unto the said ______________________________, heirs and assigns, forever, as fully and as absolute as I, as Sheriff aforesaid, can convey by virtue of said Order of Sale. It is understood and agreed that by virtue of said Judgment and Order of Sale, writ of possession will issue within twenty days after the period of redemption shall have expired, but not until then.

IN TESTIMONY WHEREOF, I have hereunto set my hand

this ________ day of __________________________, A.D. 19 _________.

____
Sheriff _______________ County
Texas

THE STATE OF TEXAS

COUNTY OF __________________

Before me, the undersigned authority, on this day personally appeared ______________________________, Sheriff, known to me to be the person whose name is subscribed to the foregoing instrument and acknowledged to me that he executed the same as Sheriff aforesaid, for the purposes, consideration and in the capacity therein expressed.

Given under my hand and seal of office, this __________

day of ________________________________, A.D. 19 ___________.

____

____

__________________ County, Texas

FIGURE 7-7 (*continued*).

The biggest difference in the tax sale and any other type of execution or foreclosure is that the tax sale provides for a specific right of the debtor, termed the *equity of redemption*; that is, the debtor has the right to buy back his property within two years if he pays the statutory penalties for doing so.

The debtor may not assert any limitation statutes as his defense because limitations in tax rules do not apply against the taxing authority (*Tex. Rev. Civ. Stat. Ann.*, art. 7898). However, personal property is sold first, and only after the sale of personalty is deemed insufficient do authorities sell the real property (*Tex. Rev. Civ. Stat. Ann.*, art. 7274); and no deficiency judgment against the debtor is provided for in the event the sale of the real estate is insufficient to pay the debtor's liability. The subject of tax sales is discussed in greater detail in Chapter 17.

Escheat

Escheat is the statutory provision of the State of Texas that provides for the transfer of real estate belonging to any person who dies without a will and has no heirs; or where the owner of any real property shall be absent for a term of seven years and is not known to exist, leaving no heirs or will. Such real estate shall escheat to and vest in the State of Texas. This simply provides for the State of Texas to get title to real estate so that no parcels of property will be unaccounted for. It is a tool to effect valid conveyance of real estate when there are no other possible means of conveyance. The methods for this conveyance are controlled very strictly by statute. It is generally safe to assume that the state does not want to become the proprietor of various odd tracts of land throughout the state, and so escheat is used only as a last resort. The process of escheating land is done through a court proceeding in a district court in the county in which the land is located. Upon such final judgment being rendered, title to the land is forwarded to the Commissioner of the General Land Office in Austin, Texas, and is dedicated to the Permanent Free School Fund for the State of Texas. The commissioner may lease or sell this property as he sees fit if it is determined (by the commissioner) to be in the state's best interest.

SUMMARY

Conveyancing can generally be divided into two categories: voluntary conveyances and involuntary conveyances. Voluntary conveyances are conveyanced by deed and will. Involuntary conveyances include adverse possession, condemnation, foreclosure, intestacy, tax sales, and escheat.

The deed is by far the most voluntary form of conveyance. Types of deeds normally used in Texas include the general warranty deed, special warranty deed, quitclaim deed, bargain and sale deed, trustee's deeds, and court-ordered deeds. Deeds, like all other real estate contracts, have specific requirements in order to be enforceable and to be upheld. The requirements are construed by case law and by statute.

Wills are basically of three types: a witnessed will, a holographic will, or a nuncupative will. Each type has its own requirements in order to be enforceable and upheld.

Eminent domain is a right by which some public entity with the power of condemnation can take an individual's property for public use provided that there is just compensation. Adverse possession, on the other hand, is the right of a private individual to obtain full title to someone else's property by virtue of his possession of that property. Intestate succession is a statutory procedure that determines who has the right to decedent's estate if he dies leaving no will. Foreclosure is a statutory method of selling property because of a default in his mortgage. Tax sales are sales by some governmental entity for past due and delinquent taxes. Escheat is the statutory provision of the state of Texas that provides for the transfer of real estate to the capital estate of Texas when a person dies leaving no will or no heirs.

8

ACKNOWLEDGMENTS, RECORDING, AND CONSTRUCTIVE NOTICE

Recording and Constructive Notice

The State of Texas, through a series of laws commonly called the *Recording Act*, has provided for a means of registration that is available to all individuals who have an interest in real estate. Through these laws, anyone who has an interest in real estate may put the world on notice of his interest in the real estate by recording the instrument reflecting that interest in the real property records of the county in which the land is located. The act provides that the following instruments may be recorded:

> Deeds, mortgages, conveyances, deeds of trust, bonds for title, covenants, defeasances, or *other instruments of writing concerning any lands or tenements* [emphasis supplied], goods or chattels, or movable property of any description (*Vernon's Ann. Civ. St.*, art. 6626).

Therefore, virtually all instruments may be recorded.

The effect of recording one's interest in real estate in this fashion is to put all subsequent purchasers for valuable consideration and all creditors on notice of the claimant's interest in that particular piece of property. Subsequent purchasers and creditors, then, are under a duty of care to search the records of real property in the county in which the land is located to assure themselves of proper title or of priority lien interests in the real estate that may adversely affect them. Texas law further provides that unless these instruments are recorded, they are void as to all such subsequent purchasers and creditors (*Tex. Rev. Civ. Stat.*, art. 6627).

Therefore, the basic premises behind the Recording Act are:

1. To protect the individual who owns an interest in real estate; and
2. To assure subsequent purchasers and creditors as to the status of the title of that real estate.

It is important to note, however, that any instrument that is not recorded is still binding between the parties; but it is not notice to third parties or subsequent creditors or purchasers of the property, and therefore would not be binding against them. The process of recording the interest in the real estate is performed in the county clerk's office in the county courthouse in the county in which the land is situated. Once the instrument has been properly recorded in the county clerk's office and made of public record, that the entire world is legally on notice of that interest in the real estate. This type of notice is termed *constructive notice* and is considered to be as good as actual notice because the law requires subsequent purchasers and creditors to search the records, *Clear Lake Apartments, Inc.* v. *Clear Lake Utilities Co.*, 537 S.W.2d 48 (Tex. Civ. App.—Houston, 1976).

Constructive notice differs from actual notice. *Actual notice* exists when the subsequent purchaser or creditor has express information about something—something that reasonable, diligent inquiry and exercise of the means of information would disclose, *O'Farrel* v. *Coolidge*, 225 S.W.2d 582 (Tex. Civ. App.—Texarkana, 1949). *Constructive notice* is information or knowledge of a fact imputed by law to a person. Knowledge of the county real property records, as well as knowledge of anyone in actual possession of the property, constitutes constructive notice, *Park* v. *Sweeten*, 270 S.W.2d 687 (Tex. Civ. App.—San Antonio, 1954).

The Recording Process

There are four basic requirements that an instrument must have to be properly recorded such that it is deemed to be constructive notice.

1. The instrument must be the original instrument, not a copy (which means that the signature must be original); and
2. The instrument must be in English and not a foreign language; and
3. The instrument must be properly acknowledged or properly witnessed (acknowledgment and witnessing will be discussed in more depth later in this chapter); and
3. It must be recorded in the county where the property is located.

When the foregoing requirements are complied with and the instrument is recorded, the recording process is determined to have been "perfected" such that subsequent purchasers and creditors are on notice.

Chain of Title

In the lesser populated Texas counties, the instruments are recorded in the county clerk's records in books provided specifically for that purpose. When recordation is referred to in describing an instrument in those counties, one refers to a deed recorded by the volume and page number of the deed records of the county in which the land is located. The entries are often made by hand in separate volumes, one volume kept for deed records, one for mortgage records, and so forth. Recordation of such instruments is recorded in the following manner:

> . . . recorded in Volume ______,
> Page ______ of the ____________________
> Records of ____________________ County, Texas.

In more populated counties, the Texas legislature has provided for a method of recording by microfilming the documents, rather than keeping the entries recorded in large volumes. In these counties, the interest in the real estate is recorded in one main microfilm library, known as the Official Public Records of Real Property. When referring to the recording information on deeds recorded in this manner, one refers to a deed recorded under the clerk's file number and film code number of the Official Public Records of Real Property of the county in which the real estate is located. Recordation of these instruments is reflected in the following manner:

> Filed for record in the Official Public Records of Real Property of ____________________ County, Texas, under Clerk's File No. ____________________ and recorded under Film Code No. ____________________.

When the proper recording has been made by the county clerk, it becomes apparent that the real property records of that county would have a list of the grantors and grantees, as well as of all of the instruments that have been recorded against the subject property as far back as records have been kept. This, of course, goes back to the original grant from the Sovereign of Texas in 1836. This *list* of instruments and of grantor-grantee records, when established in chronological order, creates what is called a *chain of title*, which should establish a complete line of fee title from the original grant from the Sovereign of Texas down to the most current property owner. When all of the recorded *instruments* (as contrasted to *list* of same) relating to a parcel of real estate are assembled in chronological order, these are collectively called an *abstract of title*.

Individuals who wish to search the title records of the county are, of course, allowed to do so since all of these records are public. All courthouses keep what is called an *index of grantors and grantees*, and an individual may trace the chain of title through the grantor-grantee index in order to perform his own title search. Private abstract companies, in addition to the grantor-grantee index, also keep records of the titles of real property for each particular tract of land. This type of indexing system is called a *tract indexing system* and is most convenient when one is trying to determine who has interests in a particular parcel of real estate.

Lis Pendens

In addition to the recording information in the Official Public Records of Real Property, or the volume and page reference, there are additional records that allow for the recordation of other instruments, such as the *plat record* (recording of subdivision plats), *condominium records* (recording of condominium regimes), and another, rather unique, recording of instruments called *lis pendens notices*. Literally translated, *lis pendens* means that the "law is pending." This establishes constructive notice to subsequent creditors, purchasers, and other third parties that there is a lawsuit pending that involves an interest to that property. Anyone who buys that property with notice of the *lis pendens* buys it subject to the outcome of the lawsuit affecting the property.

Although *lis pendens* serves as a very effective method of protecting parties in litigation, it can be abused when used to cloud the title to somebody's property, because the claim has virtually no adverse effect on the claimant. This is because a *lis pendens* is considered "privileged" since it is part of a lawsuit that has been filed and is currently pending, *Kropp* v. *Prather*, 526 S.W.2d 283 (Tex. Civ. App.—Tyler, 1975). To clarify the theory underlying this concept, it should be explained that *privilege* is an exemption from libel and slander given to a party during judicial proceedings. It is well understood that during litigation any allegations can be made in pleadings, or in the courtroom, and no individual can be liable for libel or slander if those allegations are made in good faith. This encourages the free exchange of ideas and attitudes in the courtroom, and helps solicit certain facts that otherwise might not be brought into the legal proceeding. A *lis pendens* notice, being a part of a lawsuit, is given the same status, unless filed maliciously, or in bad faith.

Acknowledgments

As previously discussed, an acknowledgment is one of the requirements for making instruments recordable. This, and only this, is the primary purpose of an acknowledgment. It does not make the instrument "official" or "legal"; it simply makes the instrument recordable. Acknowledgments are not the only method of making an instrument recordable, however; instruments can also be made recordable by signatures of two subscribing witnesses, or by the testimony of a person to the handwriting of the signatory party and witnesses.

The requirements to make an effective acknowledgment consist of the following:

1. The person who executed the instrument must appear before the person authorized to take the acknowledgment.
2. The officer taking the acknowledgment must know or have satisfactory evidence that the person making such acknowledgment is the individual who executed the instrument.
3. The signer must acknowledge to the officer taking the acknowledgment that he executed the instrument for the purposes and consideration therein expressed, and in the capacity therein stated.
4. The acknowledgment must be signed by the authorized officer, and be sealed with his seal of office.

The foregoing requirements of an acknowledgment are self-explanatory if one takes the time to carefully read an acknowledgment. The statutory form for an ordinary certificate of acknowledgment (*Tex. Rev. Civ. Stat. Ann.*, art 6607) is shown in Figure 8-1.

The State of ____________________

County of ____________________

Before me ____________________ (here insert the name and character of the officer) on this day personally appeared ____________________, known to me (or proved to me on the oath of ____________________) to be the person whose name is subscribed to the foregoing instrument and acknowledged to me that he executed the same for the purposes and consideration therein expressed.

(Seal) Given under my hand and seal of office this ____________________ day of ____________________, A.D., 19 ______.

____

FIGURE 8-1.

Persons Authorized to Take Acknowledgments

The acknowledgment or proof of an instrument of writing may be made in this state before:

1. A clerk of the district court;
2. A judge or a clerk of the county court; or
3. A notary public.

An acknowledgment may be made outside of the State of Texas, but within the physical limits of the United States of America, before:

1. A clerk of some court of record having a seal;
2. A commissioner of deeds duly appointed into the laws of this state; or
3. A notary public.

An acknowledgment or proof of an instrument may be made outside the physical limits of the United States and its territories before:

1. A minister, commissioner, or charge d'affairs of the United States, resident and accredited in the country where the proof of the acknowledgment is made;
2. A consul general, consul, vice consul, commercial agent, vice commercial agent, deputy consul, or consular agent of the United States, resident in the country where the proof of acknowledgment is made; or
3. A notary public.

In addition to the above methods, the acknowledgment may be made by a member of the armed forces of the United States before any commissioned officer of the armed forces of the United States or the auxiliaries thereof. Acknowledgments of this type do not necessarily require a seal as do other types of acknowledgments.

The certificate of acknowledgment must be substantially the same as provided for by the statute. An officer authorized to take acknowledgments must be a disinterested party. If he has an interest in the transaction, the acknowledgment is void; but this does not disqualify or make the instrument itself void.

Venue

Due to a recent change in Texas law, the *venue* (jurisdiction) of a notary public after August 29, 1977, is coextensive with the boundaries of the state, irrespective of the county in which he (the notary public) is appointed. Therefore, it can be assumed that a notary public who is commissioned in any county in Texas may take acknowledgments in any other county in the State of Texas. Note, however, that the notary's jurisdiction is confined to the State of Texas. For instance, take the example of a deed signed in Massachusetts to convey title to real property in Harris County, Texas. If that deed is acknowledged in Massachusetts, a Massachusetts notary public would take the acknowledgment, and the jurisdiction of that notary would be the State of Massachusetts. There is no requirement that an instrument conveying property in a particular county be notarized in that county. It can be acknowledged anywhere before any authorized officer, so long as his jurisdiction is properly noted on the acknowledgment certificate.

Construction of an Acknowledgment

Since the acknowledgment performs a particularly important function (to accomplish the requirements of proper recordation), the courts have rather liberally construed the requirements of an effective acknowledgment. For instance, the failure of a notary to show the date of his commission expiration does not invalidate the certificate, but the certificate is invalid without the official seal. There has been a recent Texas case where the name of the person making the acknowledgment (signer of the instrument) was omitted, but it did not render it fatally defective, *Sheldon* v. *Farinacci*, 535 S.W.2d 938 (Tex. Civ. App.—San Antonio, 1976). It appears that as long as the acknowledgment is signed by the person *taking* the acknowledgment, sealed, and in substantially the same form as prescribed by statute, it will be considered an effective and valid acknowledgment, and acknowledgment will not be literally construed so as to render them ineffective.

Proofs Other Than by Acknowledgment

The proof of an instrument for the purpose of being recorded may be given by one or more subscribing witnesses personally appearing before some officer authorized to take said proof, and stating under oath that he or they saw the person who executed the instrument subscribe to same and that this person had executed the same for purposes and consideration therein stated. The witnesses appearing to testify to said proof must be personally known to the officer taking the proof, or must prove by their oath that they are the witnesses testifying to said proof. A form of a certificate where the execution of the instrument is proved by a witness is substantially as shown in Figure 8-2.

An execution of an instrument may also be established for record by proof of the handwriting of the grantor and of at least one subscribing witness under certain circumstances, as when the signatory party of the instrument and the witnesses are dead, or nonresidents, or their residences are unknown, or for some reason the signatory parties and witnesses are incompetent to testify. The same general rules apply if there is a signatory party who has made his mark rather than signed his name.

Record of Acknowledgment

Article 6619 of Texas Revised Civil Statutes requires that all officers authorized or permitted by law to take acknowledgments shall keep a well-bound book and in that book they shall enter and record a short

The State of ____________________

County of ____________________

Before me, ____________________ (here insert the name and character of the officer), on this day personally appeared ____________________, known to me (or proved to me on the oath of ____________________), to be the person whose name is subscribed as a witness to the foregoing instrument of writing, and after being duly sworn by me stated on oath that he saw ____________________, the grantor or person who executed the foregoing instrument, subscribe the same (or that the grantor or person who executed such instrument of writing acknowledged in his presence that he had executed the same for the purposes and consideration therein expressed), and that he had signed the same as a witness at the request of the grantor (or person who executed the same).

(Seal) Given under my hand and seal of office this ____________________ day of ____________________, A.D., 19 ____.

____

FIGURE 8-2.

statement of each acknowledgment or proof taken by them, which statement shall be signed by them officially. The statement should recite the true date on which the acknowledgment was taken, the name of the grantor and grantee of the instrument, its date, if proved by the subscribing witness, the name of the witness, and the residence of the witness, and whether such witness is personally known or unknown to the officer.

Any person injured by the failure, refusal, or neglect of any officer to comply with the requirements of the law shall have a cause of action against the officer so failing, before any court of competent jurisdiction for recovery of all damages resulting from such neglect, failure, or refusal.

Jurat

A *jurat* is a certificate of an officer or person before whom a writing was sworn to. This certificate is made before the same people who have the authority to take acknowledgments. However, a jurat is not, and should not be confused with, an acknowledgment. A jurat normally simply states:

Subscribed and sworn to before me on this ____________ day of ____________________, 19 ________.

____

Notary Public in and for
____________________ County, Texas

In a jurat, the signatory party is swearing that the facts contained in the instrument are true, and not simply that he signed same for the purposes and consideration therein expressed. The acknowledgment and the jurat are entirely different certificates for entirely different purposes. The acknowledgment makes the instrument recordable. The jurat verifies the facts contained in the instrument, and is usually used in affidavits when testimony is taken for court proceedings or other evidentiary use.

SUMMARY

The state of Texas has the Recording Act, a means of registration that is available to all individuals who have an interest in real estate. The effect of recording one's interest in real estate is to put all subsequent purchasers for valuable consideration and all creditors on notice of the claimant's interest in that particular piece of real estate. The public is then on constructive notice of the claimant's interest in that property. Through recording each claimant's interest in real estate, we establish what is referred to as a chain of title. When all of the instruments have been assembled in chronological order, it is called an abstract of title.

A *lis pendens notice* is a notice that a lawsuit is pending which involves title to the real estate. It may only be filed after a lawsuit has been commenced.

An acknowledgment is one of the requirements for making instruments recordable. An acknowledgment may be taken before a notary public, a judge, or a clerk of the district court. A notary's jurisdiction encompasses the entire state of Texas. Acknowledgments are liberally construed, and there are other methods of proving the veracity of an instrument besides an acknowledgment.

A jurat, often confused with an acknowledgment, is a statement by the notary that the document has been sworn to as true. A jurat is not required to make an instrument recordable, but an acknowledgment is.

9

MORTGAGES

The financing of real estate is one of the key factors in the ability to consummate a sale. The real estate agent who understands the key details and legal ramifications of various methods of financing real estate has a clear advantage over his competitors, in that he can advise his clients on much more than just the fair market value and sales price. By recognizing the full value of the various financing techniques, the agent can understand why most deals are contingent upon the purchaser obtaining financing. To understand these various financing techniques, one must also understand the basics of the various types of mortgages in Texas since these are the primary legal documents that secure the purchaser's indebtedness.

Instruments

Most mortgage procedures in Texas require the execution of two instruments: the *promissory note* and the *deed of trust*. In financing real estate transactions, the promissory note used is generally referred to as a *real estate lien note*. This note is the actual promise to pay. The only difference between a real estate lien note and other forms of promissory notes is the reference to the real estate used as security for the payment of the note.

Real Estate Lien Note

Figure 9-1 shows a standard form real estate lien note published by the State Bar of Texas. Notice that it contains the actual promise to pay to the order of the mortgagee (1), the amount (2), the interest rate (3), and the additional interest provisions for past due unpaid principal and interest (4). (The term *matured* as used in the note in Figure 9-1 indicates that the entire amount of the note is due and payable.)

In this particular real estate lien note, the payment clause is a simple one for monthly payments for the term of the note (5), and, for illustration purposes, there is a clause for prepayment (prepayment clause) (6), which specifies a penalty for the prepayment and a provision for the application of said prepayments for the remainder of the note.

The default clause (7) is standard in most promissory notes and provides for the entire indebtedness to be matured in the event of default; it also provides for payment of attorneys' fees in the event legal proceedings are required in order to enforce payment (8).

The next clause, normally referred to as the *waiver* (9), is also standard; it provides that the maker of the note does not have to be invoiced for each and every payment, but the obligation to make those payments is absolute without any notice whatsoever (10).

The next clause is the security clause (11), which, in this case, specifies the vendor's lien retained in the deed, the lien created by the deed of trust, and the legal description of the real estate (12) to be used as security for the payment of the note.

The last item in this real estate lien note is, of course, the space provided for the signatures (13) of the makers of the note.

The real estate lien note is normally not a recorded instrument since it does not create the lien interest in the real estate. It therefore does not usually contain an acknowledgment. The lien interest in the real estate, of course, is created by the mortgage instrument itself.

Deed of Trust

The most commonly used mortgage in Texas is referred to as the *deed of trust*. A deed of trust is often described as a mortgage with a *power of sale*. A typical deed of trust form, as published by the State Bar of Texas, is shown in Figure 9-2. You will note that it has many of the same characteristics of the deed. However, as you recall the discussion in Chapter 2, legal title does not pass in a deed of trust. The lender gets only a lien since Texas is a lien theory state.

The deed of trust is most easily defined as a conveyance by the borrower (called the *grantor* in the deed of trust) to a third-party *trustee* (nominee of the lender) as security for a debt for money loaned by the lender (called the *beneficiary* in the deed of trust), subject to a condition of defeasance; that is, the conveyance of the trustee does not become effective until there has been a default in the payments of the promissory note, and the trustee must exercise the powers conferred upon him in the deed of trust. When the note has been paid in full, the deed of trust, by its own

Prepared by the State Bar of Texas for use by Lawyers only.
To select the proper form, fill in blank spaces, strike out form provisions or insert special terms constitutes the practice of law. No "standard form" can meet all requirements.

REAL ESTATE LIEN NOTE

$ 50,000.00 Houston, Texas, February 30th 1994

For value received, I, We, or either of us, as principals, promise to pay to the order of Friendly Lender Savings and Loan Association ①

in the City of Houston, Harris County, Texas, the sum of ② Fifty-Thousand and no/100-- Dollars ($50,000.00), in legal and lawful money of the United States of America, with interest thereon from date hereof until maturity at the rate of nine per cent (③ 9 %) per annum; the interest payable monthly as it accrues; matured unpaid principal and interest shall bear interest at the rate of ten per cent (10%) per annum from date of maturity until paid. ④

This note is due and payable as follows, to-wit:

⑤ In equal monthly installments of FOUR HUNDRED FIFTY AND NO/100 DOLLARS ($450.00) each, including interest, the first of such installments shall be due and payable on the 1st day of March, 1994, and a like installment shall be due and payable on the same day of each succeeding month thereafter until fully paid. Each installment shall be applied first to the payment of accrued interest due on the unpaid principal balance and the remainder of each installment shall be applied to the reduction of unpaid principal.

⑥ The makers hereof reserve the right to prepay, prior to maturity, all or any part of the principal of this note without penalty, and interest shall immediately cease on any amount so prepaid.

It is expressly provided that upon default in the punctual payment of this note or any part thereof, principal or interest, as the same shall become due and payable, the entire indebtedness secured by the hereinafter mentioned lien shall be matured, at the option of the holder; and in the event default is made in the prompt payment of this note when due or declared due, and the same is placed in the hands of an attorney for collection, or suit is brought on same, or the same is collected through Probate, Bankruptcy or other judicial proceedings, then the makers agree and promise to pay ten per cent (10%) additional on the amount of principal and interest then owing, as attorney's fees. ⑦ ⑧

Each maker, surety and endorser of this note expressly waives all notices, demands for payment, presentations for payment, notices of intention to accelerate the maturity, protest and notice of protest, as to this note and as to each, every and all installments hereof. ⑨

FIGURE 9-1. A real estate lien note.

Payment hereof is secured by a Deed of Trust of even date herewith, executed by the makers hereof to Charles J. Jacobus, Trustee, upon the following described property, to wit;

⑩

Lot 1, Block 1, Shakey Acres Subdivision,
Harris County, Texas, as shown of record ⑪
at Volume 7, Page 3, of the Map Records
of Harris County, Texas.

⑫ May B. Debted

N. Debted

REAL ESTATE LIEN NOTE

TO

PREPARED IN THE LAW OFFICE OF:

FIGURE 9-1 (*continued*).

NOTICE Prepared by the State Bar of Texas for use by Lawyers only. Revised 1-1-76
To select the proper form, fill in blank spaces, strike out form provisions or insert special terms constitutes the practice of law. No "standard form" can meet all requirements.

DEED OF TRUST

THE STATE OF TEXAS
COUNTY OF HARRIS } KNOW ALL MEN BY THESE PRESENTS:

GRANTING CLAUSE AND PROPERTY DESCRIPTION

That N. DEBTED and wife, MAY B. DEBTED

of Harris County, Texas, hereinafter called Grantors (whether one or more) for the purpose of securing the indebtedness hereinafter described, and in consideration of the sum of TEN DOLLARS ($10.00) to us in hand paid by the Trustee hereinafter named, the receipt of which is hereby acknowledged, and for the further consideration of the uses, purposes and trusts hereinafter set forth, have granted, sold and conveyed, and by these presents do grant, sell and convey unto Charles J. Jacobus, Trustee, of Harris County, Texas, and his substitutes or successors, all of the following described property situated in Harris County, Texas, to-wit:

Lot 1, Block 1, Shakey Acres Subdivision,
Harris County, Texas, as shown of record
at Volume 7, Page 3 of the Map Records
of Harris County, Texas.

FIGURE 9-2. A deed of trust.

HABENDUM AND WARRANTY CLAUSE

TO HAVE AND TO HOLD the above described property, together with the rights, privileges and appurtenances thereto belonging unto the said Trustee, and to his substitutes or successors forever. And Grantors do hereby bind themselves, their heirs, executors, administrators and assigns to warrant and forever defend the said premises unto the said Trustee, his substitutes or successors and assigns forever, against the claim, or claims, of all persons claiming or to claim the same or any part thereof.

TRUST CLAUSE

This conveyance, however, is made in TRUST to secure payment of ...... one ...... promissory note ...... of even

NOTE AND DEBT SECURED CLAUSE

date herewith in the principal sum of FIFTY THOUSAND AND NO/100ths-----------------------------------

--Dollars ($50,000.00 ......)

executed by Grantors, payable to the order of ...... Friendly Lender Savings and Loan Association ......

....

in the City of ...... Houston ......, ... Harris ...... County, Texas as follows, to-wit:

As therein provided.

FIGURE 9-2 (*continued*).

bearing interest as therein stipulated, providing for acceleration of maturity and for Attorney's fees;

Should Grantors do and perform all of the covenants and agreements herein contained, and make prompt payment of said indebtedness as the same shall become due and payable, then this conveyance shall become null and void and of no further force and effect, and shall be released at the expense of Grantors, by the holder thereof, hereinafter called Beneficiary (whether one or more).

Grantors covenant and agree as follows:

That they are lawfully seized of said property, and have the right to convey the same; that said property is free from all liens and encumbrances, except as herein provided.

To protect the title and possession of said property and to pay when due all taxes and assessments now existing or hereafter levied or assessed upon said property, or the interest therein created by this Deed of Trust, and to preserve and maintain the lien hereby created as a first and prior lien on said property including any improvements hereafter made a part of the realty.

To keep the improvements on said property in good repair and condition, and not to permit or commit any waste thereof; to keep said buildings occupied so as not to impair the insurance carried thereon.

To insure and keep insured all improvements now or hereafter created upon said property against loss or damage by fire and windstorm, and any other hazard or hazards as may be reasonably required from time to time by Beneficiary during the term of the indebtedness hereby secured, to the extent of the original amount of the indebtedness hereby secured, or to the extent of the full insurable value of said improvements, whichever is the lesser, in such form and with such Insurance Company or Companies as may be approved by Beneficiary, and to deliver to Beneficiary the policies of such insurance having attached to said policies such mortgage indemnity clause as Beneficiary shall direct; to deliver renewals of such policies to Beneficiary at least ten (10) days before any such insurance policies shall expire; any proceeds which Beneficiary may receive under any such policy, or policies, may be applied by Beneficiary, at his option, to reduce the indebtedness hereby secured, whether then matured or to mature in the future, and in such manner as Beneficiary may elect, or Beneficiary may permit Grantors to use said proceeds to repair or replace all improvements damaged or destroyed and covered by said policy.

That in the event Grantors shall fail to keep the improvements on the property hereby conveyed in good repair and condition, or to pay promptly when due all taxes and assessments, as aforesaid, or to preserve the prior lien of this Deed of Trust on said property, or to keep the buildings and improvements insured, as aforesaid, or to deliver the policy, or policies, of insurance or the renewal thereof to Beneficiary, as aforesaid, then Beneficiary may, at his option, but without being required to do so, make such repairs, pay such taxes and assessments, purchase any tax title thereon, remove any prior liens, and prosecute or defend any suits in relation to the preservation of the prior lien of this Deed of Trust on said property, or insure and keep insured the improvements thereon in an amount not to exceed that above stipulated; that any sums which may be so paid out by Beneficiary and all sums paid for insurance premiums, as aforesaid, including the costs, expenses and Attorney's fees paid in any suit affecting said property when necessary to protect the lien hereof shall bear interest from the dates of such payments at ten per cent (10%) per annum, and shall be paid by Grantors to Beneficiary upon demand, at the same place at which the above described note is payable, and shall be deemed a part of the debt hereby secured and recoverable as such in all respects.

FIGURE 9-2 (*continued*).

POWER OF SALE

That in the event of default in the payment of any installment, principal or interest, of the note hereby secured, in accordance with the terms thereof, or of a breach of any of the covenants herein contained to be performed by Grantors, then and in any of such events Beneficiary may elect, Grantors hereby expressly waiving presentment and demand for payment, to declare the entire principal indebtedness hereby secured with all interest accrued thereon and all other sums hereby secured immediately due and payable, and in the event of default in the payment of said indebtedness when due or declared due, it shall thereupon, or at any time thereafter, be the duty of the Trustee, or his successor or substitute as hereinafter provided, at the request of Beneficiary (which request is hereby conclusively presumed), to enforce this trust; and after advertising the time, place and terms of the sale of the above described and conveyed property, then subject to the lien hereof, for at least twenty-one (21) days preceding the date of sale by posting written or printed notice thereof at the Courthouse door of the county where said real property is situated, which notice may be posted by the Trustee acting, or by any person acting for him, and the Beneficiary (the holder of the indebtedness secured hereby) has, at least twenty-one (21) days preceding the date of sale, served written or printed notice of the proposed sale by certified mail on each debtor obligated to pay the indebtedness secured by this Deed of Trust according to the records of Beneficiary, by the deposit of such notice, enclosed in a postpaid wrapper, properly addressed to such debtor at debtor's most recent address as shown by the records of Beneficiary, in a post office or official depository under the care and custody of the United States Postal Service, the Trustee shall sell the above described property, then subject to the lien hereof, at public auction in accordance with such notice at the Courthouse door of said county where such real property is situated (provided where said real property is situated in more than one county, the notice to be posted as herein provided shall be posted at the Courthouse door of each of such counties where said real property is situated, and said above described and conveyed property may be sold at the Courthouse door of any one of such counties, and the notices so posted shall designate the county where the property will be sold), on the first Tuesday in any month between the hours of ten o'clock A.M. and four o'clock P.M., to the highest bidder for cash, selling all of the property as an entirety or in such parcels as the Trustee acting may elect, and make due conveyance to the Purchaser or Purchasers, with general warranty binding Grantors, their heirs and assigns; and out of the money arising from such sale, the Trustee acting shall pay first, all the expenses of advertising the sale and making the conveyance, including a commission of five per cent (5%) to himself, which commission shall be due and owing in addition to the Attorney's fees provided for in said note, and then to Beneficiary the full amount of principal, interest, Attorney's fees and other charges due and unpaid on said note and all other indebtedness secured hereby, rendering the balance of the sales price, if any, to Grantors, their heirs or assigns; and the recitals in the conveyance to the Purchaser or Purchasers shall be full and conclusive evidence of the truth of the matters therein stated, and all prerequisites to said sale shall be presumed to have been performed, and such sale and conveyance shall be conclusive against Grantors, their heirs and assigns.

It is agreed that in the event a foreclosure hereunder should be commenced by the Trustee, or his substitute or successor, Beneficiary may at any time before the sale of said property direct the said Trustee to abandon the sale, and may then institute suit for the collection of said note, and for the foreclosure of this Deed of Trust lien; it is further agreed that if Beneficiary should institute a suit for the collection thereof, and for a foreclosure of this Deed of Trust lien, that he may at any time before the entry of a final judgment in said suit dismiss the same, and require the Trustee, his substitute or successor to sell the property in accordance with the provisions of this Deed of Trust.

Beneficiary shall have the right to purchase at any sale of the property, being the highest bidder and to have the amount for which such property is sold credited on the debt then owing.

Beneficiary in any event is hereby authorized to appoint a substitute trustee, or a successor trustee, to act instead of the Trustee named herein without other formality than the designation in writing of a substitute or successor trustee; and the authority hereby conferred shall extend to the appointment of other successor and substitute trustees successively until the indebtedness hereby secured has been paid in full, or until said property is sold hereunder, and each substitute and successor trustee shall succeed to all of the rights and powers of the original trustee named herein.

In the event any sale is made of the above described property, or any portion thereof, under the terms of this Deed of Trust, Grantors, their heirs and assigns, shall forthwith upon the making of such sale surrender and deliver possession of the property so sold to the Purchaser at such sale, and in the event of their failure to do so they shall thereupon from and after the making of such sale be and continue as tenants at will of such Purchaser, and in the event of their failure to surrender possession of said

FIGURE 9-2 (*continued*).

property upon demand, the Purchaser, his heirs or assigns, shall be entitled to institute and maintain an action for forcible detainer of said property in the Justice of the Peace Court in the Justice Precinct in which such property, or any part thereof, is situated.

It is agreed that the lien hereby created shall take precedence over and be a prior lien to any other lien of any character whether vendor's, materialmen's or mechanic's lien hereafter created on the above described property, and in the event the proceeds of the indebtedness secured hereby as set forth herein are used to pay off and satisfy any liens heretofore existing on said property, then Beneficiary is, and shall be, subrogated to all of the rights, liens and remedies of the holders of the indebtedness so paid.

It is further agreed that if Grantors, their heirs or assigns, while the owner of the hereinabove described property, should commit an act of bankruptcy, or authorize the filing of a voluntary petition in bankruptcy, or should an act of bankruptcy be committed and involuntary proceedings instituted or threatened, or should the property hereinabove described be taken over by a Receiver for Grantors, their heirs or assigns, the note hereinabove described shall, at the option of Beneficiary, immediately become due and payable, and the acting Trustee may then proceed to sell the same under the provisions of this Deed of Trust.

ASSIGNMENT OF RENTALS

As further security for the payment of the hereinabove described indebtedness, Grantors hereby transfer, assign, and convey unto Beneficiary all rents issuing or to hereafter issue from said real property, and in the event of any default in the payment of said note or hereunder, Beneficiary, his agent or representative, is hereby authorized, at his option, to collect said rents, or if such property is vacant to rent the same and collect the rents, and apply the same, less the reasonable costs and expenses of collection thereof, to the payment of said indebtedness, whether then matured or to mature in the future, and in such manner as Beneficiary may elect. The collection of said rents by Beneficiary shall not constitute a waiver of his right to accelerate the maturity of said indebtedness nor of his right to proceed with the enforcement of this Deed of Trust.

It is agreed that an extension, or extensions, may be made of the time of payment of all, or any part, of the indebtedness secured hereby, and that any part of the above described real property may be released from this lien without altering or affecting the priority of the lien created by this Deed of Trust in favor of any junior encumbrancer, mortgagee or purchaser, or any person acquiring an interest in the property hereby conveyed, or any part thereof; it being the intention of the parties hereto to preserve this lien on the property herein described and all improvements thereon, and that may be hereafter constructed thereon, first and superior to any liens that may be placed thereon, or that may be fixed, given or imposed by law thereon after the execution of this instrument notwithstanding any such extension of the time of payment, or the release of a portion of said property from this lien.

In the event any portion of the indebtedness hereinabove described cannot be lawfully secured by this Deed of Trust lien on said real property, it is agreed that the first payments made on said indebtedness shall be applied to the discharge of that portion of said indebtedness.

CONDEMNATION

Beneficiary shall be entitled to receive any and all sums which may become payable to Grantors for the condemnation of the hereinabove described real property, or any part thereof, for public or quasi-public use, or by virtue of private sale in lieu thereof, and any sums which may be awarded or become payable to Grantors for damages caused by public works or construction on or near the said property. All such sums are hereby assigned to Beneficiary, who may, after deducting therefrom all expenses actually incurred, including attorney's fees, release same to Grantors or apply the same to the reduction of the indebtedness hereby secured, whether then matured or to mature in the future, or on any money obligation hereunder, as and in such manner as Beneficiary may elect. Beneficiary shall not be, in any event or circumstances, liable or responsible for failure to collect, or exercise diligence in the collection of, any such sums.

Nothing herein or in said note contained shall ever entitle Beneficiary, upon the arising of any contingency whatsoever, to receive or collect interest in excess of the highest rate allowed by the laws of the State of Texas on the principal indebtedness hereby secured or on any money obligation hereunder and in no event shall Grantors be obligated to pay interest thereon in excess of such rate.

FIGURE 9-2 (*continued*).

If this Deed of Trust is executed by only one person or by a corporation the plural reference to Grantors shall be held to include the singular and all of the covenants and agreements herein undertaken to be performed by and the rights conferred upon the respective Grantors named herein, shall be binding upon and inure to the benefit of not only said parties respectively but also their respective heirs, executors, administrators, grantees, successors and assigns.

Grantors expressly represent that this Deed of Trust and the Note hereby secured are given for the following purpose, to-wit:

PARTIAL RELEASE

It is further agreed that prior to any default in the payment of the hereinabove mentioned note, Grantors, their successors or assigns, shall be entitled to have released from the liens securing such note one or more contiguous parcels, upon payment to holder of $5,000 per parcel, which amount shall be applied toward the payment of principal last falling due on such note.

CALL CLAUSE

In the event of any sale, either judicial or voluntary, of the property above described, or any part thereof, Beneficiary shall have the right, at Beneficiary's option, to declare the entire indebtedness hereby secured due and payable.

NO PERSONAL LIABILITY

Notwithstanding anything to the contrary contained herein, or in the note secured hereby, Grantor shall in no event be liable for a money judgment in the event of a default hereunder or under such note, it being understood that the holders of such note may look only to the security provided by this Deed of Trust to enforce payment of the indebtedness.

EXECUTED this 30th day of February A. D. 1994

N. Debted

May B. Debted

FIGURE 9-2 (*continued*).

(Acknowledgment)

THE STATE OF TEXAS }
COUNTY OF }

Before me, the undersigned authority, on this day personally appeared

known to me to be the person............whose name.................subscribed to the foregoing instrument, and acknowledged to me that .... he........ executed the same for the purposes and consideration therein expressed.

Given under my hand and seal of office on this the day of , A. D. 19

....
Notary Public in and for County, Texas.

(Acknowledgment)

THE STATE OF TEXAS }
COUNTY OF }

Before me, the undersigned authority, on this day personally appeared

known to me to be the person............ whose name ....subscribed to the foregoing instrument, and acknowledged to me that ....he .... executed the same for the purposes and consideration therein expressed.

Given under my hand and seal of office on this the day of , A. D. 19

....
Notary Public in and for County, Texas.

FIGURE 9-2 (*continued*).

DEED OF TRUST

TO

TRUSTEE FOR

PREPARED IN THE LAW OFFICE OF:

PLEASE RETURN TO:

(Corporate acknowledgment)

THE STATE OF TEXAS }
COUNTY OF }

Before me, the undersigned authority, on this day personally appeared ,
of ,
a corporation, known to me to be the person whose name is subscribed to the foregoing instrument, and acknowledged to me that he executed the same for the purposes and consideration therein expressed, in the capacity therein stated and as the act and deed of said corporation.

Given under my hand and seal of office on this the 30th day of February , A. D. 1994

Notary Public in and for County, Texas.

FIGURE 9-2 *(continued)*.

terms, renders the conveyance to the trustee null and void and of no further force and effect. A complete release of the lien holder's interest is normally effected by filing a release of lien, a copy of which is shown in Figure 9-3. The illustration in Figure 9-4 may help orient your thoughts about the deed of trust, the release of lien, and the parties' interrelationships in the standard deed of trust situation.

Requirements. There are basically five requirements that make a deed of trust legally enforceable in Texas. If you refer to the deed of trust form in Figure 9-2, it may be helpful in showing how these five requirements coordinate with each other to create the enforceable obligation. The individual clauses are discussed below.

Granting Clause and Property Description. The granting clause and property description define the grantor (this is the grantee of the deed—the purchaser of the property). The clause effects a conveyance, in trust, of the therein described real estate. As stated previously, true legal title does not pass to the trustee, only title sufficient enough to create an interest in the property, in the event of a default. Note that in Figure 9-2 there is both a legal description of the real estate itself as well as a description of some personal property that is to pass with that real estate. With this type of legal description, the deed of trust form can be used not only as a mortgage that secures the debt with the real property but also as a security agreement and financing statement for personal items to perfect the mortgagee's interest in the personalty. These types of provisions are normally used in loans when the personalty is to be secured by the deed of trust as part of the entire financing agreement. This is often done when purchasing income-producing property or when constructing new improvements. Please recall that some of these conflicts were discussed in Chapter 4, Fixtures and Easements.

Habendum and Warranty Clause. The habendum and warranty clause is very similar to that of a deed, as discussed in Chapter 7, and basically binds the grantor to the warranty, so that his legal title in the real estate is good and sufficient.

Trust Clause. The trust clause specifically sets out that this conveyance is made *in trust* to secure the payment of the promissory note. This limits the title that is being passed and clearly sets out the trust relationship and reinforces the limited nature of the conveyance generally.

Note and Debt Secured. The note and debt provision indicates the amount of the note that is being secured and defines the beneficiary (this is the lender or mortgagee). The terms of the note may be specified in this

NOTICE Prepared by the State Bar of Texas for use by Lawyers only. 9-73–10M
To select the proper form, fill in blank spaces, strike out form provisions or insert special terms constitutes the practice of law. No "standard form" can meet all requirements.

RELEASE OF LIEN

THE STATE OF TEXAS
COUNTY OF HARRIS } KNOW ALL MEN BY THESE PRESENTS:

THAT the undersigned, of the County of Harris, and State of Texas, the legal and equitable owner and holder of that one certain promissory note in the original principal sum of FIFTY THOUSAND AND NO/100------------------------------------- Dollars ($50,000.00) dated February 30, 1994, executed by N. Debted and wife, May B. Debted, payable to the order of Friendly Lender Savings and Loan Association, more fully described in a deed of trust, duly recorded under Clerk's File No. Q123456 and Film Code No. 45880618 of the Official Public Records of Real Property of Harris County, Texas; said note being secured by said deed of trust lien against the following described property, to-wit:

Lot 1, Block 1, Shakey Acres Subdivision,
Harris County, Texas, as shown of Record
at Volume 7, Page 3 of the Map Records of
Harris County, Texas.

FIGURE 9-3.

for and in consideration of the full and final payment of all indebtedness secured by the aforesaid lien or liens, the receipt of which is hereby acknowledged, has released and discharged, and by these presents hereby releases and discharges, the above described property from all liens held by the undersigned securing said indebtedness.

EXECUTED this 4th day of April, A. D. 1994.

Friendly Lender Savings and Loan Association

By: ______________________________

Wynn Friendly, President

FIGURE 9-3 (*continued*).

(Acknowledgment)

THE STATE OF TEXAS }
COUNTY OF }

Before me, the undersigned authority, on this day personally appeared

known to me to be the person........... whose name.................... subscribed to the foregoing instrument, and acknowledged to me that........ he ...... executed the same for the purposes and consideration therein expressed.

Given under my hand and seal of office on this the day of , A. D. 19

....
Notary Public in and for County, Texas.

(Acknowledgment)

THE STATE OF TEXAS }
COUNTY OF }

Before me, the undersigned authority, on this day personally appeared

known to me to be the person .... whose name...................... subscribed to the foregoing instrument, and acknowledged to me that........ he ....executed the same for the purposes and consideration therein expressed.

Given under my hand and seal of office on this the day of , A. D. 19

....
Notary Public in and for County, Texas.

FIGURE 9-3 (*continued*).

RELEASE OF LIEN

TO

PREPARED IN THE LAW OFFICE OF:

PLEASE RETURN TO:

(Corporate acknowledgment)

THE STATE OF TEXAS }
COUNTY OF }

Before me, the undersigned authority, on this day personally appeared ,
of ,
a corporation, known to me to be the person whose name is subscribed to the foregoing instrument, and acknowledged to me that he executed the same for the purposes and consideration therein expressed, in the capacity therein stated and as the act and deed of said corporation.

Given under my hand and seal of office on this the day of , A. D. 19

Notary Public in and for County, Texas.

FIGURE 9-3 *(continued)*.

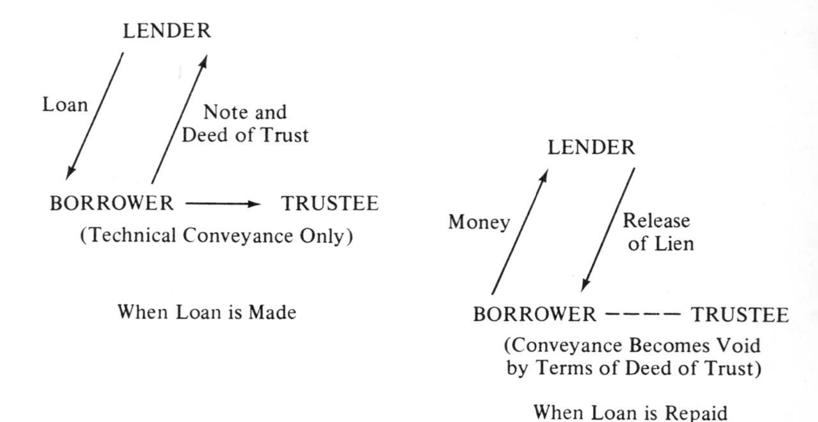

FIGURE 9-4. Typical Texas deed of trust transaction.

provision. However, since the terms of an individual's payments may be quite lengthy and confidential, the words "as therein provided" are often used as sufficient reference to the terms of the note.

Power of Sale. The power of sale clause is the specific provision that makes the deed of trust mortgage unique when compared with other types of mortgages. The clause provides for an out-of-court foreclosure in the event of a default in the payments of the real estate lien note. The power of sale provision, of course, must comply with the Texas law of executions, pursuant to sales under a deed of trust, as set out below:

Art. 3810. Sales under deed of trust

All sales of real estate made under powers conferred by any deed of trust or other contract lien shall be made in the county in which such real estate is situated. Where such real estate is situated in more than one county then notices as herein provided shall be given in both or all of such counties, and the real estate may be sold in either county, and such notice shall designate the county where the real estate will be sold. Notice of such proposed sale shall be given by posting written notice thereof at least 21 days preceding the date of the sale at the courthouse door of the county in which the sale is to be made, and if the real estate is in more than one county, one notice shall be posted at the courthouse door of each county in which the real estate is situated.

In addition, the holder of the debt to which the power is related shall at least 21 days preceding the date of sale serve written notice of the proposed sale by certified mail on each debtor obligated to pay such debt according to the records of such holder. Service of such notice shall be completed upon deposit of the notice, enclosed in a postpaid wrapper, properly addressed to such debtor at the most recent address as shown by the records of the holder of the debt, in a post office or official depository under the care and custody of the United States Postal Service. The affidavit of any person having knowledge of the facts to the effect that such service was completed shall be prima facie evidence of the fact of service. Such sale shall be made at public vendue between the hours of 10:00 A.M. and 4:00 P.M. of the first Tuesday in any month.

The power of sale clause generally provides that in the event of default in the payment of the real estate lien note, the trustee, upon request, will post a notice at the courthouse door (there are generally bulletin boards located near the courthouse door for such purposes), informing the public of the sale of the property referenced in the deed of trust. A copy of this notice must be sent by certified mail to the last known address of the grantor in the deed of trust so that he will have notice that such sale is to take place. The notice must be posted at least 21 days preceding the date of the sale. The date of the sale, pursuant to the power of sale clause, is always on the first Tuesday of the month following the 21-day notice posted at the courthouse door. Then, believe it or not, on the first Tuesday of the following month after the notice has been posted, the trustee holds a public sale of the real estate on the courthouse steps. Anyone is allowed to purchase at the sale, including the grantor (defaulting borrower) or the lender, but the purchase price must be paid in cash, unless otherwise agreed to. The sale is held between 10:00 A.M. and 4:00 P.M. and at any courthouse door, not necessarily the front door, *Micrea, Inc.* v. *Eureka Life Ins. Co. of America*, 534 S.W.2d 348 (Tex. Civ. App.—Ft. Worth, 1976). If there is an intention to buy property at a foreclosure sale, it is suggested that one find the trustee (he can hold the sale at any time between the hours of 10:00 A.M. and 4:00 P.M.) to determine how much he will accept for the property, and at which courthouse door (if more than one) he will be holding the sale. However, once these facts have been determined, and the buyer produces cash to the trustee, the conveyance is made to the subsequent purchaser by use of a trustee's deed, which passes full legal title to the purchaser.

Lien Priority

When a foreclosure sale of property secured by a deed of trust takes place, all other lien interests that are inferior to the deed of trust are "wiped out," and the inferior lien holders, as well as the grantor, lose all of their interest in the property. If there is a prior lien holder's interest, superior to the deed of trust under which the foreclosure sale took place, the property is bought subject to that prior security interest. In that situation, the purchaser buying the property obtains the right to make the payments due on the prior existing indebtedness.

Lien priorities, in any situation, follow what has been called the "barber shop rule"; that is, the first in time gets priority. The first lien in time is generally the lien created by the purchase money mortgage, usually created by the first lien deed of trust. The second lien in time (which may be a second lien note to acquire funds to aid in purchasing the property, or perhaps to construct additional improvements on the property), then, takes a second position in priority, and so forth.

If the deed of trust foreclosure is a second lien deed of trust, and a first lien deed of trust is outstanding, the purchaser at the second lien foreclosure sale also purchases what is termed an *equity of redemption*, which gives the purchaser the right to redeem (make payments on, or pay off) the first lien note. He is considered to be *subrogated* (put in the place of) the original grantor on said second lien deed of trust. The purchaser, therefore, acquires good title and the right to pay off the previously existing note. In the foreclosure process, the purchaser is said to *redeem up*, and the trustee *forecloses down*, indicating that all the inferior interests are dissolved, and the purchaser acquires the right to pay off the superior interests.

Additional Deed of Trust Provisions

It is often said that lenders operate under what iscalled the "golden rule"; that is, they have the gold, so they make the rules! Therefore, one often finds that there are additional provisions in a deed of trust that are added to protect the lender's interest. The lender needs to be sure that no additional conflicting claims may arise in his security, and that the real estate is kept in good enough condition so that the value of his security in the real estate is not impaired. Provisions included in the deed of trust instrument in Figure 9-2 include the requirements for payment of all taxes and assessments, requirements to keep the property adequately insured, provisions for a substitute trustee, and provisions for bankruptcy. Other common provisions that one may encounter while reading various deed of trust instruments are shown in the example in Figure 9-2 and include the following:

Assignment of Rentals. Assignment of rentals normally assures the lender that in the event that the subject property is leased or rented, he is entitled to the rentals obtained from that property if he so requests.

Condemnation. Condemnation generally provides that upon condemnation, all the proceeds of said condemnation are to go to the lender and are to be applied to the unpaid balance of the note, since the lender has provided the money to purchase the property. If any part of the property is lost by means of condemnation or other damage claim, the lender deserves to get the proceeds instead of the owner of the property.

Partial Releases. Partial releases provide that certain elements of the property may be released without releasing the entire property. These releases are very common when one has a deed of trust against a very large piece of property and wishes to construct improvements on only a portion of the property at a time.

Call Clause. The call clause normally provides that the grantor of the deed of trust may not convey the property to another party without paying off the note. This precludes any chance of the grantor selling the real estate on an assumption of the mortgage without the prior written consent of the mortgagee. Provisions like this protect the mortgagee from having a noncredit-worthy purchaser assume the responsibilities of the individual to whom the loan was made. Although there has been some question as to the legality of this particular clause, it has been consistently upheld as being a valid method of protecting the mortgagee's interest, *Ashley* v. *Leitch*, 533 S.W.2d 831 (Tex. Civ. App.—Eastland, 1975).

No Personal Liability. On occasion, a purchaser is fortunate enough to have a lender who is so confident as to the value of the real estate that he will provide that in the event of default he will not seek a money judgment against the purchaser, but will limit his remedies to foreclosing and retaking possession of the real estate.

Although there are many variations of each of the foregoing clauses, the ones shown in Figure 9-2 are illustrative of clauses of this type generally found in deeds of trust.

Why Have Two Instruments?

There is one question that is anticipated when discussing mortgages, and that is, Why are there two separate instruments—the promissory note and the deed of trust? The reason for this is fairly simple but is often overlooked. The promissory note, being the actual promise to pay, is considered a negotiable instrument. This means that the promissory note, similar to a bank draft, can be endorsed on the back and can be sold to an investor. This is a very common practice in the mortgage business where mortgage companies will often sell millions of dollars in loans using the promissory note as the primary instrument of transfer.

The deed of trust, on the other hand, is a mortgage that evidences a lien interest against the real estate. This is normally recorded to reflect the lender's interest in the real estate and becomes part of the official public records of the county in which the property is located.

Both instruments serve entirely different functions, but are dependent on each other to effect a sufficient promise to pay and perfect a lien interest in real estate.

Although the deed of trust per se may be a rather difficult concept to grasp, there is one misunderstanding that always seems to creep into the student's mind unnoticed. This is the concept that the deed of trust is a deed. The deed of trust *is not a deed—it is a mortgage*.

Other Types of Mortgages

Although the deed of trust is by far the most commonly used mortgage instrument in Texas, there are a number of other types of mortgages and mortgaging techniques. Some of these mortgages are different types of mortgage instruments altogether (they contain no power of sale clause), whereas others may be deeds of trust with special provisions to achieve a particular purpose.

Absolute Deed as a Mortgage

There are times when a lender will request that the mortgagor (borrower-purchaser) give the lender a deed to the property as a method of mortgaging. Although a transfer of legal title does take effect, the parties intend the transfer to be security for a loan rather than to effect a complete sale of the property. When such a situation exists, one normally finds that the grantor of the real estate retains possession of the premises, and that the market value of the property is in excess of the consideration given for the transfer. This is similar to mortgages in title theory states (where the lender is determined to have legal title and the owner merely a lien on the real estate). In such a case, when the property is fully paid for, the mortgagee executes another deed, sometimes called a *release deed*, to reconvey the property back to the original owner. When an absolute deed is used as a mortgage, it is a necessity that parol evidence be allowed to show the clear import of the deed, even though the deed may be clear and unambiguous on its face. This is one of the few exceptions to the parol evidence rule discussed in Chapter 6.

Sale Lease-back

The instruments used for a mortgage in the sale lease-back method normally include a deed and a lease; and, if the sale is not for cash, there may also be the execution of a deed of trust. In a typical sale lease-back situation, the owner of a property will sell the property for cash to an investor, and then simultaneously execute a lease to the purchaser for the use and occupancy of the premises. This guarantees a definite rate of return on an investment for the purchaser. For instance, Manufacturing Company, Inc. may sell its plant, improvements, and other facilities to B. T. Operator for a cash payment of $100,000. At the same time the deed is signed, Manufacturing Company, Inc. executes a lease, as tenant, with B. T. Operator, as landlord, at a rate of \$11,000 per year (which guarantees an 11% return cash-on-cash investment for B. T. Operator). Figure 9-5 graphically illustrates this transaction.

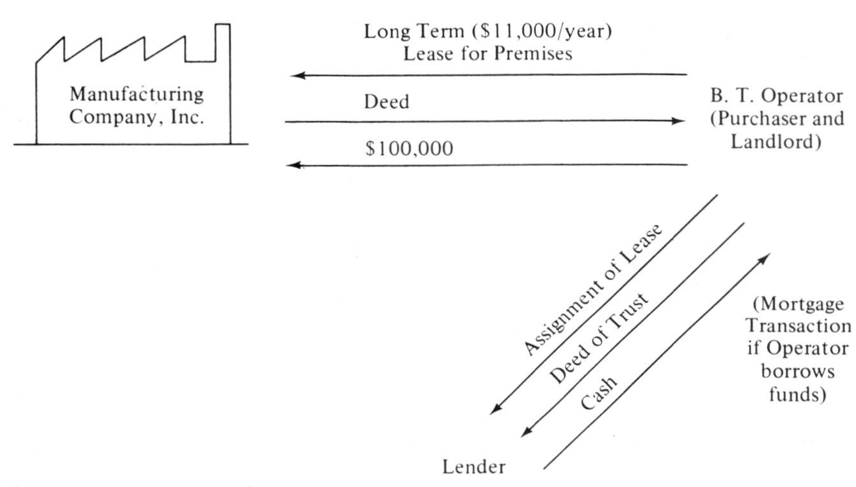

FIGURE 9-5.

Advantages. In the above transaction, Manufacturing Company, Inc. obtains a free and clear \$100,000 in working capital, which it can use to expand, make capital improvements, and streamline its manufacturing efficiency, rather than invest in real estate. Most companies would like to utilize their money in income-producing manufacturing methods rather than as a capital investment in nonincome-producing real estate. To make the investment more attractive, there may be a provision in the lease for an option to buy the property back for \$1 at the end of 30 years (the regular amortization period of a loan).

The sale lease-back transaction benefits the purchaser tremendously because he is allowed to have a definite return on his investment. He can also deduct the depreciation for the improvements on the property. If he has borrowed the money to finance the transaction, he can further deduct the interest paid on his loan. This offers a very good tax advantage for the purchaser.

The advantages for the seller, Manufacturing Company, Inc., are that it can pay a tax-deductible lease payment every month, and it receives a large influx of working capital (which is normally utilized to improve its monthly cash flow). It may also get a capital gain tax treatment upon the sale of the property, and have an excellent chance to repurchase the property if repurchase options are included in the lease.

Disadvantages. Although the above sale lease-back example may indicate to the reader that there is a perfect relationship where everyone appears to come out ahead, it must be remembered that there are also disadvantages to this type of arrangement. The primary disadvantage is the possible adverse position of the Internal Revenue Service. If the transaction is not carefully done, or if there is too close a relationship between the buyer and the seller, the IRS may choose to treat the transaction as a loan rather than as a true sale. If such is the case, the tax breaks are dramatically different. In determining how to treat the sale lease-back transaction, the IRS normally looks to the intention of the parties surrounding the circumstances of the lease agreement itself, whether or not the option to repurchase is legitimate or appears to be a sham, whether or not the price of the sale is related to fair market value, and the appropriateness and size of the rental payments.

If done properly, the sale lease-back can be a tremendous benefit as a mortgage instrument, both for the purchaser and the seller, if they can avoid the pitfalls of the IRS code, and if the transaction is done in good faith and is not a sham.

Installment Sale Contracts

An installment sale contract is a very effective means of providing a mortgage, particularly for low income transactions. An installment sale contract provides for seller financing pursuant to the terms of the installment land contract. Since the seller is financing the sale himself, he can establish his own criteria as to the credit-worthiness and risks involved in evaluating the purchaser. The purchaser buys the house in accordance with the installment land contract, usually for a small down payment, and when he has completed the full number of monthly payments, normally for a term of years, the seller will convey the property to the purchaser by execution of a deed.

As discussed in Chapter 6, there is no concern of foreclosure—the contract is simply forfeited and rescinded in the event of default. Although there are risks involved for the purchaser, if the seller operates in good faith, it provides a very efficient means by which lower income families can buy housing without having to qualify for a loan or go through the red tape of mortgage insurance and financial statements, or having to sit across from the glare of a suspicious lender's investigation. The contract document itself is the mortgage instrument and may contain many onerous provisions. Again, the "golden rule" applies.

There are also additional tax breaks for the seller in that he can use the installment sale method of reporting his income over a period of years, rather than taking all of his profit on the sale of the house in his first year. However, there are pitfalls, in that the Internal Revenue Service may consider the installment land contract to be a lease rather than an actual sale. The seller would then have to declare the income as normal income rather than as capital gains. As in the sale lease-back situation, great care should be taken to be sure that the transaction is truly bona fide and not a sham.

Construction Mortgages

A construction mortgage normally utilizes the standard deed of trust form, but it contains special provisions: (1) because of the short-term nature of this type of mortgage, (2) because of the requirements of partial advances while construction is in progress, and (3) because of the incorporation of certain items of personalty into the real estate in which the lender wants to maintain prior security interest.

Mortgages of this type are often set up as "tri-party agreements"—where the permanent lender (mortgagee), the construction lender, and the mortgagor enter into an agreement by which the permanent lender promises to pay off the construction lender's mortgage upon completion of the construction to the permanent mortgagee's satisfaction. When the construction lender is paid by the permanent lender, the mortgagor then begins making his monthly payments to the permanent lender. The interest rate on construction loans is generally somewhat higher than that of the permanent loan, and the construction lender is normally a local financing institution that can personally inspect the construction on a daily basis, whereas the permanent lender is often located in another state and is not staffed to maintain this type of inspection policy on a routine day-to-day basis.

Special provisions that one may find in a construction loan deed of trust normally include what we call a *dragnet clause* or *future advance clause*, which secures all sums loaned or advanced by the beneficiary (construction lender) to the account of the mortgagor. The deed of trust may also include an *additional property clause* which provides for any property attached at a later date to the premises to also be secured by the deed of trust. However, it should be pointed out that even if there are additional property clauses contained in the construction deed of trust, a mechanic's and materialman's lien is superior to that deed of trust if the additional property placed there by that mechanic or materialman can be removed without material injury to the property, *First National Bank in Dallas* v. *Whirlpool Corporation*, 502 S.W.2d 185 (Tex. 1974).

Assumptions and Subject To

There are two methods by which property can be conveyed without having to change the terms of, or pay off, the original mortgage instrument. This is accomplished through the means of an *assumption* of the existing indebtedness, or buying the property *subject to* the existing indebtedness.

Assumption

In the *assumption* loan situation, the grantee of the property becomes primarily liable on the note and deed of trust, whereas the grantor in the situation operates as a surety in the event the note is not paid in full. In this situation, if there is a default on the note, the lender must pursue his remedy against the grantee first; but if the grantee cannot satisfy the indebtedness, the lender has the remedy of also pursuing a cause of action against the original grantor, who is also the original signatory party on the note and deed of trust. It is sometimes a surprise to the grantor (when he sells his house on an assumption basis) that if there is a subsequent default, he may still be liable on that note at some later date. Figure 9-6 graphically shows how the assumption procedure takes effect.

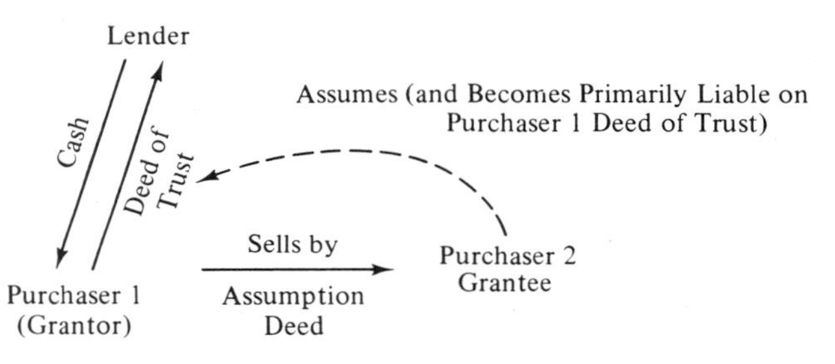

FIGURE 9-6.

Subject To

When property is sold *subject to* an existing mortgage, the grantee does not become obligated to pay the mortgage but merely has the option of paying that mortgage if he so chooses.

In the "subject to" situation, the grantor still remains primarily liable on the note, and the grantee has no obligation at all to the original lender. Figure 9-7 graphically illustrates how the "subject to" mortgage situation takes effect.

If there is a call clause in the original deed of trust, the assumption situation normally cannot take effect until the subsequent grantee has been approved by the lender. In the "subject to" situation, however, since the original mortgagor remains primarily liable on the note, there is some question as to whether or not it requires the approval of the lender before such a conveyance can take place. After all, his security is not impaired because the original mortgagor is still personally liable on the note, whereas this fact does not exist in the assumption situation.

Wrap-Around Mortgage

Commercial transactions and land syndication schemes have made widespread use of the "subject to" mortgage, more commonly called a *wrap-*

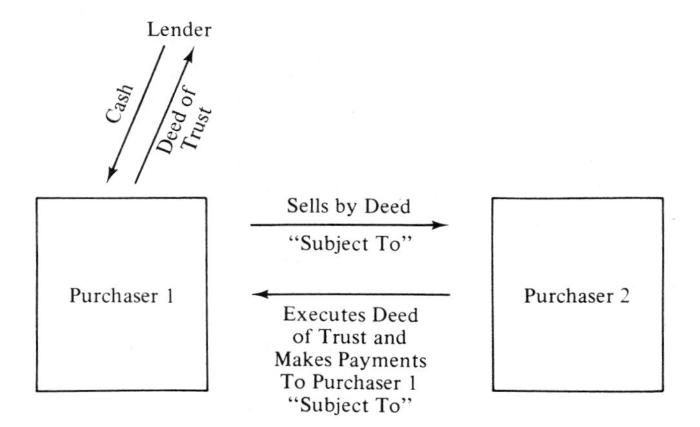

FIGURE 9-7.

around mortgage. The property is conveyed by a deed "subject to" the existing mortgage, and, of course, the second mortgage between the grantor and grantee is signed by the grantee "subject to," but not promising to pay, the prior existing mortgage. The wrap-around mortgage has basically the same effect as creating a second lien deed of trust, except that the obligation of the grantee is to pay the entire mortgage amount to the grantor, and the grantor, in turn, pays the lender (first lien holder).

This type of financing became so common during the rampant real estate syndication craze in the early 1970s that it was not uncommon to see extended chains of wrap-around mortgages, similar to the illustration in Figure 9-8.

Advantages. The wrap-around mortgage provides advantages to both the buyer and the seller similar to those of installment land contracts. Since the grantor is selling to the grantee subject to the existing mortgage, there is

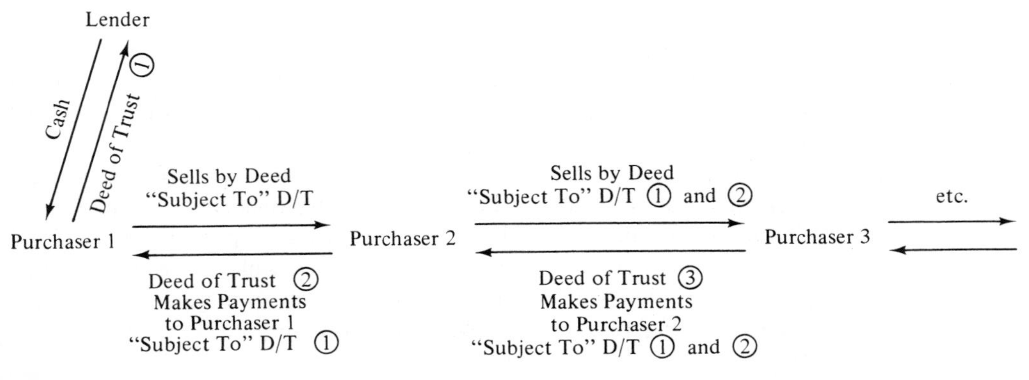

FIGURE 9-8.

normally no outside financing that has to be obtained by the grantee, and this results in the basic seller-financing situation. Since the grantee pays the grantor, this method also avoids the risks of the more typical second lien situation since the grantee must pay the grantor directly. The grantor, then, is always sure that the first lien mortgage payments are being made. If there is a default in the initial payment, the grantor is immediately on notice and can exercise his right of foreclosure to reinstate his interest in the property before there is a default to the primary lender. The terms on a sale of this kind are usually more attractive than sales utilizing more conventional financing techniques. The sales price is normally higher; there is a higher interest yield; and the seller can normally take an installment sale advantage as a tax benefit.

The buyer's advantage generally centers around the fact that he deals with the seller and lender directly, so he can get more attractive terms (interest only, or perhaps longer terms), and there are no credit requirements or loans to apply for.

Disadvantages. The disadvantages to a wrap-around note and mortgage are basically that the buyer runs the risk that the seller may not pay off the prior lien note(s) and may default. Thus, even though the purchaser has paid his note, he may lose his interest when the prior lender forecloses. This problem can sometimes be overcome by the use of a third-party escrow agent. In that event, the grantee pays the escrow agent, and the escrow agent pays part of the payment to the lender and the remainder to the grantor. This assures the subsequent grantee that all obligations pursuant to the prior existing mortgages have been met.

There has been little case law to date and little information as to the effect that the court will give these mortgages. Each grantee may also find additional liability as he changes his status from grantee to grantor because he may undertake the additional obligation to assure his grantee that the prior mortgage payments are made, *Newsom* v. *Starkey*, 541 S.W.2d 468 (Tex. Civ. App.—Dallas, 1976).

Another recent Texas case to construe wrap-around mortgages is *Tanner Development Co.* v. *Ferguson* 561 S.W.2d 777 (Tex. 1977). This case was the first such case to construe wrap-around mortgages in a usury context. This will be described in greater detail in Chapter 10, Interest and Finance Charge.

The wrap-around mortgage has proved to be a very effective tool for creating installment sales and for obtaining easy financing. For investment groups, it has not been at all uncommon for the property to be conveyed using the wrap-around mortgage several times without the primary lien holder ever being paid in full. The more this type of mortgage is used in a sequencing chain of sales and purchases, however, the bigger the risks the subsequent grantees are forced to take.

SUMMARY

The most common mortgage procedure in Texas requires the execution of two instruments: the promissory note and the deed of trust. The promissory note is the purchaser's promise to pay, and the deed of trust is the mortgage instrument most commonly used in Texas. The deed of trust is basically a mortgage with a power-of-sale provision. The power-of-sale provision allows the lending institution, by request to the trustee, to sell the property at public auction in the event of a default by the mortgagor (borrower). Other types of mortgages in Texas include the absolute deed as a mortgage, the sale lease-back, installment land contracts, and construction mortgages.

There are two methods by which property can be conveyed without paying off the original mortgage. One is selling the property on an "assumption," where the subsequent purchaser assumes the existing mortgage. The second method is "subject to," which allows the subsequent purchaser to purchase the property without assuming the mortgage but simply acknowledging the mortgage's existence and excepting it from title. A common utilization of the "subject to" mortgage is the wraparound mortgage.

10

INTEREST AND FINANCE CHARGE

The mortgagor-mortgagee relationship is one of those last vestiges of true free enterprise. The lender (mortgagee) makes an effort to maximize the return on investment, and the borrower (mortgagor) "shops around" at various savings and loan associations, mortgage companies, and other primary lending sources in an effort to find the best rates for his loan. There has been serious effort, however, on the part of the State of Texas and the U. S. government to protect borrowers and consumers from loan sharks, "sharpies," and con artists who abuse their expertise in the mortgage and lending business. The tongue-in-cheek "golden rule" that has been referred to in the previous chapter cannot extend itself to violate public policy, to discriminate, or to promote unconstitutional objectives. In addition, the legislatures (both state and federal) have made a concerted effort to effect disclosure of loan costs (finance charges) and to limit the amount of interest that can be charged. There are few areas of lending that have been more often litigated, or that more directly affect the consumer, than the areas of interest and finance charge.

Finance Charge

To begin with, there are two distinctly separate areas of the law that deal with the cost of obtaining money: one is a state law, the other is a federal law.

Originally passed in 1968, the Federal Consumer Credit Protection Act, under Title I of the Truth-in-Lending Act (T-i-L Act), required extensive disclosure by creditors when making loans to consumers. The T-i-L Act placed the job of implementing the act on the Board of Governors of the Federal Reserve System. This was accomplished by the board's promulgation of Regulation Z (Reg. Z), an exhaustive publication dealing with almost every imaginable area of extension of credit. There are entire sets of books written on these regulations alone (not to mention the interpretative rulings, public information letters, staff opinions, or published forms), and there will be little attempt made here to explain anything but the most general applications of the T-i-L Act.

The purpose of the T-i-L Act is to assure that everyone being extended commercial credit by a creditor covered by the act is given meaningful disclosures with respect to the cost of the credit being extended. The disclosures must be clear and according to the statutory forms published pursuant to the T-i-L Act and Reg. Z.

Creditors covered by the T-i-L Act must comply fully with all Reg. Z requirements if they, in the ordinary course of business, regularly extend or arrange for the extension of consumer credit, and if the credit is payable by agreement in more than four installments (Reg. Z, Sections 226.1(a), 226.2). The disclosures must be made in terms of deferred *finance charge* and *annual percentage rate* (APR), so that the consumer will clearly understand what is being disclosed to him.

Finance charge is defined as:

> . . . the sum of all charges, payable directly or indirectly by the creditor as an incident to or as a condition of the extension of credit, whether paid or payable by the customer, the seller, or any other person on behalf of the customer to the creditor or a third party . . . [Reg. Z, Section 226.4(a)].

The APR is the rate charged (expressed as a percentage) as determined by applying the federal government's definition of *finance charge* to the federal government's definition of *consumer credit*. The APR is not *interest* as defined by Texas statute. A form Reg. Z disclosure is shown in Figure 10-1. It is important to note that there are exemptions and exclusions from the determination of finance charges as they apply to certain real estate transactions (primarily in buying homes). However, good practice favors disclosure of the items, to assure compliance. One should also note that there is no ceiling (limitations) to finance charges; the requirements only specify that the charges be disclosed.

Interest

In contrast to the federal government's determination of finance charge is the Texas definition of *interest*. *Interest* is defined as "the compensation allowed by law for the use or forbearance or detention of money" (Tex.

(CASH DISCOUNT)

THE FOLLOWING DISCLOSURES ARE MADE IN ACCORDANCE WITH THE CONSUMER CREDIT PROTECTION ACT

	Cash Purchase	Installment Purchase
1. Price of Lot	$______	$______
2. Discount for Cash Purchase	$______	$______(1)
3. Cash Price of Lot	$______	$______
4. Cash Down Payment — Date Received		
(a) $______		
(b) $______		
Total Down Payment	$______	$______
5. Unpaid Balance of Cash Price	$______	
6. Amount Financed		$______(1)
7. Discount not Allowed on Installment Purchase		$______(1)
8. Principal Amount of Note		$______(1)
9. FINANCE CHARGE:		
(a) Discount not allowed on installment purchase		$______(1)
(b) Prepaid interest from closing to the end of the month of closing at ____% annual percentage rate on principal amount of note		$______(2)
(c) Interest from the end of the month of closing to maturity at ____% annual percentage rate on principal amount of note		$______
TOTAL FINANCE CHARGE		$______(1)(2)
10. Total of Payments (Amount Financed plus Total Finance Charge)		$______(2)
11. Deferred Payment Price (Cash Price of Lot plus Total Finance Charge)		$______(2)
12. ANNUAL PERCENTAGE RATE		$______%(1)

NOTES:

(1) PURCHASER is entitled to a ____% discount from the Price of Lot if the lot is purchased for cash at the time of closing. Under the Consumer Credit Protection Act, if this Cash Discount is not taken, such amount must appear as a Finance Charge rather than in the Amount Financed. Consequently, this will cause a lower Amount Financed and a greater Finance Charge, which in turn results in a higher Annual Percentage Rate than that which is evidenced by the note that will be executed. The note that will be executed will bear interest at the annual rate of ____% on the Principal Amount of Note (Item 8).

(2) The closing has been preliminarily scheduled for ____________, 19____; in the event such closing occurs on a different date, the "Prepaid interest from closing to the end of the month of closing at ____% annual percentage rate on principal amount of note," "Total Finance Charge," "Total of Payments" and "Deferred Payment Price" shall be adjusted accordingly at the time of closing.

PURCHASER hereby agrees to pay to SELLER or its assigns at the offices of SELLER or such other place as may, from time to time, be designated by SELLER or its assigns the Total of Payments (Item 10) as follows:

$__________ [Item 9(b)] at closing (see Note (2) above) and $__________ [Items 6, 9(a) and 9(c)] in ______ equal monthly installments of $________ each, the first installment being due and payable on the first day of __________, 19____, with subsequent installments being due and payable on the first day of each month thereafter until the principal and interest are fully paid; the final payment of principal and interest, if not sooner paid, shall be due and payable on the first day of __________, 19____.

If any deficiency in the payment of any installment, as provided above, is not paid within ten (10) days after its due date the note shall, at the option of the holder thereof, become immediately due and payable without notice. All past due installments of principal and interest shall bear interest from maturity at the rate of ten percent (10%) per annum.

The transaction contemplated hereby will result in the creation and retention of a security interest in the Premises purchased hereunder in favor of SELLER or its assigns, to wit: The Principal Amount of Note (Item 8) will be evidenced by a Promissory Note, secured by a Vendor's Lien and Deed of Trust on such property from PURCHASER to SELLER. ADDITIONAL PAYMENTS OR TOTAL PREPAYMENT MAY BE MADE UPON THE UNPAID PRINCIPAL AMOUNT OF THE NOTE AT ANY TIME WITHOUT PENALTY. Improvements which shall become affixed to the real property shall be subject to said security interest.

EXECUTED by PURCHASER this ____ day of __________, 19____.

____
PURCHASER

____
PURCHASER

FIGURE 10-1. Reg. Z disclosure form.

Rev. Civ. St., art. 5069-1.01). *Usury* is charging an interest rate in excess of that allowed by law. In Texas, there are three statutes dealing with the maximum legal rates of interest:

(1) For noncorporate borrowers, the rate cannot exceed 10% simple interest per annum (Tex. Rev. Civ. St., art. 5069-1.02).
(2) For corporate borrowers, the rate cannot exceed 1½% per month (Tex. Rev. Civ. St., art. 1302-2.09).
(3) Noncorporate borrowers may agree to pay the same rate of interest as corporations on any loan in the principal amount of $500,000 or more for the purpose of construction, financing, or refinancing improvements on real property (Tex. Rev. Civ. St., art. 5069-1.07).

Interest charged in excess of the foregoing statutory provisions is illegal and usurious.

There are other statutory provisions that allow for higher rates of interest in special situations (i.e., consumer credit transactions, F.H.A insured and V.A. guaranteed loans—*Tex. Rev. Civ. Stat. Ann.*, art. 5069–1.09). However, for most loans secured by real estate that are not consumer credit transactions, or controlled by federal statute, the above interest statutes are controlling.

Determination of Interest

The most difficult question to date has been, What constitutes interest? as a charge for the "forbearance or detention" of money. There are an almost indeterminable number of fees that have been tacked on, added to, credited to, paid collaterally with, and given in exchange for, all kinds of loan transactions. Most of these charges incurred when obtaining a loan are clearly established and understood. The lender must be very careful in requiring these charges, so that the interest charged will not be considered to be usurious. Therefore, the determination of these charges as "interest" is very important to the lender's business practice. Some of the more common charges for obtaining a loan may constitute interest and deserve more detailed discussion.

Points, Commitment Fees, and Loan Brokerage Fees. Points, commitment fees, and loan brokerage fees are fees paid to a lender or loan broker when obtaining a loan. The value of these fees is normally measured in *points*, each point being 1% of the loan value. For instance, a $100,000 loan requiring three points would require a fee of $3000. Although often used interchangeably, points, commitment fees, and loan brokerage fees are for separate and distinct purposes.

The definition of *points*, for the purposes of this discussion, will be deemed to be a fee charged for entering into a loan contract charged by, and paid to, the lending institution that is making the loan. The general rule in determining whether or not points are construed to be interest is determined by what the points are to be used for. If the points are not directly attributable to expenses incurred by the lender in making such loan, the points *will* constitute interest, *Terry* v. *Teachworth*, 431 S.W.2d 917 (Tex. Civ. App.—Houston, 1968); *Gonzales County Savings and Loan Association* v. *Freeman*, 534 S.W.2d 903 (Tex. 1976). However, if the points are charged for a definite expense, rationally related to making the loan, they will *not* constitute interest.

A *commitment fee*, on the other hand, is normally a fee charged for the promise of securing the funds at some future date. This does not fall within the definition of interest. A commitment fee can be characterized as an option to enter into a future loan, and as long as the fee was reasonably related to the risks taken by the lender, it will not be construed to be interest (*Gonzales County Savings and Loan Association, supra*).

Brokerage fees (fees charged by mortgage brokers for placing the loan with a lender) will not normally be considered interest if the fee does not go to the lender itself, and if there is no joint control or agreement between the lender and the broker (as in the case of points as defined above). It is common for a mortgage company or savings and loan association to operate as a mortgage broker and to charge one to five points as a fee for finding another lender to make the loan. In this capacity, the institution is serving only as a mortgage broker. In such case, the fee is not used as a cost for obtaining the loan, but instead is a fee for paying the broker for finding a lender, *Crow* v. *Home Savings Association*, 522 S.W.2d 457 (Tex. 1975); *Greever* v. *Persky*, 165 S.W.2d 709 (Tex. 1942).

Prepayment Penalties and Partial Release Fees. *Prepayment penalties* (also measured in points) are the fees that a lender charges the borrower for paying off a loan prematurely. It may seem unreasonable for a lender to charge a fee to pay off a loan. However, as a practical matter, when a borrower has entered into a contract to pay 9% interest over a period of 30 years, he has normally contracted to pay a certain determinable amount of interest over that 30-year period. Thus, if the contract is terminated prematurely (by prepayment), there is a certain amount of interest that will not be paid. Therefore, the lender charges a certain number of points as a prepayment penalty. This charge would appear to be within the legitimate expectation of damages on the lender's part.

There has been some indication that Texas courts would not construe prepayment penalties as interest but rather as consideration for the termination of the loan contract, *Boyd* v. *Life Insurance Company*, 546 S.W.2d

132 (Tex. Civ. App.—Houston, 1977); *Gulf Coast Investment Corp.* v. *Prichard*, 438 S.W.2d 658 (Tex. Civ. App.—Dallas, 1969). However, the Texas Supreme Court in *Gonzales County Savings and Loan Association, supra*, indicated that penalties for prepayments may be considered as interest if they are not reasonable expenses in light of the actual amount of work done, and do not bear some reasonable relationship to the amount of loss or inconvenience suffered by the lender due to the prepayment.

There is a similar theory regrading the payment of *partial release fees*. Normally, when a borrower requests that the lender release a portion of the secured real estate, the lender would charge not only a premium for the portion to be released, but also a partial release fee. This fee is normally attributable to the preparation of instruments, bookkeeping, and clerical costs for releasing the security and for the resulting adjustment of the principal balance due under the terms of the loan. Partial release fees of this type are not considered to be interest.

Compensating Balances. It is also a common practice for a lending institution to require the borrower to make certain deposits or to purchase certificates of deposit to be pledged to the lender. These arrangements are often verbal transactions and are not made part of the loan documents themselves. The compensating balances generally create a separate and independent obligation (on which interest is paid by the lender) and are not deemed interest, *Commerce Savings Association* v. *GGE Management Company*, 543 S.W.2d 862 (Tex. 1976); *Moss* v. *Metropolitan National Bank*, 533 S.W.2d 397 (Tex. Civ. App.—Houston, 1976). However, if the lender freezes the loan proceeds or requires the compensating balance in the loan document, it *may* be considered interest; but the authorities on this theory of interest revolve closely around the fact situations of each case, *Miller* v. *First State Bank*, 551 S.W.2d 89 (Tex. Civ. App.—Ft. Worth, 1977); *Community Finance and Thrift Corporation* v. *State of Texas*, 343 S.W.2d 232 (Tex. 1961).

Matured Interest. Most promissory notes have penalty provisions in the event there is a default on the payments. Figure 9-1 in the previous chapter shows a typical provision of this type. The provision usually states that the entire principal amount is matured; and matured unpaid principal and interest will bear interest at the rate of 10% per annum until paid. This is sometimes referred to as *interest on interest*. However, this penalty provision does not constitute interest as far as the loan transaction itself is concerned. In a very old Texas case of *Crider* v. *San Antonio Real Estate Building and Loan Association*, 34 S.W.1047 (Tex. 1896), the Texas Supreme Court held that such a provision represents a new obligation once the default has taken place, and the interest on the note and the interest on the past due principal payments do not, together, constitute a new, higher rate of interest.

Compulsory Loan Retirement. It is also a common practice for a lender to require that a borrower pay off all of his preexisting indebtedness before obtaining a new loan. This normally is not considered interest. However, such a requirement *may* be considered interest if there is a required prepayment penalty on the loan to be paid off.

Turn-Around Sales. In the interesting case of *Commerce Savings Association* v. *GGE Management Company, supra*, there was a requirement that the borrower sell a project to the lender for $349,000. The lender resold the property to the borrower for $400,000. Not surprisingly, the extra costs charged in this transaction was determined by the jury to be interest and a transaction disguised to evade the usury statute.

Equity Participation. Lenders have become increasingly aware of their ability to participate in the equity and development of the project without any additional cost to themselves as lenders. The key determination when a lender is involved in equity participation is whether or not the lender is taking a risk similar to that of the borrower. If the borrower gets a preferred return on his investment, this may be determined to be interest, and possibly usurious, *Johns* v. *Jabe*, 518 S.W.2d 857 (Tex. Civ. App.—Dallas, 1974), but such is not always the case. If the lender shares in the risks, and the return on his investment is not readily ascertainable, he is considered to be a true equity participant. However, this entire area revolves very closely around the facts involved in each particular loan, and there are a number of interesting cases on both sides of this issue.

Required Incorporation. Since the law allows corporations to pay interest at higher rates than those of noncorporate borrowers, lenders sometimes simply require that the noncorporate borrower either incorporate or guarantee a corporation's indebtedness. In one of the more profound cases, *Skeen* v. *Glenn Justice Mortgage Company*, 526 S.W.2d 252 (Tex. Civ. App.—Dallas, 1975), the court held that the requirement by a lender for the borrower to form a corporation as a condition of the loan does not, by itself, indicate that the corporation was created to cover up for a fraudulent transaction or to evade usury statutes. The mere fact that a corporation was formed to obtain the loan did not, in itself, render the transaction void or illegal.

Another practice permitted that the lender require that an individual guarantee a corporation's indebtedness. There was some speculation that perhaps this might constitute usury. However, there have been two very recent cases that indicate that since the loan was made to the corporation and not to the individual, the transaction did not constitute usury, *Loomis Land and Cattle Company* v. *Diversified Mortgage*, 533 S.W.2d 420 (Tex. Civ. App.—Tyler, 1976); *Micrea, Inc.* v. *Eureka Life Insurance Company of America*, 534 S.W.2d 348 (Tex. Civ. App.—Ft. Worth, 1976).

There has been additional speculation as to whether two corporations, constituting a partnership, should pay the maximum corporate rate or the maximum noncorporate rate because of their partnership status. A Texas attorney general's opinion (No. H-589) determined that a partnership composed solely of two corporations is not a "corporation" for purposes of usury, and, therefore, such partnerships are subject to the 10% ceiling on interest rates for noncorporate borrowers. However, there are many unanswered questions in transactions of this type, and applicable attorney general's opinions, by themselves, should not be relied on as controlling on subsequent court decisions.

Spreading

Once it has been determined that these extra charges, such as points, turn-around sales, and other additional payments to secure loans, are, in fact, "interest," there is a question as to how that interest is to be calculated to determine whether or not it is usurious. Texas has recently enacted a new usury statute (Tex. Rev. Civ. St. Ann., art. 5069-1.07, effective September 1, 1975), which has indicated that Texas has adopted the concept of "spreading." The spreading doctrine refers to the fact that the points for fees and commitments and other charges attributable to the loan transaction itself (although they are one-time charges) can be "spread" over the life of the loan to determine whether or not it would constitute usury over the entire period. For instance, if one made a loan at 9% per annum but had to pay three points to the lender as consideration for making the loan, the charge for making the loan would be determined by taking the 9% interest and adding to it one-thirtieth of the three points for each year. The 9% interest is then added to the one-thirtieth times three points to determine whether or not the annual interest charge would exceed 10% per annum. Since the loan is made for a period of 30 years, it is assumed that the three points paid prior to obtaining the loan can be spread over this 30-year period to determine the true effective interest rate. Calculating the interest in this manner, it can be seen that a large number of points can be calculated and be added to an interest rate before it can achieve the actual 10% ceiling.

Although there may have been some question as to the applicability of Article 5069-1.07 to notes prior to enactment of the statute, the Texas Supreme Court confirmed the spreading statute as applying the intent of a prior statute (Art. 5069-1.06). In the same case, *Tanner* v. *Ferguson, Tex.*, 561 S.W.2d 777 (Tex. 1977), the Texas Supreme Court further confirmed that *prepaid* interest (interest paid in advance) could also be "spread" in determining whether or not a transaction is usurious.

The penalties for usury are not treated lightly in Texas, and the law of usury is strictly construed against the lender. The statutory penalty provides basically as follows:

1. The lender is to forfeit to the obligor (borrower) twice the amount of interest contracted for and reasonable attorneys' fees fixed by the court.
2. Any person who contracts for or receives interest in excess of double the amount of interest allowed by the law shall forfeit all principal as well as interest and all other charges and shall also pay a reasonable attorney's fee set by the court.

It is not difficult to see that the risks of charging usurious interest far outweigh the small advantage that might be obtained by the extra dollars that might be charged. The penalties are far too severe for most lenders who want to intentionally assume this type of risk.

SUMMARY

There are few areas of lending that have been litigated more often than the areas of interest and finance charge. *Finance charge* is a term used under the Federal Consumer Credit Protection Act (commonly called the Truth-in-Lending Act). This law requires extensive disclosures by creditors when making loans to consumers.

Interest, on the other hand, is covered by state law. Charging a fee for money in excess of the maximum allowable interest rate in Texas is called usury. There are criminal and civil penalties for charging usurious interest. Many lenders have tried to get around charging "interest" by charging additional fees to produce or maintain a loan. There have been various constructions by courts in Texas as to what does or does not constitute "interest" as a fee charge for procuring a loan.

11

METHODS OF TITLE ASSURANCE

Evidence of Title

Once a purchaser has made up his mind that he wants to purchase an interest in real estate, he wants to be absolutely sure that he is fully advised of the status of the title to that real estate. The real estate agent's function is important in this area because it is part of the real estate agent's obligation to inform the purchaser, in writing, that he (the purchaser) should have the abstract to real estate examined prior to closing or that he should obtain title insurance to assure himself of the status of the title to that real estate. There are a number of ways that the purchaser can assure himself of good title, and those to be discussed will include the Torrens system of title registration, personal warranty of the grantor, a lawyer's title opinion, an abstractor's opinion, and title insurance policies.

The Torrens System of Title Registration

The Torrens system of title registration is not utilized in Texas, but it is a rather interesting method of title assurance that has proved effective in other states. In this method of title assurance, the title to the real estate is reflected by a registration certificate, similar to that used in Texas for an automobile title. A registration certificate of this type would simply have a proper legal description of the real estate on the certificate, and, on the face of that certificate, all liens against the real estate would also be reflected. When a lien is placed on the property, one turns in his title registration certificate and receives a new one reflecting the new lien. The old registration certificate is then destroyed. Therefore, in each parcel of real estate, there is only one registration certificate outstanding, and there can never be any doubt as to the status of the title since it is reflected on the face of that certificate, unless due to fraud or forgery.

Although this system seems to greatly facilitate the passage of title and the assurance of proper title, there are certain drawbacks as to its effectiveness, particularly in a state like Texas. The primary difficulty in the Torrens registration system involves the final determination of title. If one is going to convert to the Torrens registration system, the final status of title must be judicially determined in order to assure proper title in every single case as it pertains to every ascertainable parcel of real estate. Unless a special judicial system could be set up to ascertain property title, the burden on the existing court system, and accompanying costs, would probably be insurmountable in order to achieve a proper shift from our existing methods of title assurance to the Torrens system. In addition, there would have to be certain changes in our recording act, in insurance codes as they relate to title insurance, and in methods of recordation in the county courthouses. Such changes, of course, would require legislative action, which would mean another very difficult process of shifting to the Torrens system. One also should not underestimate the function of the lobbyists representing the lawyers and title insurance companies in the State of Texas, although this would be one of the lesser problems in making a shift of this type. Such individuals might be adversely affected by a shift to a title registration system.

Personal Warranty of the Grantor

A second method of title assurance is the personal warranty of the grantor. As discussed in Chapter 7, Conveyancing, and depending on the type of deed utilized in the conveyance, the grantor gives certain warranties to the title of the real estate upon execution of the deed. If there is a defect in the title, the purchaser has the right to pursue a cause of action against the grantor on his warranty. The difficulty here, of course, involves the quality of the warranty of the grantor, who may not be alive, in existence (if a corporation or other business entity), or financially solvent enough to stand behind the warranty or to pay damages to an aggrieved purchaser. However, the personal warranty of the grantor, coupled with the effect of the adverse possession statutes, does provide some method of title assurance after the purchaser has maintained possession of the real estate beyond the 3-, 5-, 10-, and 25-year statutes of limitations.

There are situations, of course, when the personal warranty of the grantor is a very good method of title assurance, especially when the grantor is large, solvent, and reputable. A solvent grantor probably provides better assurance than some title companies.

Lawyer's Title Opinion

The lawyer's title opinion at one time was one of the most common methods of title assurance. It is still quite frequently used in some of the more rural areas of Texas. It is also used in cases where the chain of title and abstracts to a parcel of property may be so involved and complicated that the purchaser would prefer his own attorney's opinion as to the effect of each document, rather than a blanket policy of title insurance or personal warranty of the grantor.

The lawyer's title opinion is a functional and effective method of title assurance, but it has several main disadvantages, as listed below:

1. Most lawyers, in an effort to do a good job, often find that reading the abstracts and writing opinions is a very time-consuming process; and many purchasers find that it is too slow when trying to complete or consummate the closing of a fairly complicated real estate transaction.
2. The lawyer, in reading an abstract, always runs the risk that the abstract compiled for his review may have been improperly prepared or may be missing some instruments in the chain of title.
3. There is no guarantee in the event that title fails that the purchaser can have any recovery. Although most lawyers carry malpractice insurance in the event of errors and omissions, the purchaser may still find that his recovery may not be enough to cover the damages he may have incurred.
4. As in every other profession, there is always the problem of incompetency, errors in judgment, and mistakes.

There has been considerable effort in recent years on the part of the legal community to reinstate lawyers in the business of insuring title to real property. It is felt by some members of the legal community that the role of the lawyer has become too diminished in the function of assuring title because of the widespread use of title insurance companies. In 1975, the Texas legislature passed an act creating the Attorney's Title Insurance Company, regulated by Article 9.56 of the Texas Insurance Code. The Attorney's Title Insurance Company has regulations similar to those of title insurance companies generally. However, there has not been a dramatic shift toward utilizing this method to date.

Abstractor's Certificate

An abstractor is a person who is employed to compile abstracts that affect certain parcels of real estate. The abstract reflects a complete chain of title to a particular piece of real estate from the current date back to the origin of title to the property, but it gives the purchaser no protection in and of itself.

An abstract is usually furnished to an attorney as a basis for the lawyer's title opinion, as discussed above. An abstractor, however, is normally bonded, and in the event there is an error or omission in the abstract, one may proceed against his (the abstractor's) bond in order to effect a recovery. If the abstractor's bond is sufficient, it will cover the damages suffered by the purchaser. However, there is no requirement that an abstractor carry bonds in any great amount. Therefore, there is probably a good chance that the bond would not be sufficient to reimburse the purchaser's damages. In addition, the purchaser might have to prove negligence on the part of the abstractor. There is no malpractice insurance available for abstractors. Furthermore, an abstractor's opinion normally only lists the instruments affecting the property, rather than the specific encumbrances that are reflected by those instruments. In addition, as you may recall, interpreting an instrument and its effect on the property is a legal function, and unless the abstractor is a lawyer, an interpretation of the instruments is practicing law without a license, so the abstractor will probably not offer a legal opinion.

Title Insurance

Title insurance is by far the most common method of title assurance used in Texas. It actually incorporates several methods of title assurance that have already been mentioned. Title companies originally grew as the result of the need for an insurance policy for a lawyer's title opinion. Title insurance allows for spreading of the risk and offers a greater possibility of solvency in the event that damages were incurred by the purchaser. Most title companies have their own abstract plans and their own abstractors. They also have their own lawyers for title opinions. In addition, they are insured by a solvent insurance company that has been authorized to do business in Texas. So, for practical purposes, this is probably the most efficient method of title assurance, with the greatest probability of solvency for the buyer's benefit. Furthermore, since title insurance can be concentrated into a volume business, it normally provides a faster, more efficient service to the customer. It also provides an advantage to the seller in that he has no liability on his warranty to the purchaser since the title company agrees to indemnify the purchaser from any claims, although he (the seller) may have some liability to the title company. The buyer, of course, gets the absolute assurance that the title is good and in the event that he does have a cause of action, he can proceed against a solvent insurer who has guaranteed to him that he will be protected in the event of title failure.

A title insurance policy is a contract of indemnity. For a one-time premium charge, it guarantees that the insured will be indemnified (protected) from any cause of action or loss in the event his title fails for any defect that accrued prior to the effective date of the policy. Therefore, there is no affirmative duty on the title company to clear the title, only to defend the title from adverse claims. The rates for title policies are set by the State Board of Insurance, so there is no advantage to "shopping around" for a better price on a title insurance policy. It should be remembered also that title insurance and title insurance commitments are not transactions in real estate, but merely transactions incidental to a transaction in real estate. The provisions of the title insurance policy are governed by the insurance code and not Texas real estate law, *American Title Insurance Company, et al.* v. *Byrd, et al.*, 348 S.W.2d 683 (Tex., 1964).

Types of Title Insurance. There are normally two policies issued: one issued and made payable to the mortgagee, and one issued and made payable to the mortgagor (new owner). The *mortgagee's title policy* (for the purpose of this discussion, this policy will not be discussed in great detail) is generally issued at a nominal cost (if issued simultaneously with the owner's policy) to the purchaser, and it assures the mortgagee (the lender) that the title is good. This policy generally has better warranties and somewhat better title coverage than does the more expensive *owner's title policy*, which is issued to insure the mortgagor's title. Upon the sale of the real estate, the owner's policy of title insurance converts to a warrantor's policy. If the mortgage is foreclosed by the mortgagee, the mortgagee's title insurance policy converts to an owner's policy, effective as of the original date of issuance.

Scope of Coverage. The basic duty of a title company is not to disclose the defects of the title, but only to indemnify the insured against any loss from defects in the title, *Prendergast* v. *Southern Title Guaranty Company*, 454 S.W.2d 802 (Tex. Civ. App.—Houston, 1970). It insures the real estate at the purchase price, and does not increase in coverage as the value of the real estate increases. The duty to defend any causes of action against that title is generally set out in the terms of the title policy.

A copy of the standard Texas Owner's Title Insurance form is shown in Figure 11-1 for your reference, with pertinent parts underlined for emphasis. Note that in this standard form, the title insurance company is obligated to defend the insured in every action or proceeding adverse to the title of the real estate or interest of the land as guaranteed. The company is *not* required to defend any claims except those entered in the policy under Schedule B of the standard form (the standard exceptions).

It should also be noted that the parties entitled to defense (the insured party) must, within a reasonable time after any action against the title of that property has commenced, give the company written notice of the pendency and authority to defend. The company is not liable for any damages until it has reached the court of last resort and such adverse interest or claim has been established. This provision has been construed strictly in favor of the title company. If it appears that a defect in the title is cured, the damages would be no more than nominal, regardless of the

OWNER POLICY OF TITLE INSURANCE

_____ TITLE INSURANCE COMPANY, a _________________________________ corporation, hereinafter called the Company, for value does hereby guarantee to the herein named Insured, the heirs, devisees, executors and administrators of the Insured, or if a corporation, its successors by dissolution, merger or consolidation, that as of the date hereof, the Insured has good and indefeasible title to the estate or interest in the land described or referred to in this policy.

The Company shall not be liable in a greater amount than the actual monetary loss of the Insured, and in no event shall the Company be liable for more than the amount shown in Schedule A hereof, and shall, except as hereinafter stated, at its own cost defend the Insured in every action or proceeding on any claim against, or right to the estate or interest in the land, or any part thereof, adverse to the title to the estate or interest in the land as hereby guaranteed, but the Company shall not be required to defend against any claims based upon matters in any manner excepted under this policy by the exceptions in Schedule B hereof or excluded by Paragraph 2, "Exclusions from Coverage of this Policy", of the Conditions and Stipulations hereof. The party or parties entitled to such defense shall within a reasonable time after the commencement of such action or proceeding, and in ample time for defense therein, give the Company written notice of the pendency of the action or proceeding, and authority to defend. The Company shall not be liable until such adverse interest, claim, or right shall have been held valid by a court of last resort to which either litigant may apply, and if such adverse interest, claim, or right so established shall be for less than the whole of the estate or interest in the land, then the liability of the Company shall be only such part of the whole liability limited above as shall bear the same ratio to the whole liability that the adverse interest, claim, or right established may bear to the whole estate or interest in the land, such ratio to be based on respective values determinable as of the date of this policy. In the absence of notice as aforesaid, the Company is relieved from all liability with respect to any such interest, claim or right; provided, however, that failure to notify shall not prejudice the rights of the Insured if such Insured shall not be a party to such action or proceeding, nor be served with process therein, nor have any knowledge thereof, nor in any case, unless the Company shall be actually prejudiced by such failure.

Upon sale of the estate or interest in the land, this policy automatically thereupon shall become a warrantor's policy and the Insured, the heirs, devisees, executors and administrators of the Insured, or if a corporation, its successors by dissolution, merger or consolidation, shall for a period of twenty-five years from date hereof remain fully protected according to the terms hereof, by reason of the payment of any loss he, they or it may sustain on account of any warranty of title contained in the transfer or conveyance executed by the Insured conveying the estate or interest in the land. The Company shall be liable under said warranty only by reason of defects, liens or encumbrances existing prior to or at the date hereof and not excluded either by the exceptions or by the Conditions and Stipulations hereof, such liability not to exceed the amount of this policy.

IN WITNESS HEREOF, the _____ TITLE INSURANCE COMPANY has caused this policy to be executed by its President under the seal of the Company, but this policy is to be valid only when it bears an authorized countersignature, as of the date set forth in Schedule A.

Attest: _____ TITLE INSURANCE COMPANY

(SEAL)

_________________________ By _________________________

Secretary President

Countersigned at _________________________, Texas.
(Location and Use Optional)

____

Authorized Countersignature
(Location in policy discretionary)

September 1, 1975

FIGURE 11-1.

SCHEDULE A

GF No. or File No.: (Optional)

Owner Policy No.: Date of Policy:

Name of Insured:

Amount:

1. The estate or interest in the land insured by this policy is: (fee simple, leasehold, easement, etc.—identify or describe)

2. The land referred to in this policy is described as follows:

SCHEDULE B

This policy is subject to the Conditions and Stipulations hereof, the terms and conditions of the leases or easements insured, if any, shown in Schedule A, and to the following matters which are additional exceptions from the coverage of this policy:

1. Restrictive covenants affecting the land described or referred to above.

2. Any discrepancies, conflicts, or shortages in area or boundary lines, or any encroachments, or any overlapping of improvements.

3. Taxes for the year 19_____ and subsequent years.

4. The following lien(s) and all terms, provisions and conditions of the instrument(s) creating or evidencing said lien(s):

CONDITIONS AND STIPULATIONS

1. Definitions

The following terms when used in this policy mean:

(a) "land": The land described, specifically or by reference, in Schedule A, and improvements affixed thereto which by law constitute real property.
(b) "public records": Those records which impart constructive notice of matters relating to the land.
(c) "knowledge": Actual knowledge, not constructive knowledge, or notice which may be imputed to the Insured by reason of any public records.
(d) "date": The effective date, including hour if specified.

2. Exclusions from the Coverage of this Policy

This policy does not insure against loss or damage by reason of the following:

(a) The refusal of any person to purchase, lease or lend money on the land.
(b) Governmental rights of police power or eminent domain unless notice of the exercise of such rights appears in the public records at the date hereof; and the consequences of any law, ordinance or governmental regulation including, but not limited to, building and zoning ordinances.
(c) Any titles or rights asserted by anyone including, but not limited to, persons, corporations, governments or other entities to tidelands, or lands comprising the shores or beds of navigable or perennial rivers and streams, lakes, bays, gulfs or oceans, or to any land extending from the line of mean low tide to the line of vegetation, or to lands beyond the line of the harbor or bulkhead lines as established or changed by any government, or to filled-in lands, or artificial islands, or to riparian rights, or the rights or interests of the State of Texas or the public generally in the area extending from the line of mean low tide to the line of vegetation or their right of access thereto, or right of easement along and across the same.

September 1, 1975

FIGURE 11-1 (*continued*).

(d) Defects, liens, encumbrances, adverse claims against the title as insured or other matters (1) created, suffered, assumed or agreed to by the Insured at the date of this policy, or (2) known to the Insured at the date of this policy unless disclosure thereof in writing bythe Insured shall have been made to the Company prior to the date of this policy; or loss or damage which would not have been sustained if the Insured were a purchaser for value without knowledge; or the homestead or community property or survivorship rights, if any, of any spouse of any Insured.

3. Defense of Actions

(a) In all cases where this policy provides for the defense of any action or proceeding, the Insured shall secure to the Company the right to so provide defense in such action or proceeding, and all appeals therein, and permit it to use, at its option, the name of the Insured for such purpose. Whenever requested by the Company, the Insured shall give the Company all reasonable aid in any such action or proceeding, in effecting settlement, securing evidence, obtaining witnesses, or defending such action or proceeding.

(b) The Company shall have the right to select counsel of its own choice whenever it is required to defend any action or proceeding, and such counsel shall have full control of said defense.

(c) Any action taken by the Company for the defense of the Insured or to establish the title as insured, or both, shall not be construed as an admission of liability, and the Company shall not thereby be held to concede liability or waive any provision of this policy.

4. Payment of Loss

(a) No claim shall arise or be maintainable under this policy for liability voluntarily assumed by the Insured in settling any claim or suit without written consent of the Company.

(b) All payments under this policy, except payments made for costs, attorney fees and expenses, shall reduce the amount of the insurance pro tanto; and the amount of this policy shall be reduced by any amount the Company may pay under any policy insuring the validity or priority of any lien excepted to herein or any instrument hereafter executed by the Insured which is a charge or lien on the land, and the amount so paid shall be deemed a payment to the Insured under this policy.

(c) The Company shall have the option to pay or settle or compromise for or in the name of the Insured any claim insured against by this policy, and such payment or tender of payment, together with all costs, attorney fees and expenses which the Company is obligated hereunder to pay, shall terminate all liability of the Company hereunder as to such claim. Further, the payment or tender of payment of the full amount of this policy by the Company shall terminate all liability of the Company under this policy.

(d) Whenever the Company shall have settled a claim under this policy, all right of subrogation shall vest in the Company unaffected by any act of the Insured, and it shall be subrogated to and be entitled to all rights and remedies of the Insured against any person or property in respect to such claim. The Insured, if requested by the Company, shall transfer to the Company all rights and remedies against any person or property necessary in order to perfect such right of subrogation, and shall permit the Company to use the name of the Insured in any transaction or litigation involving such rights or remedies.

5. Policy Entire Contract

Any action, actions or rights of action that the Insured may have, or may bring, against the Company, arising out of the status of the title insured hereunder, must be based on the provisions of this policy, and all notices required to be given the Company, and any statement in writing required to be furnished the Company, shall be addressed to it at ______________________________.

6. This policy is not transferable.

Form T-1: Owner Policy of Title Insurance

September 1, 1975

FIGURE 11-1 (*continued*).

MORTGAGEE POLICY OF TITLE INSURANCE

_____ TITLE INSURANCE COMPANY, a ____ corporation, hereinafter called the Company, for value received, will pay to the Insured named in Schedule A hereof, as interest may appear, all loss or damage not exceeding the amount stated in Schedule A which the Insured, or the executors, administrators, successors or assigns of the Insured may sustain or suffer by reason of the failure of, defects in, encumbrances upon, or liens or charges against the title of the mortgagors or grantors to the estate or interest in the land described in the mortgage or trust deed identified in Schedule A, existing at or prior to the date of this policy, including mechanics' and materialmen's liens now having priority, or now existing but incomplete, which may hereafter be completed so as to gain priority over the lien of the Insured, and not excepted to in Schedule B hereof, subject to the Conditions and Stipulations hereof.

Subject to the provisions of Schedule B and the Conditions and Stipulations, the Company insures that at the date of filing said mortgage or trust deed for record, the title to the estate or interest in the land described therein was as shown in Schedule A, and said mortgage or trust deed was a valid first lien thereon unless superior liens are set out in Schedule B. The Company insures that any assignments noted in Schedule A, whether recorded or not at the date hereof, are good and valid and vest title to said mortgage or trust deed in the Insured free and clear of liens, except as specified in Schedule B.

This policy inures to the use and benefit of the lawful owner or owners of the evidence of debt identified herein and to any subsequent owner or owners thereof, under and in accordance with the terms and conditions hereof; provided always that it shall not be the duty of the Company to trace the ownership of such evidence of debt or of this policy; and, in the absence of satisfactory proof of such ownership at the time liability hereunder accrues, any payment made to the named Insured, or a legally appointed successor, upon surrender of this policy for endorsement, shall be deemed to be in satisfaction of all demands hereunder pro tanto.

IN WITNESS HEREOF, the _____ TITLE INSURANCE COMPANY has caused this policy to be executed by its President under the seal of the Company, but this policy is to be valid only when it bears an authorized countersignature, as of the date set forth in Schedule A.

Attest: _____ TITLE INSURANCE COMPANY

(SEAL)

______________________________ BY ______________________________

Secretary President

Countersigned at ______________________, Texas.
(Location and Use Optional)

____

Authorized Countersignature
(Location in policy discretionary)

SCHEDULE A

GF No. or File No.: (Optional)

Mortgagee Policy No.: Date of Policy:

Name of Insured:

Amount:

1. The estate or interest in the land described or referred to in this policy is: (fee simple, leasehold, easement, etc.—identify or describe)

2. Title to the estate or interest covered by this policy at the date hereof is vested in:

3. The mortgage or trust deed and assignments thereof, if any, under which title or interest is vested in the Insured are described as follows:

4. The land referred to in this policy is described as follows:

September 1, 1975

FIGURE 11-1 (*continued*).

complications this defect might have caused between the time it was apparent and the time the title company cured same, *Southern Title Guaranty Company* v. *Prendergast*, 494 S.W.2d 154, 158 (Tex. 1973).

The liability of the title company is further limited by what is called the *Proportionate Reduction Clause Formula*. This clause has been consistently upheld by the Texas Supreme Court, and the formula is stated as follows:

> The liability of the insurance company (X) is to the whole liability of the policy limit (A) as the value of the outstanding interest (B) is to the value of the whole property without an outstanding interest (C), or (X) divided by (A) equals to (B) divided by (C) (*Southern Title Guaranty Company* v. *Prendergast, supra*).

Each of these figures, (X), (A), (B), and (C), is determined by the court, or by the jury, in order to establish what the liability of the insurance company is. This is more simply set out as follows:

$$\frac{\text{(X)}}{\text{Policy Limit (A)}} = \frac{\begin{array}{c}\text{Value of Outstanding Interest (B)}\\ \text{[Jury Question]}\end{array}}{\begin{array}{c}\text{Value of Entire Property without}\\ \text{the Outstanding Interest (C)}\\ \text{[Jury Question]}\end{array}}$$

For instance, let us assume that there were 100 acres purchased and the title was insured for \$100,000 (A). Then (X) is equal to the amount of the liability of the title insurance company. The determination of (B) and (C) are jury questions. If the jury was to find that the title failed on one-tenth of the property, and that the value of that outstanding interest (B) is \$12,000, and the value of the property without the outstanding interest (C) is \$80,000, the formula would be calculated as follows:

$$\frac{\text{(X)}}{\$100{,}000} = \frac{\$12{,}000}{\$80{,}000}$$

In calculating this amount using the Proportionate Reduction Clause Formula, we would determine that the *total damages* that the title company would be liable for to the purchaser would be \$15,000. However, as stated earlier, if the title company cures the defect in title, at any stage of the proceeding, the title company is only liable for nominal damages, and not the calculated amount.

In addition, if the plaintiff alleges and proves reasonable value of legal services rendered in enforcing the terms of the policy against the issuing company, he is also entitled to attorneys' fees in addition to his damages.

Standard Exceptions. There are certain standard title exceptions included in the title policy against which the title policy will not insure the purchaser, unless an additional premium is paid or unless special riders are attached to the policy. These exceptions are listed under Schedule B of the Standard Owner's Policy of Title Insurance shown in Figure 11-1. They are as follows (italics indicate actual wording as shown in Schedule B):

1. *Restrictive covenants affecting the land described or referred to above.*

   The title company, if requested, may put a notation in their "none of record" or "none of record except . . ." that would effectively inform the owner that there are no restrictions, at least of record, in the county affecting his property.

2. *Any discrepancies, conflicts, or shortages in area or boundary lines, or any encroachments, or any overlapping of improvements.*

   This exception clearly states in both the owner and mortgagee title policies that any shortages in area, encroachments, or overlapping improvements simply are not insured against. This exception might come as quite a shock to people who buy homes and find that the neighbors have an encroachment on their property, or perhaps that they as the new home purchasers have an encroachment on their neighbor's property. This exception (except for the "shortages in area" exception) can be deleted for an additional premium in an amount equivalent to 15% of the basic rate or a minimum fee of $20. This would normally require the title company to use an approved surveyor, and to make the determination of whether or not it feels that the title to the property is an insurable risk. Of course, the title company always has the option of not insuring the title to the property in the event it finds the encroachment or overlapping improvements. Courts have been rather hard on title companies in the past, and generally construe the title insurance policy against the insurer in the event there is a title defect due to a shortage or boundary conflict, *Clements* v. *Stewart Title Company*, 537 S.W.2d 126 (Tex. Civ. App.—Austin, 1976); *Dallas Title and Guaranty Company* v. *Valdes*, 445 S.W.2d 26 (Tex. Civ. App.—Austin, 1969); *Chanoux* v. *Title Insurance Company*, 258 S.W.2d 866 (CCA El Paso, 1953, W.E.R.N.R.E.).

3. *Taxes for the current year and subsequent years.*

   Everyone is considered by law to be on notice of taxes and tax liens. Taxes arise at the first of every year and will stay with the property until paid. The title insurance policy, though, does insure that all taxes prior to the current year have been paid and that the only taxes that the purchaser will be liable for are those for the current year and subsequent year.

4. The fourth exception notes all liens and instruments creating any evidence of said liens in the property, and normally lists whatever might still be of record at the time the title search is performed.

There is an additional exception that most title companies include in the title insurance form even though it is not part of the standard form, and that is the exception to the *rights of parties in possession*. The title company may add this exception to either the owner's or mortgagee's title policy where the purchaser waives the inspection of the land by the title company. If the purchaser is not willing to waive the inspection by the title company, the title company may charge an additional fee for personal on-the-site inspection of the property. It should also be pointed out that the first paragraph of Schedule B indicates that the policy is subject to the conditions and stipulations of any leases or easements shown in Schedule A, which works hand in hand with the rights of parties in possession exception to the title policy. The courts have consistently held that a purchaser has a duty of inspection to the property because the right of parties in possession is equivalent to that of constructive notice as required by the recording act, *Bell* v. *Smith*, 532 S.W.2d 680 (Tex. Civ. App.—Ft. Worth, 1976). This exception also applies to easements or any other obvious encumbrance on the property that would have been obvious to the purchaser had he personally inspected the property. Upon a personal inspection of the property, the purchaser would have known of such rights of parties in possession, even though the title insurance company does not, *Halvorson* v. *National Title and Abstract Company*, 391 S.W.2d 112 (Tex. Civ. App.—Tyler, 1965).

Although it may appear that the title insurance business seems to be ''ducking'' most obvious liabilities and limiting its exposure of liability to such a great extent, it should also be pointed out that compared to other methods of title assurance, title insurance is probably the quickest, cheapest, and most available type for most real estate transactions.

Disadvantages. Title insurance does have certain limitations, but these are usually conditions that are out of the ordinary for most standard real estate transactions. The most obvious limitation in a title insurance policy would be the insuring of a very valuable piece of property, the value of which may exceed the value of the title insurance company's assets. This is often the case in purchasing an office building that is worth tens of millions of dollars. Similar exception would be the purchase of a block of a downtown major metropolitan center like Houston. If the block costs $250 per square foot and the title policy is limited to the cost of the property, it would not cover the cost of the subsequent improvements erected on that property, unless the title policy has specific provisions for renewal in the event of construction of the specified improvements. Since the title policy is for a fixed amount, the same disadvantage applies to normal inflationary increases in real estate values (these are not covered by a title policy).

Another major exception is one where the grantor of a piece of property is probably more solvent than the title company. In such event, one may well find that the grantor would be a better insurer of the title of that property through his personal warranty than the title insurance company would be using the Proportionate Reduction Clause Formula. However, in this circumstance, the purchaser would have the affirmative duty and expense of filing the lawsuit, whereas the title insurance company is required to provide the indemnification at no expense to the purchaser.

SUMMARY

It is part of the real estate agent's obligation in Texas to inform the purchaser in writing that the purchaser should have the abstract to real estate examined prior to closing or that the purchaser should obtain title insurance to assure himself of status of title to that real estate.

The Torrens system is a system of title registration that is not utilized in Texas. The personal warranty of the grantor gives a full warranty as to the title of the property, but it is only as good as the solvency of the grantor. A lawyer's title opinion is a commonly used method of title assurance. However, in the event of default or title failure there is little ability for recovery short of a suit for malpractice, unless the lawyer has insurance on his opinions. An abstractor's certificate, or a certificate of title, does not give a legal opinion nor is there a solvent fund for recovery in the event of mistakes, omissions, or errors. Title insurance is a method by which a state-regulated insurance company, with a proven source of solvent funds, provides an insurance policy to assure the purchaser that his title is good and indefeasible. Title insurance is issued on standard forms which are promulgated by the Insurance Board of the state of Texas.

12

CLOSINGS

The Closing Process

The final consummation of a real estate transaction is commonly termed the *closing*. It is at the closing that the documents are signed and transmitted to the parties, the funds are distributed, and, hopefully, all obligations of all parties have been fulfilled. A closing is not a purely legal function; it is considered by most to be a business function. In a well-planned closing, the papers are normally prepared by the attorneys and are reviewed by the clients prior to the closing, to eliminate potential misunderstandings.

The vast majority of closings in Texas are held at title companies, or a third-party escrow serves as a depositary for instruments and funds. The escrow agent is normally a noninterested third party who accumulates the various and sundry instruments and funds into "escrow," for final distribution upon consummation of the sale, pursuant to the terms of the earnest money contract or formal escrow instrument. The widespread use of escrows and escrow agents during closings creates very little need for all the parties to attend the closing together. In fact, it is suggested by some that all parties should not attend the closing at the same time. Depending on the circumstances surrounding the sale (especially residential sales), there is often an air of tension or emotionalism that may serve to hinder the actual closing process rather than help it.

In the typical residential transaction, there are actually two closings involved rather than just one. First, there is the closing of the sale from the seller to the purchaser; and second, there is the closing of the loan, involving the mortgagee and the purchaser. In the actual sale closing between the seller and the purchaser, the mortgagee is not interested in any part of the transaction except the fact that the purchaser is getting a clear, unencumbered title, subject only to the mortgagee's new lien to be created at the closing. For the loan-closing transaction, the seller has no concern as to the papers and documents to be signed between the purchaser and the lender, but only with the papers he (the seller) is supposed to secure to complete the actual sale of the property.

It should be pointed out at this point that there are closings in which *no* sale transaction takes place. This type of closing, referred to as a *loan closing*, normally only involves the refinancing of real estate by the owner, or the borrowing of money that is to be secured by the owner's real estate. The loan closing (very common among real estate developers, contractors, and investors) does not involve a sale of property at all, just the borrowing of money to be secured by the real estate.

Escrows

The escrow function, whether it is served by a title company or by a disinterested attorney, is one of the keys to a successful closing. The escrow officer is normally one who is trusted by both parties, he helps ease the air of suspicion or distrust that may exist in a transaction when the parties think of themselves as adversaries. The escrow is created pursuant to an escrow agreement with specific instructions for the escrow officer. If not written as specific escrow instructions, the intent and specifications for the escrow may be contained in the earnest money contract, *Covert* v. *Calvert*, 287 S.W. 117 (Tex. Civ. App.—Amarillo, 1926); *Campbell* v. *Barber*, 272 S.W.2d 750 (Tex. Civ. App.—Ft. Worth, 1954). Such escrows are generally considered irrevocable. Although this general rule may seem to be harsh, it must be remembered that the escrow officer, in placing himself in a position of trust, cannot act detrimentally to the interest of either party. Since the escrow is irrevocable, it may somewhat ease the burden of the escrow officer having to respond to the whims and capricious desires of either party. The escrow officer holds the instruments and funds in trust from the time they are deposited with him until the conditions and specific obligations required in the earnest money contract or escrow instructions are performed. At the time that all conditions have been performed, he distributes the funds and signed instruments, and the transaction is considered complete.

Relation Back Doctrine

Since escrow agreements are normally considered to be irrevocable, and since the escrow function is dictated by certain obligations and performances that must be completed prior to distribution, a legal doctrine has been applied to the escrow function relating to the time of performance. This doctrine is called the *Relation Back Doctrine*. This can be briefly summarized by stating that when a document is given to an escrow officer (when authorized by the escrow agreement) for delivery to the grantee upon compliance with specified conditions, the date of delivery relates back to the time of deposit into escrow so as to constitute delivery to the grantee upon delivery into escrow. However, title does not pass to the grantee until all the conditions have been performed and the document has been delivered by the escrow agent. This document has particularly pertinent application when instruments are disposed into escrow and the grantor subsequently dies or becomes insane. The Relation Back Doctrine supports the theory of irrevocability by vesting delivery from the grantor at the time of deposit into escrow.

Closing into Escrow

The escrow function also performs a very valuable accommodation to the parties by allowing different closing times for each of the parties. One party who may be forced to leave town at an early date can sign all the instruments as required by the contract and leave them with the escrow agent. This is called *closing into escrow*. The other party, then, upon performance of his obligations as required by the contract, may go in at some later date and close at his convenience. As long as all contracting parties performed their obligations within the time specified, there normally should not be any conflicts in utilizing the escrow function in this manner. As stated previously, it is sometimes recommended that the parties do not close at the same time because of the amount of emotion and tension that sometimes exist at a closing. One only needs to leave a closing once with all the parties crying (including the real estate agents and escrow officer) to realize how valuable this escrow function can be.

Liability of Escrow Agent

The escrow agent is held to a duty of due care, honesty, and integrity when operating as an escrow agent. Normally, the full liability of the escrow officer in the event of a mistake or negligent error is to pay the expense of restoring the status quo, *Texas Reserve Life Insurance Company* v. *Security Title Company*, 352 S.W.2d 347 (Tex. Civ. App.—San Antonio, 1961).

One of the more perilous undertakings by the escrow officer in a closing is when one of the parties indicates that the other party has breached the contract. When certain obligations and functions have not been performed, the escrow agent normally waits for a judicial determination before returning any of the documents or earnest money to either party. For example, take the case where one party claims that there has been a breach of the transaction, but the other party denies that such breach has taken place. The escrow agent, as a third party, normally will choose not to take sides and will only perform his function as ordered by a court of competent jurisdiction. This is a very important thing to remember. Even though the earnest money contract may be very clear as to the parties' obligations, if one of the parties claims a breach, the escrow agent is not going to undertake the responsibility of disbursing funds or instruments. This would be running the risk of breaching one's duty of care in the escrow function.

Documents for the Closing

Virtually all documents needed for a closing are deposited into escrow. Sometimes there are difficulties in determining exactly what instruments are supposed to be at the closing. Therefore it is good advice for realtors and lawyers to make a closing checklist before attending the closing. This is a very simple thing to do, and can save tremendous embarrassment. There are few situations more humiliating than to leave the closing (after representing a client) and discover that certain documents have not been properly signed or the proper amount of funds have not been distributed.

The closing checklist is very simply created by sitting down and carefully reading the earnest money contract and making a list of which documents and which funds your client should have in his possession upon leaving the closing. In creating this list you should also keep in mind that there are going to be certain documents that will not leave the closing but will be transferred to the courthouse for recordation before being distributed to the proper parties. A typical closing checklist may include the following items if representing the seller:

1. Cash in an amount which should be predetermined (this may be delayed upon funding of the purchaser's loan);
2. The deed of trust (if the seller is going to finance the transaction);
3. A promissory note (if the seller is going to finance the transaction).
4. Hopefully, a smile.

If representing the purchaser:

1. The deed (which is normally forwarded to the courthouse for recording before being delivered to the purchaser);
2. Warranties as requested or required [(1) mechanical equipment

inspection, (2) termite inspection, (3) slab inspection, (4) roof inspection];
3. The owner's title policy;
4. A bill of sale (if any personalty is to be transferred);
5. Estoppel certificates to evidence the payoff figure for the underlying indebtedness, if any;
6. A receipt for the purchase price paid.

If the purchase concerns income-producing property, the buyer may walk away with the following additional items:

1. Estoppel letter by tenants;
2. Landlord's estoppel certificates signed by the prior landlord;
3. Assignments, which may include the following:
   (a) Service contracts,
   (b) Warranties on mechanical equipment,
   (c) Rents and depsoits,
   (d) Escrow funds that may be contained in the seller's mortgage account,
   (e) Insurance policies.
4. A letter from the seller to the tenants indicating the new ownership;
5. A letter to the building manager indicating the change in ownership;
6. The rental rolls (normally certified);
7. Copies of leases;
8. Employment contracts;
9. Assignment of trade name.

If the property purchased is a condominium, the following additional items may be obtained:

1. The master deed or condominium declaration;
2. The bylaws of the condominium home owners' association;
3. Builders' warranties.

The use of a closing checklist of any of the foregoing, or a more abridged version for simpler transactions, provides a very easy method of assuring that the closing will go properly, and that no documents are misplaced or funds misappropriated.

Parties to a Closing

Two of the more important aspects of a smooth closing transaction that all parties should understand are: (1) what the closing is supposed to accomplish, and (2) what role or function each of the parties should assume to assure a proper closing and adequate representation of the client.

The various roles of the parties at a closing normally include these four categories:

1. The escrow officer,
2. The seller and purchaser,
3. The real estate agent(s), and
4. The attorneys.

(This is assuming the worst of all possible situations when all the parties show up at the same time!)

The escrow agent, especially if a title company, performs only two functions, that of being an escrow agent, and that of being the agent of the title guarantor, as previously discussed. The escrow agent's duties are not to be a "gopher," negotiator, soothsayer, or salver of all wounds. His job is a professional one; and he should not be involved with the problems of either party, or of the respective real estate agents or attorneys, unless such involvement relates to his particular function as an escrow agent. It is not his job to make phone calls, check on loan proceeds, or talk to anyone's relatives or friends with respect to said closing. The escrow officer normally has enough responsibility without having to be concerned with all the other parties' problems.

The purchaser, or seller is normally a client whose property and funds are involved in consummating the sale. He is represented by a real estate agent and preferably also by an attorney. It is anticipated that this client is a true "consumer," one who is not a professional real estate licensee, attorney, or individual involved in the business of transacting real estate. It is the interest of the consumer that must be protected.

The real estate agent's role is primarily one of being the chief negotiator and arbiter between the parties. He can be of tremendous help in making sure that all parties stay convinced that they have each made a good deal, and that there is a complete understanding of all the facts involved. The transfer of real estate is normally considered a very personal transaction; that is, it is people-oriented. Therefore the assistance of a qualified real estate agent should help to solve many problems since he understands the relationship between the parties and what each party is expecting to obtain from the consummation of the sale.

Although the closing is not particularly a legal function, it is the author's personal opinion that all clients should be represented by an attorney (just as they should also be represented by their real estate agent). It is the attorney who understands the technical legal ramifications of the escrow agent's function, the representations made by both parties, and the interpretations of the instruments used at the closing. He is uniquely valuable in being the only individual at the closing who is capable of explaining an individual's legal rights as these pertain to the transaction. Anyone else who attempts to interpret the documents or to explain an individual's legal rights is practicing law without a license. This applies to the escrow agent as well as to the real estate agent (provided that neither are licensed to practice law).

All four of the above separate roles and functions overlap to a certain degree. However, each one can be maintained separately, individually, and in coordination with each of the other parties' rights, providing all parties can maintain their professional attitudes.

The Real Estate Settlement Procedures Act

Most closings are relatively simple and do not last very long, depending on the complications involved and the number of parties required to consummate the transaction. However, there have been a number of severe criticisms of closings generally, because of the amount of fees and costs that are taken out of the purchaser's and seller's funds—expenses that were not disclosed prior to the closing. It was as a result of some of these imprudent practices across the country that the Congress felt compelled to pass a new law called the *Real Estate Settlement Procedures Act*, which required certain disclosures to all parties prior to a closing and the use of certain forms during the closing. These requirements are of particular importance in residential transactions, and therefore will be discussed here in some detail.

The Real Estate Settlement Procedures Act (RESPA) was originally passed in 1974. Amendments in the act, as well as in the applicable regulations, were passed in 1975 and 1976. Most of the provisions of RESPA were passed so as to control practices of certain states that had a large number of fees going to the escrow officer, attorneys, and other various and sundry parties—fees that came as a surprise to the consumer when he attended the closing. As in most other cases, the statutes were passed at the national level for the benefit of all people who needed this protection. On a national scope, Texas is not considered one of the states with a reputation for charging a large amount of costs incident to the closing process. In fact, Texas passed regulations affecting title companies that are very similar to those of RESPA; these regulations are contained in Articles 9.53 and 9.54 of the Insurance Code. However, all the provisions of the federal act, of course, apply to Texas, as they do to all the other states.

Transactions Covered

Just as the federal Truth-in-Lending Act passed Regulation Z to establish guidelines for the enforcement of the Truth-in-Lending Act, so the Department of Housing and Urban Development passed what we call *Regulation X*, which establishes the guidelines for enforcement of the Real Estate Settlement and Procedures Act (RESPA). Under Regulation X, RESPA is construed to apply to all "federally related loans," which are loans that meet *all four* of the following requirements:

1. The loan proceeds must be used to finance the purchase or transfer of title to the mortgaged property;
2. The loan must be secured by a first lien on property upon which there is located a one- to four-family residential structure, either presently existing or to be constructed from the loan proceeds, or a condominium or co-op unit;
3. The mortgaged property must be located in a state;
4. The loan must be made by a lender whose accounts are insured by, or the lender is regulated by, an agency of the federal government; RESPA also requires that the lender, other than a state agency, invest in more than one million dollars per year in residential real estate loans; or the loan must be insured, guaranteed, or assisted by the federal government; or the loan must be made in connection with the Housing and Urban Development program administered by the government; or the loan must be intended to be sold to FNMA, GNMA, FHLMC, or to a lender who intends to sell the mortgage to FHLMC.

It is not difficult to see that RESPA applies to all institutional lenders and to virtually all residential transactions.

Exemptions from RESPA

There are specific exemptions from coverage under RESPA, which include the following:

1. A loan to finance the purchase or transfer of 25 or more acres;
2. A home improvement loan, refinance, or other loan where the proceeds are not used to finance the purchase or transfer of legal title to the property;
3. A loan to finance the purchase or transfer of a vacant lot;
4. An assumption, novation, sale, or transfer subject to a preexisting loan, unless it involves the use of or conversion of a construction loan to a permanent mortgage to finance the purchase by the first user;

5. A construction loan, unless it is used as and/or converted to a permanent loan to finance the purchase by the first user;
6. A permanent loan to finance the construction of a one- to four-family structure where the lot is already owned by the borrower;
7. A loan to finance the purchaser's property intended primarily for resale; or
8. Execution of a land sales contract or an installment land contract in a situation in which the legal title is not transferred to the purchaser.

The general requirements of RESPA, similar to those of the Truth-in-Lending Act, simply involve disclosure of all costs and items applicable to a particular closing transaction. We will now discuss some of these disclosures that are important to the purchaser—disclosures that involve the lender, the escrow agent, and the title companies.

Lender Requirements

The requirements of RESPA imposed on the lender consist primarily of the lender giving a "special information booklet in any RESPA-covered transaction to every person who submits a loan application in writing" [Rev. Reg. X, Section 3500.6(a)]. The purpose of the booklet is to provide as much information as possible about the borrower's rights and obligations in connection with the closing of the loan transaction. The booklet must be provided to the borrower not later than the third business day after the lender receives the loan application [Rev. Reg. X, Section 3500.6(a)]. The book is basically in the format provided by HUD, although certain variations are allowed to be made by the lender as long as it is HUD-approved.

In addition to the special information booklet, the lender must also furnish the borrower with a good faith estimate of the settlement charges that the borrower is likely to incur in connection with the loan transaction [Rev. Reg. X, Section 3500.7(a)]. Although there is some discretion allowed for the "good faith estimate," it is required that the form used must include the lender's name, must be clear and concise, and must inform the borrower that other charges may be incurred at the time of closing [Rev. Reg. X, Section 3500.7(d)].

Settlement Agent's Requirements

Whereas Texas requires the settlement agent (escrow agent) to use the State Board of Insurance-promulgated closing forms in all non-RESPA transactions, RESPA requires that the escrow agent must use the standard settlement or closing statement, often referred to as *HUD-1* [Rev. Reg. X, Section 3500.8(a)]. There are exceptions provided where the borrower is not required to pay any closing costs; but, at least to date, this option has not been widely utilized in the State of Texas. There have been some complaints about the use of the HUD-1 form because it is confusing in parts and sometimes difficult to explain to prospective purchasers during the closing transaction.

There is a basic requirement to itemize all charges paid by the borrower and seller, except for those that are not imposed by the lender and are paid for outside of the closing. If there are any costs required by the lender, even if paid outside the closing, they must still be noted on the settlement form; these would be marked "P.O.C." to indicate their payment outside of the closing. It is interesting to note that both the buyer's and seller's expenses are noted on the same form. There have been some complaints that the buyer and the seller preferred to keep their parts of the transaction confidential. Therefore, RESPA regulations now provide that the seller's columns may be deleted from the buyer's copy and the buyer's columns may be deleted from the seller's copy [Rev. Reg. X, Section 3500.8(b)]. There is additionally a general requirement that the settlement agent must provide the lender with a copy of each settlement statement.

One of the more fundamental disclosures that is required is that upon the buyer's request, the settlement agent must permit the borrower to inspect the HUD-1 form at any time during the business day before the scheduled closing. There is some limitation on this, however, in that the escrow officer need only complete the items known at the time, and has no obligation to furnish information not available prior to the closing date. With a few exceptions, the final settlement statement is to be delivered to the borrower and seller, or to their agents, at or before the time of the settlement.

Required Title Companies

There has evidently been some problem in closings as to the seller requiring the buyer to purchase title insurance from a particular title company. Since the seller in Texas normally purchases the title insurance, it is rather questionable as to whether or not this requirement has any technical application under normal Texas real estate practice. However, it deserves mentioning that such a requirement does exist, and any seller who violates this provision is liable to the buyer in an amount equal to three times the charge for such title insurance [RESPA, Section 9(b)].

Escrow Accounts

There has been a common practice among lenders to require the borrower to maintain an escrow account for the payment of taxes and insurance during the term of the mortgage. There have been some complaints made by the borrowers that they are required to pay certain advanced amounts into the escrow account that exceed the amount that would be required to pay for the tax and insurance requirements. The new RESPA rules provide that any amounts collected for escrow accounts for payments of taxes and insurance can only be so much as would equal the amount to be sufficient to pay such taxes, insurance premiums, and other charges attributable to the period between the closing and the time the amount is to be paid. All future collections for payment into the escrow account are limited to one-twelfth of the charges to become due within the next year.

The foregoing is, of course, not even a slight attempt at explaining all the RESPA rules. As in the case of the Truth-in-Lending Act, there are extensive amounts of publications available that explain most of the provisions of the RESPA Act and Regulation X in much greater detail than can be given here.

SUMMARY

The closing is the final consummation of a real estate transaction. The vast majority of closings in Texas are held at title companies, where a third party escrow agent serves as a depositary for instruments and funds. In the typical residential transaction, there are actually two closings involved rather than one. There is closing of the sale (from the seller to the purchaser), and there is closing of the loan (involving the contractual relationship between the mortgagee and the mortgagor-purchaser).

The escrow function involves the use of a disinterested third party, which helps ease the air of suspicion and distrust that may exist in a transaction. By utilizing escrow the parties may also "close into escrow," which greatly facilitates most closing transactions.

Since there is a diversity of documents utilized in a closing, it is often helpful for the real estate agent to prepare a closing checklist to help him monitor the instruments that are to be signed. It is also important that all parties to a transaction recognize what function each party to the closing is to perform.

In an attempt to clarify and disclose some of the pertinent closing functions, the federal government passed the Real Estate Settlement Procedures Act (RESPA), which covers virtually all residential transactions and all institutional lenders, although there are specific exemptions.

13

LIENS

A *lien*, generally defined, is a charge on the property of a person for the payment or discharge of a debt or duty owed by that person. It is also defined as a claim against a person's real estate that exists as a security interest for some obligation to be discharged. It has been long understood that when one party is indebted to a creditor, the creditor has the right to an interest in the first party's real estate under certain specified circumstances. In some circumstances, the creditor may even force the sale of that real estate to satisfy the debt. The only liens to be discussed in this chapter will consist of liens that attach directly to real estate, since UCC and chattel mortgage liens have been discussed in Chapter 4.

Real estate liens are generally categorized according to the source from which they are derived. For the purposes of this discussion, equitable liens (implemented upon principles of equity), statutory liens (implemented by statute), constitutional liens (implemented by the state constitution), and contractual liens (liens created by contracts) will be discussed.

Equitable Liens

An equitable lien, as its name implies, is recognized and enforced by courts under equitable principles. As in other equitable principles, this lien is founded on an express or implied contract pertaining to some specific real property, and will not be applied when there is an adequate remedy at law. The only significant requirement of an equitable lien is that the lien holder must show an intention on his part to charge the property with a debt. An equitable lien, since it is not usually recorded, is not good against a subsequent purchaser or creditor without notice of the lien.

Equitable liens normally fall into two categories. One is a *vendor's lien*, and the other is normally referred to as a *tenant's lien*. In Texas, a *vendor's lien* is well established as being implied every time there is a transfer of real property by a deed and the purchase money was not paid in full. The deed with a vendor's lien is interpreted as a mortgage, coupled with a power of rescission (right to rescind the contract) in the event of default. The vendor's lien must be judicially imposed, and can only operate as security for payment of the purchase price of the real estate, and not for any other type of indebtedness. In most transactions, there are deed of trust liens, mechanics' and materialmen's liens, and other express liens that can be recorded and are good against innocent purchasers and subsequent creditors. These are such widely accepted methods of implementing and charging property with liens that the vendor's lien situation normally only occurs in the most severe fact situations. The vendor's lien is normally felt to be the "last resort" to create a lien interest in real estate if there is a default by the purchaser. When such situations occur, the courts generally hold that the purchaser holds title to the property in trust for the seller until the purchase price is paid. However, the vendor's lien is often expressly reserved and is assigned to financing institutions to create a record on the *face of the deed*.

Another equitable lien, a *tenant's lien*, is easy to envision and sometimes creates unanticipated headaches for negligent landlords. In the typical tenant lien situation, the tenant constructs some improvement on the real property (with the landlord's knowledge, and with the expectation of being paid) that increases the value of that property such that the landlord would be unjustly enriched if the tenant was not adequately reimbursed. One can easily envision a tenant constructing an improvement, with the landlord's full knowledge, and the landlord refusing to reimburse the tenant for the cost of the improvement. In this type of situation, the tenant's only recourse may be to petition a court of equity to assure his reimbursement at some future date.

Statutory Liens

There are basically two types of statutory liens that affect real property in Texas: (1) judgment liens, and (2) mechanics' and materialmen's liens.

Judgment Liens

In order to obtain a judgment lien under Texas law, the creditor must obtain a judgment of a state or federal court of competent jurisdiction against the debtor. After the judgment has been obtained, it takes 30 days for it to become final. When the judgment is final, the creditor must then cause the judgment to be "abstracted" and indexed in the judgment records maintained by the county clerk in the county in which the land is located. This recording process is called *filing an abstract of judgment*. Obtaining the judgment, by itself, does not create a lien until the abstract of judgment has been filed and perfected. Once the abstract of judgment has been perfected, however, the lien attaches to all nonexempt real estate owned by the judgment debtor within the county, as well as to any other real estate acquired by that debtor in the county during the life of the judgment lien. The abstract of judgment may be filed in as many counties as the judgment creditor desires, and it creates an independent lien in each county where it is recorded. Judgment liens generally follow the "barber shop rule," and have priority against all subsequent liens and interests in the real property, with the exception of federal tax liens and state and county tax liens provided for by Texas law (Tex. Rev. Civ. Stat. Ann., art. 7172).

It is important to note that judgment liens do not attach to exempt homestead property. Likewise, the proceeds of the sale of the homestead remain exempt from forced sale for six months after the homestead is sold. If the proceeds are reinvested in another homestead, the new home is also exempt from forced sale. Texas has such liberal exemptions from judgment liens that it has often been called *the debtor's state*. When a judgment lien has been attached to the real estate, however, most title companies will not guarantee title until the lien has been satisfied. Therefore, as a practical matter, the judgment lien is often given more credence than the law may technically provide for.

Mechanics' and Materialmen's Liens

Mechanics' and materialmen's liens (more commonly called *M and M liens*) were created by the legislature to protect the mechanic or materialman in the event of nonpayment of funds due him for material or labors he supplied to improve real property. Virtually anyone who furnishes labor or materials pursuant to an agreement for construction of improvements on real property can claim the benefit of this statutory lien [Tex. Rev. Civ. Stat. Ann., art. 5452(2)(b)]. The liens must be perfected in the manner prescribed by law, and are strictly construed.

The method of securing the liens is very specifically described by statute [Tex. Rev. Civ. Stat. Ann., art. 5453]. The statute stipulates two different requirements in creating the lien, depending on whether the contractor was the *original contractor* (one who has a direct contractual relationship with the owner) or a *subcontractor* (one who has a direct contractual relationship with the original contractor). The statute further delineates differences in the filings for subcontractors, depending on the type of labor that was performed. The M and M lien takes inception from the time that labor or materials are furnished to the job, but the lien arises only upon perfection of that lien interest by recording it in the county courthouse in the manner prescribed by law.

Original Contractors' Liens. If there is an original contractor who wishes to perfect a lien, he must do so by filing an affidavit with the county clerk 120 days after the indebtedness accrues. He must additionally send two copies of the affidavit to the owner by certified mail. The affidavit must be substantially in the same form as provided by statute (Tex. Rev. Civ. Stat. Ann., art. 5455) and must contain the following:

1. A sworn statement of the contractor's claim, including the amount; a copy of the written agreement or contract, if any, may be attached.
2. The name of the owner or reputed owner, if known.
3. A general statement of the kind of work done or materials furnished.
4. The name of the person by whom the contractor was employed or to whom he furnished the materials or labor, and the name of the original contractor.
5. A description of the property to be charged with the liens legally sufficient for identification (an adequate legal description).

It should be noted that there are two important facts concerning the original contractor's perfecting his lien: (1) there is no advance notice required to be given to the owner of the property before the affidavit is filed; and (2) the lien, as far as money accrued is concerned, is considered to relate back to the date of inception, which is the day that materials or labor was first performed on the project. This protects the contractor and assures that he gets paid the full amount for labor and materials used in constructing improvements on the property. This doctrine of the lien arising as of the time of inception is referred to as the *Relation Back Doctrine*. However, it should not be confused with the Relation Back Doctrine referred to when speaking of escrow accounts.

Subcontractors' Liens. Subcontractors are more properly called *derivative claimants*. Derivative claimants include suppliers, artisans, laborers, lumber dealers, and other people who have an "accrued indebtedness" as defined by statute. For the purposes of this discussion, derivative claimants will be discussed primarily with respect to subcontractors. *Subcontractors* are defined by statute as a person, firm, or corporation who has furnished labor or materials to fulfill an obligation to an original contractor, or another subcontractor, to perform all or part of work required by an original contractor.

Before discussing the legal requirements for perfecting a lien by a derivative claimant, it is important to understand that such liens are rather technical, but for a special reason; that is, there is no original contract between the derivative claimant (subcontractor) and the owner of the property. In the normal situation, the owner of the property contracts with an original contractor, who, in turn, employs the subcontractors. Therefore, there is no *privity of contract* (direct contractual relationship) between the owner and subcontractor. Since the subcontractor has the ability to cloud the title to the owner's property, he is held to a high degree of care in perfecting his claim to a lien on that property.

For a subcontractor to perfect his lien, he must give the required *notice* to the owner in order to secure his lien as provided by statute under Article 5453(2). (Remember that the original contractor is not required by statute to give notice.) The statute provides for three different types of notices from the subcontractor, which have been customarily called the *2a notice,* the *2b notice,* and the *2c notice,* depending on which provision of the statute is utilized.

According to the conditions under which the work was performed, a *2a notice* provides that if an agreement for a *retainage* (escrowed funds) exists between the claimant and the original contractor, or between the claimant and any other subcontractor, the derivative claimant may give written notice to the owner of his right to perfect a lien. The notice must be given not later than 36 days after the tenth day of the month following the making of such retainage agreement. A copy of the notice must also be given to the original contractor. The notices must be sent by certified or registered mail, properly addressed to the owner and to the original contractor. The notice must state the amount to be retained and indicate the nature of the retainage agreement. This type of notice does not impound any funds and only serves as a proceeding to collect against a bond or retainage agreement, if such agreement is in full force and effect and funds have not been disbursed out of the retainage or bond funds to another claimant. This is not considered one of the more protective provisions of notices required by the statute.

A *2b notice*, on the other hand, is generally considered to be one of the most protective for the subcontractor because it has the effect of impounding funds that are in the hands of owners and are owing to the original contractor. Normally, when this happens, the owner will withhold any funds from the original contractor until he is sure that the subcontractor has been paid. It is not uncommon for an owner to make the check payable to both the original contractor and the subcontractor to be sure that both parties are aware that payment has been made by the owner and that the funds have been properly distributed. When making a check out jointly, the owner is at least assured that the proper funds have been paid, and if the subcontractor does not get his share of those funds, it was not due to the owner's negligence or lack of diligence.

The notice provided for under the 2b provision of Article 5453 must: (1) state the unpaid balance of the claim, (2) provide a copy of the statement billing in the usual and customary form, and (3) contain some form of statement to the owner that if the bill remains unpaid, the owner may be personally liable and his property may be subjected to a lien unless he withholds payment from the contractor for the payment of such statement or unless the bill is otherwise paid or settled. The 2b notice must be sent by the claimant to the owner not later than 90 days after the tenth day of the month next following each month in which the labor was performed. This notice is an absolute requirement to authorize the owner to retain funds, *Trinity Universal Insurance Company* v. *Palmer*, 412 S.W.2d 691 (Tex. Civ. App.—San Antonio, 1967). The 2b notice must also be given to the original contractor not later than 36 days after the tenth of the month next following each month in which the claimant's labor was done or performed. These notices to the contractor must be given each and every month that work is performed or materials are delivered and the derivative claimant is not paid.

There is an additional problem for the subcontractor, in that if he waits until the 120 days or 90 days after the work was performed before he sends his notice, all funds could have already been distributed to the original contractor upon completion of the work. In this case, it may be too late to trap any substantial amount of funds to assure the derivative claimant of payment. Therefore, it is sometimes common practice for a subcontractor to file his notice automatically at the end of the month, to be sure to protect his interest and to impound any funds that may be available before distribution to the original contractor. This sometimes serves to put the owner on notice that the lien may exist in the event of nonpayment. Of course, the owner does not know the terms of the contract between the original contractor and subcontractor, and the subcontractor may be sending the notice without any right to do so. However, its use normally only serves to effect proper notice to the owner, as required by statute, and does not serve to cloud the title to the property.

A *2c notice* is a notice used when the derivative claimant's claim is for a specially fabricated item. The 2c notice must also be given to the owner not later than 36 days after the tenth day of the month next following the receipt of the acceptance of the order for such specially fabricated material. This notice must be sent by certified or registered mail addressed to the owner, and to the original contractor where required. A 2c notice does not provide for impoundment of funds and must be followed by a 2b notice to perfect the lien after the material has been delivered to the job.

In addition to the foregoing notices, the subcontractor must also file an affidavit pursuant to the same requirements that the original contractor must file; he must file this affidavit within 90 days after the indebtedness accrues. Two copies of the affidavit are sent to the owner, and the lien must be filed in the lien records of the county courthouse.

Statutory Retainage. An often overlooked area of mechanics' and materialmen's liens is the statute that provides for a claimant's fund with preference to mechanics and artisans (Tex. Rev. Civ. Stat. Ann., art. 5469). The purpose of this statute is to create a special fund for the benefit of mechanics and artisans, and to grant them a preference over materialmen and subcontractors. The statute basically provides that it is the duty of the owner, or his agent, to retain in his hands, during the progress of work and for 30 days after the work is completed, 10% of the contract price of such work (or 10% of the value of same). This secures the payment of artisans and mechanics who perform labor and services, and also secures the payment of any other claimant furnishing material, material and labor, or specially fabricated material for any contractor, subcontractor, agent, or receiver.

All persons who send notice as required by the mechanics' and materialmen's lien statute (not later than 30 days after the work is completed) shall have a lien upon that retained fund with preference given to artisans and mechanics. The claimants share ratably to the extent of their claims, so there is a good chance that a claimant may only get a small proportional part of the money due him. However, he will have a preference claim to the funds remaining if he files his claim within 30 days. After the artisans and mechanics are paid, the remainder of the fund, if any, goes to the other participating claimants, also ratably shared.

The statute further states that if the owner fails to comply with this statutory provision, he shall be liable for the liens, at least to the extent of the 10%, implying that there might be unlimited liability on the part of the owner for failing to keep this statutory 10% retainage. There have been quite a number of cases that support the artisan's claim to the statutory retainage, implying that the owner may have an unlimited liability, *Hayek* v. *Western Steel Company*, 478 S.W.2d 786 (Tex. 1972), and, further, that if the statutory retainage is not properly kept, the 30-day period for claiming liens is not applicable as a limitation time for lien claimants, *General Air Conditioning Co.* v. *Third Ward Church of Christ*, 426 S.W.2d 541 (Tex. 1968).

Mechanic and Materialmen Lien Priorities—Severable Improvements. With the foregoing statutory mechanic and materialmen lien provisions, both for notice and affidavits, along with the statutory retainage provision, one would normally think that the mechanic and materialman, particularly the artisan and laborer, would be well protected under Texas law. However, this is not necessarily the case. Owners who have to keep the statutory retainage are often corporations with little or no assets. These owners may be construction companies, or developers' subsidiaries, and claims for damages against them may be difficult to recover. This problem is compounded by the fact that the subcontractors or contractors do not have to file their claims for 120 days or 90 days, respectively, so these claims for liens may be too late to be constructive notice to a subsequent purchaser for value. Therefore, the law puts a high duty of care on the contractor, subcontractor, and mechanic and materialman in perfecting their interest.

In an effort to protect the mechanic's and materialman's interest, the courts have liberally construed the statutes so as to protect them when possible. Starting with one of the oldest landmark cases in Texas, *Oriental Hotel Company* v. *Griffiths*, 33 S.W. 652 (Tex. 1896), the courts have consistently held that the lien, regardless of when filed, relates back to the date of inception, that is, the date that any work was done or materials were brought to the premises, so that the mechanic's and materialman's claim would be prior in time to anything brought subsequently. Derivative claimants take the same inception date as that of the general contractor.

The mechanics' and materialmen's lien is also superior to a prior recorded deed of trust lien, where the improvements can be removed without material injury to the land and preexisting improvements, *First National Bank* v. *Whirlpool Corp.*, 517 S.W.2d 262 (Tex. 1974). It is interesting to note that there have been a number of cases that distinguish what can be removed without material injury to the building (these improvements are termed *severable* improvements). Severable improvements have been held to include a ticket booth, a speaker stand and a screen at a drive-in theatre, a partially completed structure attached to a concrete foundation and frame building, garbage disposals, built-in dishwashers, heating and air-conditioning systems, and compressors and air-handling units inside of air-conditioning units. Nonseverable improvements have included a house, painting and plastering, roof repairs, window frames, and cabinets. There will probably be a lot of litigation in the future to determine what other improvements could be construed as being severable.

This doctrine of mechanic and materialman lien priority, plus the concept of severable improvements, is virtually absolute except in a circumstance where the interim lender (the bank) may have a deed of trust that specifies a prior lien for money advanced to the general contractor (future advance clause). If such a mortgage is filed before the materialman begins delivery of his materials, that deed of trust lien is prior to the materialman's lien with respect to the advances made, with notice, actual or constructive, of the materialman's lien, *Coke Lumber & Mfg. Co.* v. *First National Bank in Dallas*, 529 S.W.2d 612 (Tex. Civ. App.—Dallas, 1975). The doctrine favoring the interim lender is fairly limited, and is construed according to the covenants contained in the deed of trust instrument with respect to future advances.

In addition to the foregoing, it should be pointed out that mechanics and materialmen are also protected by the attorneys' fees statute (Tex. Rev. Civ. Stat. Ann., art. 2226). This statute entitles the lien holder to attorneys' fees in the event he is forced to hire legal counsel to represent him in pursuing a cause of action for payment of his services.

Constitutional Liens

The Texas Constitution provides for an automatic lien under Article 16, Section 37—as another means for protecting the mechanic and materialman and artisan. This type of lien is available only to an original contractor (one who is in direct contractual relationship with the owner), but it does apply to all mechanics, artisans, and materialmen, and those who furnish labor and materials for the erection and repair of a building.

The lien becomes effective automatically, with the only exception being the homestead exemption provided by Article 16, Section 50, of the Texas Constitution. This lien becomes effective as of the time the owner entered into the contract or at the time of first delivery of material or labor, whichever is first. However, like a vendor's lien, if it is not recorded, it would not be good against an innocent purchaser unless the contractor filed his affidavit in accordance with the mechanics' and materialmen's lien statutes. In this manner, a filed constitutional lien becomes a statutory lien.

The importance of a constitutional lien, of course, is that one does not have to rely on the whims and caprices of the legislature, and the lien exists regardless of whether or not one meets the filing deadlines as provided under the mechanics' and materialmen's lien statutes. Even if the lien is filed late, and not within the statutory guidelines, one still has a constitutional basis for establishing that lien as a mechanic or materialman.

Contractual Liens

The liens discussed thus far have been those provided for by statute or by law of equity. The contractual lien, on the other hand, can exist simply when two parties wish to establish the lien as security for some type of obligation. Examples of contractual liens would be mortgages, in that they offer proper security for money to be loaned. Leases are also a very common source of contractual liens. Or one often finds that the tenant offers his furniture and personalty in the leased premises as security for his payment of his rental obligations under his lease. There are also provisions for statutory landlords' liens and owners' of buildings liens, which will be discussed in greater detail in the next chapter.

Redemption

In the event of default on any secured obligation in Texas, including liens, the only right one has is to buy the property at the foreclosure sale, which is generally for cash. *Texas has no right of redemption unless specifically provided for by agreement*. As you recall from Chapter 9, debtors do have the right to "redeem up" if they are not in default and have an equity of redemption in the property. However, if such equity of redemption is in default, and the property is subject to foreclosure, there is no right to pay the entire indebtedness except by buying at the foreclosure sale. From a practical standpoint, the lender or lien holder normally allows the debtor to pay the obligations rather than having to go through the foreclosure procedure. However, this is not always the case. One must remember that mere lack of consideration, by itself, is not enough to set aside a foreclosure sale, and that the law is that the foreclosure is proper unless there are some material irregularities in that foreclosure.

SUMMARY

A lien is a charge on the property of a person for the payment or discharge of a debt or duty owed by that person. Equitable liens are imposed by a court of jurisdiction to help prevent an unfair result, since it is not recorded as not good against a subsequent purchaser or creditor without notice of the lien. Statutory liens have a significant impact in Texas. They consist of judgment liens and mechanics' and materialmen's liens. A judgment lien is a lien which is perfected by the property party filing an abstract of judgment. This abstract of judgment can only be filed after a court of competent jurisdiction rules in favor of the creditor. Mechanics' and materialmen's liens were created by the legislature to protect mechanics or materialmen in the event of nonpayment of funds owed to the mechanic or materialmen. The methods of perfecting liens are very specifically set out by a statute. There are different requirements for perfecting the lien, depending on whether or not the contractor is a general contractor or a subcontractor. There are complicated questions of priorities when dealing with mechanics' and materialmen's liens. The ability to sever the improvements and remove them without material injury to the building is another effective method of protecting the contractor.

Constitutional liens protect the contractor and artisan. These liens have no recording requirements and become effective automatically after the work is performed on all property except homestead property. Texas has no right of redemption for defaults unless specifically provided for by an agreement.

14

LANDLORD AND TENANT RELATIONSHIPS

The existence of a landlord (lessor) and tenant (lessee) relationship creates a nonfreehold estate, which we term a *leasehold estate*. A leasehold estate is also referred to as a *tenancy*. Tenancy implies more than just a mere use of the premises because it includes occupancy and possession of the premises superior to the rights of anyone else except the landlord. Even the landlord's rights are limited, both by statute and by case law. In the recent past, the landlord was given very high priority in determining rights between the landlord and tenant. New statutes, however, have given much greater effect to the rights of the tenant in possession of the property. In most cases, the landlord finds that his hands are tied when making an effort to remove the tenant from the premises very quickly. The tenant, if he is represented by good lawyers, often finds he can maintain his occupancy for a couple of months before he would ever have to leave the premises. This chapter will discuss the statutory law and case law relating to landlord and tenant relationships, the law applicable to forcible entry and detainer proceedings, and some procedural court problems that arise in a normal eviction proceeding.

Tenancies

There are four types of tenancies, leasehold estates, and nonfreehold estates:

1. An estate for years.
2. An estate from period to period.
3. An estate at will.
4. An estate at sufferance.

Estate for Years

An estate for years has a definite term, and almost necessarily implies the existence of a lease. The Statute of Frauds (Section 26.01) specifically provides that a lease for real estate for a term longer than one year is not enforceable unless it is in writing and is signed by the person to be charged. One normally envisions estates for years as being long-term office leases, ground leases, or those rare instances when one may find a residential lease for longer than one year. One of the more interesting examples of an estate for years was created as a lifetime tenancy for a lessee under an oral lease. The tenant, in this case, contended that the entire estate for years was dependent on whether or not she lived for longer than one year, and, therefore, was not within the Statute of Frauds. Believe it or not, this contention was upheld, *McCloud* v. *Knapp*, 507 S.W.2d 644 (Tex. Civ. App.—Dallas, 1974). The basic fundamentals of leases will be discussed later in this chapter as a separate topic.

Estate from Period to Period

An estate from period to period normally includes an estate from month to month, or an estate from year to year, renewable at the option of the parties. It has an indefinite duration. The estate from month to month is not normally in writing, and is probably the most common form found in Texas. Unless there is a written agreement to the contrary, tenancies from month to month must have a 30-day notice before they are terminated.

Estate at Will

An estate at will is an estate that is terminable at the will of either the lessor or the lessee. It has an indefinite duration.

Estate at Sufferance

An estate at sufferance is an estate that exists when a person wrongfully continues possession of the land after the termination of his right to possession. Normally, in an estate at sufferance, the tenant's right to possession is the result of the landlord's neglect or lack of diligence. The tenant, as a tenant at sufferance, has no obligation to pay rent, nor any other rights under his estate at sufferance. It is equal to having no estate at all. In Texas, a tenant in this holdover capacity is normally liable for rents during his occupancy under the same terms and conditions that he enjoyed prior to the end of his lease term and before the holdover period.

Statutes

As a general rule, the rights of landlord and tenant are set out either by statute or by the requirements of the lease. Texas passed a number of statutes that have particularly useful application to protect tenants' rights; most of these statutes became effective September 1, 1973. Since these statutes are so specific, and so important in interpreting day-to-day landlord and tenant problems, they are reproduced here in their entirety for the student's benefit, with some additional comment as to the application of the statutes. Please note that there is emphasis supplied in some portions of the statute in order to bring pertinent points to the student's attention:

> **Art. 5236a. Notice for terminating certain tenancies**
>
> (a) A monthly tenancy or tenancy from month to month may be terminated by the landlord or the tenant by *one month's notice* given to the other party. When the rent reserved in a lease is payable at periods of less than a month, the time of the notice of termination is sufficient if it is equal to the interval between the times of payment. The notice is not void merely because it mentions a day for the termination of the tenancy not corresponding to the conclusions or commencement of the rent-paying period, but rather the notice terminates the tenancy at the end of a period equal in time to that in which the rent is made payable, unless a later date is specified.
>
> (b) If the notice required by Subsection (a) of this section terminates the tenancy on a day which does not correspond to the conclusion or commencement of a rent-paying period, *the tenant is liable only for rent up to the date of termination and not liable for rent for the balance of the rent-paying period*.
>
> (c) Subsection (a) of this section does not apply when
>
> (1) *by written agreement, signed by the landlord and tenant, a different period of notice, or no notice, is to be given*; or
>
> (2) *there is any breach of contract recognized by law*.

Please note that the foregoing statute provides for a specified notice for terminating the tenancy, primarily in the event that there is no written agreement or lease between the landlord and tenant that provides for other terms of termination.

Art. 5236b. Landlord's Agent for Service of Process

Authorized agent

Section 1. In any lawsuit by a tenant founded on an oral or written rental agreement for a residential dwelling or in any lawsuit to enforce a legal obligation of the owner in his capacity as landlord, the owner's management company, on-premise manager, or rent collector serving such dwelling unit shall automatically be the owner's authorized agent for service of process unless the owner's name and business street address has been furnished in writing to the tenant.

Management company as agent

Sec. 2. Provided, however, if the residential dwelling unit is managed by a management company whose name and business street address has been furnished in writing to the tenant, only such management company shall be the owner's agent for such service of process under Section 1 above.

This provision provides generally for the same type of protection and privilege for service of process that the law of principle and agency provides. In this instance, the landlord is considered the agent for the owner.

Art. 5236c. Willful Interruption of Utilities and Willful Exclusion by Landlord

Interruption of utilities

Section 1. It shall be unlawful under any circumstances for a landlord or his agent to interrupt or cause interruption of utilities *paid for by the tenant directly to the utility company*.

Willful exclusion of tenant

Sec. 2. *It shall be unlawful for a landlord or his agent to willfully exclude a tenant from the tenant's premises in any manner except by judicial process*. Willful exclusion shall mean preventing the tenant from entering into the premises with intent to deprive the tenant of such entry. Provided, however, *a landlord or his agent shall not be prevented from removing the contents of the premises when the tenant has abandoned the premises or from changing door locks when the tenant's rentals are in fact delinquent in whole or in part*. When such door lock is changed under such circumstances, a written notice shall be left on the tenant's front door describing where the new key may be obtained *at any hour* and describing the name of the individual who will provide the tenant with such key; *and such key shall be provided regardless of whether the tenant pays any delinquent rentals*.

Bona fide repairs, construction or emergencies

Sec. 3. The landlord or his agent shall not be guilty of a violation of this Article if the action complained of resulted from bona fide repairs, construction, or emergencies.

Remedies of tenant; damages; attorneys fees

Sec. 4. Upon violation of this Article by the landlord or his agent, the tenant may recover possession or terminate the rental agreement; and, *in either case, the tenant may recover actual damages, plus one month's rent, plus reasonable attorneys fees, less any delinquent rentals or other sums for which the tenant is liable*.

Waiver of rights and liabilities void and unenforceable

Sec. 5. Any provision of an oral or written rental agreement between the landlord and tenant which provision purports to exempt the landlord or tenant from any liability or duty imposed herein or which provision purports to waive the rights and liabilities granted under this Article, *shall be void and unenforceable*.

Rights consistent with article undiminished

Sec. 6. Nothing in this Article shall serve to affect or diminish any of the rights of the landlord or tenant under contract, statute, or common law which are consistent with the provisions hereof.

This particular statute is one of the key provisions of the new landlord and tenant law put in effect in 1973. It imposes very strong restrictions on the landlord in that he cannot willfully interrupt any utilities if paid for by the tenant directly to the utility company, and may not exclude a tenant from the premises without due process of law. *Due process of law* means court action. This means the landlord must take a tenant to court and have a formal eviction proceeding before he can exclude that tenant from his premises. This applies even if the lease provides for an automatic eviction, since Section 5 of the statute prohibits any waiver by oral or written agreement for the rights contained in this particular statute.

Section 2 specifies that the landlord can change the locks on a tenant's doors but must provide a key for the tenant so that he (the tenant) can gain entrance into his apartment at any time of the day or night. The net effect of this particular provision is that the tenant must approach the landlord and at least talk to him on a face-to-face basis before he can get the key to his apartment. Although this statute might seem to be totally unfair to the landlord, there are methods of making this provision a little more effective for the landlord's benefit. For instance, the landlord might post the notice on the man's door that his key is available at some very questionable all-night bar and grill by asking for ''Fat-Face Ernie.'' It is a rare tenant who will attempt to go get his key under these conditions.

A particularly important provision of this statute is Section 4, which provides for the damages that the tenant may recover in the event of a violation of that statute by the landlord. Note that the tenant may recover actual damages, plus one month's rent, plus reasonable attorneys' fees, less any delinquent rentals or other sums for which the tenant is liable. Those are pretty stiff penalties for noncompliance on the part of the landlord. This particular statute has been held to apply to all tenancies, both residential and commercial, regardless of their duration (Op. Atty. Gen. 1974, No. H-337).

Art. 5236d. Landlord's Lien for Rent

Lien on property for unpaid rent

Section 1. The operator of any residential house, apartment, duplex, or other single or multi-family dwelling, shall have a lien upon all property found within the tenant's dwelling and upon all property stored by the tenant within a storage room for all rentals due and unpaid by the tenant, except that property specifically exempted hereinafter.

Exemptions

Sec. 2. Notwithstanding any other statute to the contrary, there shall be exempt from the lien set out in Section 1 above, the following: (1) all wearing apparel, (2) all tools, apparatus and books belonging to any trade or profession, (3) school books, (4) one automobile and one truck, (5) family library and all family portraits and pictures, (6) household furniture to the extent of one couch, two living room chairs, dining table and chairs, (7) all beds and bedding, (8) all kitchen furniture and utensils, (9) all food and foodstuffs, (10) all medicine and other medical supplies, (11) all goods known by the landlord or his agent to belong to persons other than the tenant or other occupants of such dwelling, (12) all goods known by the landlord or his agent to be subject to a recorded chattel mortgage lien or financing agreement, and (13) all agricultural implements.

Waiver of rights, liabilities or exemptions void and unenforceable

Sec. 3. Any provision of an oral or written rental agreement between the landlord and tenant which purports to waive or diminish the rights, liabilities, or exemptions granted herein, shall be void and unenforceable to the extent herein limited.

Enforceability; conspicuously printed in agreement

Sec. 4. A contractual landlord's lien shall not be enforceable unless underlined or printed in conspicuous bold print in the rental agreement.

Unlawful seizures of property

Sec. 5. It shall be unlawful for any landlord or his agent to seize any property exempt under Section 2 above, under any circumstances. It shall be unlawful for a landlord or his agent to seize any property not exempt under Section 2 above, unless pursuant to the terms of a written rental agreement between the landlord and the tenant.

Removal of contents when tenant has abandoned premises

Section 6. Nothing herein shall prevent a landlord or his agent from removing the contents of the premises when the tenant has abandoned the premises.

Remedies of tenant; damages; attorneys fees

Sec. 7. Upon willful violation of this Article by the landlord or his agent, the tenant may recover one month's rent, plus actual damages, plus reasonable attorneys fees, less any delinquent rentals or other sums for which the tenant is liable.

Rights consistent with article undiminished

Sec. 8. Nothing in this Article shall serve to affect or diminish any of the rights of the landlord or tenant under contract, statute, or common law which are consistent with the provisions hereof.

Added by Acts 1973, 63rd Leg., p. 1227, ch. 441, § 3, eff. Sept. 1, 1973.

There is some question as to whether or not the foregoing statute is constitutional, in that it does allow the landlord the right to certain properties of the tenant without due process of law. However, to date, there has not been a precedent-setting decision that holds the statute unconstitutional. It is important to note the exemptions under Section 2 are rather broad, and there would be probably very little that a tenant would have that would be subject to the lien anyway. In this statute, similar to the previous one, we have nonwaiver of rights for the tenant, as well as a stiff remedy for the landlord in the event he violates any provision of the act.

Art. 5236e. Security deposits; minimum age for entering into rental agreements

Definitions

Section 1. As used in this Act:

(1) "Security deposit" means any advance or deposit of money, regardless of denomination, the primary function of which is to secure full or partial performance of a rental agreement for a[1] residential premises. "Security deposit" does not include advance rentals.

(2) "Landlord" means the owner, lessor, or sublessor of a residential dwelling unit. "Landlord" also includes any legal entity shown as a managing agent or leasing agent on a written rental agreement.

(3) "Tenant" means any person entitled under a rental agreement to occupy a dwelling unit to the exclusion of others.

(4) "Premises" means a rental unit, appurtenances thereto, grounds and facilities held out for the use of the tenants generally, and any other area or facility whose use is promised to the tenant.

(5) "Rental agreement" means any agreement, written or oral, which establishes or modifies the terms, conditions, rules, regulations, or any other provisions regarding the use and occupancy of a residential rental unit.

(6) "Normal wear and tear" means that deterioration which occurs, based upon the use for which the rental unit is intended, without

negligence, carelessness, accident, or abuse of the premises or equipment or chattels by the tenant or members of his household, or his invitees or guests.

Landlord's obligation to refund security deposit

Sec. 2. (a) Security deposits must be refunded by the landlord to the tenant within 30 days after the tenant surrenders the premises. A tenant shall give advance notice of surrender as may be required by the rental agreement. However, advance notice may not be a condition for refund unless the requirement of advance notice is underlined or printed in conspicuous, bold print in the rental agreement.

(b) The landlord shall keep accurate records of all security deposits. The tenant's claim to the security deposit shall be prior to any creditor of the landlord, excluding a trustee in bankruptcy.

Landlord's obligation to furnish accounting of security deposit

Sec. 3. (a) In the event actual cause exists for retaining all or any portion of the security deposit, the landlord shall return to the tenant the balance of the security deposit, if any, together with a written description and itemized list of all deductions. Such deductions shall be limited to damages and charges for which the tenant is legally liable under the rental agreement or as a result of breaching the rental agreement. No security deposit may be retained to cover normal wear and tear as defined in Paragraph (6), Section 1, of this Act. The burden of proving the reasonableness of such damages or charges shall be on the landlord.

(b) A landlord is not required to furnish a description and itemized list of deductions if there are any rentals due and unpaid at the time the tenant surrenders possession of the premises and there is no controversy over the amount of rentals due and unpaid.

Landlord's failure to comply

Sec. 4. (a) A landlord who in bad faith retains a security deposit in violation of this Act is liable for $100 plus treble the amount of that portion of the deposit which was wrongfully withheld from the tenant, and shall be liable for reasonable attorneys fees in a lawsuit to recover the security deposit.

(b) A landlord who in bad faith fails to provide a written description and itemized list of damages and charges pursuant to the requirements of this Act, forfeits all rights to withhold any portion of the security deposit or to bring suit against the tenant for damages to the premises and is liable to the tenant for reasonable attorneys fees in a lawsuit to recover the security deposit.

(c) In any court action brought by a tenant under this Act, the landlord bears the burden of proving that his retention of the security deposit or any portion thereof was reasonable. In this court action the landlord is

[1]So in enrolled bill.

not liable for the penalty, treble damages, or attorneys fees referred to in Subsections (a) and (b) of this section unless the landlord is found to have acted in bad faith. Failure to return a security deposit within 30 days or failure to provide a written description and itemization of deductions within 30 days is prima facie evidence and a presumption that the landlord acted in bad faith.

Cessation of owner's interest

Sec. 5. (a) On cessation of the owner's interest in the premises (whether by sale, assignment, death, appointment of a receiver, or otherwise), the new owner is liable for the return of security deposits pursuant to the terms of this Act, from the date title to the premises is acquired by the new owner. However, this subsection is not applicable to acquisition of title at foreclosure by real estate mortgage lien holders.

(b) On cessation of the owner's interest in the premises (whether by sale, assignment, death, appointment of a receiver, or otherwise), the owner remains liable for security deposits received by the owner or his agent until such time as the new owner or his agent has delivered to the tenant a signed statement, acknowledging that the new owner has received and is responsible for the tenant's security deposit. The acknowledgment shall specify the exact dollar amount of the tenant's security deposit.

Tenant's obligation regarding security deposit

Sec. 6. (a) The tenant shall furnish the landlord with a written copy of the tenant's forwarding address for purposes of security deposit refunding. A tenant's right to security deposit refund and description of damages and charges is never forfeited for mere failure to furnish a forwarding address to the landlord. Notwithstanding any other provision of this Act, a landlord is not obligated to return the security deposit or furnish a written description of damages and charges until the tenant has furnished the forwarding address.

(b) The tenant shall not withhold payment of the last month's rental, or any portion thereof, on grounds that the security deposit serves as security for the unpaid rentals. If a tenant in bad faith fails to abide by the requirements of this subsection, the tenant is liable to the landlord for treble the amount of the rentals wrongfully withheld and for reasonable attorneys' fees in a lawsuit to recover the rentals. Withholding a portion of the last month's rental on grounds that the security deposit serves as security for the unpaid rentals, is prima facie evidence and a presumption that the tenant acted in bad faith.

Waiver of rights void

Sec. 7. Any provision of an oral or written rental agreement between the landlord and tenant which purports to exempt the landlord or tenant from any liability or duty imposed by this Act or which purports to waive the rights and liabilities granted under this Act, is void and unenforceable.

Other rights not affected

Sec. 8. Nothing in this Act shall affect or diminish any of the rights of the landlord or tenant under contract, statute, or common law which are consistent with provisions of this Act.

Minimum age

Sec. 9. Except where specifically exempted by the constitution or statutes of this state, a person 18 years of age or older has the legal capacity to enter into a binding written rental agreement or written security deposit agreement for residential property, and shall be bound by all the provisions of this Act.

Laws in conflict

Sec. 10. All laws in conflict herewith are repealed to the extent of the conflict.

Effective date

Sec. 11. This Act shall take effect on September 1, 1973, and shall apply to all residential rental agreements executed or entered into after that date.

Saving

Sec. 12. If any word, phrase, clause, paragraph, sentence, part, portion, or provision of this Act or the application thereof to any person or circumstance is held to be invalid or unconstitutional, the remainder of this Act shall nevertheless be valid, and the legislature hereby declares that this Act would have been enacted without such invalid or unconstitutional word, phrase, clause, paragraph, sentence, part, portion, or provision or application.

This statute is very specific with respect to security deposits, and provides very stiff penalties under Section 4 in the event that the landlord fails to comply with the statute. The subject of security deposits was an area of heavy conflict prior to the passage of this statute. The statute, coupled with the new Deceptive Trade Practices—Consumer Protection Act, makes the landlord's liability far greater than any enrichment he might receive from the amount of the deposit. Of course, the tenant's obligations under Section 6 must be strictly complied with in order to maintain an action under the statute.

Art. 5237. [5489] [3250] Tenants shall not sub-let

A person renting said lands or tenements shall not rent or lease the same during the term of said lease to any other person without first obtaining the consent of the landlord, his agent or attorney. Id.

The foregoing statute makes it quite clear that no tenant may assign or sublet his premises without the prior written approval of the landlord.

Lease Agreements

Leases are obviously contracts involving the transfer of interest of real property. As such, the provisions of the Statute of Frauds are applicable for any lease in excess of one year. It is well accepted that the contractual nature of real property leases is interpreted pursuant to the strict construction of contracts, rather than the law of real property. Most leases, especially the more sophisticated varieties for office space and retail (shopping center) space, have become so detailed that it is necessary to secure the services of a lawyer to make sure that a party is adequately protected. The rules governing the interpretation of contracts and construction of contracts are the same when applied to leases.

A harsh result was reached in the recent case of *Reynolds-Penland Company* v. *Hexter & Lobello, et al.*, 567 S.W.2d 237 (Tex. Civ. App.—Dallas, 1978), which construed the lease in strict accordance with its terms and disallowed the intervention of equity, even though it resulted in hardship for one of the parties. The court stated that in the absence of circumstances such as fraud, misleading statements, or acts by the lessor, or waiver, the rules of equity could not be interposed to rewrite a lease.

It is very important to point out that as a result of a recent Texas Supreme Court decision, *Kamarath* v. *Bennett*, 568 S.W.2d 658 (Tex. 1978), Texas now recognizes an implied *warranty of habitability*, which arises as a consequence of the landlord-tenant relationship. In this landmark case, the Texas Supreme Court held that the implied warranty of habitability exists and is imposed by law as a matter of public policy. It is very important to recognize, however, that the case specifically did not address the question of the landlord's breach of warranty constituting a deceptive trade practice in violation of the Deceptive Trade Practices—Consumer Protection Act.

The criteria constituting ''habitability'' are lengthy and indefinite. The court stated that in order to constitute a breach of the warranty, the defect must be:

> of a nature which will render the premise unsafe, or unsanitary, or otherwise unfit for living therein. The nature of the deficiency, its affect on habitability, the length of time which it persisted, the age of the structure, the amount of the rent, the area in which the premise is located, whether the tenant waived the defects, and whether the defects resulted from malicious, abnormal, or unusual use by the tenant are among the factors to be considered in deciding.

If there is a breach of the warranty, the court specifically stated that:

> the existence of a breach is usually a question of fact to be determined by the circumstance of each case.

Evidently, this makes any breach of implied warranty a fact to be decided at a trial, and is not a question of law.

It has also been held that when a lessor retains possession or control of a portion of the leased premises, he is charged with the duty or ordinary care in maintaining that portion so as not to damage the lessee, *McCreless Properties, Ltd.* v. *F. W. Woolworth Company*, 533 S.W.2d 863 (4th Ct. Civ. App.—San Antonio, 1976). Thus, it must be impressed upon all lessees, as well as lessors, that the rights set out in the lease agreement will probably control any fact situation as it arises, with possible implied warranties on the part of the landlord. Since these rights have become so important under contractual terms, we will discuss the requirements of the lease, types of leases, and certain aspects of assignment and subletting.

Lease Requirements

In discussing the requirements of a lease, we will find that they are very similar to those of other contracts for real estate generally. These requirements are as follows:

1. The lease must be in writing and must be signed by the party to be charged;
2. It must include a specific, identifiable landlord and tenant (the parties to the lease);
3. It must contain the intent of the landlord to grant to the tenant the right to enter and possess the designated premises for a fixed consideration;
4. It must include an adequate description of the leasehold premises;
5. It must give a specific period of time of occupancy;
6. It must have been delivered and accepted.

Except for item 6, most of these provisions are self-explanatory. Delivery and acceptance, being a fact question, is normally implied when the lessor takes possession of the premises, which will bind him as effectively as an express acceptance. It is important to note that even if the lessor sells the property, the lease gives the lessee an estate in land that is not terminated by the sale unless it is expressly provided for in the lease, *Zale Corp.* v. *Decorama*, 470 S.W.2d 406 (Tex. Civ. App.—Waco, 1971). The lessee may further wish to protect his interest by recording the lease. If this is the case, the lease will also need to be acknowledged.

Types of Leases

There are four types of leases, depending on the manner in which the rent is paid:

1. A lease for a fixed term (gross lease).
2. A percentage lease.
3. A net lease.
4. A ground lease.

It is important to note that any one of the above types of leases is going to have its own character, depending on the type of premises it is intended to transfer. For instance, the terms of a gross lease vary widely, depending on whether the premises are a single-family residence, office space, or an apartment. No one standard lease form is applicable to all situations.

Gross Lease. A gross lease is most often used for a fixed term and for a fixed sum of money. In more current years, the fixed rental provisions are subject to some rental adjustment for operation, costs, and utility escalation. However, for the most part, the gross lease is considered to be one of a fixed term and fixed rental amount. This type of lease is commonly used when leasing office space, apartments, and other residential properties.

Percentage Lease. A percentage lease is most often used for lessees in retail premises. A retail premise would include shopping centers, shopping malls, strip centers, and any other type of use that may deal directly with a lessee whose income is contingent upon access to the shopping public.

The unique rental payment provisions make the percentage lease different from most other types of leases. The lease normally provides that the lessee will occupy the space at a relatively low base rent. This rent is usually just enough for the lessor to meet his mortgage payment with perhaps a small amount of profit. The remainder of the lessee's lease payments are contingent upon a percentage of the gross sales that the lessee experiences. This percentage interest may vary from 2 to 11%, depending on the size of the lessee. Large, major lessees normally pay a much lower percentage because their volume of business is much higher and they are often a "draw" for smaller lessees. The percentage rentals may be paid monthly (after preliminary accounting for gross income), quarterly, or annually. Because of the volatile nature of costs in recent years, most lessors prefer that this percentage rental be paid monthly to cover the increasing uncontrolled costs for utilities, taxes, and insurance.

The percentage lease provides many advantages to both the lessor and the lessee by creating some dependence on each party. The lessee gets a lower base rate for his rentals and only has to pay an increased rent if, in fact, his volume of business justifies it. The lessor, on the other hand, is not only assured of having his mortgage payments paid, but stands to make higher profits if the lessee makes higher profits. Therefore it is to the advantage of the lessor to maintain his shopping center in such a manner as to make it attractive and accessible to old potential shoppers. There is an incentive on the part of both the lessor and the lessee to make their respective businesses as successful as possible. As a general rule, the percentage lease never creates a partnership agreement between the lessor and the lessee.

Net Lease. A net lease is generally one in which, in addition to rent, the lessee pays all of the expenses of operation, and the lessor's only obligation is to pay the mortgage payment. Although this type of lease has no true legal significance, the term *net lease* is standard jargon in the real estate business to describe certain types of leases. Normally, a *net lease* is one in which the tenant pays real estate taxes and special assessments in addition to his rent. A *net-net* lease usually implies that in addition to the foregoing, the tenant pays his own insurance premiums, both for hazard and liability insurance. A *net-net-net* lease (often called a *triple net* lease) usually implies that the tenant also pays the cost of repairs and maintenance of the property.

As one might have suspected, the net lease is the perfect investment tool for the passive investor-lessor who has a solvent, credit-worthy tenant for the premises. Most retail fast-food establishments prefer to use triple net leases to give themselves absolute control over the maintenance and attractiveness of the premises, as well as over certain operating costs, in order to keep their rental rates at a minimum. The investor-lessor is normally guaranteed a fixed rate of return after his mortgage payment has been made. This lease plan also guarantees a fixed rental rate for the lessee. In some situations, the lender will even request that the lessee pay his lease payments directly to him (the lender), and the lender merely sends a difference check to the landlord (investor-lessor) after the mortgage payments and other costs have been deducted. This assures the lender of timely payments and provides the owner-lessor-investor with very little room to complain. In most of these situations, the lender loans money based on the quality of the tenant rather than on the financial statement of the investor.

Ground Lease. A ground lease is normally a long-term leasehold estate that has lease payment provisions similar to those of a gross lease. This type of lease is basically simple, providing primarily for a fixed monthly or annual payment to the lessor. The peculiarities of this type of lease, however, involve a rather complicated method of mortgaging the leasehold estate, so that the lessee can borrow money for the construction of improvements, subject to the underlying leasehold estate. This type of lease usually has provisions that allow for *subordination* of the leasehold premises, making the underlying lease inferior to the construction mortgage to provide an incentive for a lender to make the loan by giving him a first lien position. A ground lease often has fairly liberal provisions for assignment and subletting, since the lease is for such a long term. It is also one of the basic tools for the sale lease-back mortgaging technique discussed in Chapter 9.

Assignment and Subletting

Although Texas has a statutory provision prohibiting the right of a lessee to assign or sublet the premises without the lessor's prior written consent, it should be understood that assignment and subletting are very functional and operational parts of the leasing process, and most lessors do not unreasonably withhold their consent. The transfer of interest of the lessee, however, can become rather complicated when the mortgaged premises involve a long-term ground lease. In this case, the parties would include the original landlord and the new lessee under the long-term ground lease. In the event there is a subsequent transfer of interest to the property, the lessee becomes either a *sublessor* or *assignor*. The subsequent interests are then held by the *sublessee* or the *assignee*, depending on the type of transfer used.

In the *sublease* situation, there is still a direct contractual relationship (privity of contract) between the lessor and the lessee. There is also a privity of contract between the lessee (sublessor) and the sublessee. There is no privity of contract between the sublessee and the original lessor. This makes the lessee (sublessor) still primarily liable on payments to be made to the original lessor.

In the *assignment* situation, all rights, title, and interest of the original lessee (assignor) are assigned to the assignee, who then has a direct privity of contract with the original lessor. The liabilities change then, in that the assignee has a direct obligation to the lessor.

Texas law tends to favor the sublease, and it has been held that if the original lessee (sublessor) maintains any right of reversion at all, the instrument will be held to be a sublease rather than an assignment. The original lessee (sublessor) is still held to be primarily liable on any breach of covenants to the original lessor. The diagram as shown in Figure 14-1 graphically illustrates how the assignment/sublease relationship exists.

Special Provisions

A lease can have as many special provisions as the mind can possibly imagine. The scope of these lease provisions has become so large in recent years that one finds typical office leases or retail leases bound in book form, rather than stapled together as a short-form document. Because of the variety of applicable special provisions in any given situation, we will not discuss any of these special provisions. There are extensive treatises on lease law that would be of greater benefit to the more advanced student than any further discussion that could be given here.

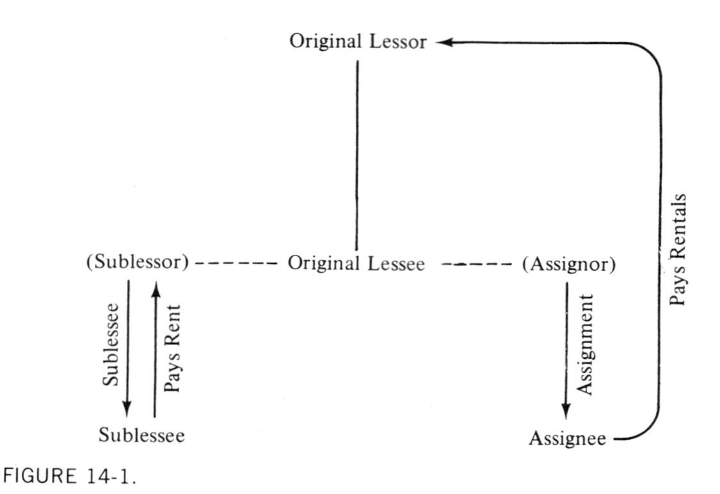

FIGURE 14-1.

Forcible Entry and Detainer

Forcible entry and detainer is the proper cause of action for a lessor to pursue when he chooses to eject or remove a lessee from the premises, more commonly known as *eviction proceedings*.

Forcible Detainer Statutes

Technically, a cause of action exists for forcible entry and detainer if any person makes an entry into any lands, tenements, or any other real property, or shall make such entry by force, or shall willfully and without force hold over any lands, after demand has been made in writing for the possession thereof by the lessor (Tex. Rev. Civ. Stat. Ann., art. 3973). Prior to bringing an action for forcible entry and detainer, the lessor must give the lessee a minimum of three (3) days' written notice to vacate such premises prior to filing his action for forcible entry and detainer (Tex. Rev. Civ. Stat. Ann., art. 3975a). This 3-day requirement should not be confused with the 30-day notice for terminating certain tenancies under the previously mentioned statutes. Rather, this is a notice requirement *prior to* filing a suit for forcible entry and detainer. You may recall that a lessee may not be dispossessed from the premises without due process of law. The forcible entry and detainer statutes provide the procedure to effect a valid due process of law action by filing the suit for forcible entry and detainer to initiate the court proceeding.

Procedural Rules

Beyond the two basic statutory provisions, the law of forcible entry and detainer becomes one of procedural matters rather than one of substantive legal matters. Assuming the lessor has properly given notice and has filed his cause of action that the lessee has committed such acts as to constitute forcible entry and detainer, the procedure for evicting that lessee is then initiated. The rules for effecting the dispossession after filing the forcible entry and detainer are contained in the Texas Rules of Civil Procedure (a part of the Texas Statutes).

Original jurisdiction for an action for forcible entry and detainer is vested in the justice of the peace court in the precinct of the county in which the premises are located. When the suit has been filed, the justice is required to issue a citation to the defendants to appear not less than six days nor more than ten days after service of citation. Said service of citation can be left with anybody at the premises above the age of 16 years. Upon request, and supported by an affidavit, the trial may be postponed by either party showing good cause for a period not to exceed six days. (One can see that there is at least a statutory attempt to make a quick proceeding out of the forcible entry and detainer process.)

The only issue that may be argued at the justice of the peace court is *possession of the premises*, which necessarily includes an interpretation of the lease, if there is one. Although the justice of the peace court has only a $200 maximum jurisdiction, the value of the lease rights is not involved when it comes to an issue of possession and of forcible entry and detainer, *Walther* v. *Anderson*, 114 S.W. 414 (Tex. Civ. App.—1958). However, the $200 jurisdictional limit of the justice of the peace court does prevent either party from suing for damages in excess of the $200 in another court having the proper jurisdiction.

If judgment is awarded to the plaintiff (lessor), a *writ of restitution* (which awards the possession of the premises to the lessor) will be issued to give the plaintiff possession. The writ cannot be issued until five days after the judgment is entered. If one of the parties appeals, however (which appeal must be perfected within five days after the judgment), and after a proper bond has been posted, the decision may be appealed to the county court where the issue of possession is tried once again. The second trial is not considered a true appeal process since the issue is tried once again as if the first trial had never happened. This process is called a trial *de novo*. After the appeal bond is filed, the judge in the justice of the peace court must file a transcript within six days. The trial in the county court is heard at any time after five full days from the date of filing the transcript in county court. If no answer is filed at the county court level, there is a judgment entered by default. When judgment is rendered at the county court level, the case is finally and completely disposed of as to the issue of possession, and no further appeals are allowed, except when the judgment exceeds $100 in damages. The lessor may also maintain an action for attorneys' fees if he gives a tenant ten days' notice by registered or certified mail prior to filing the suit.

Understanding that the reader has just been exposed to a flurry of laws and procedural rules, the graphic illustration shown in Figure 14-2

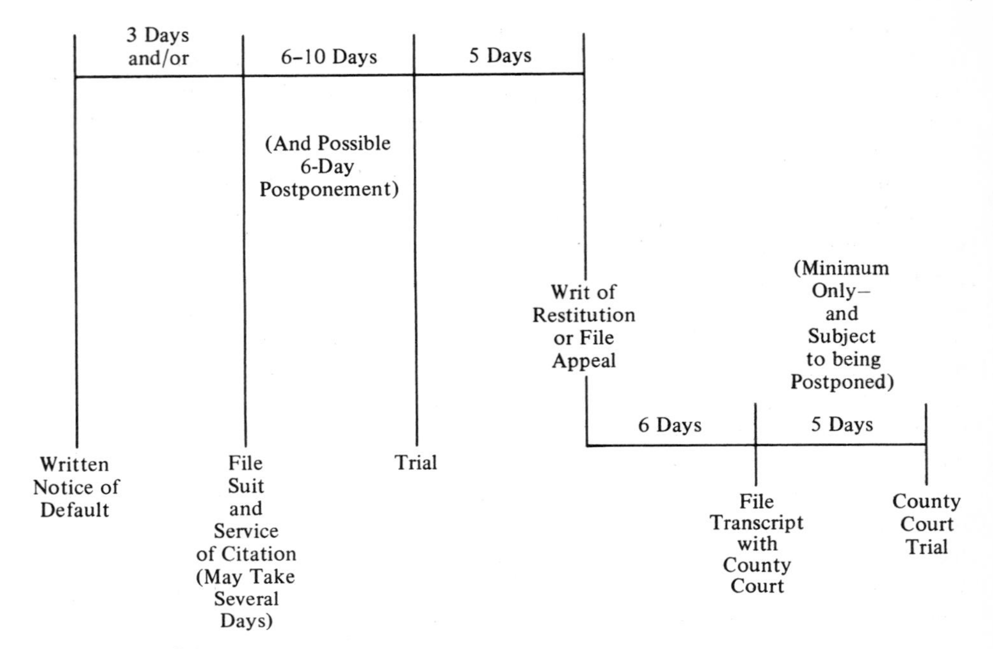

FIGURE 14-2.

may be helpful in illustrating the time concepts and some of the alternatives available in the forcible entry and detainer process. A good lessee, with a good lawyer, can sometimes postpone an actual dispossession of the premises for as long as 60 to 90 days, during which time the lessee is usually not paying any rent. If there are substantial damages involved, as there often are, the lessor must bring a separate suit in either county or district court (depending on the amount of damages in controversy) in order to recover whatever damages he may have suffered.

At first impression, it appears that most of the laws seem to have been "stacked" against the landlord, particularly when coupled with the provisions of the Deceptive Trade Practices—Consumer Protection Act. However, as in most consumer-oriented laws, it must be remembered that there would have been no need to have such protective legislation if it had not been for the unscrupulous practices of some landlords.

SUMMARY There are four types of nonfreehold estates: an estate for years, an estate from period to period, an estate at will, and an estate at sufferance. Many landlord and tenant relationships are construed by statute unless those rights are determined by an existing lease agreement. Lease agreements are construed similarly to other real estate contracts, and the same general rules of construction apply. There are four basic types of real estate leases: gross leases, percentage leases, net leases, and ground leases. Leases are not assignable by the lessee unless agreed to in writing by the landlord.

Forcible entry and detainer are commonly referred to as eviction proceedings. There must be a court proceeding in order to obtain a legal eviction proceeding. There are statutory requirements for notice and procedure which can extend the time of eviction for several weeks if contested vigorously.

15

CONDOMINIUMS AND COOPERATIVES

Condominiums have been one of the biggest booms that the Texas housing industry has seen for a number of years. Particularly in more urban areas, the condominium has become one of the cheapest and more efficient methods of home ownership. Cooperatives, although not as common in Texas, have equally as good an attraction in low cost, but Texans have been a little more hesitant to accept cooperative ownership. It is probably safe to say that the full effect of condominium and cooperative ownership has not yet been felt in Texas and may not be felt for some time to come. Only a small amount of Texas has been urbanized to the point that condominiums and cooperatives could become an acceptable means of home ownership.

There is no common-law derivation of the concepts of condominium or cooperative in the United States. The creation of these two forms of housing has been one of statute and purely legal theory. As a result, this type of housing has been called *housing built on a statutory foundation*. A more current term reflecting both of these forms of ownership has been *shared facilities housing*.

Condominiums

It is perhaps easier, for purposes of our explanation, to think of condominiums as ownership of single apartment units. If one can visualize the more typical garden-type apartment project, along with the individual ownership of each of those apartments, one begins to understand the true concept behind condominium ownership. Condominiums are generally cheaper to build than single family houses or townhouses (for example, there are no major firewall requirements in most cities), and they (the condominiums) constitute a very high utilization of land. Also, more units can be built, and built faster, than comparable single-family residences. However, each unit has its own individual mortgage, as in other single-family residences. The condominium units may either be built new, or be converted to condominiums from existing apartment projects.

Statutory Definitions

Since condominiums are, by their nature, housing built on a statutory foundation, it stands to reason that the statute controlling the creation of a condominium and its function deals with a number of areas rather specifically. In 1963, Texas passed the *Condominium Act* (Tex. Rev. Civ. Stat. Ann., art. 1301a). Before discussing any details of the three different types of ownership a condominium creates, it is imperative to understand how this act defines pertinent terms of condominiums and how these terms are used in relation to condominium ownership.

The act defines *condominium* as:

> the separate ownership of single units or apartments in a multiple-unit structure or structures *with common elements* [emphasis supplied]. Tex. Rev. Civ. Stat. Ann., art. 1301(a), Section 2(d).

A *condominium project* is further defined as:

> a real estate condominium project; a plan or project whereby four (4) or more apartments, rooms, office spaces, or other units in existing or proposed buildings or structures are offered or proposed to be offered for sale. Tex. Rev. Civ. Stat. Ann., art. 1301a, Section 26c.

This implies that any condominium housing must consist of at least four units. Therefore, a duplex could not be a condominium project, nor could a triplex. Note also that condominium projects can include much more than just residential units or apartments. They include office spaces or "other units," which indicates that even the parking sections in parking garages could be converted to condominiums (condominiumized).

An *apartment* as defined by the act means:

> an enclosed place consisting of one (1) or more rooms occupying all or part of a floor in a building of one (1) or more floors or stories regardless of whether it be designed for residence, for office, for the operation of any industry, business, or for any other type of independent use, pro-

> vided it has direct exit to a thoroughfare or to a given common space leading to a thoroughfare.

This definition indicates that virtually any type of structure can become a condominium as long as it has individual apartments or units contained therein. Therefore, the physical structure itself has no bearing on whether or not a project is a condominium. A condominium can be a high-rise project, a townhouse project, a garden-type apartment project, or a four-plex unit, as long as the units meet the statutory criteria.

Now that the basics of apartment and its fee simple ownership, and condominium and its character, are understood, we can proceed to define *common elements*. Each owner holds his proportionate share of the common elements as a tenancy in common with the other apartment owners. There are two types of common elements, *general* common elements and *limited* common elements. The act defines general common elements to mean and include:

> the land, whether leased or in fee simple, on which the building stands;
>
> the foundations, bearing walls and columns, roofs, halls, lobbies, stairways, and entrances and exits or communication ways;
>
> the basements, flat roofs, yard, and gardens, except as otherwise provided or stipulated;
>
> the premises for the lodging of janitors or persons in charge of the building, except as otherwise provided or stipulated;
>
> the compartments or installation of central services such as power, light, gas, cold and hot water, refrigeration, central air condition and central heating, reservoirs, water tanks and pumps, swimming pools, and the like;
>
> the elevators and shafts, garbage incinerators and, in general all devices or installations existing for common use; and
>
> all other elements of the building desirable or rationally of common use or necessary to the existence, upkeep and safety of the condominium regime, and any other elements described in the declaration. . . .

It is easy to see from the above that the bulk of the real esate in a condominium project is owned by the owners as shared facilities and as tenants in common.

Limited common elements are common elements for only some of the owners, and are statutorily defined as:

> those common elements which are agreed upon by all of the co-owners to be reserved for the use of a certain number of apartments to the exclusion of the other apartments, such as special corridors, stairways and elevators, sanitary services common to the apartments of a particular floor, and the like.

Types of Ownership and Ownership Rights

Once the concept of apartment (unit) ownership is understood, one needs to recall the more fundamental theory of ''estates in land'' to grasp the full meaning of what this ownership means. To begin with, the condominium owner gets three separate, indivisible, and distinct types of ownership:

1. Fee simple to a portion of the common elements, which must be shared in common with the others; and
2. Fee simple title to the condominium unit (compartment); and
3. An exclusive easement for air space, which that unit may occupy from time to time.

Each of these types of ownership will now be discussed separately.

Tenancy in Common. The fee-simple ownership of a portion of the common elements is an undivided interest in the unit owner's proportionate share of the common elements. *Common elements* can generally be described as all of the real property existing outside of the individual's unit that technically belongs to all of the homeowners in undivided interests as tenants in common (it cannot be partitioned). The interests in the common elements must remain undivided, and cannot be used such that they encroach upon the rights of the other owners. The concept of encroaching upon the rights of others is probably one of the more important concepts for understanding what shared facilities housing really means. The unit owner's portion of the common elements may be determined in two ways. First, it may be determined by the amount of square footage the owner occupies with respect to the entire condominium project, such as:

$$\text{unit} = 1{,}500 \text{ square feet}$$
$$\text{project} = 150{,}000 \text{ square feet}$$
$$\frac{1{,}500}{150{,}000} = .01 \times 100 = 1\%$$

(proportionate ownership of the common elements)

The owner of the 1500 square foot unit would thus own an undivided 1% of the common elements, shared in common with the other unit owners.

Second, the owner's proportionate share of the common elements may be determined by the unit versus the number of units in the project. For instance, if there are 300 units in the project and the unit owner owns one of the 300 units, his proportionate share of the common elements would be:

$$\frac{1}{300} = .00333 \times 100 = .333\%$$

(proportionate share
of the common elements)

Fee Simple to Unit. The fee simple title to the unit refers to only the interior of the unit that the owner occupies. This is sometimes referred to as the *air space* contained *inside* the apartment unit itself. More common theories of ownership indicate that the owner owns from *paint to paint* and from *ceiling to carpet*, including the *non*load-bearing walls. Load-bearing walls are not included because it is understood that a load-bearing wall is probably critical to the unit ownership of another apartment owner, and demolition or removal of a load-bearing wall may affect the other owner's rights significantly.

Easement. The third type of ownership is an easement to the air space that the unit may occupy from time to time. This concept of easement for air space is particularly functional in high-rise structures. Since it is understood that air space for the unit may shift due to a variety of factors, and this may affect the owner's use. Rather than worrying about older, more difficult concepts of metes and bounds descriptions and rights of parties in the property of others, it is simpler to consider the air space that the unit may occupy from time to time as an easement for reasonable enjoyment and use, so long as it does not affect the rights of other unit owners. This gives the unit owner particular rights to permit access through his unit to part of the common elements that may be contained therein, whether it be a roof, foundation, certain plumbing fixtures, or other common element items that the other owners may have a right to.

All three of these ownership rights must be conveyed together and cannot be conveyed separately under any circumstances (Tex. Rev. Civ. Stat. Ann., art. 1301a, Section 9). An example of a deed used to convey a condominium unit is shown in Figure 15-1.

Creation

The creation of a condominium project is very similar to creating a subdivision. The statute provides that every county clerk shall provide a suitable well-bound book, to be called *condominium records*, in which shall be recorded all master deeds, master leases, or declarations. As a subdivision developer draws a survey and records the subdivision plat, the condominium developer files a master deed, master lease, or declaration to create the condominium regime (Tex. Rev. Civ. Stat. Ann., art. 1301a, Section 3). The declaration must contain the legal description of the land with the location of each building or proposed building to be located

WARRANTY DEED TO A CONDOMINIUM APARTMENT UNIT

STATE OF TEXAS)
) KNOW ALL MEN BY THESE PRESENTS:
COUNTY OF HARRIS)

That we, I. M. SELLER and wife, HAPPY SELLER, hereinafter called "Grantor," for and in consideration of the sum of TEN AND NO/100 ($10.00) DOLLARS and other good and valuable considerations in cash to me in hand paid by N. DEBTED and wife, MAY B. DEBTED, hereinafter called "Grantee", have GRANTED, SOLD and CONVEYED and by these presents do GRANT, SELL and CONVEY unto the said Grantee of Harris County, Texas, subject to and upon the covenants, restrictions, limitations, conditions and other matters hereinbelow stated, the following described Apartment-type Unit, Parking Space and Undivided franctional interest in the Common Elements (together constituting and hereinafter collectively referred to as an Apartment Unit) located in and being part of SHAKEY ACRES CONDOMINIUMS, a condominium project in the City of Houston, Harris County, Texas, according to the Enabling Declaration thereof (hereinafter called the "Declaration") and the survey plats and by-laws attached as Exhibits to such Declaration as part thereof, dated September 32, 1978, filed for record in the Office of the County Clerk of Harris County, Texas, on September 33rd, 1978, under said Clerk's File No. Q106738, of the Condominium Records of Harris County, Texas, reference to all of which and said record thereof being hereby made for all purposes, which said condominium apartment project known as SHAKEY ACRES CONDOMINIUMS, is situated on the project tract of land described as 5.63 acres of land in the Charles Patrick Survey, Abstract No. 1076, City of Houston, Harris County, Texas, according to the plat thereof recorded in Volume 120, page 97 of the Harris County May Records, which constitutes the project tract of land for SHAKEY ACRES CONDOMINIUMS, and which said Apartment, Parking Space and Undivided fractional interest in the Common Elements constituting the Apartment Unit hereby conveyed are described as follows, to-wit:

(a) SHAKEY ACRES CONDOMINIUMS Apartment No. 301, and the space encompassed by the boundaries thereof, located in BUILDING H;

FIGURE 15-1.

(b) PARKING SPACE NO. 301A, and the space encompassed by the boundaries thereof, located in BUILDING NO. H; and

(c) AN UNDIVIDED .956% ownership interest in and to the common elements of the Condominium Project known as SHAKEY ACRES CONDOMINIUMS;

according to and as such apartment unit, parking space and undivided fractional interest in the common Elements are more particularly described in said Declaration and the survey plats attached as exhibits thereto.

This grant and conveyance is made and accepted subject to (a) the provisions of the Condominium Act of the State of Texas, hereby incorporated herein and made part hereof (b) the provisions, covenants, easements, restrictions, limitations, covenants and conditions contained and set out in said Declaration and/or shown on the survey plats attached as exhibits thereto, and all easements, covenants, restrictions and conditions otherwise appearing of record and affecting the project tract of land or part thereof, and (c) the said By-Laws of SHAKEY ACRES CONDOMINIUMS and all amendments hereafter lawfully made thereto.

By acceptance of this deed and as part of the consideration therefor, the Grantees hereinabove named, their heirs, executors and administrators, personal representatives, successors, grantees, assigns and all future owners of said apartment unit or interest therein, covenant and agree and shall be bound and obligated (1) to abide by and comply with each of and all of the provisions of said Act, Declaration and By-Laws and the government and administration of said condominium apartment project in accordance therewith (2) to observe and comply with all lawful decisions and resolutions at any time made by the Board of Administration, the Council of Co-Owners and/or the unit owners of said condominium apartment project and (3) to promptly pay, as the same becomes due and payable his prorata share and part of all common expenses and other valid charges and expenses assessed pursuant to the provisions of said Act, Declaration and/or By-Laws, all of which common expenses and assessments shall be and constitute a lien upon and against the hereinabove described apartment unit at the time the same becomes due and payable, which lien shall be subject to, secondary and inferior to (a) all liens for taxes and special assesments levied by governmental and taxing authorities and (b) all liens securing sums due or to become due under any mortgage, Vendor's Lien or Deed of Trust filed for record prior to the time such prorata share of common expenses, charges and assessments become due, and (3) in general to fulfill and discharge all of his obligations, duties and responsibilities as an owner of an apartment unit in the condominium apartment project known as SHAKEY ACRE CONDOMINIUMS.

TO HAVE AND TO HOLD and said Apartment unit, Parking Space and Undivided fractional ownership interest in common elements, hereinabove described and together constituting an Apartment Unit, together with all and singular the rights, hereditaments and appurtenances thereto in any wise belonging, unto the said Grantee hereinabove named, its successors and assigns forever. And, subject to each and all of the matters hereinabove stated, the Grantor herein does hereby bind himself, his heirs, executors and administrators, to WARRANT AND DEFEND the title to said Apartment Unit herein and hereby conveyed unto the said Grantee, its successors and assigns, against every person whomsoever lawfully claiming or to claim the same of any part thereof.

EXECUTED this the 30th day of February, A.D., 1994.

____
I. M. Seller

____
Happy Seller

FIGURE 15-1 (*continued*).

thereon. Each building must be denoted by a letter (A, B, C, etc.). The declaration must also contain a general description and the number of each unit, including its square footage, location, and other data necessary for its proper identification. The information is depicted by a plat of each floor of each building, showing also the letter of the building and the number of the floor, along with the number of each unit. The declaration must also contain a general description of each garage, carport, or any other area subject to individual ownership and exclusive control; plus a description of the general common elements and limited common elements; and a statement of the fractional or percentage interest that the unit bears to the entire condominium regime expressed in fractions or percentages. The declaration may also provide for other provisions if desired by the developer. There are often a number of special provisions referring to peculiarities of each project that will change from project to project.

Most of the detailed information concerning maintenance and control of the condominium is contained in the condominium bylaws, which are administered through the "council of co-owners," who may amend the bylaws as changes are needed.

Control and Maintenance

A *co-owner* is defined as a person, firm, corporation, partnership, association, trust, or other legal entity who owns an apartment or apartments within the condominium project, Tex. Rev. Civ. Stat. Ann., art. 1301a, Section 2(h). The *council of co-owners* means all of the co-owners, as defined by the statute. As a practical matter, the council of co-owners forms a homeowners' association, which is usually a corporation with the specific function of maintaining the common elements and the day-to-day activity of the condominium project. Normally, if the project is a new one being built by the developer, the developer maintains control of the council of co-owners because of his ownership of the unsold number of apartments until the number of co-owners becomes sufficient to outvote the developer.

The maintenance of the common elements is one of the primary functions of the council of co-owners. Whether it chooses to appoint its own administrator (or board of administration) or to hire an outside management firm, the day-to-day maintenance of the common elements is determined by the council of co-owners. All co-owners are obligated to contribute pro rata toward the expense of the administration of the maintenance and repairs of the common elements. This is normally accomplished by the owners' monthly contributions to a *maintenance fund*, which is established by the condominium's bylaws. The statute specifically provides that no owner shall be exempt from contributing toward such expenses by any waiver of his use of the enjoyment of the common elements or by abandonment of the apartment that he owns. Again, we see where the shared facilities housing concept plays a very large part in creating an interdependence between the co-owners in the condominium project.

The council of co-owners decides on how the premises are to be maintained (usually by majority vote). The premises maintained by the council of co-owners are the common elements, and, in applicable cases, the limited common elements. In addition to this, the bylaws normally specify that the individual unit owner may not maintain, change, or alter any of the general common elements or limited common elements without the approval of the council of co-owners.

The council of co-owners, then, takes the pro rata contributions made by all the co-owners into a general fund and uses this fund for maintenance and operation of the condominium project. It is up to the council to determine which area is going to be maintained and how well it is to be maintained. It is not uncommon for people to move into a condominium project and later find that their pro rata share of the contributions (generally referred to as the *maintenance fund*) increases drastically in an effort to maintain the condominium regime in a "first-class manner." If the exterior of the door to any condominium unit, or the windows, roof, foundation, or other common elements need any sort of alteration or repair, it is up to the council of co-owners to see that such repairs are taken care of properly. The obvious problem that arises from this maintenance by the council of co-owners is one where an element of the common elements (for instance, the roof) is in need of repair, but it only affects one of the condominium owners (the man who lives on the top floor!). Sometimes it may be difficult for this one owner to convince the rest of the co-owners to spend the necessary capital funds to see that the roof is properly fixed. One can expect similar problems from cracked slabs, cracked exterior walls, broken windows, and other similar common element repairs that may affect only a very small minority of the co-owners.

Specific Problem Areas

A condominium ownership does, in fact, provide many of the benefits of home ownership along with the benefits of apartment ownership, which basically make the project free from the worries that accompany the ownership of a single-family residence. However, there are drawbacks to condominium ownership that need to be discussed in greater detail.

Casualty Insurance.

A recurring problem of condominium ownership is casualty insurance. Normally, the council of co-owners maintains a casualty insurance policy in the event of fire, accident, or other hazard that may destroy the project or any individual unit. Therefore, there is a practical problem of whether or not the individual unit owner should also carry insurance in the event the policy owned by the council of co-owners lapses or is inadequate to fully protect the homeowner. This results in a duplication of insurance to assure proper coverage for the same unit.

Taxation. Taxation provides another area of controversy in condominium ownership. The condominium owner will pay the ad valorem taxes for his individual unit; and the council of co-owners will pay the taxes on the common area facilities out of the maintenance fund. However, a critical problem arises about the monthly contributions from the homeowners to this maintenance fund. The homeowners' association must normally report this income for the maintenance fund (along with the other contributions for insurance, maintenance, etc.) each month as a taxable income, since this income is subject to taxation like any other income for an organization that falls under the jurisdiction of the Internal Revenue Service. Therefore, there is a double taxation achieved, once when income is taxed going to the individual co-owner, and again when it is contributed to the maintenance fund.

This problem has been solved to some extent, however, by the 1976 Tax Reform Act, which provides that a condominium management association may elect to be treated as a tax-exempt organization. If such an election is made, the association is not taxed on fees, membership dues, and assessments from the members of the association who own residential units in the particular condominium or subdivision, applicable to taxable years beginning after December 31, 1973 [I.R.C. Section 528(c)1(A)]. The association's taxable income is only that equal to the excess of the gross income over actual operating costs, less any deductions and exempt income. To qualify for the exempt tax qualification, substantially all of the units must be used as residences. There are additional requirements, too, in that the association must have at least 60% of the association's gross income solely from dues, fees, and assessments; and at least 90% must be expended to acquire, construct, manage, maintain, care for, or improve association property [I.R.C. Section 528(c)1(B)]. Although these provisions still leave many unanswered questions, at least some steps have been made toward eliminating a difficult problem.

Tort Liability. Tort liability is another area that has come under controversy in recent years. Take, for instance, the fact situation where a young 28-year-old neurosurgeon breaks his hands on a negligently maintained exercise machine owned by the homeowners' association. There is a good chance that the homeowners' association may have an insurance policy that would provide for certain coverage in that case. However, if the limit on that insurance policy is too low, one may wonder where the doctor will pursue additional causes of action once he has surpassed the limits of the insurance policy maintained by the homeowners' association. There is at least some authority that the doctor may be able to take his cause of action against the homeowners individually, *White* v. *Cox*, 17 Cal. App. 3d 824 (1973).

Security Regulations. The most significant problem in purchasing a condominium unit is in the area of securities regulations. If the unit may be construed to be a security, rather than an interest in real estate, it will fall under the jurisdiction of the Securities and Exchange Commission and the Acts of 1933 and 1934. In the often-cited case of *SEC* v. *Howey*, 328 U.S. 293 (1946), it was determined that if one invests in a condominium unit that may be rented to others when it is not in use by the owner, and the owner expects profits from that investment through the efforts of a third-party manager, the unit will be construed to be a security. Therefore, condominium ownership is not simply an interest in real estate, and all offerings for sale may be subject to the regulation and disclosure requirements of the securities acts. This opinion has had particular application in regard to *time-sharing* condominiums (contractual arrangements among co-tenants for an agreed time of occupancy), *interval ownership* condominiums (fee title for a specified period—one to four weeks—that the owner is entitled to possession), resort condominiums, and other types of condominiums that lend themselves to investment opportunities. Condominiums are considered good investments since condominiums can be owned and operated with very low maintenance requirements for the owner. A private investor can buy a condominium and assure himself that at least the exterior and general common elements will be maintained in an acceptable manner. This is a luxury he does not have in a single-family residence because there is no homeowners' association to maintain the exterior and structural parts of the unit.

Homestead Provisions. The last problem to be discussed is one that is peculiar to Texas. Condominium ownership is protected by the constitutional homestead provisions available to all other residential units. The difficulty with the homestead statute exists when an owner owns his unit but refuses to pay his maintenance fund fees for maintenance and improvement of the common areas. It is logically assumed that due to the effect of the constitutional homestead laws, there is virtually no action one can take against such a unit owner. He clearly cannot be forced to sell the unit to satisfy any debts that may be incurred as a result of his nonpayment of his maintenance fees. The only recourse that the homeowners' association may have is to file a lien against the unit, in order to recover what obligations may be due and owing to the homeowners' association upon the subsequent sale of the unit (Tex. Rev. Civ. Stat. Ann., art. 1301a, Section 18). You may recall that a homestead may not be sold to satisfy any debts except for purchase money, taxes, and home improvements. Therefore, unless these are escrow accounts maintained by the owner's lender, there is simply no provision that allows an enforcement of any type of homeowners' association dues other than the statutory lien specified above.

Cooperative Housing

Cooperative ownership is another method of apartment ownership or shared facilities housing. It is very similar to condominium ownership, but with a few major, distinct differences. The co-ownership and interdependence of the individual owners have much the same drawbacks of any multifamily housing project. However, there are distinct differences in methods of control and type of unit ownership as used by cooperatives in comparison to condominiums.

Creation

A cooperative can take one of three forms: (1) tenancy in common, (2) the trust form, or (3) the corporate form.

The *tenancy in common* form is fairly widespread in California and basically consists of the tenancy in common estates that were discussed in Chapter 2. In this form, the homeowner owns his share of the cooperative project in undivided proportionate shares, along with a lease, or certificate of occupancy, for a particular unit. Rights and liabilities of tenancy in common generally apply, and, to some extent, this form does not create the problems of interdependence as much as do the other two forms of ownership.

The *trust* form of ownership is an ownership in severalty by a trust (a single entity), which executes a single blanket mortgage for the entire cooperative housing regime. The basis for the creation of this form of cooperative ownership is the trust instrument under which the trust derives its ownership and control. In the trust form of ownership, there is a single mortgage and management function, operated solely through the trust.

The *corporate form* of ownership, also an ownership in severalty, is similar to the corporate ownership of the homeowners' association in a condominium. The basis for this type of ownership arises out of the charter and bylaws of the corporation as created according to the laws of the State of Texas. Similar to the trust form of ownership, the corporation executes the mortgage on behalf of all the owners and maintains the actual control and ownership of the building throughout the life of the cooperative.

Ownership and Control

The ownership and control under a tenancy in common cooperative is based on each individual owner's proportionate share of ownership in the cooperative regime. The owners normally elect a homeowners' association, which is primarily responsible for the maintenance and operation of the premises. The trust and corporate forms of ownership (both involving ownership in severalty) also have one blanket mortgage which is secured by the entire cooperative as a unit. This type of cooperative ownership usually relies on the lender's being willing to take the proportionate liability of each of the owners as satisfactory security for the blanket mortgage that has been issued to cover the entire cooperative housing unit.

The trust (or board of trustees), or corporation, holds legal title to the property. The co-owners get a lease, or certificate of occupancy, under which they have the exclusive right to occupy their proportionate share of the property. To simplify this, you might want to think of a larger apartment project as an example. A corporation or trust would hold legal title to the project, and each of the occupants of the apartments, being a shareholder of the corporation (or beneficial owner of the trust), has the exclusive right of occupancy of his individual unit. This type of ownership normally involves obligations in the bylaws (or trust instruments) that require each individual unit owner to pay his fractional percentage of the mortgage each and every month, as well as his fractional percentage of the utilities, insurance, costs, and maintenance.

The certificate of occupancy (or lease) is regarded as personal property, not real estate. As in condominium ownership, there are fairly detailed and finite rules and regulations under the trust instrument or bylaws, which each and every unit owner must comply with, so that he will not have a detrimental effect on the other unit owners. Normally, upon termination of the certificate of occupancy, or the lease, the unit owner must surrender possession of the unit (by sale or otherwise) to the corporation or trust, who, in turn, may resell that interest to another subsequent occupant. The charter and bylaws (or trust instrument) usually contain provisions whereby the corporation or trust has the right of first refusal to buy the certificate of occupancy and proportionate interest when the unit owner decides to terminate his residency. Since there is a great amount of interdependence because of the proportionate payments of mortgages, maintenance fees, and payments (much more so than the condominium ownership), it is critical that there be a strictly enforced agreement between the co-owners, carefully setting forth what all the rights and obligations are in order to ensure adequate functioning and maintenance of the cooperative housing development.

Advantages

Cooperative housing developments have had particularly good application in retirement and resort areas. Because of the lower construction costs of cooperative housing, similar to those of condominiums, cooperatives are substantially cheaper to build than are other forms of single or multifamily residential ownership; thus the cost of these units is likewise much cheaper. In the retirement situation, you can understand why a person, in his old age, may decide to retire to a senior citizens' cooperative housing development (normally restricted to people being 65 years of age or over), buying a 1200 to 1500 square foot unit for the price of $12,000 to $20,000 (perhaps his life savings). His future contributions, then, would be used only to pay utilities and maintenance fund costs for the rest of his life. He would get all the benefits of living in an apartment, but with all the attributes of home ownership. He would have no mortgage payments to pay (assuming his unit was paid for), and any future conveyance of his cooperative unit would be subject only to the right of first refusal of the homeowners' association, corporation, or trust. Thus, he would be much more comfortable being able to live on a fixed retirement income. He also would probably have a higher quality of housing than he would have if he tried to buy a single-family residence or townhouse, or even a condominium unit, at the same price.

Disadvantages

The disadvantages of cooperative housing stand out primarily because of the extreme role of interdependence played in this type of housing. For instance, if each unit owner has the obligation to pay his proportionate share of the mortgage payment, what would happen if several unit owners could not make their payment for one month? The obvious answer is that the remaining unit owners must come up with the rest of the money in order to assure that the mortgage payment is paid. The same is true of insurance, taxes, and other maintenance costs. In the condominium ownership situation, a mortgage company can foreclose on one unit. The cooperative form of ownership, however, does not allow for this type of independence, except possibly in the tenancy in common type of cooperative ownership.

Thus, *financing* is the first major disadvantage of cooperative ownership. For example, a loan can be made only to the corporation or trust, and not to any of the unit owners independently. This disadvantage also exists in all services, utilities, and other obligations that may be undertaken by the cooperative housing association. There is, of course, the usual problem of trying to ascertain the appraised value of the property for loan purposes because of the interdependence and multiownership facets of cooperative housing.

The second major difficulty and complication arising out of cooperative ownership is that of *securities*. Since this form of ownership is evidenced by a certificate of occupancy, or "shares" of ownership, one may think that it would automatically be affected by the securities laws. This was a very heavily litigated area for some time. In 1975, the Supreme Court of the United States, in a landmark decision involving cooperative housing, *United Housing Foundation* v. *Foreman*, 421 U.S. 837 (1975), indicated that the housing aspect of a transaction that involved the purchase of stock in the co-op corporation was not making an *investment*, as that term is used in securities law, even though it was possible for the cooperative owners to sell their "shares" at a later time and even for a profit. Since the housing units themselves were used as primary residences by the occupants, the purchaser is seeking a place to live, regardless of how the cooperative was financed or sold. The shares of stock in this case were completely tied to the proprietary leases, a fact that negates some of the attributes of ownership and investment that most stock shares exhibit. The court also emphasized that the voting rights under the ownership in a cooperative unit were not one vote per share of stock, but rather, one vote per homeowner.

So at least in very closely identified situations, the shares of ownership in a cooperative will not automatically be considered to be securities. However, this does not indicate that all cooperatives are not securities. As in condominium ownership, there can always be a situation involving the marketing, selling, and retransfer of the interest in the cooperative housing that would make securities an extremely troublesome situation if handled improperly.

Tort liability for corporate or trust form cooperatives is not nearly the problem that it is under condominium ownership because the owners are, of course, insulated through the corporate veil or the trust form of ownership. Anyone who has a claim against the cooperative housing unit would have to sue the trust or corporation, and the homeowners would understandably be sufficiently insulated from liabilities so that they would not be personally liable. The same is true of most contractual liabilities.

It is assumed that the tort or contractual liability of a tenancy in common cooperative is the same as that of tenancy in common generally, rendering the owner liable only for his proportionate share, although the owner's personal liability may be unlimited.

In summary, it can be easily seen that both condominiums and cooperatives are heavily dependent on the shared facilities housing concept and that the mutual interdependence of both types of ownership may create problems. However, we are going to have to learn to live with these problems because single-family housing is becoming more and more expensive in various parts of the country. In dealing with a purchaser or seller of a condominium or cooperative unit, the wise and astute attorney, and the real estate agent, must understand the various complications that are involved through securities, tort liability, organization of the ownership entity, and various aspects of interdependent living, all of which may make a substantial difference (especially to the purchasing client). Recalling the terms of Section 15(4)(A) of the new Real Estate Licensing Act, almost any of these facts and criteria listed above could be a material consideration for a reasonable and prudent purchaser who is interested in purchasing a unit. It is therefore particularly important that the real estate agent be familiar with this type of housing if he chooses to concentrate his marketing efforts in this area.

SUMMARY

There is no common-law derivation of the concepts of condominium or cooperative ownership in the United States. The creation of these two forms of housing has been one of statute and legal theory. Condominium ownership involves the ownership of the fee to the apartment, ownership of the common elements as a tenant in common, and an easement to the space that that unit may occupy for ingress and egress to that unit. The rights of the parties involved in condominiums are governed generally by the Texas Condominium Act. A condominium project in Texas must consist of at least four apartments. The rights of condominium ownership necessarily involve the interdependence of the rights of the other unit owners in the condominium project. This creates specific problem areas, some of which have yet to be resolved.

Cooperative ownership is similar to condominium ownership with a few major, distinct differences in ownership and methods of control and operation of the project. The entire project is normally owned by one entity—a corporation or a trust. Each of the individual shareholders in that corporation or trust then has a right to occupancy of a specific unit. Cooperative ownership creates more interdependence in that, if one party defaults, the other parties are obligated to make up the difference to prevent a default in the obligations of corporation or trust. Real estate agents should take particular care in representing the purchasing parties' rights when attempting to sell either condominium or cooperative housing because of the new provisions of the Real Estate Licensing Act and provisions of the Deceptive Trade Practices—Consumer Protection Act.

16

GOVERNMENTAL REGULATION OF REAL ESTATE

In our form of government, as in any form of government, there must be certain priorities that the government has with respect to the land contained within its jurisdiction, which has higher priority than any other individual or entity.

In the United States, the government has four chief methods for controlling land use or ownership. These are as follows:

1. Eminent domain procedures
2. Taxation
3. Escheat
4. Police power.

The fundamentals of eminent domain and escheat were discussed in Chapter 7. Taxation is discussed in Chapter 17. The scope of this chapter is to dwell on the fourth governmental power, which is government regulation pursuant to the police power.

It is by the use of *police power* that the government regulates and enforces laws and regulations that pertain to land use control. This is a relatively inexpensive process because, there is no "taking" of property (as in eminent domain), and therefore no requirement for just compensation.

There has been such a voluminous amount of land use control legislation passed at the federal level that it cannot all be discussed within the scope of this chapter, or even within this text. Therefore, in discussing federal land use control, we will attempt only to highlight some of the more important legislative efforts, just so the reader can keep his sanity. Beyond the federal land use controls, we will discuss controls at the state and county level, as well as those at the municipal and local level.

Federal Land Use Control

In an attempt to categorize federal land use control as succinctly as possible, we will discuss each federal agency under which land use is controlled. The agencies to be covered are the Securities and Exchange Commission, the Department of Housing and Urban Development, the Federal Trade Commission, and the Environmental Protection Agency. From a land use control aspect, it should be remembered that every time a new restrictive regulatory law is passed, some developers and investors will stop investing in the type of project being regulated, forcing their funds into other areas, and ultimately changing certain land use patterns.

Securities and Exchange Commission

The Securities and Exchange Commission (SEC) regulates certain forms of land use, which, in their opinion, involve securities, investment contracts, or sale of equity interests. Thus, the SEC has been very effective in regulating real estate investment trusts, real estate syndications, and certain types of condominium offerings that involve investments, interstate sales promotions, and sales made with a promise of profit or a high rate of return.

In the eyes of the SEC, virtually any investment scheme or contract to purchase real estate with the expectation of profit makes that particular real estate transaction a security, and requires certain disclosures pursuant to the Securities and Exchange Acts of 1933 and 1934. There are only two provisions of the 1934 act that exempt real estate investment transactions from being classed as securities. These are:

1. Section 4(a)2 of the act, which exempts offerings that are made only to close friends, business associates, family relations, and other "close" offerings that are not made to the public in general; and
2. Section 3(a)11 of the act, which exempts offerings that do not go interstate, but are kept wholly as an intrastate offering. This means that the sales promotion cannot use any of the means of interstate commerce (the telephone, newspaper advertising, the U.S. mail, etc.).

The SEC has severely curtailed certain investment schemes and syndication offerings that became very common in Texas in the early 1970s.

The expense of registering a security to comply with the Securities and Exchange Act is so great that most developers now prefer to restrict their offerings, or to go into a different type of real estate development altogether, instead of complying with the securities regulations. If any real estate offering has even the possibility of being considered a security, and the exemption may be in question, the real estate broker should work very closely with a lawyer well qualified in the area of real estate and securities laws.

The Department of Housing and Urban Development

The Department of Housing and Urban Development (HUD) has made great strides in controlling and regulating real estate. The agencies under HUD control to be discussed include the Office of Interstate Land Sales Registration, the Federal Housing Administration, the Government National Mortgage Association, the Federal National Mortgage Association, and the Federal Insurance Administration.

The Office of Interstate Land Sales Registration was established to administer the rules, regulations, and statutes pertaining to the Interstate Land Sales Full Disclosure Act. This act makes it unlawful for any land developer (except for certain exempt developers) to sell or lease, by use of the mails or by use of any means of interstate commerce, any land offered as a part of a common promotional plan, unless such land has been registered with the Secretary of Housing and Urban Development, *and* a printed property report (in a format established by HUD) is furnished to the purchaser or lessee in advance of the signing of any agreement for sale or lease. Although originally meant to affect sales of lots in resort-type subdivisions (an industry that badly needed regulating), the act has been recently changed to include a new definition of *lot*:

> . . . any portion, piece, division, unit, or undivided interest in land, if such interest includes the right to exclusive use of a specific portion of the land.

This means that literally any parcel of land, or ''unit'' of real estate, could ultimately be regulated by the Office of Interstate Land Sales Registration. Can you imagine having to register an office building for tenant leasehold space, or a parking garage for contract parking, or condominiums, or even apartments? This may sound ridiculous, but it is a real possibility since there are no guidelines limiting the government's authority.

The Federal Housing Administration (FHA) was originally established in 1933 to provide for and encourage improvement in housing standards and conditions and to provide for an adequate home financing system. All homes qualifying for FHA loans must pass an FHA inspection to assure adequate housing standards for the purchaser. This is also true of homes qualifying for Veterans' Administration (VA) guaranteed loans.

FHA also provides insurance for private lenders against loss on mortgage financing of homes, multifamily projects, and land-development projects. FHA covers virtually every area of the housing industry and has been one of the better incentives to induce lenders to make low equity loans. It has been a major contributor toward Americans being able to secure 90 to 95% loans when buying homes. When FHA changes its requirements of insurable loans, it affects the availability of certain segments of the American public to buy homes. When FHA is in an expansion posture, one will find that more loans are being made to stimulate the housing industry. When FHA chooses to take a less expansive posture, the housing industry will quickly feel the effect as fewer people can qualify for loans.

The Government National Mortgage Association (GNMA), commonly called *Ginnie Mae*, and the Federal National Mortgage Association (FNMA), commonly called *Fannie Mae*, were originally created to purchase, service, and sell mortgages insured or guaranteed by FHA and VA in the *secondary market*. The secondary market is a market to purchase mortgages from the primary lending sources (savings and loans, mortgage companies, and mortgage brokers). When the primary lending institutions sell their mortgages to Fannie Mae or Ginnie Mae, it gives the primary lending institutions more cash to make additional loans. Both Fannie Mae and Ginnie Mae put requirements on these primary lending institutions, such as requiring the lenders to buy back the mortgages if requested, and establish certain discount rates (sales price) for smaller mortgage lenders. This, in effect, allows Fannie Mae and Ginnie Mae to select what types of loans they will buy from the primary lenders. Whatever type of loan they buy from the primary lender automatically gives the incentive to the primary lender to make loans to the public in that area. For instance, if Fannie Mae or Ginnie Mae wishes to increase the amount of money being made available for apartment construction, it has the ability to specify that it will purchase apartment loans rather than single-family loans. This, in turn, encourages the primary lender to lend on apartment projects rather than single-family residences.

Ginnie Mae in recent years has taken a less active posture in purchasing in the secondary market and has turned more toward managing and liquidating the government's loan portfolios. The Federal Home Loan Mortgage Corporation (FHLMC), commonly called *Freddie Mac*, serves a similar function to that of Fannie Mae. Freddie Mac creates a secondary market for savings and loan associations only.

The Federal Insurance Administration was created to provide insurance for loss of properties as defined in standard insurance contracts. It has been particularly influential in providing for federal flood insurance under the National Flood Insurance Act. This act, along with the Flood Disaster Control Act of 1973, was designed to provide previously unavailable flood insurance to property owners in flood-prone areas. As almost all real estate agents know, the government's designation of flood-prone areas has taken a rather broad sweep along the Texas gulf coast and certain others areas near rivers, reservoirs, and even minor tributaries. The Flood Disaster Control Act basically makes it unlawful for any lending institution with funds underwritten or guaranteed by the federal government (which includes basically all lending institutions) to make loans on improvements in flood-prone areas unless the borrowers have flood insurance. There has been considerable controversy over how the "flood-prone areas" were designated by the U.S. Army Corps of Engineers, and a large amount of litigation has developed since the act was first passed.

One of the major concerns in the area of flood insurance has been the cost of obtaining the flood insurance. This is currently a relatively low cost. However, after a major flood, the rates may go up significantly, and this is a cost that the homeowner must bear. If the rates do go up, the homeowner has no choice but to continue to purchase the flood insurance (regardless of the cost) to satisfy the requirements that have been imposed by his lender. It is arguable that this requirement for flood insurance makes a significant difference in the purchase price of a house built in a "flood-prone" area, since the purchaser mayhave an undetermined future expenses.

The Federal Trade Commission

The Federal Trade Commission has recently come into the limelight because it has strongly expanded its scope from financial areas to those of consumer protection and consumer credit. The rules and regulations of the Federal Trade Commission are implemented and enforced by the Federal Reserve Board. Some of the primary functions of this board are to oversee the implementation and enforcement of such legislation as the Federal Truth-in-Lending Act, the Equal Credit Opportunity Act, the Fair Credit Reporting Act, and the Home Mortgage Disclosure Act.

The Truth-in-Lending Act was originally passed to require lenders to make certain meaningful disclosures as to interest rates and costs of obtaining loans. The Equal Credit Opportunity Act (ECOA) went into effect in 1975 to prohibit discrimination in any aspect of a credit transaction on the basis of sex or marital status. In 1976, amendments were added to the ECOA to prohibit discrimination on the basis of race, color, religion, national origin, age, and other arbitrary requirements. The Fair Credit Reporting Act has its most significant application to credit bureaus. Prior to the passage of this act, it was possible to have a "bad" credit rating, and the person who had the bad credit rating could not find out the source of that information, even if it was untrue. The Fair Credit Reporting Act has opened up the vaults of credit bureaus such that consumers can find out what their credit rating is, and hopefully alleviate some mistakes, if there are any. The Home Mortgage Disclosure Act was passed in 1975 to force lenders to disclose in what areas of a town or metropolitan region they were making loans. This is to prevent "redlining" (making loans to only specified areas of town) and to encourage lenders to make loans in all areas of a town.

The Environmental Protection Agency

In a continuing effort to make our environment more habitable, the Environmental Protection Agency (EPA) has passed voluminous laws and regulations to control the use of real property if such use is considered to be a direct source or an indirect source of environmental pollution. EPA has made an effort to control virtually every area of air, water, and industrial pollution, and many of the regulations have resulted in extreme controversy. The EPA administers the Clean Air Act, which was designed to maintain a national air quality standard, whether the source of pollution was from a stationary, mobile, or indirect source of pollution. EPA also passed land use regulations under the Federal Water Pollution Control Act, which provides for area-wide planning. The EPA has not had very much success at the courthouse, however, and many of its attempts at regulating the land use control through these laws have been substantially altered or struck down altogether. The Clean Air Act and its indirect source rule have been somewhat more successful in controlling the construction of certain sources of pollution, such as shopping centers, office buildings, etc. These examples constitute indirect sources of pollution due to the number of cars that the structures attract, thereby creating a large amount of exhaust and carbon monoxide pollution.

Net Effect

One can easily see that in land use control, the federal government has been fairly significantly involved in a number of different areas. Through the Securities and Exchange Commission, it controls the methods by which we can offer parcels of real estate for sale, or present investment prospectuses and real estate promotional schemes. The federal government also regulates the sale of units of real estate through the Office of Interstate Land Sales Registration, the quality of housing and the availability of loans through the Federal Housing Administration, closing disclosure requirements through the Real Estate Settlement and Procedures Act, and availability of certain funds to primary lenders through Fannie Mae, Ginnie Mae, and Freddie Mac. The federal government also protects the consumer from himself by requiring flood insurance for homes in governmental-designated flood-prone areas. Through the Federal Trade Commission, the federal government requires that certain disclosures be made to the consumer as provided by the federal Truth-in-Lending Act; it also requires disclosures under the Fair Credit Reporting Act; and it provides for additional disclosures to be made through the Home Mortgage Disclosure Act by the requirements imposed on lenders. The Environmental Protection Agency also helps in controlling land use by its regulations on construction through the Clean Air Act and the Federal Water Pollution Control Act. These acts significantly affect where factories and industry can be located, and major traffic patterns may be substantially altered if the federal government feels that these may hurt our pollution standards. Most of these regulations require an extensive amount of funds to be paid by the people regulated, and, ultimately, by you, the consumer.

Some of the governmental functions have been outstanding in contributing to the overall welfare of the American public. However, this is not always the case. The most disturbing area of federal land use control comes from the extended implementation of the acts as passed by Congress. Each of the foregoing federal agencies passes its own regulations in an attempt to clarify its positions, and sometimes an agency expands upon the authority given to it under the original statutes. It must be emphasized that although these regulations are not passed by Congress, they have the force of law until they are challenged in the federal courts. Challenging any federal regulation is an expensive, time-consuming, and high-risk process on the part of any private land developer. Not only does he run the risk of losing the case, but he also runs the risk of incurring the wrath of that federal government agency he chooses to challenge. In addition, there is no control whatsoever on these federal government agencies as they pass these regulations. They are not subject to any system of checks and balances, and there is no authority to discipline them if there is any type of injustice or selective (unfair) enforcement involved, other than through the federal courts. If there is a basic injustice in any of the federal land use controls, it is that there are no watchdogs over the federal government, whereas the federal agencies are being the watchdogs over the private land owner and developer.

An interesting anomaly to the land use control pattern of the federal government has been the proposal of a National Land Use Planning Act. This article of legislation provides incentives for national land use control (often referred to as *national zoning*). This legislation has been introduced into both houses of Congress for several years and has not been passed to date. Oddly enough, one of the major lobbying efforts in attempting to stop passage of the act has been because "we do not want the federal government to control our land use."

State Land Use Control

The Tenth Amendment to the U.S. Constitution reserves all powers not specifically delegated to the federal government to the states. So, subject to other constitutional provisions, the states do have the right to pass reasonable regulations and to exercise their police power to promote the health, safety, and welfare of the community. The states regulate land use through a number of different means, the most important of which are state agencies, land management, enabling acts, special-purpose districts, and regulation of natural resources.

The state of Texas has the Texas Highway Commission, the General Land Office, the Texas Water Development Board, the Texas Water Rights Commission, the Texas Parks and Wildlife Department, and various and sundry other state agencies. Each agency has jurisdictional control over all lands that are maintained under that agency's specified scope of control. Most of these agencies are appointed by the governor and are relatively autonomous as to implementation and enforcement, and there is very little coordination between them.

Land management in Texas is accomplished through a number of different regional planning commissions, which have been inactive in recent years. Through independent authorities such as the Houston-Galveston Area Council, the Coastal Zone Management Commission, and other regional planning authorities, Texas is making its first attempt at regional land planning, to achieve the best land use, both economically and environmentally, for areas of strategic environmental concern.

Special-purpose districts have been very important to the Texas development pattern. Through the authority of the legislature, special districts have been established whose boards ultimately regulate almost every type of land use imaginable. These districts have their own jurisdictional boundaries, which often overlap with other authority's boundaries (cities, school districts, etc.). Special levee districts (to protect water hazards in flood-prone areas), water districts, water improvement districts, and utility districts have been instrumental in allowing vast expansion for most Texas cities when the municipal authorities did not have sufficient utility capacity to serve new subdivisions. Other special-purpose districts that have been particularly instrumental are the navigation districts, water conservation districts, soil conservation districts, and subsidence districts.

Regulation of natural resources has been the primary responsibility of the state Railroad Commission. The Railroad Commission has authority to regulate production capacities and to set restrictions on oil and gas production in Texas. The General Land Office has authority over certain uses of these resources offshore.

County Regulations

Texas has no particular provisions for county land use control. The only real areas of control that a county has are subdivision regulations and road construction and maintenance. The subdivision controls assure minimum street widths, drainage standards, plat approvals for new subdivisions, and utility requirements. In planning and maintaining county roads, the county commissioners are given exclusive authority in establishing traffic patterns, which, in an urban area, can make a significant impact on the direction and planning that a city's future growth potential may have. In 1977, there was significant effort in the state legislature to authorize counties to pass much more restrictive subdivision and land use control. This legislation did not pass, but it is expected to be brought up again at the next legislative session.

Municipal Land Use Control

Cities do not have any inherent law-making powers except those granted by the state. Therefore, the state has passed certain enabling acts that grant cities the authority to regulate land use. Typical examples of this type of delegation of power are reflected in the zoning statutes, indirect municipal land use controls, municipal enforcement of deed restrictions, and certain powers of annexation.

Zoning

Zoning is the most extensive method of regulating land use in cities, and its use was upheld in Texas in 1934 in the case of *Lombardo* v. *City of Dallas*, 73 S.W.2d 475 (Tex. 1934). Zoning is a police power, and one of the strongest powers a city has to regulate land use. In fact, once a zoning ordinance has been passed, the law favors its validity. If a party contests the ordinance, the burden is on the complaining party to show that the city acted arbitrarily and capriciously in passing the ordinance. This is a very difficult burden of proof.

Purpose. Article 1011a is the specific grant of authority to the cities by the state for the power of zoning. The statute specifically sets out that zoning is for the purpose of promoting health, safety, and morals; for the protection and preservation of places and areas of historical and cultural importance and significance; and for the general welfare of the community. This power specifically gives the municipality the authority to regulate and restrict the height, number of stories, and size of buildings and other structures; the percentage of a lot that may be occupied; the size of the yards, courts, and other open space; the density of population; and the location and use of buildings, structures, and land for trade, industry, residence, or other purpose. In the case of designated places and areas of historical and cultural importance, the city also has the power to regulate and restrict the construction, alteration, and reconstruction or razing of buildings and other structures. One must always keep in mind the specific purpose of the zoning enabling legislation, because the purpose per se is one of the fundamental criteria the courts look to to determine whether or not a zoning ordinance will be upheld. The process relies on sound land planning practices, and is not subject to popular demand, nor subject to a referendum, *San Pedro North, Ltd.* v. *City of San Antonio* (Tex. Civ. App.—San Antonio, 1978).

The procedural aspects of zoning ordinances and zoning changes are critically important to the legality of any ordinance. If the proper procedures are not strictly adhered to, the ordinance is in imminent danger of being tested by opponents. One of the basic underlying principles of the zoning concept is that the zoning regulations (and changes thereto) must be made in accordance with a *comprehensive plan* (Tex. Rev. Civ. Stat. Ann., art. 1011c). There is some question as to exactly what constitutes a comprehensive plan, and municipal planners often have their own ideas and criteria for what will constitute a valid comprehensive plan. There is no particular comprehensive plan format or criteria that must be followed, but the plan must be a uniform one that can act as a basis for justification to effect further zoning changes, or the refusal of same. The regulations, according to statute, must also be designed to accomplish the following:

1. To lessen congestion in the streets;
2. To secure safety from fire, panic, and other danger;
3. To promote health and the general welfare;
4. To provide adequate light and air;
5. To prevent the overcrowding of land;
6. To avoid undue concentration of population; and
7. To facilitate adequate provision for transportation, water, sewage, schools, parks, and other public requirements.

The statute further authorizes the city to divide the municipality into districts of such number and shape and area as to carry out the purposes of the ordinance and to regulate and restrict construction and reconstruction, alteration, and repair, and use of building structures or land inside of each district. All regulations are to be uniform for each class or kind of building throughout each district, but the regulations may differ from one district to the other.

Zoning Procedure. The zoning regulations (as well as any amendments, supplements, or changes of same) cannot become effective until the legislative body holds a public hearing with respect to said changes, at which all parties and interested citizens can have an opportunity to be heard. At least 15 days' notice of the time and place of such hearing shall be published in an official paper in such municipality (Tex. Rev. Civ. Stat. Ann., art. 1011d). In the event the proposed regulations are protested by the owners of 20% of the area of the lots or persons within 200 feet of the property proposed to change, a three-fourths vote of the legislative body is necessary to enact the amendment or change (Tex. Rev. Civ. Stat. Ann., art. 1011e).

The ultimate decision as to how an area is going to be zoned depends on the legislative body of the muncipality, i.e., the august body of elected officials who bear the burden of running the city. These individuals are aided by a group of appointed officials referred to as *zoning commissioners*, whose appointment and function are specifically authorized by statute.

In the normal zoning procedure, the applicant appears before the zoning commission, who, after a preliminary review, sets a public hearing for the applicant's proposed zoning change. After proper statutory notice has been given, a public hearing is held to determine the public's views and attitudes on said proposed change. After the public hearing has taken place, the zoning commission then proceeds to make its recommendations and decisions on the proposed zoning change. It may propose the change exactly as it was proposed, or it can modify it and recommend a modified proposal, or it can reject the proposal entirely.

If the commission chooses to recommend the proposed change, the proposal then goes to the city council, who, after proper statutory notice, has its own public hearing and makes the final decision as to whether or not the zoning change will be accepted or rejected. The legislative body (city council, in this case) cannot make a decision until it has received a recommendation from the zoning commission. If the recommendation from the zoning commission was against the change, it would take a three-fourths majority of the council to overrule the recommendation of the zoning commission. The same is not true of a recommended change, however. If the zoning commission recommends the change, the city council can overrule it by mere majority vote.

If the applicant feels he has been unjustly treated, he may appeal his case to another appointed body, the *board of adjustment*. The board of adjustment is limited to hearing appeals from administrative decisions and to granting *special exceptions* and *variances*. The board is also empowered by statute to hear and decide appeals when there is an error in the decision by an administrative official in enforcing an ordinance. The board can also hear and decide special exceptions under the terms of the ordinance and can even authorize a variance from the terms of the ordinance when there are special circumstances, or if the ordinance creates an unnecessary hardship.

A *special exception* is a use that is permitted in a certain zone, but such use is subject to control or supervision by the municipal authorities. If there is an objection to the use in that zone, the special exception can be revoked, and the use is no longer permitted.

A *variance* is a use that literally violates the terms of the zoning ordinance, but the variance is permitted to stand because otherwise an unnecessary hardship would be created for the owner of the property. A variance can only be granted to solve location and construction violations.

Any appeal beyond the board of adjustment has to be taken to the nearest court of competent jurisdiction.

Zoning Issues. There are a number of issues that continually recur in the zoning process that bear some additional discussion. Those to be considered will be "taking" issue, spot zoning, contract zoning, nonconforming use, and exclusionary land use controls.

"Taking" Issue. There has long been an argument that zoning a property for a particular use is, in fact, "taking" that property from the owner who can no longer determine its highest and best use and perhaps cannot even build for a profit. An example of this would be a piece of prime commercial frontage property, which, for various reasons, is rezoned for residential use. In this situation, the owner, expecting to sell the property for a commercial use, feels that his rights to build on the property profitably have been taken from him. The courts have consistently held, however, that this is a legal regulation of land use and *not* "taking." Therefore, there is no requirement for just compensation, and the city is not liable for any just compensation as it would be in an eminent domain proceeding.

Spot Zoning. Spot zoning has been described as the process of singling out a small parcel of land for a use classification that is different and inconsistent with that of the surrounding zoned areas. Zoning of this type is normally to the benefit of the lot owner but to the detriment of the surrounding area. An example of this would be to allow a townhouse zoning use in the middle of a single-family residential area (by permitting one of the owners to sell his lot off to a townhouse developer who may build four or five townhouses on that property). This use would not fit into the overall land use of the neighborhood or of that section of the city, and creates a spot zoning issue. Spot zoning is illegal and prohibited in Texas, *Burket* v. *City of Texarkana*, 500 S.W.2d 242 (Tex. Civ. App.—Texarkana, 1973).

Contract Zoning. Contract zoning is an agreement by a governing body to enact a change in land use classification in exchange for certain concessions to be granted by the developer or applicant. It is "zoning by agreement," which does not fit into the criteria of providing for the health, safety, and welfare of the citizens. This has been held to be invalid as an improper "bargaining away" of the city's police power, *City of Farmers Branch* v. *Hawnco, Inc.*, 435 S.W.2d 298 (Tex. Civ. App.—Dallas, 1968).

Nonconforming Use. Nonconforming use relates to a zoning change or a new zoning designation. The nonconforming use is maintaining the previous use of an area, a use that does not properly fit into the new zoning classification. For instance, if a particular area of town was zoned R1-residential, and, at the time of the zoning change, there were two commercial uses in that zoning district, the two commercial uses would be allowed to remain, but they could not be materially changed or altered (or even improved) if they did not comply with the new existing zoning classification. The theory behind this is that if the area has been properly planned, and a new zoning designation has been given, the nonconforming uses are supposed to eventually cease to function, and the new classification designated by the plan would be the only existing classification. There have been successful efforts at putting a limit to the use of the nonconforming structure by designating a certain number of years by which that nonconforming use must cease to exist, *City of Garland* v. *Valley Oil Company*, 482 S.W.2d 342 (Tex. Civ. App.—Dallas, 1972).

Exclusionary Land Use Control. There has been considerable litigation in recent years over what rights the city has to zone properties to exclude certain uses. This practice is referred to as *exclusionary zoning*. If zoning, for instance, is used to limit construction to homes on two-acre lots, and the city contains no apartments, no middle-income housing, or no low-income housing, that city may be determined to be using an exclusionary zoning technique, which would be illegal. Basically, the court would say that the city is excluding certain people from living in the town, which would be a violation of an individual's right to travel interstate, as provided for by the U.S. Constitution, *N.A.A.C.P.* v. *Button*, 371 U.S. 415; *Southern Burlington County N.A.A.C.P.* v. *Township of Mount Laurel*, 336 A.2d 713 (Supreme Ct.—New Jersey, 1975). There have been two recent cases, however, that reaffirm the city's ability to use wide discretion in zoning its areas, as long as it has a permissible, constitutional objective for its land use regulation, *Construction Industry Association of Sonoma County* v. *City of Petaluma*, 375 F.Supp. 574 (1975); *Village of Belle Terre* v. *Boraas*, 416 U.S. 1 (1974).

Annexation—Extraterritorial Jurisdiction

The Texas legislature has passed an additional method of land use control giving the city certain annexation powers and certain rights within its extraterritorial jurisdiction (Tex. Rev. Civ. Stat. Ann., art. 970a). *Extraterritorial jurisdiction* has been defined as the unincorporated area, not a part of any other city, that is contiguous to the corporate limits of any city. The size of the extraterritorial jurisdiction changes depending on the number of inhabitants in that city. The governing body of any city has the right, according to this statute, to extend by ordinance to all the area under its extraterritorial jurisdiction, all the city's ordinances establishing rules and regulations governing the plats and subdivision of land. In addition to this, the city is given additional power to annex the area within its extraterritorial jurisdiction up to certain specified limits.

This statute has unusually broad application in a city like Houston, which has a five-mile extraterritorial jurisdiction (ETJ). When the city annexes additional property, it automatically increases its ETJ another five miles beyond the limits of the new annexed area. The Houston city limits are peculiar in that they have adopted what is called *spoke annexation*. Houston has annexed a lot of property in satellite communities around it by doing this, and has effectively increased its ETJ to include almost all of Harris County. The graphic illustration in Figure 16-1 shows how Houston has accomplished this feat.

There has been considerable litigation concerning Houston's power to annex and service these outlying areas. The basis behind the annexation ordinance is a very solid one, however. One finds that in the Houston area, as the city continues to expand beyond its perimeters, it cannot be surrounded by other incorporated suburban communities. It has been the opinion of some land planners that this encirclement by suburban communities (of most cities) has been one of the major contributions to decay of the inner city and white flight, because the city's inhabitants can flee to the suburbs. In Houston, however, the inhabitants cannot escape to an outlying subdivision to escape the city's problems, tax base, or other municipal difficulties. Today, Houston is one of the few cities in the United States that has seen a revival of its downtown area, so the ETJ and annexation ordinance may be significant factors in this development.

Indirect Municipal Land Use Controls

Cities carry significant impact in being able to regulate land use control through indirect sources, that is, sources that do not directly affect the use of property. One of these methods is the *building code*. This code regulates

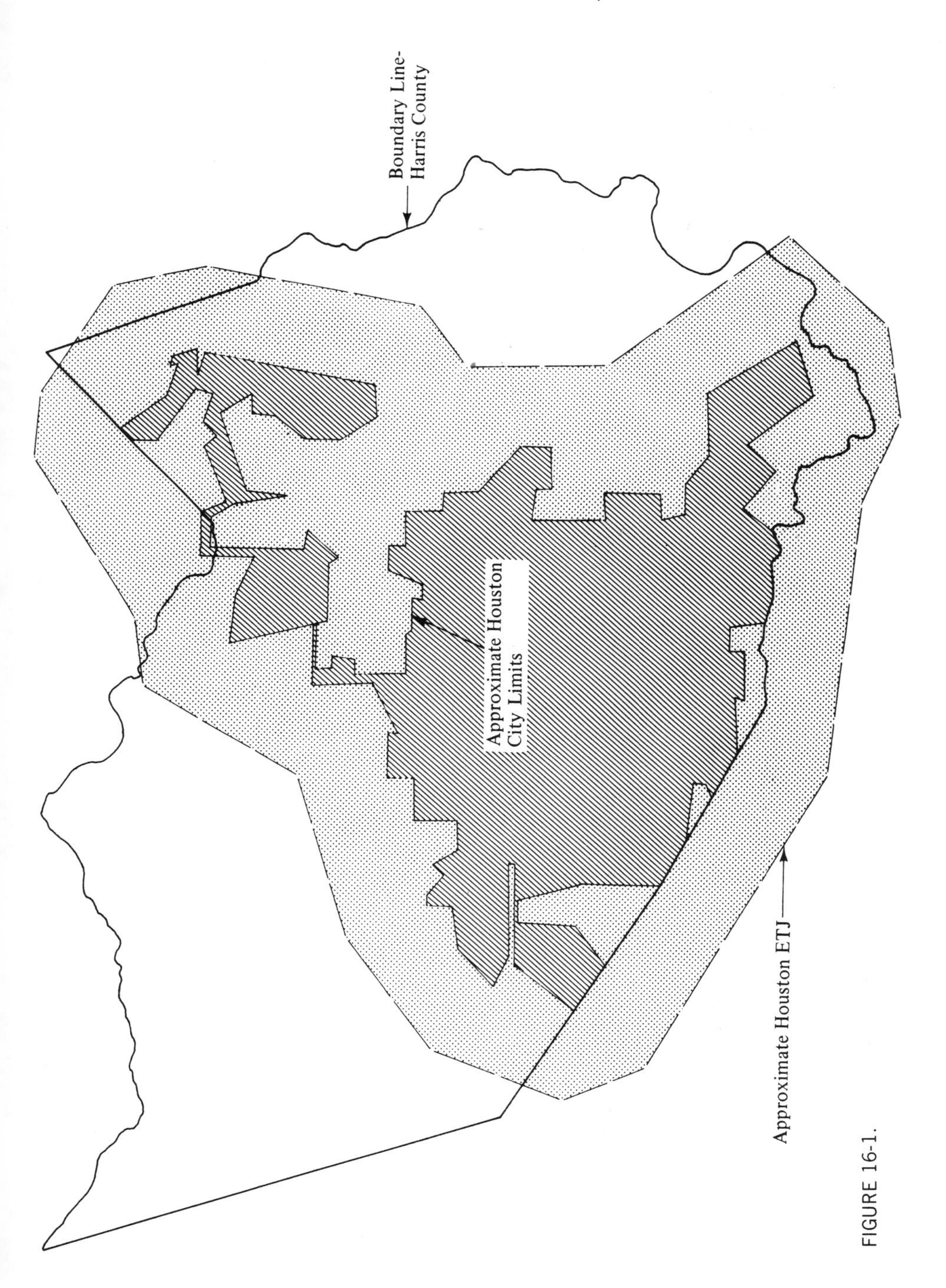
Boundary Line-
Harris County
Approximate Houston
City Limits
Approximate Houston ETJ

FIGURE 16-1.

the minimum standards of construction for building within the city. The municipality has additional power through the control of *utility extensions* and capacities for those utilities as they are extended. For instance, if the city constructs a utility system in a particular subdivision that has just enough capacity for single-family homes, this literally denies the use for any multifamily homes or higher density use for that property. *Maintenance and construction of city streets* also have a particular impact on where and what direction the city will expand and how fast. *Subdivisions' regulations* are controlled through the city planning department, through which all land plans and subdivision plats must be submitted for approval, so that the city can check the proposed development versus the capacity of existing utilities and traffic control problems. Thus, major city concerns can be monitored to be sure that the new development would not be one that creates a difficulty for the city's existing facilities. The city is additionally given certain powers under the new federal statutes to enforce provisions of federal legislation such as the Clean Air Act and the Clean Water Act.

Deed Restrictions

Creation

Deed restrictions are the primary private method of land use control. These restrictions are generally created in one of two ways: (1) They are incorporated into the subdivisions as part of a developer's overall plan for maintaining the quality and environment for the subdivision, or (2) they are included as a reservation in a particular deed when an owner sells the adjacent property, either to maintain the quality and environment of the existing conditions, and/or because of his proximity to the sold parcel. Since deed restrictions are normally recorded, they are on constructive notice for all subsequent purchasers and creditors, *Smith* v. *Bowers*, 463 S.W.2d 222 (Tex. Civ. App.—Waco, 1970).

Control

Deed restrictions are particularly valuable in that they are construed as an agreement between parties rather than a land use control. Therefore, there can be a lot more controls in deed restrictions since they can include more than just the health, safety, and welfare of the community. Common provisions in many deed restrictions include the quality requirements of roof shingles, minimum square footages, and building materials that must be used in the construction of a house. In contrasting these requirements with those of zoning or of building permits, it is apparent that deed restrictions go far beyond the health, safety, and welfare of the community. In fact, the only prohibitions of deed restrictions are those in violation of the rights under the U.S. Constitution (i.e., racial discrimination), *Shelly* v.

Kraemer, 334 U.S. 1 (1948). Since these restrictions are private restrictions that are enforced by contract between the parties, it is important to note that only a party who gets a benefit from these deed restrictions (i.e., the other property owners in the subdivision) can maintain a cause of action to try to enjoin any violation of those restrictions, or attempt to enforce those restrictions.

Enforcement

In enforcing deed restrictions, the rule of construction of contracts generally applies. When there is an ambiguity, the restrictive covenants will be construed in favor of the less restrictive use of the property and against the restriction, *Southampton Civic Club* v. *Couch*, 322 S.W.2d 516 (Tex. 1958). However, that does not mean that the restrictions will not be strictly enforced, *Stephenson* v. *Perlitz*, 532 S.W.2d 954 (Tex. Sup. Ct.—1976). There is at least some authority that the covenants can run perpetually, *Moore* v. *Smith*, 443 S.W.2d 552 (Tex. 1969), but they are usually restricted by their own terms for a number of years. Changing deed restrictions is also controlled by the restrictions' own terms; however, in the absence of specific procedure for change, it normally takes a vote of 100% of the people affected by those deed restrictions, *Norwood* v. *Davis*, 345 S.W.2d 944 (Tex. Civ. App.—Austin, 1961), to make a change.

There has been concern over enforcing these deed restrictions because of the expense of litigation involved and maintaining said enforcement. Some relief to this has been given under Tex. Rev. Civ. Stat. Ann., art. 1293b (effective August 29, 1977), which allows for attorney's fees to the prevailing party who asserted an action for a breach of restrictive covenant.

Municipal Enforcement of Deed Restrictions

An additional method of municipal land use control has surfaced in Texas, primarily due to Houston's lack of zoning and its abundance of subdivision deed restrictions, and that is, municipal enforcement of deed restrictions. The Texas legislature has passed two enabling statutes to effect this method of land use control (Tex. Rev. Civ. Stat. Ann., art. 974a-1 and art. 974a-2). Under these statutes, the city is authorized to pass an ordinance that requires uniform application of the statutes to all property and citizens. These statutes also give the incorporated city the power to sue in any court of competent jurisdiction to enjoin or abate a violation of a deed restriction contained in a duly recorded plan, plat, replat, or other instrument affecting the subdivision inside its boundaries. Article 974a-2 specifically prohibits the issuance of commercial building permits if it is in violation of existing subdivision deed restrictions. This particular statute provides that the city may join with an interested property owner in a suit to enjoin further construction activity by someone who does not have a permit in compliance with the act. Thus, both of these statutes provide a possible alternative to zoning in cities that rely primarily on deed restrictions as a means of land use control.

There are two difficult issues, however, and possible constitutional questions concerning the validity of these statutes. The first is that the Texas Constitution, under Article III Section 52(a), prohibits the expenditure of public funds that provide individual benefit at public expense. Deed restrictions clearly inure to the benefit of the private property owners who seek to have them enforced. The city, however, must use tax funds (and the city's legal staff) to enforce these restrictions. This seems to be a clear violation of the constitutional provision. There is a second legal question, which is whether or not the city can maintain an action to enforce these restrictions, since the city would not properly be considered an aggrieved party, as the deed restrictions do not normally apply to the city but only to the lot owners affected thereby. To date, there has not been a precedent setting judicial determination of either of the issues.

SUMMARY

It is by use of police power that the government regulates and enforces laws and regulations that pertain to land use control. This involves no "taking" of the property, as in eminent domain, and therefore, no requirement for just compensation to the landowner. Land use controls are normally broken down into federal land use controls, state land use controls, county land use controls, and municipal and local land use controls.

Federal land use regulations involve the Securities Exchange Commission, Department of Housing and Urban Development, Federal Trade Commission, and the Environmental Protection Agency. State land use controls involve various state agencies in their control over parts of the real estate business. County regulations are minimal except for their road maintenance and construction authority. Municipal land use control consists basically of zoning, building permit procedures, road construction, repair and maintenance, extraterritorial jurisdiction, and attempts at enforcing private deed restrictions. Deed restrictions are purely a private method of land use control and are important in cities where there is no zoning.

17

REAL ESTATE TAXATION

No one pretends that taxation of real estate is an easy subject and the various tax laws affecting real estate are so complex that only a very basic approach to taxation will be made in this text. Hopefully, this chapter will provide the foundation for further research and inquiries for assistance from trained professionals, since tax advice often constitutes legal advice and is not within the scope of most licensees' employment. Advice from a competent tax lawyer and Certified Public Accountant is indispensable to any licensee who plans a career in investment and income-producing property.

For the purposes of this chapter, the only areas of taxation considered are ad valorem taxation and certain provisions of federal income taxation which have unique application to real estate.

Ad Valorem Taxes

In these times of taxpayer revolt, Proposition 13, and general taxpayer dissatisfaction with the government, the most fundamental concepts of *ad valorem* taxation are often questioned. However, it is a system that will not easily be changed since there are numerous statutes and constitutional provisions dealing with ad valorem taxation which have etched this concept in Texas law over many years.

Constitutional Provisions

Ad valorem is a Latin phrase which translates literally to "according to value." Accordingly, ad valorem taxes are taxes which are assessed on real property, the tax being based on the property's fair market value. The Texas Constitution specifically provides for ad valorem taxation under Article VIII, § 1, which states that,

> all property in this state, . . . shall be taxed in proportion to its value, which shall be ascertained as may be provided by law.

It also provides that the taxes shall be "equal and uniform" (Article VIII, § 2). The Constitution further provides that each county is to elect an Assessor and Collector of Taxes (or sheriff, depending on the size of the county) to perform all the duties necessary for the collection of taxes, and equalization of taxes. The annual tax assessment is considered a special lien which arises automatically at the first of every year. The Constitution also provides for seizure of the property for delinquent taxes (Article VIII, § 13), which will be discussed in greater detail later in this chapter.

On the lighter side, there is a Constitutional limit to taxation in that the fair market value of the property may not be exceeded by the assessment. The Constitution also provides for certain exemptions. These exemptions are primarily for land put to agricultural use (Article VIII, § 1-d), property owned by governmental entities for public purposes, and other property devoted exclusively to the use and benefit of the public (Article XI, § 9). The Constitution also enables the legislature to exempt from taxation a large number of other properties, consisting primarily of those used for religious, charitable, and school purposes. Oddly enough, in light of all of the Constitutional and statutory provisions, the State of Texas has abolished ad valorem taxes for state purposes except for those levied against certain institutions of higher learning (Article VIII, § 1-e). The vast bulk of ad valorem taxes are paid at the county and local tax levels.

Statutory Provisions

The Constitutional provisions have several enabling statutes authorizing the legislature to pass further tax laws. Specifically, procedures for assessment, foreclosure, determination of fair market value, tax equalization, and procedures for collecting delinquent accounts are left to the legislature's ability to balance government needs against the taxpayer's ability to pay. Before any of these statutory provisions are discussed in detail, we should understand the basic formula for calculating the tax an individual pays on his real estate. Simply stated, the formula is as follows:

$$\text{Assessed value} \times \text{tax rate} = \text{tax payment}$$

To understand the full meaning of the formula, one must first investigate the significance of each of its parts, as specifically determined by the statutes.

Assessed Value. As shown in the formula, one's taxes are a multiple of the *assessed value*. The statutes provide for an Assessor and Collector of Taxes to be elected at the regular biennial election and who shall hold office for two years. In counties with populations of less than 10,000, the sheriff may be the Assessor Collector (Tex. Rev. Civ. Stat., art. 7245). The Assessors are obligated by statute to make a list of all taxable property between the first day of January and the thirtieth day of April of each year (Tex. Rev. Civ. Stat., art. 7189). The Assessor then fixes a fair market value of the property, usually determined by the taxing authorities' appraisers. The manner and form of assessing is according to normal appraisal methods and is relatively simple when applied to real property, specifying the legal description as closely as practicable and assessing values on the improvements separate from the value of the land.

Assessed Value vs. Fair Market Value. The fair market value that is determined, however, is seldom the assessed value. Taxes are paid according to assessed value which is generally set at a percentage of the fair market value. This sounds confusing, and well it should, since there are no statutory provisions which allow the Assessor to do this. Some taxing districts, especially water districts, often set the assessed value at 100% of (and therefore equal to) the fair market value, but most municipalities and school district taxes do not. Dallas's assessed value, for instance, is 66⅔% of fair market value. The City of Houston's assessed value is 53% of the total fair market value.

Tax Review. The tax assessor prepares a list of all property subject to taxation in the taxing district. When the assessment lists are completed, they are turned in to the board of equalization for inspection, correction or equalization, and approval. The board of equalization is the commissioner's court for county taxes; cities and school districts generally appoint their own tax equalization board. Whenever the board feels that assessments need to be raised, it must give notice to the owner so that he or she may have an opportunity to contest the increased assessment. As a practical matter, most assessed values are set well below the actual fair market value and are difficult to contest, even after substantial increases.

Tax Rate. The tax rate is set by the taxing authority in accordance with the following formula set out in Article 7043 of the Texas Revised Civil Statutes:

1. Subtract the total which may be expected to be paid out by the taxing authority from the total amount expected to be paid to the taxing authority. This determines the *total sum* needed from collection of ad valorem taxes.
2. Determine the total valuation of the property in the taxing jurisdiction (values assessed by Assessor).
3. Divide 1 by (2 divided by 100). This final quotient shall be the number of cents per $100 of valuation to be collected for the current year. The rates normally vary between $1 and $2 per $100 of assessed valuation.

For instance, the county has determined that, after all income is received, it will need $10,000,000 to provide an adequate budget to meet its needs. The Assessor has determined that the assessed valuation of the property in the county is worth $400,000,000. To determine the tax rate, the calculation would be as follows:

$$\$10{,}000{,}000 \div \frac{400{,}000{,}000}{100} = \text{Tax Rate}$$

$$\frac{10{,}000{,}000}{4{,}000{,}000} = \$2.50$$

Therefore, the tax rate to be paid would be $2.50 per $100 of assessed valuation. All taxpayers would pay the same *rate* of taxation, but their total taxes would depend completely on the valuation of their properties.

As stated previously, there has been a serious concern by legislature on rising ad valorem taxes, and Texas is not different. Recently, the Texas legislature voted to restrict increases in property taxes by local taxing units; this law is to become effective on January 1, 1979 (H.B. No. 18 approved August 14, 1978). The statute basically provides that the governing body may not adopt a tax rate that exceeds the rate for the previous year by more than 3 percent until the governing body has: (1) given public notice of its intention to adopt a higher rate; and (2) held a public hearing on the proposed increase. The hearing must be on a week day that is not a public holiday and must begin after 5:00 P.M. and before 9:00 P.M. There are also provisions for notice to the property owners if the property value has been increased over the preceding tax year. The governing body of the taxing unit may decrease the official tax rate for the current year at any time.

Tax Payment. Once it has been finally determined that tax is due and payable by the taxing authority and all appeals have been exhausted, there is no provision for the reduction of taxes. However, the statutes provide that the taxing authority may allow a specified discount for early payment.

State of Texas and county taxes are due January 31 of each year. Most other taxes are at the rate of 6% per annum from the date of their delinquency.

Taxes may be paid in semiannual installments (Tex. Rev. Civ. Stat., art. 7336). If a person pays one-half of the taxes imposed on or before December 30 for the year in which the assessment was made, he shall have until June 30 of the following year to pay the other one-half of the taxes without penalty or interest. Past-due taxes paid in this manner incur a penalty of 8% of the amount of the unpaid taxes. There are no other provisions for the installment payment of taxes currently in force in Texas.

Delinquency. Interest penalties for delinquent taxes are normally considered to be more of an inconvenience than a penalty. One can seldom borrow money for rates comparable to 6% or 8% in today's money market. Instead, the real penalties occur in the form of forced sale of the property and the statutory penalties one must pay in order to redeem the property.

While summary seizure and sale is provided for in both the Constitution and the statutes, it has been effectively eliminated by the enactment of Article 732a, Tex. Rev. Civ. Stat. This statute provides that all sales of real estate (personalty is not included) made for the collection of delinquent taxes can be made only after judicial foreclosure of the tax lien by a court of competent jurisdiction. The suit for the foreclosure of tax liens must also be in accordance with the existing statutes pertaining to tax suits, which are very specific as to notice, citation, and petition, to allow for adequate notice to and response from the property owner. Once judgment has been obtained, the court orders the sheriff to execute the sale. It's the sheriff who signs the deed effecting conveyance of the property.

Redemption. The unique attribute of tax foreclosures in Texas is there is a redemption period during which the owner, his heirs, or representatives may pay the taxes due (plus statutory costs and penalties incurred during and after the tax sale) and once again receive full title to the property. Courts have held that the statutes providing for redemption are to be construed liberally in favor of the right to redeem.

Before the Tax Sale. The law provides that the delinquent taxpayer, or anyone else having an interest in the property, may redeem the same at any time *before the lands are sold* for taxes by paying to the collector all the taxes due thereon, plus interest at 6% per annum, all lawfully accrued court costs, and a penalty of 10% (Tex. Rev. Civ. Stat., art. 7339).

After the Tax Sale. If the state, city, or town becomes the purchaser at the tax sale, the owner, or anyone else having an interest in the real estate, has the right to redeem the property at any time within two years from the *date of the sale* upon payment of the amount of taxes, interest, penalties, and costs on or against said land at the time of the redemption (Art. 7340). There is some conflict, however, since the Constitution (Art. VIII, Sec. 13) authorizes redemption of the land within two years from the *date of filing of the purchaser's deed of record*. As a practical matter, however, the dates would probably be the same.

Transfer of the Tax Lien. The statutes also provide for a transfer of the taxing authority's tax lien to any person or company that pays the taxing authority any taxes due upon real property at the request of the owner of said property. The holder of the transferred lien may bring suit to foreclose after 12 months. The owner then has the right to redeem within one year after said foreclosure after paying attorney's fees, amount of judgment at foreclosure, and costs and interest accrued in the judgment, plus 10%.

Article 7345b. The key statute which covers tax foreclosure situations most comprehensively is Article 7345b. Regarding apparent conflict with earlier tax statutes, most authorities feel that this statute, passed more recently, supercedes those earlier ones that seem to conflict. Article 7345b provides for court proceedings in some detail and provides for an order of sale to foreclose the tax liens. The procedure for sale is basically the same as provided for in Article 3810, which is used in foreclosures of deeds of trust, as discussed in Chapters 7 and 9. The property may not be sold to anyone other than the taxing unit for less than the adjudged value of the property or the aggregate amount of judgments against the property rendered in the tax foreclosure suit. If there is an excess at the sale, the proceeds are to go to the owner after all costs of sale have been paid. However, the burden is on the owner to file a petition and have a hearing to determine whether he or she is entitled to these funds. If there is no claim for the excess funds within four years, they are transferred to the state's general revenue fund.

The statute provides that the period of redemption in all suits brought under the authority of 7345b shall be within two (2) years from the date of the filing for record of the purchaser's deed, on the following basis:

(1) Within the first year of the redemption period, upon the payment of the amount of the bid for the property by the purchaser at such sale, including a One Dollar ($1) tax deed recording fee and all taxes, penalties, interest and costs thereafter paid thereon, plus twenty-five per cent (25%) of the aggregate total.

(2) Within the last year of the redemption period, upon the payment of the amount bid for the property at such sale, including a One Dollar ($1) tax deed recording fee and all taxes, penalties, interest and costs thereafter paid thereon, plus fifty per cent (50%) of the aggregate total; and no further oradditional amount than herein specified shall be required to be paid to effect any such redemption.

The purchaser of the property at the sale takes the title free and clear of all liens and claims for ad valorem taxes delinquent at the time of judgment in the tax suit. However, the purchaser may not take possession of the premises until 20 days after the redemption period has lapsed, creating a waiting period of approximately two years and 20 days after the recording of the tax deed before the purchaser can take possession.

Homestead Old Age Exemption

As a final note, it is comforting to know that Snidely Whiplash doesn't exist in Texas. In 1971 the legislature passed an exemption from forced sale for taxes of property that is (1) homestead, and (2) occupied by a person 65 years or older claiming the homestead exemption. When the tax foreclosure suit is filed, all that is required of the claimant is to file an affidavit containing the following information:

1. The birth date of the affiant,
2. Legal description of the homestead, and
3. Signature of the affiant, along with an ackowledge or proof of record.

The effect of the statute is only to delay the proceeding. The taxes, interest, and penalties continue to exist as a prior lien against t e property, and the taxing unit can foreclose when the homestead is no longer held by the claimant. However, this exemption can provide a refuge from the increasing taxes that can be so burdensome on the elderly. Too often elderly people on fixed incomes can't cope with the constantly increasing ad valorem taxes. This statute gives considerable relief from that problem.

Federal Income Taxation

There are few areas more frustrating to the layman and lawyer alike than federal income taxation. The statutes and regulations are constantly updated, revised, reviewed, and so randomly enforced that sometimes none of it seems to make sense. However, it is safe to say that tax advantages and incentives are a significant part of federal income taxation, and there are certain benefits in federal income taxation that apply to ownership and development of real estate. These incentives tend to attract the type of investment that encourages construction of housing, office space, retail centers, and other developments which affects all of us and stimulates the economy of which we all form a part.

Since the subject of federal income taxation involves volumes of treatises at the professional level, only the fundamentals of taxation most significant to real estate will be discussed here. These are:

1. Depreciation,
2. Capital gains tax treatment,
3. Tax free exchanges, and
4. Installment sales.

Depreciation

Depreciation is generally defined as an allowance for loss of value. The federal government, through the Internal Revenue Service, recognizes the intrinsic loss of value of improvements (land may not be depreciated) and allows the taxpayer to provide for this loss of value by allowing these decreases in value to be a deduction from gross income before the income is taxed. This, in effect, reduces the amount of taxes the taxpayer will pay, even though he has made no actual or "out-of-pocket" expenditures. Depreciation is often used synonymously with the term "tax shelter" because it is a deduction from gross income even though: 1. no payment is made, 2. no actual loss is suffered, and 3. depreciation is allowed in excess of the owner's equity invested. Since land cannot be depreciated, an allocation of the purchase price must be made between the improvements and land purchased. The most common allocation method used is the ratio of fair market value of the component (land or improvements) to the total value.

There are specific rules for determining which depreciation method a taxpayer can use, and in the final analysis, neither the Service nor the courts will allow an individual to take more depreciation than he is entitled to. Additionally, depreciation is limited to commercial (industrial and office space) and investment (residential rental) property. One's primary residence cannot be depreciated. Each taxpayer should consult his tax counsel and accountant to determine if depreciation is applicable, and if it is, which of the depreciation methods is more advantageous for his particular needs.

There are two basic methods of depreciation: 1. straight line, and 2. accelerated depreciation. Accelerated depreciation is further subdivided into the *sum of the years digits* (S.Y.D.) method, and the *declining balance* method. Subdivisions of the declining balance method are the 125, 150, and 200 percent methods. The depreciation methods previously discussed are graphically illustrated in Figure 17-1. To depreciate an improvement by any of the foregoing methods, a useful life must be assigned to that improvement. That is, the improvement has a limited period during which it will functionally, economically, or physically "wear out." For instance, a building is generally depreciated over 30 or 40 years. A dishwasher, however, is generally depreciated over 5 years. In an effort to help, the IRS has published a list of "guideline lives" which gives the taxpayer a good rule of thumb for depreciation. Taxpayers can vary from the published list of

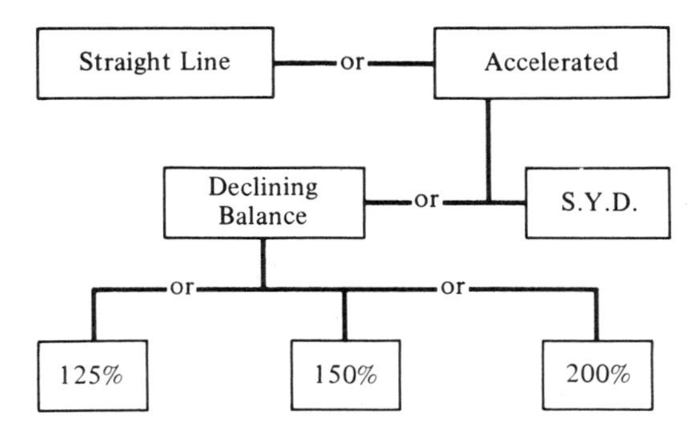

FIGURE 17-1. Depreciation methods.

guideline lives, but should be prepared to support the life used if questioned by the Internal Revenue Service.

While it may seem obvious from a cash flow standpoint, it is generally always to the taxpayer's benefit to use the shortest guideline life possible, allowing larger deductions in any given year.

For instance, if the asset will last only two years, it will lose 50% of its value each year. If it has an economic life of ten years, it loses 10% of its value annually. If its economic life is 50 years, it will lose 2% of its value annually. Therefore, the shortest guideline life the taxpayer chooses to use results in greater deductions in each year of the asset's life.

As discussed earlier, there is a similar variation in the method of depreciation the taxpayer may use. If he uses accelerated depreciation, he can deduct more in the initial years but less in the later years. This can be better understood if we discuss each of the depreciation methods individually for more detailed study.

Straight Line Method. The straight line method of depreciation is the one type of depreciation that can always be used. The first step in determining the amount of straight line depreciation is to establish the correct useful life of the asset. In computing the straight line rate, one takes the basis (cost or value of the improvement), less the estimated salvage value of the asset, and divides the remainder by the number of years of economic life the taxpayer intends to use for that improvement. For instance, if a dishwasher costs $200, has a five-year life, and has no salvage value, the taxpayer is allowed 20% each year ($40) as a depreciation deduction from gross income. If a two-year life is used for the dishwasher, 50% each year ($100) can be deducted.

Sum of the Years Digits Method. The *sum of the years digits* method of depreciation is calculated by multiplying a changing fraction by the depreciating value of the property. The numerator of this fraction is the remaining number of years of useful life of the property, and the denominator is the sum of the years of life of the property. For example, if a property has a five-year life and cost $30,000, the fraction used in depreciating for the first year would be 5/15, five being the number of remaining years of life, and fifteen being the sum of 1 plus 2 plus 3 plus 4 plus 5, or the *sum of the years*. For the second year, the fraction would be 4/15 of the depreciable cost of the property and so on. The depreciation schedule for five years would be as follows:

Year	*Fraction*	*Cost*	*Allowable Depreciation*
1st	5/15	$30,000	$10,000
2nd	4/15	$30,000	8,000
3rd	3/15	$30,000	6,000
4th	2/15	$30,000	4,000
5th	1/15	$30,000	2,000

If the property has a ten-year life and cost $30,000, the fraction used in computing depreciation for the first year would be 10/55, fifty-five being the sum of 1 plus 2 plus 3 plus 4 plus 5 plus 6 plus 7 plus 8 plus 9 plus 10. The depreciation schedule for sum of the years digits using a ten-year life would be as follows:

Year	*Fraction*	*Cost*	*Allowable Depreciation*
1st	10/55	$30,000	$5,454.54
2nd	9/55	$30,000	$4,909.09
3rd	8/55	$30,000	$4,363.64
4th	7/55	$30,000	$3,818.18
5th	6/55	$30,000	$3,272.73
6th	5/55	$30,000	$2,727.27
7th	4/55	$30,000	$2,181.82
8th	3/55	$30,000	$1,636.36
9th	2/55	$30,000	$1,090.91
10th	1/55	$30,000	$ 545.45

Declining Balance Method. As discussed previously, the declining balance method can be 200%, 150% or 125% of the straight line rate. Assuming the same facts as the sum of the years digit method, and using a five-year life for the asset, the straight line method depreciation rate would be 20% of the cost or value of the asset in the first year, or $6,000.00. The 200% declining balance method, therefore, would give the taxpayer the right to deduct double the straight line rate (40% or $12,000); the 150% declining balance would be 30%, or $9,000; and the 125% declining balance would be 25% of the cost or value to be depreciated, or $7,500. The *basis* (cost or initial value of the improvement) is reduced by the sum of depreciation claimed in years prior to the current year, so the amount to be depreciated is reduced each year. If we assume the same facts as the five-year life on the sum of the years digits method described above, we would come out with the following figures:

	Year	Rate	Basis Prior to Depreciation	Allowable Depreciation
200% Rate				
	1	40%	$30,000	$12,000
	2	40%	$18,000	$ 7,200
	3	40%	$10,800	$ 4,320
	4	40%	$ 6,460	$ 2,592
	5	40%	$ 3,888	$ 1,556
	Total Depreciation			$27,668
150% Rate				
	1	30%	$30,000	$ 9,000
	2	30%	$21,000	$ 6,300
	3	30%	$14,700	$ 4,410
	4	30%	$10,290	$ 3,088
	5	30%	$ 7,202	$ 2,160
	Total Depreciation			$24,958
125% Rate				
	1	25%	$30,000	$ 7,500
	2	25%	$22,500	$ 5,626
	3	25%	$16,874	$ 4,218
	4	25%	$12,656	$ 3,164
	5	25%	$ 9,491	$ 2,374
	Total Depreciation			$22,882

After comparing all of the depreciation methods, the taxpayer may find certain advantages, depending on how his personal tax structure might change over the years. The accelerated depreciation methods clearly allow a much greater amount to be deducted in the earlier years than the straight line method; however, the straight line method allows more to be deducted in later years and less in the first years, as shown below:

Year	Methods of Depreciation				
	Straight Line	S.Y.D.	200%	150%	125%
1	6,000	10,000	12,000	9,000	7,500
2	6,000	8,000	7,200	6,300	5,626
3	6,000	6,000	4,320	4,410	4,218
4	6,000	4,000	2,592	3,088	3,164
5	6,000	2,000	1,556	2,160	2,374
Total Depreciation	30,000	30,000	27,668	24,958	22,882

As stated previously, there are some guidelines and rules for using each of the depreciation methods. Simply stated, the 200% method can be used only by the first owner of any new residential rental property; the 150% method for new commercial and industrial property; the 125% method for used residential rental property having a remaining useful life of twenty years or more.

From the chart above you will notice that if the declining balance method of depreciation is used, the total depreciation never achieves the full value of the property, as it does in the straight line and sum of the years digit methods. Further, there is a point where a taxpayer can change from an accelerated method and depreciate the remaining balance (cost less the sum of prior year's depreciation) over the remaining life of the asset. The Internal Revenue Service allows a taxpayer to begin claiming depreciation using an accelerated method and later switching to straight line; however, the taxpayer generally does not have the right to change from the straight line method to an accelerated method of depreciation.

Recapture. One negative aspect of an accelerated depreciation method is that it may convert long-term capital gain to ordinary income when the asset is sold for a gain. This procedure is called the *recapture* of the excess depreciation. When depreciation is computed using an accelerated method, the excess amount of that depreciation over a hypothetical straight line amount must be reported as ordinary income upon disposition of the property. It may come as quite a shock for someone using accelerated depreciation to discover that when he sells the asset, a large amount of his profits may be taxed at ordinary income because it was allocated to excess depreciation. The amount of recapture depends on the type of asset disposed of, either personal or real property, and the amount of gain realized on the disposition. As previously stated, only excess depreciation must be recaptured on the disposition of real property, but all depreciation claimed must be recaptured on the sale of personal property. Recapture on both types of property is limited to the lesser of the recapture amount or the gain.

Component Depreciation. Component depreciation is a procedure in which the taxpayer apportions the total asset cost among the various elements of the asset, and uses separate lives to depreciate each item. The straight line and accelerated methods of depreciation are applied to each component of the improvement rather than depreciating the entire improvement over its physical life. For instance, a building generally has a forty-year guideline life, however, within that building are components (sheet rock walls, kitchen appliances, air-conditioning equipment, furnaces, and other particular component items) that will have a shorter useful life than the structure of the building. Therefore, instead of lumping the entire cost of the building and depreciating it over forty years, the cost of each component can be determined with a separate useful life and depreciation computed for each of the components. Thus, a taxpayer can increase depreciation by assigning a shorter useful life to the air-conditioning system, interior walls, and so forth, allowing him to take advantage of the shorter useful lives for each of the components within the improvement. This will result in increasing the depreciation deductions of the taxpayer even if the straight line method is used for each of the components.

Capital Gains Tax Treatment

While depreciation cannot be claimed on residences, capital gains tax treatment *does* apply to residential property, and is a major incentive to home ownership. Capital gains tax treatment refers to the special tax rate paid on profits from the sale of capital assets. A "capital asset" is generally defined as property which is *not* stock in trade (inventory), property used in a trade or business of a kind subject to depreciation, and notes and accounts receivables acquired in the course of a trade or business.

There are two types of capital gains: long-term and short-term capital gain. Long-term capital gain is gain on the sale of a capital asset held for more than one year. A short-term capital gain is gain on the sale of a capital asset held for less than one year. Short-term gains are taxed as income at normal rates, depending on the taxpayer's bracket. Long-term capital gains are taxed as follows: one half of the gain is tax-free; the other half is added to the taxpayer's income and taxed at ordinary income tax rate, or at the taxpayer's option the capital gain can be taxed at 25% of the first $50,000 and at a maximum rate of 35% of amounts over $50,000. The tax to be paid is applied to the *profit* made, which is calculated as the *sales price* less the *adjusted basis* (discussed next) the taxpayer has in the property. A confusing part of computing capital gains is determining the *basis* (the original cost or value) of the assets at the time of its acquisition.

Basis is generally considered to be of two types: *original basis*, which is the original cost of the asset, and *adjusted basis*, which is original basis plus the cost of capital improvements less any allowances for any depreciation. Graphically, adjusted basis may be shown as follows:

$$\text{Original Base} + \text{Capital Improvement} - \text{Depreciation} = \text{Adjusted Basis or,}$$

$$OB + CI - D = AB$$

As an example of how capital gains may be calculated, suppose that Mr. Garrison acquires a building at a cost of $100,000, which is his *original basis*. After holding the property for one year, he sells it for $200,000. The amount to be taxed would be calculated by deducting the basis ($100,000) from the sales price ($200,000), which determines how much of the income ($100,000, or his profit) is to be taxed at capital gains rates.

If the building has been depreciated, the *adjusted basis* must be used. For example: Mr. Garrison purchases the property for $100,000. During the course of his ownership he adds capital improvement in the amount of $25,000 and depreciates the asset over a 20-year life, yielding a straight line depreciation allowance of 5% of $100,000, or $5,000. His adjusted basis, therefore, would be his original basis $100,000, plus capital improvement of $25,000 minus depreciation, which in this case is $5,000. Using the formula AB = OB + CI − D, this would give him a taxable income of only $80,000, since the *adjusted basis* is subtracted from his sales price of $200,000.

Dealer Property. When practicing real estate, it must be remembered that there is a particular problem in determining capital gains rates peculiar to dealers in real estate. The normal capital gains rates are applicable to investment property. They are not applicable to *dealer property*. *Dealer property* is characterized by a real estate developer buying a large amount of la d, subdividing and developing it, and selling it off in his normal course of business. This man is termed a dealer in real property and the profits from his sales are taxed at normal rates rather than capital gains rates. This type of tax treatment is often responsible for the very complicated organizational structures of real estate developers and their investors, since everyone would usually prefer to take advantage of the lower capital gains tax treatment.

Tax-Deferred Exchanges

Tax-deferred exchanges are often referred to as tax-free exchanges. However, nothing could be further from the truth, as the tax will ultimately be paid. The tax-deferred exchange procedure allows only for deferment of taxes. The theory behind tax-free exchanges is that the exchange of property of value for other "like kind" (same type) property of the same value or higher value should not result in taxable income to the exchanging parties, with certain exceptions. If the trade is for property of higher value and a gain is realized, the gain is not taxed (recognized) until the taxpayer chooses to sell the property at a later date.

As an example, assume that Mr. Martin buys some apartments for$50,000. He has a contract to sell them for $100,000; however, instead of effecting a sale and taking a $50,000 profit, he trades for like kind property, owned by the purchaser, which is worth $100,000. There is no taxable gain to Mr. Martin on that particular transaction. If Mr. Martin trades for property worth $150,000 and sells later for $200,000, he would have to pay tax on the gain buy only upon the sale of the second piece of property. In determining the amount of gain on the sale, Mr. Martin's original basis in the first project (which may have been quite low) would carry over to the newly acquired property. He would subtract it from the new sales price. Therefore, he would pay capital gains tax on a much larger amount of money, but the advantage would be that he could defer this gain until he is ready to sell the second piece of property, or he trades it again for a more expensive piece of property to be sold at some subsequent date.

In this manner, Mr. Martin may continue to "trade up" to other pieces of more expensive property, realizing that on the sale of the final piece of property he will have a very large tax liability, even at capital gains rates. However, one would assume that he will wait to sell the property when his overall personal income tax rates would be lower.

The concept of tax-free exchange applies to all "like kind" real estate, even personal residential real estate.

Installment Sales

One of the simplest major tax advantages of owning real estate is the installment sale benefit. It applies to all types of real estate, including residential property. To qualify for installment sales tax treatment, the taxpayer must sell his property, but may accept no more than 30% of the sales price in the first year of the sale. The remainder of the income is taxed as it is received over the future years. This allows the taxpayer to sell his property, for example, over ten years, yielding a $100,000 total profit. However, instead of paying tax on $100,000 profit in one year (which may be taxed at a very high rate), the taxpayer is allowed to spread this profit over ten years at $10,000 each year (which would probably be taxed at a much lower rate, depending on the taxpayer's tax bracket). This is why one often finds that a seller wants a 29% down payment on the sale of a property. That seller wants to take advantage of the installment sale method.

Over 65 Exemption

The federal government has also seen fit to provide a special tax benefit to help the elderly. A taxpayer over 65 may sell his principal personal residence where he has lived for five of the last eight years tax-free if the sales price is $35,000 or less. If the sales price of the house is in excess of $35,000 it is only partially tax-free. The amount that is tax-free bears a proportion to the actual sales price, computed as follows:

$$\frac{\text{Tax-Free Sales Price}}{\text{Actual Sales Price}} \times \text{Total Gain} = \text{Tax-Free Gain}$$

For instance, if Don Dotage, age 65, sells his personal residence for $50,000 and he purchased it years ago for $10,000, how much of the gain is taxable? The tax-free gain would be computed as follows:

$$\frac{\$35{,}000}{\$50{,}000} \times \$40{,}000 = \$28{,}000$$

Therefore, instead of paying taxes on a $40,000 gain, the taxpayer gets $28,000 tax free and only $12,000 is to be taxed, resulting in a substantial tax saving. This exclusion may be used only once, however, so if one has a client who is a taxpayer at age 64, he may want to advise him to wait until he is 65 before he sells so that he can take advantage of the tax-free Over-65 Exemption. The agent may use this very simple mathematical calculation to explain what advantage it may have for his client. However, the concerned agent wll probably refer the entire matter to the homeowner's accountant if he chooses to investigate the matter in greater detail.

As one might see, there are a number of different tax ramifications in any single transaction. To be sure, the foregoing was only a very cursory explanation. Each of the individual tax benefits of real estate ownership is very lengthy, involved, and should be left to people who are trained in the business. However, it is an astute real estate agent who has at least a good working knowledge of tax benefits, so that he may advise his client as to the initial ramifications that a transaction *might* have. One has only to read the Internal Revenue Code, or one provision thereof, to get an inkling of how complicated the tax laws, rules, regulations, bulletins and tax court decisions can be. To compound the problems and responsibilities of the real estate licensee, one only has to remember the duty of care to which all American citizens are held. Ignorance of the law is no excuse!

SUMMARY

The primary concerns in real estate taxation are *ad valorem* taxes and special tax benefits under federal income taxation.

Ad valorem taxation is assessed on real property in proportion to its value which shall be ascertained as provided for by law. The formula for determining the tax payment is:

$$\text{Assessed Value} \times \text{Tax Rate} = \text{Tax Payment}$$

The assessed value is determined by the assessor and collector of taxes who determines an assessed value, which may or may not be equal to fair market value. The tax collector assesses the real estate according to the budget requirements for the taxing jurisdiction. The tax rate is set by the taxing authority in accordance to statutory formula.

In the event ad valorem taxes are delinquent, there is a penalty and procedure for judicial foreclosure against the property. In the event a foreclosure occurs, there is a two year right of redemption where the property owner can redeem his property after payment of taxes, fees, and penalties.

The advantages of federal income taxation are primarily attributable to depreciation, capital gains tax treatment, tax free exchanges, and installment sales. Depreciation is an allowance for loss of value and can be calculated several different ways. Capital gains tax treatment is a special tax rate paid on the profits of sale of capital assets. This tax treatment can be either long-term or short-term capital gains. A long-term capital gain receives special tax benefits. Short-term capital gains are taxed at normal rates. Tax deferred exchanges are a means by which an owner may exchange property and defer the payment of taxes until the sale of the second piece of property. The installment sale benefit applies to any seller who sells his property with less than 30% of that property being paid to the seller in the first year of the sale. The remainder of the income is taxed as the seller receives it over future years.

TEXAS REAL ESTATE LICENSING ACT

Art. 6573a. The Real Estate License Act

Short title; license required; responsibility for acts and conduct; compensation and commissions

Section 1. (a) This Act shall be known and may be cited as "The Real Estate License Act."

(b) It is unlawful for a person to act in the capacity of, engage in the business of, or advertise or hold himself out as engaging in or conducting the business of a real estate broker or a real estate salesman within this state without first obtaining a real estate license from the Texas Real Estate Commission. It is unlawful for a person licensed as a real estate salesman to act or attempt to act as a real estate agent unless he is, at such time, associated with a licensed Texas real estate broker and acting for the licensed real estate broker.

(c) Each real estate broker licensed pursuant to this Act is responsible to the commission, members of the public, and his clients for all acts and conduct performed under this Act by himself or by a real estate salesman associated with or acting for the broker.

(d) No real estate salesman shall accept compensation for real estate sales and transactions from any person other than the broker under whom he is at the time licensed.

(e) No real estate salesman shall pay a commission to any person except through the broker under whom he is at the time licensed.

Definitions

Sec. 2. As used in this Act:

(1) "Real estate" means a leasehold, as well as any other interest or estate in land, whether corporeal, incorporeal, freehold, or nonfreehold, and whether the real estate is situated in this state or elsewhere.

(2) "Real estate broker" means a person who, for another person and for a fee, commission, or other valuable consideration, or with the intention or in the expectation or on the promise of receiving or collecting a fee, commission, or other valuable consideration from another person:

(A) sells, exchanges, purchases, rents, or leases real estate;

(B) offers to sell, exchange, purchase, rent, or lease real estate;

(C) negotiates or attempts to negotiate the listing, sale, exchange, purchase, rental, or leasing of real estate;

(D) lists or offers or attempts or agrees to list real estate for sale, rental, lease, exchange, or trade;

(E) appraises or offers or attempts or agrees to appraise real estate;
(F) auctions, or offers or attempts or agrees to auction, real estate;
(G) buys or sells or offers to buy or sell, or otherwise deals in options on real estate;
(H) aids, attempts, or offers to aid in locating or obtaining for purchase, rent, or lease any real estate;
(I) procures or assists in the procuring of prospects for the purpose of effecting the sale, exchange, lease, or rental of real estate; or
(J) procures or assists in the procuring of properties for the purpose of effecting the sale, exchange, lease, or rental of real estate.

(3) "Broker" also includes a person employed by or on behalf of the owner or owners of lots or other parcels of real estate, at a salary, fee, commission, or any other valuable consideration, to sell the real estate or any part thereof, in lots or parcels or other disposition thereof. It also includes a person who engages in the business of charging an advance fee or contracting for collection of a fee in connection with a contract whereby he undertakes primarily to promote the sale of real estate either through its listing in a publication issued primarily for such purpose, or for referral of information concerning the real estate to brokers, or both.

(4) "Real estate salesman" means a person associated with a Texas licensed real estate broker for the purposes of performing acts or transactions comprehended by the definition of "real estate broker" as defined in this Act.

(5) "Person" means an individual, a partnership, or a corporation, foreign or domestic.

(6) "Commission" means the Texas Real Estate Commission.

(7) If the sense requires it, words in the present tense include the future tense; in the masculine gender, include the feminine or neuter gender; in the singular number, include the plural number; in the plural number, include the singular number; the word "and" may be read "or"; and the word "or" may be read "and."

Exemptions

Sec. 3. The provisions of this Act shall not apply to any of the following persons and transactions, and each and all of the following persons and transactions are hereby exempted from the provisions of this Act, to wit:

(a) an attorney at law licensed in this state or in any other state;
(b) an attorney in fact under a duly executed power of attorney authorizing the consummation of a real estate transaction;
(c) a public official in the conduct of his official duties;
(d) a person acting officially as a receiver, trustee, administrator, executor, or guardian;
(e) a person acting under a court order or under the authority of a will or a written trust instrument;
(f) a salesperson employed by an owner in the sale of structures and land on which said structures are situated, provided such structures are erected by the owner in the due course of his business;
(g) an on-site manager of an apartment complex;
(h) transactions involving the sale, lease, or transfer of any mineral or mining interest in real property;
(i) an owner or his employees in renting or leasing his own real estate whether improved or unimproved;
(j) transactions involving the sale, lease, or transfer of cemetery lots.

Acts constituting broker or salesman

Sec. 4. A person who, directly or indirectly for another, with the intention or on the promise of receiving any valuable consideration, offers, attempts, or agrees to perform, or performs, a single act defined in Subdivisions 2 and 3, Section 2 of this Act, whether as a part of a transaction, or as an entire transaction, is deemed to be acting as a real estate broker or salesman within the meaning of this Act. The commission of a single such act by a person required to be licensed under this Act and not so licensed shall constitute a violation of this Act.

Real Estate Commission; disposition of fees; Research Center; application of Sunset Act

Sec. 5. (a) The administration of the provisions of this Act is vested in a commission, to be known as the "Texas Real Estate Commission," consisting of six members to be appointed by the governor with the advice and consent of two-thirds of the senate present. The commissioners hold office for six years or until their successors are appointed and have qualified. Within 15 days after their appointments, they shall qualify by taking the constitutional oath of office and furnishing a bond payable to the Governor of Texas in the penal sum of $10,000, conditional on the faithful performance of their duties as prescribed by law. A vacancy for any cause shall be filled by the governor for the unexpired term. The members of the commission in office at the effective date of this Act shall constitute the commission and shall continue in office until the 5th day of October of the years in which their respective terms expire, or until their successors are appointed and have qualified. At a regular meeting in October of each year, the commission shall elect from its own membership a chairman, vice-chairman, and secretary. A quorum of the commission consists of four members.

(b) All members, officers, employees, and agents of the commission are subject to the code of ethics and standards of conduct imposed by Chapter 421, Acts of the 63rd Legislature, Regular Session, 1973 (Article 6252—9b, Vernon's Texas Civil Statutes).

(c) Each member of the commission shall be a citizen of Texas and a qualified voter, and shall have been engaged in the real estate brokerage business as a licensed real estate broker as his major occupation for at least five years next preceding his appointment.

(d) Each member of the commission shall receive as compensation for each day actually spent on his official duties the sum of $50 and his actual and necessary expenses incurred in the performance of his official duties.

(e) The commission shall have the authority and power to make and enforce all rules and regulations necessary for the performance of its duties, to establish standards of conduct and ethics for its licensees in keeping with the purposes and intent of this Act or to insure compliance with the provisions of this Act. In addition to any other action, proceeding, or remedy authorized by law, the commission shall have the right to institute an action in its own name to enjoin any violation of any provision of this Act or any rule or regulation of the commission and in order for the commission to sustain such action it shall not be necessary to allege or prove, either that an adequate remedy at law does not exist, or that substantial or irreparable damage would result from the continued violation thereof. Either party to such action may appeal to the appellate court having jurisdiction of said cause. The commission shall not be required to give any appeal bond in any action or proceeding to enforce the provisions of this Act.

(f) The commission is empowered to select and name an administrator, who shall also act as executive secretary, and to select and employ such other subordinate officers and employees as are necessary to administer this Act. The salaries of the administrator and the officers and employees shall be fixed by the commission not to exceed such amounts as are fixed by the applicable general appropriations bill. The commission may designate a subordinate officer as assistant administrator who shall be authorized to act for the administrator in his absence.

(g) When in this Act a power, right, or duty is conferred on the commission, the power, right, or duty shall be exercised by the administrator or by the assistant administrator, unless the commission directs otherwise by an order entered in the minutes of a commission meeting; and in such case, the power, right, or duty shall rest in or on the commission. Service of process on the administrator or assistant administrator shall be service of process on the commission. Reports, notices, applications, or instruments of any kind required to be filed with the commission shall be considered filed with the commission if filed with the administrator or assistant administrator. A decision, order, or act of the commission referred to in this Act, other than an order of the commission relative to the administrator or his powers, rights, or duties, means and includes an order, decision, or act of the administrator or of the assistant administrator when duly acting for the administrator. Where the commission is authorized in this Act to delegate authority or to designate agents, the administrator, or the assistant administrator when duly acting for the administrator, shall have the right and the power to delegate authority and designate agents, unless the commission shall enter its order in the minutes of a commission meeting directing otherwise. The administrator, or the assistant administrator when duly acting for the administrator, shall act as manager, secretary, and custodian of all records, unless the commission shall otherwise order, and each shall devote his entire time to his office.

(h) The commission shall adopt a seal of a design which it shall prescribe. Copies of all records and papers in the office of the commission, duly certified and authenticated by the seal of the commission, shall be received in evidence in all courts with like effect as the original.

(i) Except as provided in Subsection (j) of this section, all money derived from fees, assessments, or charges under this Act, shall be paid by the commission into the State Treasury for safekeeping, and shall be placed by the State Treasurer in a separate fund to be available for the use of the commission in the administration of this Act on requisition by the commission. A necessary amount of the money so paid into the State Treasury is hereby specifically appropriated to the commission for the purpose of paying the salaries and expenses necessary and proper for the administration of this Act, including equipment and maintenance of supplies for the offices or quarters occupied by the commission, and necessary travel expenses for the commission or persons authorized to act for it when performing duties under this Act. At the end of the state fiscal year, any unused portion of the funds in the special account, except such funds as may be appropriated to administer this Act pending receipt of additional revenues available for that purpose, shall be paid into the General Revenue Fund. The comptroller shall, on requisition of the commission, draw warrants from time to time on the State Treasurer for the amount specified in the requisition, not exceeding, however, the amount in the fund at the time of making a requisition. However, all money expended in the administration of this Act shall be specified and determined by itemized appropriation in the general departmental appropriation bill for the Texas Real Estate Commission, and not otherwise.

(j) Fifteen dollars received by the commission for each annual certification of real estate broker licensure status and $7.50 received by the commission for each annual certification of real estate salesman licensure status shall be transmitted to Texas A&M University for deposit in a separate banking account. The money in the separate account shall be expended for the support and maintenance of the Texas Real Estate Research Center and for carrying out the purposes, objectives, and duties of the center.

(k) The Texas Real Estate Commission is subject to the Texas Sunset Act;[1] and unless continued in existence as provided by that Act the commission is abolished, and this Act expires effective September 1, 1979.

[1] Article 5429k.

Licenses; qualification

Sec. 6. (a) A person desiring to act as a real estate broker in this state shall file an application for a license with the commission on a form prescribed by the commission. A broker desiring to engage a person to participate in real estate brokerage activity shall join the person in filing an application for a salesman license on a form prescribed by the commission.

(b) To be eligible for a license, an individual must be a citizen of the United States, be at least 18 years of age, and be a legal resident of Texas for at least six months immediately preceding the filing of an application, and must satisfy the commission as to his honesty, trustworthiness, integrity, and competency. However, the competency of the individual, for the purpose of qualifying for the granting of licensure privileges, shall be judged solely on the basis of the examination referred to in Section 7 of this Act.

(c) To be eligible for a license, a corporation must designate one of its officers to act for it. The designated person must be a citizen of the United States, be at least 18 years of age, and be a resident of Texas for at least six months immediately preceding the filing of an application, and must be qualified to be licensed individually as a real estate broker. However, the competency of the person shall be judged solely on the basis of the examination referred to in Section 7 of this Act.

Examinations; educational requirements

Sec. 7. (a) Competency as referred to in Section 6 of this Act shall be established by an examination prepared by or contracted for by the commission. The examination shall be given at such times and at such places within the state as the commission shall prescribe. The examination shall be of scope sufficient in the judgment of the commission to determine that a person is competent to act as a real estate broker or salesman in a manner to protect the interest of the public. The examination for a salesman license shall be less exacting and less stringent than the examination for a broker license. The commission shall furnish each applicant with study material and references on which his examination shall be based. When an applicant for real estate licensure fails a qualifying examination, he may apply for reexamination by filing a request therefor together with the proper fee. The examination requirement shall be satisfied within one year from the date the application for a license is filed. Courses of study required for licensure shall include but not be limited to the following: arithmetical calculations as used in real estate transactions; rudimentary principles of conveyancing; the general purposes and effect of deeds, deeds of trust, mortgages, land contracts of sales, leases, liens, and listing contracts; elementary principles of land economics and appraisals; fundamentals of obligations between principal and agent; principles of real estate practice and canons of ethics pertaining thereto; and the provisions of this Act and rules and regulations of the commission.

(b) The commission shall waive the examination of an applicant for broker licensure who has, within one year previous to the filing of his application, been licensed in this state as a broker, and shall waive the examination of an applicant for salesman licensure who has, within one year previous to the filing of his application, been licensed in this state as either a broker or salesman.

(c) From and after the effective date of this Act, each applicant for broker licensure shall furnish the commission satisfactory evidence that he has had not less than two years active experience in this state as a licensed real estate salesman practitioner during the 36-month period immediately preceding the filing of the application; and, in addition, prior to January 1, 1977, shall furnish the commission satisfactory evidence that he has successfully completed 180 classroom hours in real estate courses or related courses accepted by the commission. On or after January 1, 1977, an applicant for real estate broker licensure shall submit evidence, satisfactory to the commission, of successful completion at an accredited college or university of 12 semester hours of real estate or related courses accepted by the commission, or of a course of study accepted by the commission as being equivalent to the courses offered by accredited colleges and universities. On or after January 1, 1979, the number of required semester hours shall be increased to 15; on or after January 1, 1981, the number of required semester hours shall be increased to 36; and on or after January 1, 1983, the number of required semester hours shall be increased to 48. On or after January 1, 1985, an applicant for a real estate broker license shall submit evidence, satisfactory to the commission, that he has successfully completed 60 semester hours in real estate or related courses accepted by the commission from an accredited college or university, or that he has completed a course of study accepted by the commission as being equivalent to the courses offered by accredited colleges and universities. The requirement of not less than two years experience as a Texas real estate licensee during the 36-month period immediately preceding the filing of the application for broker licensure shall not apply to applications submitted on or after January 1, 1985. These qualifications for broker licensure shall not be required of an applicant who, at the time of making the application, is duly licensed as a real estate broker by any other state in the United States if that state's requirements for licensure are comparable to those of Texas.

(d) From and after the effective date of this Act, as a prerequisite for applying for salesman licensure prior to January 1, 1977, each applicant shall furnish the commission satisfactory evidence that he has completed 30 classroom hours in a basic real estate fundamentals course or related course accepted by the commission. As a condition for the second annual certification of salesman licensure privileges, the licensee shall furnish the commission satisfactory evidence that he has successfully completed an additional 30 classroom hours of real estate courses or related courses accepted by the commission, and as a condition for the third annual certification of salesman licensure privileges, the licensee shall furnish the commission satisfactory evidence that he has successfully completed an additional 30 classroom hours of real estate courses or related courses accepted by the commission. On or after January 1, 1977, an applicant for real estate salesman licensure shall submit evidence, satisfactory to the commission, of successful completion at an accredited college or university of six semester hours of real estate courses or related courses accepted by the commission, or of a course of study accepted by the commission as being equivalent to the courses offered by accredited colleges and universities. On or after January 1, 1979, the number of required semester hours shall be increased to 12; on or after January 1, 1981, the number of required semester hours shall be increased to 21; and on or after January 1, 1983, the number of required semester hours shall be increased to 36.

(e) On or after January 1, 1985, the commission shall accept applications for broker licensure only, and each license issued on or after January 1, 1985, shall be designated as a license to practice real estate.

(f) Insofar as is necessary for the administration of this Act, the commission is authorized to inspect and accredit educational programs or courses of study in real estate and to establish standards of accreditation for such programs conducted in the State of Texas, other than accredited colleges and universities. Schools, other than accredited colleges and universities, which are authorized to offer real estate educational courses pursuant to provisions of this section shall be required to maintain a corporate surety bond in the sum of $10,000 payable to the commission, for the benefit of a party who may suffer damages resulting from failure of a commission approved school or course to fulfill obligations attendant to the approval.

(g) A person who is licensed as a salesman on the effective date of this Act is not subject to the educational requirements or prerequisites of this Act as a condition for holding salesman licensure privileges. A person who is licensed as a broker on the effective date of this Act is not subject to the educational requirements or prerequisites of this Act as a condition for holding broker licensure privileges. A person who is licensed as a real estate salesman on the effective date of this Act may submit an application for broker licensure during the 24-month period immediately following such date if he furnishes evidence satisfactory to the commission that he meets the prerequirements for applying for broker licensure in force and effect on the day prior to the effective date of this Act.

Real estate recovery fund

Sec. 8. Part 1. (a) The commission shall establish a real estate recovery fund which shall be set apart and maintained by the commission as provided in this section. The fund shall be used in the manner provided in this section for reimbursing aggrieved persons who suffer monetary damages by reason of certain acts committed by a duly licensed real estate broker or salesman, or by an unlicensed employee or agent of a broker or salesman, provided the broker or salesman was licensed by the State of Texas at the time the act was committed, provided the act was performed in the scope of activity which constitutes a broker or salesman as defined by this Act, and provided recovery is ordered by a court of competent jurisdiction against the broker or salesman. The use of the fund as provided in Part 1 of this section is limited to an act that is either:

(1) a violation of Section 15(3) and (4) of this Act, or

(2) conduct which constitutes fraud, misrepresentation, deceit, false pretenses, or trickery.

(b) On the effective date of this Act, the commission shall collect from each real estate broker and salesman licensed by this state a fee of $10 which shall be deposited in the real estate recovery fund. The commission shall suspend a license issued under the provisions of this Act for failure to pay this fee. After the effective date of this Act, when a person makes application for an original license pursuant to this Act he shall pay, in addition to his original license application fee, a fee of $10 which shall be deposited in the real estate recovery fund. If the commission does not issue the license, this fee shall be returned to the applicant.

Part 2. If on December 31 of any year the balance remaining in the real estate recovery fund is less than $300,000, each real estate broker and each real estate salesman, on recertification of his license during the following calendar year, shall pay, in addition to his license recertification fee, a fee of $10, which shall be deposited in the real estate recovery fund, or a pro rata share of the amount necessary to bring the fund to $1 million, whichever is less.

Part 3. (a) No action for a judgment which subsequently results in an order for collection from the real estate recovery fund shall be started later than two years from the accrual of the cause of action. When an aggrieved person commences action for a judgment which may result in collection from the real estate recovery fund, the real estate broker or real estate salesman shall notify the commission in writing to this effect at the time of the commencement of the action.

(b) Upon the entry of a final judgment in any suit which may involve payment from the real estate recovery fund, the judgment creditor shall promptly notify the commission of the granting of the judgment. In the event payment is to be requested from the real estate recovery fund, such notice must be given at least 20 days prior to any post-judgment hearing held in accordance with this Act.

(c) When an aggrieved person recovers a valid judgment in a court of competent jurisdiction against a real estate broker, or real estate salesman, on the grounds described in Part 1(a) of this section that occurred on or after the effective date of this Act, the aggrieved person may, after final judgment has been entered, execution returned nulla bona, and a judgment lien perfected, file a verified claim in the court in which the judgment was entered and, on 20 days' written notice to the commission, may apply to the court for an order directing payment out of the real estate recovery fund of the amount unpaid on the judgment, subject to the limitations stated in Part 8 of this section.

(d) The court shall proceed on the application forthwith. On the hearing on the application, the aggrieved person is required to show that:

(1) the judgment is based on facts allowing recovery under Part 1(a) of this section;

(2) he is not a spouse of the debtor, or the personal representative of the spouse;

(3) he has complied with all the requirements of Part 3 of this section;

(4) he has obtained a judgment as set out in Part 3(c) of this section, stating the amount of the judgment and the amount owing on the judgment at the date of the application;

(5) he has made all reasonable searches and inquiries to ascertain whether the judgment debtor is possessed of real or personal property or other assets liable to be sold or applied in satisfaction of the judgment;

(6) that by the search he has discovered no real or personal property or other assets liable to be sold or applied, or has discovered insufficient real or personal property or other assets liable to be sold or applied, and that he has taken all necessary action and proceedings for the realization of satisfaction of the judgment, and that the amount realized was insufficient to satisfy the judgment, stating the amount realized and the balance remaining due on the judgment after application of the amount realized.

(e) The court shall make an order directed to the commission requiring payment from the real estate recovery fund of whatever sum it finds to be payable on the claim, pursuant to and in accordance with the limitations contained in this section, if the court is satisfied, on the hearing, of the truth of all matters required to be shown by the aggrieved person by Part 3(d) of this section and that the aggrieved person has fully pursued and exhausted all remedies available to him for recovering the amount awarded by the judgment of the court.

(f) If the commission pays from the real estate recovery fund any amount toward satisfaction of a judgment against a licensed real estate broker or real estate salesman, the license of the broker or salesman shall be automatically revoked on the issuance of a court order authorizing payment from the real estate recovery fund. No broker or salesman is eligible to receive a new license until he has repaid in full, plus interest at the rate of six percent a year, the amount paid from the real estate recovery fund on his account. A discharge in bankruptcy shall not relieve a person from the penalties and disabilities provided in this Act.

Part 4. The sums received by the real estate commission for deposit in the real estate recovery fund shall be held by the commission in trust for carrying out the purposes of the real estate recovery fund. These funds may be invested and reinvested in the same manner as funds of the Texas State Employees Retirement System, and the interest from these investments shall be deposited to the credit of the real estate recovery fund, provided, however, that no investments shall be made which will impair the necessary liquidity required to satisfy judgment payments awarded pursuant to this section.

Part 5. When the real estate commission receives notice of entry of a final judgment and a hearing is scheduled under Part 3(d) of this section, the commission may notify the Attorney General of Texas of its desire to enter an appearance, file a response, appear at the court hearing, defend the action, or take whatever other action it deems appropriate on behalf of, and in the name of, the defendant, and take recourse through any appropriate method of review on behalf of, and in the name of, the defendant. In taking such action the real estate commission and attorney general shall act only to protect the fund from spurious or unjust claims.

Part 6. When, on the order of the court, the commission has paid from the real estate recovery fund any sum to the judgment creditor, the commission shall be subrogated to all of the rights of the judgment creditor to the extent of the amount paid. The judgment creditor shall assign all his right, title, and interest in the judgment up to the amount paid by the commission which amount shall have priority for repayment in the event of any subsequent recovery on the judgment. Any amount and interest recovered by the commission on the judgment shall be deposited to the fund.

Part 7. The failure of an aggrieved person to comply with the provisions of this section relating to the real estate recovery fund shall constitute a waiver of any rights under this section.

Part 8. (a) Notwithstanding any other provision, payments from the real estate recovery fund are subject to the conditions and limitations in Subsections (b) through (d) of this part.

(b) Payments may be made only pursuant to an order of a court of competent jurisdiction, as provided in Part 3, and in the manner prescribed by this section.

(c) Payments for claims arising out of the same transaction shall be limited in the aggregate to $10,000 irrespective of the number of claimants.

(d) Payments for claims based on judgments against any one licensed real estate broker or salesman may not exceed in the aggregate $20,000 within any calendar year, but in no event may payments for claims based on judgments against any one licensed real estate broker or salesman exceed in the aggregate $40,000, until the fund has been reimbursed by the licensee for all amounts paid.

Part 9. Nothing contained in this section shall limit the authority of the commission to take disciplinary action against a licensee for a violation of this Act or the rules and regulations of the commission; nor shall the repayment in full of all obligations to the real estate recovery fund by a licensee nullify or modify the effect of any other disciplinary proceeding brought pursuant to this Act.

Part 10. Any person receiving payment out of the real estate recovery fund pursuant to Section 8 of this Act shall be entitled to receive reasonable attorney fees as determined by the court, subject to the limitations stated in Part 8 of this section.

Issuance of license; annual certification fees; expiration dates

Sec. 9. (a) When an applicant has satisfactorily met all requirements and conditions of this Act, a license shall be issued which may remain in force and effect so long as the holder of the license remains in compliance with the obligations of this Act, which include payment of the annual certification fee as provided in Section 11 of this Act. Annual certification fees shall be paid in September, October, and November of each calendar year. Each salesman license issued shall be delivered or mailed to the broker with whom the salesman is associated and shall be kept under his custody and control.

(b) An applicant is not permitted to engage in the real estate business either as a broker or salesman until a license evidencing his authority to engage in the real estate business has been received.

(c) The commission by rule may adopt a system under which licenses expire on various dates during the year. Dates for payment of the annual certification fee shall be adjusted accordingly. For the year in which the certification date is changed, annual certification fees payable shall be prorated on a monthly basis so each licensee shall pay only that portion of the license fee which is allocable to the number of months during which the license is valid. On certification of the license on the new certification date, the total annual certification fee is payable.

Refusal to issue license; review

Sec. 10. If the commission declines or fails to license an applicant, it shall immediately give written notice of the refusal to the applicant. Before the applicant may appeal to a district court as provided in Section 18 of this Act, he must file within 10 days after the receipt of the notice an appeal from the ruling, requesting a time and place for a hearing before the commission. A sponsoring broker is an applicant and must file the appeal if an application to license a person as a salesman has been disapproved. The commission shall set a time and place for the hearing within 30 days from the receipt of the appeal, giving 10 days' notice of the hearing to the applicant. The time of the hearing may be continued from time to time with the consent of the applicant. Following the hearing, the commission shall enter an order which is, in its opinion, appropriate in the matter concerned.

If an applicant fails to request a hearing as provided in this section, the commission's ruling shall become final and not subject to review by the courts.

Fees

Sec. 11. The commission shall charge and collect the following fees:

(1) a fee not to exceed $40 for the filing of an original application for real estate broker licensure;

(2) a fee not to exceed $40 for annual certification of real estate broker licensure status;

(3) a fee of $20 for the filing of an original application for salesman licensure;

(4) a fee of $20 for annual certification of real estate salesman licensure status;

(5) a fee not to exceed $10 for taking a license examination;

(6) a fee of $10 for filing a request for a license for each additional office or place of business;

(7) a fee of $10 for filing a request for a license for a change of place of business or change of sponsoring broker;

(8) a fee of $10 for filing a request to replace a license lost or destroyed;

(9) a fee of $400 for filing an application for approval of a real estate course pursuant to the provisions of Subsection (f) of Section 7 of this Act; and

(10) a fee of $200 per annum for and in each year of operation of a real estate course, established pursuant to the provisions of Subsection (f) of Section 7 of this Act.

Maintenance and location of offices; display of license

Sec. 12. (a) Each resident broker shall maintain a fixed office within this state. The address of the office shall be designated on the broker's license. Within 10 days after a move from a previously designated address, the broker shall submit applications for new licenses for himself and each salesman associated with him, designating the new location of his office, together with the required fee, or fees, whereupon the commission shall issue a license, or licenses, reflecting the new location, provided the new location complies with the terms of this section.

(b) If a broker maintains more than one place of business within this state, he shall apply for, pay the required fee for, and obtain an additional license to be known as a branch office license for each additional office he maintains.

(c) The license or licenses of the broker shall at all times be prominently displayed in the licensee's place or places of business.

(d) Each broker shall also prominently display in his place or in one of his places of business the license of each real estate salesman associated with him.

Inactive licenses

Sec. 13. (a) When the association of a salesman with his sponsoring broker is terminated, the broker shall immediately return the salesman license to the commission. The salesman license then becomes inactive.

(b) The salesman license may be activated if, within the calendar year, a request, accompanied by the required fee, is filed with the commission by a licensed broker advising that he assumes sponsorship of the salesman.

Unlawful employment or compensation; nonresident license

Sec. 14. (a) It is unlawful for a licensed broker to employ or compensate directly or indirectly a person for performing an act enumerated in the definition of real estate broker in Section 2 of this Act if the person is not a licensed broker or licensed salesman in this state or an attorney at law licensed in this state or in any other state. However, a licensed broker may pay a commission to a licensed broker of another state if the foreign broker does not conduct in this state any of the negotiations for which the fee, compensation, or commission is paid.

(b) A resident broker of another state may obtain a license as a broker in this state by complying with all requirements of this Act, provided that the nonresident broker is licensed as a broker by the state of his residence and provided that the state of his residence has legal standards of qualification which the commission finds equivalent to this Act and which state offers the same privileges to licensed brokers of this state. A nonresident licensee need not maintain a place of business within this state. The commission may license the nonresident broker without examination if he has qualified for a broker license in the state in which he resides by written examination considered equivalent to that offered by this state and if his state of residence permits licenses to be issued without written examinations to brokers resident in and licensed after passing an examination by this state. However, the commission may, in its discretion, refuse to issue a broker license to an applicant who is not a resident of this state for the same reasons that it may refuse to license a resident of this state.

(c) Each nonresident applicant shall file an irrevocable consent that legal actions may be commenced against him in the proper court of any county of this state in which a cause of action may arise, or in which the plaintiff may reside, by service of process or pleading authorized by the laws of this state, or by serving the administrator or assistant administrator of the commission. The consent shall stipulate that the service of process or pleading shall be valid and binding in all courts as if personal service had been made on the nonresident broker in this state. The consent shall be duly acknowledged, and if made by a corporation, shall be authenticated by its seal. A service of process or pleading served on the commission shall be by duplicate copies, one of which shall be filed in the office of the commission and the other forwarded by registered mail to the last known principal address which the commission has for the nonresident broker against whom the process or pleading is directed. No default in an action may be taken except on certification by the commission that a copy of the process or pleading was mailed to the defendant as provided in this section, and no default judgment may be taken in an action or proceeding until 20 days after the day of mailing of the process or pleading to the defendant.

Notwithstanding any other provision of this subsection, a nonresident of this state who resides in a city whose boundaries are contiguous at any point to the boundaries of a city of this state, and who has been an actual bona fide resident of that city for at least six months immediately preceding the filing of his application, is eligible to be licensed as a real estate broker or salesman under this Act in the same manner as a resident of this state. If he is licensed in this manner, he shall at all times maintain a place of business either in the city in which he resides or in the city in this state which is contiguous to the city in which he resides, and he may not maintain a place of business at another location in this state unless he also complies with the requirements of Section 14(b) of this Act. The place of business must satisfy the requirements of Subsection (a) of Section 12 of this Act, but the place of business shall be deemed a definite place of business in this state within the meaning of Subsection (a) of Section 12.

Investigations; suspension or revocation of license; civil or criminal liability

Sec. 15. The commission may, on its own motion, and shall, on the verified complaint in writing of any person, provided the complaint, or the complaint together with evidence, documentary or otherwise, presented in connection with the complaint, provides reasonable cause, investigate the actions and records of a real estate broker or real estate salesman. The commission may suspend or revoke a license issued under the provisions of this Act at any time when it has been determined that:

(1)(A) the licensee has entered a plea of guilty or nolo contendere to, or been found guilty of, or been convicted of, a felony, in which fraud is an essential element, and the time for appeal has elapsed or the judgment or conviction has been affirmed on appeal, irrespective of an order granting probation following such conviction, suspending the imposition of sentence; or

(B) a final money judgment has been rendered against the licensee resulting from contractual obligations of the licensee incurred in the pursuit of his business, and such judgment remains unsatisfied for a period of more than six months after becoming final; or

(2) the licensee has procured, or attempted to procure, a real estate license, for himself or a salesman, by fraud, misrepresentation or deceit, or by making a material misstatement of fact in an application for a real estate license; or

(3) the licensee, when selling, trading, or renting real property in his own name, engaged in misrepresentation or dishonest or fraudulent action; or

(4) the licensee, while performing an act constituting a broker or salesman, as defined by this Act, has been guilty of:

(A) making a material misrepresentation, or failing to disclose to a potential purchaser any latent structural defect or any other defect known to the broker or salesman. Latent structural defects and other defects do not refer to trivial or insignificant defects but refer to those defects that would be a significant factor to a reasonable and prudent purchaser in making a decision to purchase; or

(B) making a false promise of a character likely to influence, persuade, or induce any person to enter into a contract or agreement when the licensee could not or did not intend to keep such promise; or

(C) pursuing a continued and flagrant course of misrepresentation or making of false promises through agents, salesmen, advertising, or otherwise; or

(D) failing to make clear, to all parties to a transaction, which party he is acting for, or receiving compensation from more than one party except with the full knowledge and consent of all parties; or

(E) failing within a reasonable time properly to account for or remit money coming into his possession which belongs to others, or commingling money belonging to others with his own funds; or

(F) paying a commission or fees to or dividing a commission or fees with anyone not licensed as a real estate broker or salesman in this state or in any other state, or not an attorney at law licensed in this state or any other state, for compensation for services as a real estate agent; or

(G) failing to specify in a listing contract a definite termination date which is not subject to prior notice; or

(H) accepting, receiving, or charging an undisclosed commission, rebate, or direct profit on expenditures made for a principal; or

(I) soliciting, selling, or offering for sale real property under a scheme or program that constitutes a lottery or deceptive practice; or

(J) acting in the dual capacity of broker and undisclosed principal in a transaction; or

(K) guaranteeing, authorizing, or permitting a person to guarantee that future profits will result from a resale of real property; or

(L) placing a sign on real property offering it for sale, lease, or rent without the written consent of the owner or his authorized agent; or

(M) inducing or attempting to induce a party to a contract of sale or lease to break the contract for the purpose of substituting in lieu thereof a new contract; or

(N) negotiating or attempting to negotiate the sale, exchange, lease, or rental of real property with an owner or lessor, knowing that the owner or lessor had a written outstanding contract, granting exclusive agency in connection with the property to another real estate broker; or

(O) offering real property for sale or for lease without the knowledge and consent of the owner or his authorized agent, or on terms other than those authorized by the owner or his authorized agent; or

(P) publishing, or causing to be published, an advertisement including, but not limited to, advertising by newspaper, radio, television, or display which is misleading, or which is likely to deceive the public, or which in any manner tends to create a misleading impression, or which fails to identify the person causing the advertisement to be published as a licensed real estate broker or agent; or

(Q) having knowingly withheld from or inserted in a statement of account or invoice, a statement that made it inaccurate in a material particular; or

(R) publishing or circulating an unjustified or unwarranted threat of legal proceedings, or other action; or

(S) establishing an association, by employment or otherwise, with an unlicensed person who is expected or required to act as a real estate licensee, or aiding or abetting or conspiring with a person to circumvent the requirements of this Act; or

(T) failing or refusing on demand to furnish copies of a document pertaining to a transaction dealing with real estate to a person whose signature is affixed to the document; or

(U) failing to advise a purchaser in writing before the closing of a transaction that the purchaser should either have the abstract covering the real estate which is the subject of the contract examined by an attorney of the purchaser's own selection, or be furnished with or obtain a policy of title insurance; or

(V) conduct which constitutes dishonest dealings, bad faith, or untrustworthiness; or

(W) acting negligently or incompetently in performing an act for which a person is required to hold a real estate license; or

(X) disregarding or violating a provision of this Act; or

(Y) failing within a reasonable time to deposit money received as escrow agent in a real estate transaction, either in trust with a title company authorized to do business in this state, or in a custodial, trust, or escrow account maintained for that purpose in a banking institution authorized to do business in this state; or

(Z) disbursing money deposited in a custodial, trust, or escrow account, as provided in Subsection (Y) before the transaction concerned has been consummated or finally otherwise terminated; or

(AA) failing or refusing on demand to produce a document, book, or record in his possession concerning a real estate transaction conducted by him for inspection by the Real Estate Commission or its authorized personnel or representative; or

(BB) failing within a reasonable time to provide information requested by the commission as a result of a formal or informal complaint to the commission which would indicate a violation of this Act; or

(CC) failing without just cause to surrender to the rightful owner, on demand, a document or instrument coming into his possession.

The provisions of this section do not relieve a person from civil liability or from criminal prosecution under this Act or under the laws of this state.

Unauthorized practice of law

Sec. 16. A license granted under the provisions of this Act shall be suspended or revoked by the commission on proof that the licensee, not being licensed and authorized to practice law in this state, for a consideration, reward, pecuniary benefit, present or anticipated, direct or indirect, or in connection with or as a part of his employment, agency, or fiduciary relationship as a licensee, drew a deed, note, deed of trust, will, or other written instrument that may transfer or anywise affect the title to or an interest in land, or advised or counseled a person as to the validity or legal sufficiency of an instrument or as to the validity of title to real estate.

Hearings

Sec. 17. (a) Before a license is suspended or revoked, the licensee is entitled to a public hearing. The commission shall prescribe the time and place of the hearing. However, the hearing shall be held, if the licensee so desires, within the county where the licensee has his principal place of business, or if the licensee is a nonresident, the hearing may be called for and held in any county within this state. The notice calling the hearing shall recite the allegations against the licensee and the notice may be served personally or by mailing it by certified mail to the licensee's last known business address, as reflected by the commission's records, at least 10 days prior to the date set for the hearing. In the hearing, all witnesses shall be duly sworn and stenographic notes of the proceedings shall be taken and filed as a part of the records in the case. A party to the proceeding desiring it shall be furnished with a copy of the stenographic notes on the payment to the commission of a fee of $1.50 per page plus applicable sales tax and postage. After a hearing, the commission shall enter an order based on its findings of fact adduced from the evidence presented.

(b) The commission may issue subpoenas for the attendance of witnesses and the production of records or documents. The process issued by the commission may extend to all parts of the state, and the process may be served by any person designated by the commission. The person serving the process shall receive compensation to be allowed by the commission, not to exceed the fee prescribed by law for similar services. A witness subpoenaed who appears in a proceeding before the commission shall receive the same fees and mileage allowances as allowed by law, and the fees and allowances shall be taxed as part of the cost of the proceedings.

(c) If, in a proceeding before the commission, a witness fails or refuses to attend on subpoena issued by the commission, or refuses to testify, or refuses to produce a record or document, the production of which is called for by the subpoena, the attendance of the witness and the giving of his testimony and the production of the documents and records shall be enforced by a court of competent jurisdiction of this state in the same manner as the attendance, testimony of witnesses, and production of records are enforced in civil cases in the courts of this state.

Judicial review

Sec. 18. (a) A person aggrieved by a ruling, order, or decision of the commission has the right to appeal to a district court in the county where the hearing was held within 30 days from the service of notice of the action of the commission.

(b) The appeal having been properly filed, the court may request of the commission, and the commission on receiving the request shall within 30 days prepare and transmit to the court, a certified copy of its entire record in the matter in which the appeal has been taken. The appeal shall be tried in accordance with Texas Rules of Civil Procedure.

(c) In the event an appeal is taken by a licensee or applicant, the appeal does not act as a supersedeas unless the court so directs, and the court shall dispose of the appeal and enter its decision promptly.

(d) If an aggrieved person fails to perfect an appeal as provided in this section, the commission's ruling becomes final.

Penalties; injunctions

Sec. 19. (a) A person acting as a real estate broker or real estate salesman without first obtaining a license is guilty of a misdemeanor and on conviction shall be punishable by a fine of not less than $100 nor more than $500, or by imprisonment in the county jail for a term not to exceed one year, or both; and if a corporation, shall be punishable by a fine of not less than $1,000 nor more than $2,000. A person, on conviction of a second or subsequent offense, shall be punishable by a fine of not less than $500 nor more than $1,000, or by imprisonment for a term not to exceed two years, or both; and if a corporation, shall be punishable by a fine of not less than $2,000 nor more than $5,000.

(b) In case a person received money, or the equivalent thereof, as a fee, commission, compensation, or profit by or in consequence of a violation of a provision of this Act, he shall, in addition, be liable to a penalty of not less than the amount of the sum of money so received and not more than three times the sum so received, as may be determined by the court, which penalty may be recovered in a court of competent jurisdiction by an aggrieved person.

(c) When in the judgment of the commission a person has engaged, or is about to engage, in an act or practice which constitutes or will constitute a violation of a provision of this Act, the county attorney or district attorney in the county in which the violation has occurred or is about to occur, or in the county of the defendant's residence, or the attorney general may maintain an action in the name of the State of Texas in the district court of such county to abate and temporarily and permanently enjoin the acts and practices and to enforce compliance with this Act. The plaintiff in an action under this subsection is not required to give a bond, and court costs may not be adjudged against the plaintiff.

Actions for compensation or commission; abstracts or title insurance

Sec. 20. (a) A person may not bring or maintain an action for the collection of compensation for the performance in this state of an act set forth in Section 2 of this Act without alleging and proving that the person performing the brokerage services was a duly licensed real estate broker or salesman at the time the alleged services were commenced, or was a duly licensed attorney at law in this state or in any other state.

(b) An action may not be brought in a court in this state for the recovery of a commission for the sale or purchase of real estate unless the promise or agreement on which the action is brought, or some memorandum thereof, is in writing and signed by the party to be charged or signed by a person lawfully authorized by him to sign it.

(c) When an offer to purchase real estate in this state is signed, the real estate broker or salesman shall advise the purchaser or purchasers, in writing, that the purchaser or purchasers should have the abstract covering the real estate which is the subject of the contract examined by an attorney of the purchaser's own selection, or that the purchaser or purchasers should be furnished with or obtain a policy of title insurance. Failure to advise the purchaser as provided in this subsection precludes the payment of or recovery of any commission agreed to be paid on the sale.

Appendix II

STATEMENT OF PRINCIPLES BY THE STATE BAR OF TEXAS

.001. Statement of Principles by the State Bar of Texas and the Texas Real Estate Commission.

Whereas, under modern business practices and procedures, the practices of attorneys at law (hereinafter referred to as "lawyers") and the practices of real estate brokers and salesmen (both of whom are hereinafter referred to as "brokers") are, in certain instances, interrelated and interdependent; and,

Whereas, it is in the interest of the public, lawyers, and brokers that the services and efforts of both professions be coordinated; and,

Whereas, there should be a clear understanding in the minds of the practitioners of these professions as to their respective fields of endeavor and the functions to be performed by each in relation to matters in which there is an interdependence; Now, Therefore,

Be It Resolved by the State Bar of Texas and the Texas Real Estate Commission as a Statement of Principles in a joint effort to serve better the Texas public in regard to the coordination of the said functions of the members of these professions:

Article I

The Lawyer

It is the function of lawyers to give all legal advice required by the principals to or broker in a real estate transaction. It is not the function of lawyers to negotiate the sale, exchange, purchase, rental or leasing of real estate or the terms thereof, unless expressly employed by a principal or broker to perform that function. The lawyer may prepare the contract or agreement if employed to do so by one of the principals to the real estate transaction or by the broker therein.

In order to accompish his functions, the lawyer shall be governed by the following principles:

1. The lawyer who is employed in such a real estate transaction shall use his best efforts to proceed diligently to the conclusion of that transaction, and, if his availability or work load does not permit a prompt conclusion of the same, he shall inform his principal prior to accepting such employment or, thereafter, if at such later time his work load would prevent a prompt conclusion.

2. The lawyer shall not minimize the value of the broker's services nor participate or attempt to participate in the broker's commissions.

3. The lawyer, representing any principal to a real estate transaction, shall not give his opinion on the physical condition or the market value of the real estate involved in the transaction unless expressly employed by the principal to perform that function. However nothing herein shall be deemed to limit the fiduciary duty of the lawyer to disclose to his principal all pertinent facts which are within the knowledge of the lawyer, including such facts which might reflect on the physical condition or market value of the real estate.

4. The lawyer shall not accept employment by or compensation from the broker to represent any principal to a real estate transaction.

5. It is the responsibility of the lawyer who has been employed by a principal to a real estate transaction to prepare documents to be used in the real estate transaction, which documents the broker is not himself authorized to prepare.

6. A lawyer shall not represent, in the same transaction, more than one of the principals nor the broker and a principal except in those situations where the applicable canons of ethics clearly permit representations of conflicting interests by a lawyer after full and complete disclosure of the conflict of interest to those desiring such representation and upon the express consent of same.

7. Where a lawyer is also a real estate licensee, he shall not advertise or hold himself out as being able to handle a real estate transaction less expensively or better because he is such licensee as well as a lawyer nor should he act as a lawyer for any principal in the same transaction in which he proposes to act, is acting, or has acted as a real estate licensee, unless he is expressly employed by a principal in the capacity of a lawyer after a full and complete disclosure of the conflict of interest is given and expressly consented to by the principal in accordance with the applicable canons of ethics.

Article II

The Broker

It is the function of the broker to negotiate the sale, exchange, purchase, rental and leasing of real estate for his principal(s). In accomplishing such result the broker shall be governed by the following principles:

1. The broker shall not practice law, offer, give nor attempt to give advice, directly or indirectly; he shall not act as a public conveyancer nor give advice or opinions as to the legal effect of any contracts or other such instruments which may affect the title to real estate; he shall not give opinions concerning the status or validity of title to real estate; and he shall not attempt to prevent nor in any manner whatsoever discourage any principal to a real estate transaction from employing a

lawyer. However, nothing herein shall be deemed to limit the broker's fiduciary obligation to disclose to his principals all pertinent facts which are within the knowledge of the broker, including such facts which might affect the status of or title to real estate.

2. The broker shall not undertake to draw or prepare documents fixing and defining the legal rights of the principals to a transaction. However, in negotiating real estate transactions, the broker may fill in forms for such transactions, using exclusively those printed forms which have been approved by the State Bar of Texas and the Texas Real Estate Commission and promulgated by the Texas Real Estate Commission as the required standard forms to be used by all real estate licensees. When filling in such a form, the broker may only fill in the blanks provided and may not add to or strike matter from such form, except that brokers shall add factual statements and business details desired by the principals and shall strike only such matter as is desired by the principals and as is necessary to conform the instrument to the intent of the principals. Nothing herein shall be deemed to prevent the broker from explaining to the principals the meaning of the factual statements and business details contained in said instrument so long as Paragraph 1 above relating to the offering or giving of legal advice is not violated.

3. Where it appears that, prior to the execution of any such instrument, there are unusual matters involved in the transaction which should be resolved by legal counsel before the instrument is executed or that the instrument is to be acknowledged and filed for record, the broker should advise the principals that each should consult a lawyer of his choice before executing same.

4. The broker shall not minimize the value of the lawyer's services nor participate or attempt to participate in the lawyer's fees

5. The broker shall not employ, directly or indirectly, a lawyer nor pay for the services of a lawyer to represent any principal to a real estate transaction in which he, the broker, is acting as an agent. The broker may employ and pay for the services of a lawyer to represent only the broker in a real estate

transaction, including preparation of the contract, agreement, or other legal instruments to be executed by the principals to the transaction.

6. A broker shall advise the principals that the instrument they are about to execute is intended to be binding on them.

7. Where the broker is also a lawyer, he shall not advertise or hold himself out as being able to handle the complete details of a real estate transaction, including the preparation of documents other than the filling in of the blanks on standard forms approved and promulgated by the Texas Real Estate Commission as provided in Paragraph 2 above, or as being able to handle the transaction less expensively or better because he is also a lawyer. Also, he shall not act as a lawyer for any principal in the same transaction in which he proposes to act, is acting, or has acted as the broker, unless he is expressly employed by a principal in the capacity of a lawyer after a full and complete disclosure of the conflict of interest is given and expressly consented to by the principal in accordance with the applicable canons of ethics of the State Bar of Texas.

Article III

Permanent Organization

1. There is hereby created a continuing organization which shall be designated as the Texas Real Estate Broker-Lawyer Joint Committee, which shall be constituted and have those functions as hereinafter in this article set forth.

2. There shall be twelve members of this Committee, six appointed by the Texas Real Estate Commission and six appointed by the State Bar of Texas, appointed by each agency in accordance with its own procedures but with due regard and emphasis being placed on experience and expertise in the real estate field. The initial members shall be appointed, two from each agency, for a term of two years, two from each agency for a term of four years, and two from each agency for a term of six years. Every two years thereafter, members of the Committee shall be appointed to fill the expiring terms for six year terms.

Vacancies on the Committee shall be filled for the unexpired term by the agency which originally appointed the person whose absence created the vacancy.

3. The Committee shall:

(a) At all times act in the interest of the public.

(b) Consider and promote such changes in procedure and in laws relative to real estate transactions, while preserving the respective roles of the broker and lawyer, as will benefit the public, subject to the approval of the agencies approving this Statement of Principles.

(c) Promote and encourage understanding and cordial relations between brokers and lawyers throughout Texas to the end that both professions may more effectively and efficiently serve the people of Texas in real estate transactions.

(d) Consider any controversies between brokers and lawyers which may be referred to it involving any alleged violations of the principles set forth in Articles I and II hereof, inclusive, and attempt to resolve the same.

In cases where there appear to have been violations of such principles by either a broker or a lawyer and the resultant controversy cannot be resolved by the Committee, it shall refer the matter to the Texas Real Estate Commission if a broker's conduct is involved or to the State Bar of Texas if a lawyer's conduct is involved.

(e) Draft and revise uniform types of standard contract forms for use in the respective areas of the State of Texas, which forms will provide blanks for filling in strictly factual and business detail only, will expedite real estate transactions and reduce controversies to a minimum while containing safeguards adequate to protect all principals to real estate transactions, and will be capable of becoming the customary form or forms of contracts in use in the community. Such forms shall be subject to the approval of both the State Bar of Texas and the Texas Real Estate Commission and to promulgation by the Texas Real Estate Commission.

4. Cooperate with the respective organizations, as may be requested by them, in the joint dissemination to brokers, lawyers and the public of information on the conduct of real estate transactions. Promote and encourage the joint education and training of both brokers and lawyers in the real estate field through seminars, continuing education, research and development, and other related means as requested and funded by the respective organizations.

Article IV

This Statement of Principles shall be in full force and effect after having been approved by the Board of Directors of the State Bar of Texas and the Texas Real Estate Commission, at which time the Texas Real Estate Broker-Lawyer Joint Committee shall undertake the drafting of the standard real estate contract forms referred to in Article II, Paragraph 2, hereof, which forms, when approved by the Board of Directors of the State Bar of Texas and approved and promulgated by the Texas Real Estate Commission, shall become a part of this Statement of Principles as fully as if set forth herein word for word.

402.04.02. Standard Contract Forms

.001. Use of Standard Contract Forms TREC No. 1-0 and TREC No. 2-0. After March 1, 1976, all Texas real estate licensees must use standard contract forms TREC No. 1-0 and TREC No. 2-0, where applicable, for residential assumption of loan transactions, except in situations where the services of a lawyer are used to prepare the instrument for a particular sale.

Real estate brokers may supply themselves with the forms for their use in any way they desire. Copies may be purchased from the Commission at a price of $2.50 per pad of 50 copies of form TREC No. 1-0 and $2.50 per pad of 50 copies of form TREC No. 2-0. Such price includes sales tax. A $1.00 mailing and handling charge must accompany each order. Payment should be made in the form of a cashier's check or money order made payable to the Texas Real Estate Commission.

For those who desire to reproduce the form in volume, "slick proofs" are available from the Commission at a price of

$45.00 per three-page set (both forms). Such price includes sales tax. A $1.00 handling and mailing charge must accompany each order. Payment should be made for the proofs in the form of a cashier's check or money order made payable to the Texas Real Estate Commission. All "slick proofs" will be separately numbered for the purpose of control of reproduction. The control number on each proof must appear on all forms reproduced. When reproducing the form, additions or changes are prohibited except that brokers, organizations or printing services may add their name and/or logo at the top of the front page, outside of the border surrounding the form itself. Also, the real estate broker's name may be inserted on the front page of the form in the blank space provided in Section Number 10 after the words BROKER'S FEE and the broker's name and license number may be printed in the signature section on the back page.

DECEPTIVE TRADE PRACTICES—CONSUMER PROTECTION ACT

SUBCHAPTER E. DECEPTIVE TRADE PRACTICES AND CONSUMER PROTECTION [NEW]

Sec.
17.41 Short Title.
17.42 Waivers: Public Policy.
17.43 Cumulative Remedies.
17.44 Construction and Application.
17.45 Definitions.
17.46 Deceptive Trade Practices Unlawful.
17.47 Restraining Orders.
17.48 Duty of District and County Attorney.
17.49 Exemptions.
Sec.
17.50 Relief for Consumers.
17.50A. Damages; Defenses.
17.51 to 17.54. Repealed.
17.55 Promotional Material.
17.55A. Indemnity.
17.56 Venue.
17.57 Subpoenas.
17.58 Voluntary Compliance.
17.59. Post Judgment Relief.
17.60 Reports and Examinations.
17.61 Civil Investigative Demand.
17.62 Penalties.
17.63 Application.

Cross References

Texas motor vehicle commission code, see Vernon's Ann.Civ.St. art. 4413(36).

SUBCHAPTER B. DECEPTIVE ADVERTISING, PACKING, SELLING, AND EXPORTING

§§ 17.09, 17.10. Repealed by Acts 1973, 63rd Leg., p. 995, ch. 399, § 3(d), eff. Jan. 1, 1974

Acts 1973, 63rd Leg., p. 883, ch. 399, repealing these sections, enacts the new Texas Penal Code.

See, now, V.T.C.A. Penal Code, § 32.42.

§ 17.12. Deceptive Advertising

(a) No person may disseminate a statement he knows materially misrepresents the cost or character of tangible personal property, a security, service, or anything he may offer for the purpose of

(1) selling, contracting to sell, otherwise disposing of, or contracting to dispose of the tangible personal property, security, service, or anything he may offer; or

(2) inducing a person to contract with regard to the tangible personal property, security, service, or anything he may offer.

(b) No person may solicit advertising in the name of a club, association, or organization without the written permission of such club, association, or organization or distribute any publication purporting to represent officially a club, association, or organization without the written authority of or a contract with such club, association, or organization and without listing in such publication the complete name and address of the club, association, or organization endorsing it.

(c) A person's proprietary mark appearing on or in a statement described in Subsection (a) of this section is prima facie evidence that the person disseminated the statement.

(d) A person who violates a provision of Subsection (a) or (b) of this Section is guilty of a misdemeanor and upon conviction is punishable by a fine of not less than $10 nor more than $200.

Amended by Acts 1969, 61st Leg., p. 2045, ch. 701, § 1, emerg. eff. June 12, 1969.

1969 Amendment. Inserted provisions of subsec. (b).

Section 2 of the Amendatory act of 1969 was a severability clause.

Cross References

Texas motor vehicle commission code, deceptive advertising by dealers, manufacturers, etc. prohibited, see Vernon's Ann.Civ.St. art. 4413(36), §§ 5.01(2), 5.02(4).

SUBCHAPTER D. COUNTERFEITING OR CHANGING A REQUIRED MARK; MISUSE OF CONTAINER BEARING MARK

§ 17.28. Repealed by Acts 1973, 63rd Leg., p. 995, ch. 399, § 3(d), eff. Jan. 1, 1974

Acts 1973, 63rd Leg., p. 883, ch. 399, repealing this section, enacts the new Texas Penal Code.

See, now, V.T.C.A. Penal Code, § 32.21.

SUBCHAPTER E. DECEPTIVE TRADE PRACTICES AND CONSUMER PROTECTION [NEW].

This Subchapter E was enacted by § 1 of Acts 1973, 63rd Leg., p. 322, ch. 143. Section 3 of the 1973 Act repealed Chapter 10 of Title 79, Vernon's Ann.Civ.St. arts. 5069—10.01 to 5069—10.08.

DISPOSITION TABLE

Showing where the subject matter of former Chapter 10 of Title 79, Revised Civil Statutes, is now covered in this Subchapter E.

Vernon's Ann. Civ.St.Article	Subchapter E Section
5069—10.01(a)	17.45
5069—10.01(b)	17.46
5069—10.01(c)	17.45
5069—10.01(d)	17.45
5069—10.02	17.46
5069—10.03	17.49
5069—10.04	17.47
5069—10.05	17.58
5069—10.06	17.60
5069—10.07	17.61
5069—10.08	17.62

Cross References

Assumed Business or Professional Name Act, see § 36.01 et seq.

Consumer credit commissioner and division, see Vernon's Ann.Civ.St. art. 5069—2.02.

Consumer credit generally, see Vernon's Ann.Civ.St. art. 5069—2.01 et seq.

Consumer debt counseling and education, see Vernon's Ann.Civ.St. art. 5069—9.01 et seq.

Debt collection, deceptive or misleading representations, see Vernon's Ann.Civ.St. art. 5069—11.05.

Fraud in real estate and stock transactions, see § 27.01.

Fraudulent transfers, see § 24.01 et seq.

Health Maintenance Organization Act, deceptive advertising, see V.A.T.S. Insurance Code, arts. 20A.14, 20A.20(a)(8).

Home solicitation transactions, violation as deceptive trade practice, see Vernon's Ann.Civ.St. art. 5069—13.03.

Insurance, unfair claim settlement practices, see V.A.T.S. Insurance Code, art. 21.21—2.

Insurance companies,

Federal regulation, see 15 U.S.C.A. § 1011 et seq.

Unfair competition and practices, see V.A.T.S. Insurance Code, art. 21.21.

Interest, see Vernon's Ann.Civ.St. art. 5069—1.01 et seq.

Medical Liability and Insurance Improvement Act, inapplicability of this subchapter, see Vernon's Ann.Civ.St. art. 4590i, § 12.01.

Mobile Homes Standard Act, deceptive trade practices, see Vernon's Ann.Civ.St. art. 5221f, § 17(e).

Pawnshop act, see Vernon's Ann.Civ.St. art. 5069—51.01 et seq.

Prescription drug advertising, deceptive trade practices, see Vernon's Ann.Civ.St. art. 4542a, § 20A.

Removal of unauthorized vehicles from parking facilities or highways, applicability of this subchapter, see Vernon's Ann.Civ.St. art. 6701g—2, § 8.

Unfair methods of competition, see 15 U.S.C.A. § 45 et seq.

Law Review Commentaries

Amendments of 1975 to Consumer Protection Act. David F. Bragg, 28 Baylor L. Rev. (1976).

Breach of warranty and treble damages under Texas Deceptive Trade Practices and Consumer Protection Act. 28 Baylor L. Rev. 395 (1976).

Competitor's suit to enjoin criminal acts. 26 Baylor L.Rev. 267 (1974).

Consumer class action. 16 South Texas L.J. 111 (1974).

Consumer credit regulation in Texas. 49 Texas L.Rev. 1011 (1971).

Consumer credit rejoinder. S. Hugh High, 50 Texas L.Rev. 463 (1972).

Consumer legislation in Texas. Bill M. Shaw, 37 Texas Bar J. 141 (1974).

Emergence of consumer credit protection —Federal and Texas. 8 St. Mary's L.J. 794 (1977).

Measure of damages for misrepresentation under Texas Deceptive Trade Practices Act. 29 Baylor L.Rev. 135 (1977).

Deceptive Trade Practices and Consumer Protection Act. 25 Baylor L.Rev. 425 (1973).

§ 17.41. Short Title

This subchapter may be cited as the Deceptive Trade Practices-Consumer Protection Act.

Added by Acts 1973, 63rd Leg., p. 322, ch. 143, § 1, eff. May 21, 1973.

Section 2 of the 1973 Act amended V.A.T.S. Insurance Code, art. 21.21; § 3 repealed Vernon's Ann.Civ.St. arts. 5069—10.01 to 5069—10.08; and § 4 thereof provided: "If any provision of this Act or the application thereof to any person or circumstances is held invalid, such invalidity shall not affect other provisions or applications of the Act which can be given effect without the invalid provision or application, and to this end the provisions of this Act are declared to be severable."

Law Review Commentaries

A remedy for undermade and oversold products—Texas Deceptive Trade Practices Act. Michael P. Lynn, 7 St. Mary's L.J. 698 (1976).

Preservation of claims and defenses under Texas Business and Commerce Code and under Texas Consumer Credit Code. James G. Boyle, 8 St. Mary's L.J. 679 (1977).

Public and private rights and remedies under deceptive trade practices—Consumer Protection Act. Philip K. Maxwell, 8 St. Mary's L.J. 617 (1977).

Texas deceptive trade practices—Consumer Protection Act: Application to professional malpractice. 8 St. Mary's L.J. 763 (1977).

§ 17.42. Waivers: Public Policy

Any waiver by a consumer of the provisions of this subchapter is contrary to public policy and is unenforceable and void.

Added by Acts 1973, 63rd Leg., p. 322, ch. 143, § 1, eff. May 21, 1973.

Law Review Commentaries

Implied warranties: Can they still be waived in Texas? 26 Baylor L.Rev 440 (1974).

§ 17.43. Cumulative Remedies

The provisions of this subchapter are not exclusive. The remedies provided in this subchapter are in addition to any other procedures or remedies provided for in any other law. The provisions of this subchapter do not in any way preclude other political subdivisions of this state from dealing with deceptive trade practices.

Added by Acts 1973, 63rd Leg., p. 322, ch. 143, § 1, eff. May 21, 1973.

§ 17.44. Construction and Application

This subchapter shall be liberally construed and applied to promote its underlying purposes, which are to protect consumers against false, misleading, and deceptive business practices, unconscionable actions, and breaches of warranty and to provide efficient and economical procedures to secure such protection.

Added by Acts 1973, 63rd Leg., p. 322, ch. 143, § 1, eff. May 21, 1973.

§ 17.45. Definitions

As used in this subchapter:

(1) "Goods" means tangible chattels or real property purchased or leased for use.

(2) "Services" means work, labor, or service purchased or leased for use, including services furnished in connection with the sale or repair of goods.

(3) "Person" means an individual, partnership, corporation, association, or other group, however organized.

(4) "Consumer" means an individual, partnership, corporation, or governmental entity who seeks or acquires by purchase or lease, any goods or services.

(5) "Unconscionable action or course of action" means an act or practice which, to a person's detriment:

(A) takes advantage of the lack of knowledge, ability, experience, or capacity of a person to a grossly unfair degree; or

(B) results in a gross disparity between the value received and consideration paid, in a transaction involving transfer of consideration.

(6) "Trade" and "commerce" means the advertising, offering for sale, sale, lease, or distribution of any good or service, of any property, tangible or intangible, real, personal, or mixed, and any other article, commodity, or thing of value, wherever situated, and shall include any trade or commerce directly or indirectly affecting the people of this state.

(7) "Documentary material" includes the original or a copy of any book, record, report, memorandum, paper, communication, tabulation, map, chart, photograph, mechanical transcription, or other tangible document or recording, wherever situated.

(8) "Consumer protection division" means the antitrust and consumer protection division of the attorney general's office.

(9) "Knowingly" means actual awareness of the falsity or deception, but actual awareness may be inferred where objective manifestations indicate that a person acted with actual awareness.

Added by Acts 1973, 63rd Leg., p. 322, ch. 143, § 1, eff. May 21, 1973. Amended by Acts 1975, 64th Leg., p. 149, ch. 62, § 1, eff. Sept. 1, 1975; Acts 1977, 65th Leg., p. 600, ch. 216, § 1, eff. May 23, 1977.

1975 Amendment. In subd. (1) substituted "or real property purchased or leased for" for "bought for"; in subd. (2) substituted "or service purchased or leased for use," for "and services"; and in subd. (4) inserted ", partnership, or corporation".

1977 Amendment. In subd. (2) deleted "for other than commercial or business use," after "leased for use,"; in subd. (4) inserted ", or governmental entity"; and rewrote subd. (5), which prior thereto read: " 'Merchant' means a party to a consumer transaction other than a consumer."

Derivation:

Acts 1967, 60th Leg., p. 658, ch. 274, § 2.
Acts 1969, 61st Leg., p. 1504, ch. 452, § 1.
Vernon's Ann.Civ.St. art. 5069—10.01(a), (c), (d).

Cross References

Consumer credit commissioner and division, see Vernon's Ann.Civ.St. art. 5069—2.-02.

Law Review Commentaries

Amendments of 1975 to Consumer Protection Act. David F. Bragg, 28 Baylor L. Rev. 1 (1976).

1. Construction and application

Purchaser, who brought suit as purchaser of realty, not goods or services, was not "consumer" within purview of this section and thus could not bring action against vendors, limited partner of vendor and trustee in deed of trust securing purchase money notes under Section 17.50 for alleged violations of such section. Cape Conroe Ltd. v. Specht (Civ.App.1975) 525 S.W.2d 215.

In respect to plaintiff's "unfair settlement practices" theory of relief against insurance company, predicated on claim that the insurer engaged in false, misleading or deceptive acts or practices in violation of § 17.46 by, inter alia, representing that plaintiffs had unlimited use of a rental car with respect to time and mileage until the insurer obtained a replacement vehicle for them, plaintiffs did not purchase or lease the rental car and therefore were not "consumers" within definition in subd. (4) of this section and thus had no cause of action under § 17.50(b). Russell v. Hartford Cas. Ins. Co. (Civ.App.1977) 548 S.W.2d 737, ref. n. r. e.

§ 17.46. Deceptive Trade Practices Unlawful

(a) False, misleading, or deceptive acts or practices in the conduct of any trade or commerce are hereby declared unlawful.

(b) The term "false, misleading, or deceptive acts or practices" includes, but is not limited to, the following acts:

(1) passing off goods or services as those of another;

(2) causing confusion or misunderstanding as to the source, sponsorship, approval, or certification of goods or services;

(3) causing confusion or misunderstanding as to affiliation, connection, or association with, or certification by, another;

(4) using deceptive representations or designations of geographic origin in connection with goods or services;

(5) representing that goods or services have sponsorship, approval, characteristics, ingredients, uses, benefits, or quantities which they do not have or that a person has a sponsorship, approval, status, affiliation, or connection which he does not;

(6) representing that goods are original or new if they are deteriorated, reconditioned, reclaimed, used, or secondhand;

(7) representing that goods or services are of a particular standard, quality, or grade, or that goods are of a particular style or model, if they are of another;

(8) disparaging the goods, services, or business of another by false or misleading representation of facts;

(9) advertising goods or services with intent not to sell them as advertised;

(10) advertising goods or services with intent not to supply a reasonable expectable public demand, unless the advertisements disclosed a limitation of quantity;

(11) making false or misleading statements of fact concerning the reasons for, existence of, or amount of price reductions;

(12) representing that an agreement confers or involves rights, remedies, or obligations which it does not have or involve, or which are prohibited by law;

(13) knowingly making false or misleading statements of fact concerning the need for parts, replacement, or repair service;

(14) misrepresenting the authority of a salesman, representative or agent to negotiate the final terms of a consumer transaction;

(15) basing a charge for the repair of any item in whole or in part on a guaranty or warranty instead of on the value of the actual repairs made or work to be performed on the item without stating separately the charges for the work and the charge for the warranty or guaranty, if any;

(16) disconnecting, turning back, or resetting the odometer of any motor vehicle so as to reduce the number of miles indicated on the odometer gauge;

(17) advertising of any sale by fraudulently representing that a person is going out of business;

(18) using or employing a chain referral sales plan in connection with the sale or offer to sell of goods, merchandise, or anything of value, which uses the sales technique, plan, arrangement, or agreement in which the buyer or prospective buyer is offered the opportunity to purchase merchandise or goods and in connection with the purchase receives the seller's promise or representation that the buyer shall have the right to receive compensation or consideration in any form for furnishing to the seller the names of other prospective buyers

if receipt of the compensation or consideration is contingent upon the occurrence of an event subsequent to the time the buyer purchases the merchandise or goods;

(19) representing that a guarantee or warranty confers or involves rights or remedies which it does not have or involve, provided, however, that nothing in this subchapter shall be construed to expand the implied warranty of merchantability as defined in Sections 2.314 through 2.318 of the Business & Commerce Code to involve obligations in excess of those which are appropriate to the goods;

(20) selling or offering to sell, either directly or associated with the sale of goods or services, a right of participation in a multi-level distributorship. As used herein, "multi-level distributorship" means a sales plan for the distribution of goods or services in which promises of rebate or payment are made to individuals, conditioned upon those individuals recommending or securing additional individuals to assume positions in the sales operation, and where the rebate or payment is not exclusively conditioned on or in relation to proceeds from the retail sales of goods; or

Text of subd. (21) added by Acts 1977, 65th Leg., p. 601, ch. 216, § 3

(21) representing that work or services have been performed on, or parts replaced in, goods when the work or services were not performed or the parts replaced.

Text of subd. (21) added by Acts 1977, 65th Leg., p. 892, ch. 336, § 1

(21) filing suit founded upon a written contractual obligation of and signed by the defendant to pay money arising out of or based on a consumer transaction for goods, services, loans, or extensions of credit intended primarily for personal, family, household, or agricultural use in any county other than in the county in which the defendant resides at the time of the commencement of the action or in the county in which the defendant in fact signed the contract, except that it is not a violation of this subsection where the defendant resides in a county having a population of less than 250,000 and the suit was filed in the nearest county with a population of 250,000 or more; provided, however, that a violation of this subsection shall not occur where it is shown by the person filing such suit he neither knew or had reason to know that the county in which such suit was filed was neither the county in which the defendant resides at the commencement of the suit nor the county in which the defendant in fact signed the contract; and provided further that a violation of this Act shall not occur by the joinder of multiple parties to an obligation where venue is otherwise proper as to the primary obligor or to any joint obligor.

(c)(1) It is the intent of the legislature that in construing Subsection (a) of this section in suits brought under Section 17.47 of this subchapter the courts to the extent possible will be guided by Subsection (b) of this section and the interpretations given by the Federal Trade Commission and federal courts to Section 5(a)(1) of the Federal Trade Commission Act [15 U.S.C.A. 45(a)(1)].

(2) It is the intent of the legislature that in construing Subsection (a) of this section in suits brought under Section 17.50 of this subchapter the courts to the extent possible will be guided by Subsection (b) of

this section and the interpretations given by the federal courts to Section 5(a)(1) of the Federal Trade Commission Act [15 U.S.C.A. 45(a)(1)].
Added by Acts 1973, 3rd Leg., p. 322, ch. 143, § 1, eff. May 21, 1973. Amended by Acts 1977, 65th Leg., p. 601, ch. 216, §§ 2, 3, eff. May 23, 1977; Acts 1977, 65th Leg., p. 892, ch. 336, § 1, eff. Aug. 29, 1977.

1977 Amendments. In subsec. (b), chs. 216 and 336 each added a subd. (21); in subsec. (c), ch. 216 inserted "in suits brought under Section 17.47 of this subchapter" in subd. (1) and added the provisions of subd. (2).

Derivation:

Acts 1967, 60th Leg., p. 658, ch. 274, § 2.
Acts 1969, 61st Leg., p. 1504, ch. 452, § 1.
Acts 1969, 61st Leg., p. 2344, ch. 794, § 1.
Acts 1971, 62nd Leg., p. 3059, ch. 1018, § 1.
Vernon's Ann.Civ.St. arts. 5069—10.01(b), 5069—10.02.

Cross References

Insurers, unfair competition and practices in violation of this section.
Administrative class actions, see V.A.T.S. Insurance Code, art. 21.21, § 14 (a).
Cease and desist orders, see V.A.T.S. Insurance Code, art. 21.21, § 7(a).
Class actions, see V.A.T.S. Insurance Code, art. 21.21, § 17(a).
Injunctions, see V.A.T.S. Insurance Code, art. 21.21, § 15(a).
Relief to injured parties, see V.A.T.S. Insurance Code, art. 21.21, § 16(a).
Voluntary compliance, see V.A.T.S. Insurance Code, art. 21.21, § 22.

Law Review Commentaries

Consumer class action. 16 South Texas L.J. 111 (1974).

A remedy for undermade and oversold products—Texas Deceptive Trade Practices Act. Michael P. Lynn, 7 St. Mary's L.J. 698 (1976).

Deceptive Trade Practices—Consumer Protection Act: Application to professional malpractice. 8 St. Mary's L.J. 763 (1977).

Doctrine of unconscionability: A sword as well as a shield. 29 Baylor L.Rev. 309 (1977).

Emergence of consumer credit protection —Federal and Texas. 8 St. Mary's L.J. 794 (1977).

Measure of damages for misrepresentation under Texas Deceptive Trade Practices Act. 29 Baylor L.Rev. 135 (1977).

Preservation of claims and defenses under Texas Business and Commerce Code and under Texas Consumer Credit Code. James G. Boyle, 8 St. Mary's L.J. 679 (1977).

Public and private rights and remedies under Deceptive Trade Practices—Consumer Protection Act. Philip K. Maxwell, 8 St. Mary's L.J. 617 (1977).

Settlement costs: R.E.S.P.A. and other relevant legislation. 29 Baylor L.Rev. 357 (1977).

Index to Notes

In general 1
Attorney fees 3.6
Declaratory judgment 3.5
Evidence 3
Injunction 2
Instructions 3.8
Pleadings 2.5
Presumptions and burden of proof 2.9
Review 4
Venue 1.5

---

1. In general

Evidence that passenger made confirmed reservation with air carrier, that he informed carrier of fact that he was required to be at wedding rehearsal at certain time, that passenger arrived on time for flight, and that carrier ignored boarding priority rules which it had filed with Civil Aeronautics Board and refused to allow passenger to board airplane even though it had not disclosed possibility of oversales, was insufficient to constitute common-law fraud, and was outside this Act as matter of law. Smith v. Piedmont Aviation, Inc. (D.C.1976) 412 F.Supp. 641.

Legislature, in enacting Vernon's Ann. Civ.St. art. 5069—10.02 (repealed; see, now, subsec. (c) of this section), relating to unlawful deceptive practices and providing that courts to the extent possible would be guided by art. 5069—10.01(b) and by interpretations given by the Federal Trade Commission and the federal courts to specified section of the Federal Trade Commission Act, intended to rely on the vast body of law heretofore promulgated by federal courts and the FTC. Wesware, Inc. v. State (Civ.App.1972), 488 S.W.2d 844.

It cannot be a deceptive trade practice for a credit bureau to advise that an unpaid account will be referred to an attorney for civil action if the debtor does not respond. Credit Bureau of Laredo, Inc. v. State (Civ.App.1974) 515 S.W.2d 706, affirmed 530 S.W.2d 288.

Under Deceptive Trade Practices-Consumer Protection Act (this subchapter), State's right to seek restitution on behalf of identifiable persons was not limited to seeking restitution on behalf of consumers. Bourland v. State (Civ.App.1975) 528 S.W. 2d 350, ref. n. r. e.

Where seller purchased car from used car company and disclosure statement from that company disclosed 8,226 miles on odometer of car, and where disclosure statement from seller to buyer showed 8,280 miles, fact that figure was wrong did not establish that seller had violated any provisions of federal statute setting forth "odometer requirements" (15 U.S.C.A. § 1981 et seq.). Shepherd v. Eagle Lincoln

Mercury, Inc. (Civ.App.1976) 536 S.W.2d 92.

Although modification of septic tank system of new house was completed a month following effective date of the Deceptive Trade Practices Act and, at that time, was represented to be adequate, recovery could not be had under the Act where the house and lot were sold prior to effective date of lot and the alleged misrepresentations were made at such time. Littleton v. Woods (Civ.App.1976) 538 S.W.2d 800, affirmed 554 S.W.2d 662.

Interest of state in preventing unfair or deceptive competitive practices is not effectively met by § 20A, subd. II, (a), (d) of Vernon's Ann.Civ.St. art. 4542a prohibiting pharmacies from advertising drug prices, for unfair competitive practices are more effectively controlled by Consumer Protection Act. Texas State Bd. of Pharmacy v. Gibson's Discount Center, Inc. (Civ.App. 1976) 541 S.W.2d 884.

Breach of warranty as to mobile home arose under this Act once defects were known, and purchasers of mobile home therefore had no cause of action against sellers under this Act where defects became known before this Act became effective. Town & Country Mobile Homes, Inc. v. Stiles (Civ.App.1976) 543 S.W.2d 664.

In respect to plaintiffs' "unfair settlement practices" theory of relief against insurance company, predicated on claim that the insurer engaged in false, misleading or deceptive acts or practices in violation of this section by, inter alia, representing that plaintiffs had unlimited use of a rental car with respect to time and mileage until the insurer obtained a replacement vehicle for them, plaintiffs did not purchase or lease the rental car and therefore were not "consumers" within definition in § 17.45(4) and thus had no cause of action under § 17.-50(b). Russell v. Hartford Cas. Ins. Co. (Civ.App.1977) 548 S.W.2d 737, ref. n. r. e.

Appellant, only defendant found to have committed deceptive trade practice charged, could not complain of judgment finding him jointly and severally liable with codefendant. Yorfino v. Ferguson (Civ.App.1977) 552 S.W.2d 563.

Enumeration of 20 specific acts in this section which defines the term "false, misleading, or deceptive acts or practices" is not an exclusive list of acts that violate the prohibition against deceptive business practices; listing encompasses any type of business activity which deceives consumers. Spradling v. Williams (Civ.App.1977) 553 S.W.2d 143.

Definition of term "deceptive trade practice," for purpose of this chapter pursuant to which an act or series of acts constitutes a "deceptive trade practice" if it has the capacity or tendency to deceive an average or ordinary person, even though that person may have been ignorant, unthinking or credulous, represented the intention of the legislature. Id.

Where jury found that construction company failed to install swimming pool in good and workmanlike manner and that this failure was producing cause of damage, trebling of actual damages for breach of warranty of good workmanship was mandatory under this chapter. Boman v. Woodmansee (Civ.App.1977) 554 S.W.2d 33.

A sales plan in which there was no deceptive sales representation did not violate Vernon's Ann.Civ.St. art. 5069—10.01 et seq. (repealed), Op.Atty.Gen.1971, No. M-781.

1.5 Venue

In view of fact that provision of Vernon's Ann.Civ.St. art. 2390 for justice courts expressly authorized finance company to institute suit against consumer in distant forum, Vernon's Ann.Civ.St. art. 1995, subd. 5 had to be construed as constituting exception to general law found in this subchapter and accordingly, consumer was not entitled to injunction restraining finance company from engaging in certain alleged defective trade practices based on its filing of suits against consumer in distant forum; nor was consumer entitled to injunctive relief against distant forum suits which might be filed against him in county or district courts. Vargas v. Allied Finance Co. (Civ.App.1976) 545 S.W.2d 231, ref. n. r. e.

2. Injunction

Trial court did not abuse its discretion by temporarily enjoining defendants from advertising guarantee on money back basis unless the conditional nature of the guarantee was conspicuously displayed or mentioned where the conditional nature of the guarantee was shown only in obscure portion of defendants' sales kit and other advertising. R E I Industries, Inc. v. State (Civ.App.1972) 477 S.W.2d 956.

Temporary injunction which enjoined defendants from representing that automobile accessory marketed by them significantly reduced air pollution, from representing that the accessory was guaranteed on money back basis unless conditional nature of the guarantee was conspicuously displayed or mentioned, from representing the past earnings of participants in their marketing program unless those earnings reflected the earnings of substantial number of participants in Texas and from representing that it was easy for participants to recruit prospects who would engage in defendants' marketing program contained sufficient statement of reasons for issuance of the injunction. Id.

In view of testimony of mechanical engineer for Bureau of Mobile Pollution Sources that test results showed that defendants' automobile accessory had no significant effect on either increasing or decreasing vehicle emissions, trial court did not abuse its discretion in granting temporary injunction which enjoined defendants from representing that the accessory significantly reduced air pollution from automobile emissions. Id.

The portion of temporary injunction which prevented defendants from representing past earnings of participants in its marketing plan for automobile accessory unless the past earnings represented were those of substantial number of participants in Texas was sufficient to inform defendants that if they were to employ the "success story" device to gain new converts then accurate picture of the earnings of participants was to be presented rather than an atypical one and was sufficiently definite and precise so as to place defendants on notice of the acts enjoined. Id.

Where either party, to suit in which Attorney General sought to temporarily enjoin corporation from conducting pyramid sales scheme, could have insisted upon hearing on the merits, and where the corporation would be able at trial on the merits to present all defenses deemed available to prevent State from enforcing Vernon's Ann.Civ.St. art. 5069—10.01 et seq. (repealed) against the corporation's particular business practices without necessity of separate suit or cross action amounting to another suit, effect of temporary injunction was not permanent so as to entitle corporation to supersedeas bond staying effectiveness of the injunction during appeal. Wesware, Inc. v. Blackwell (Civ.App.1972) 486 S.W.2d 599.

Temporary injunction order which was entered in proceeding against alleged operator of pyramid-selling scheme for alleged violation of State Deceptive Trade Practices Act which sufficiently stated the acts prohibited and did not describe them by reference to the petition and which did not go beyond scope of the Act or destroy the status quo complied with requirements of Vernon's Ann.Rules Civ.Proc., rule 683, relating to form and scope of an injunction. Wesware, Inc. v. State (Civ.App.1972) 488 S.W.2d 844.

There was no requirement that prohibitory language of an injunction under the State Deceptive Trade Practices Act had to track any of statutory language of the Act. Id.

2.5 Pleadings

In suit by purchaser against, inter alia, vendors for alleged violations of Deceptive Trade Practices Act (§ 17.41 et seq.) purchaser's pleadings, which listed seven specific acts of vendors on which cause of action was based and alleged that each act was violation of given section of said act, did not entitle her to recover damages from vendors for breach of contract or to judgment rescinding sale of property in question. Cape Conroe Ltd. v. Specht (Civ. App.1975) 525 S.W.2d 215.

General rule requiring plaintiff to plead and prove cause of action to support venue applied to action for damages and attorney's fees under the Deceptive Trade Practices and Consumer Protection Act. Doyle v. Grady (Civ.App.1976) 543 S.W.2d 893.

2.9 Presumptions and burden of proof

To show conspiracy to engage in false, misleading, or deceptive acts or practices in violation of Deceptive Trade Practices —Consumer Protection Act (this subchapter), there must be proof of agreement to obtain money from others by engaging in course of conduct which parties know has tendency or capacity to deceive. Bourland v. State (Civ.App.1975) 528 S.W.2d 350, ref. n. r. e.

As plaintiff stated no cause of action against tort-feasor's liability insurer for a violation of subsecs. (a) and (b) of this section or V.A.T.S. Insurance Code, arts. 21.21, § 4(4) and 21.21—2, and since it was upon the acts of the insurer that plaintiffs' conspiracy theory was premised, plaintiffs failed to meet the "unlawful act" or "unlawful means" requirement of a conspiracy. Russell v. Hartford Cas. Ins. Co. (Civ.App. 1977) 548 S.W.2d 737.

3. Evidence

Evidence was sufficient to sustain finding that chain-referral or pyramid-selling scheme was in violation of State Deceptive Trade Practices Act [Vernon's Ann.Civ.St. art. 5069—10.01 et seq. (repealed)] and was as such subject to being temporarily enjoined, notwithstanding contention that since the scheme was fully explained there was no deception as to its nature or as to likelihood of market saturation and that the only element of chance involved was that common to any business venture depending on sales of goods. Wesware, Inc. v. State (Civ.App.1972) 488 S.W.2d 844.

In action by state seeking to enjoin defendants from committing certain alleged deceptive acts, for penalties, and for restitution of money for benefit of certain persons who had paid money pursuant to alleged deceptive trade practices, evidence was sufficient to support trial court's finding that the operation's attorney acquired knowledge at some time during two-year period involved that acts and practices of other defendants had capacity to deceive and that such were done for purpose of acquiring property or money from others, that attorney intended to participate therein and to share in the gains, and attorney was therefore liable to make restitution as member of conspiracy. Bourland v. State (Civ.App.1975) 528 S.W.2d 350, ref. n. r. e.

Where used car buyer did not establish, inter alia, that seller knowingly or recklessly made false representations as to used car's mileage, fact that figures shown on odometer were wrong was insufficient to prove actionable fraud. Shepherd v. Eagle Lincoln Mercury, Inc. (Civ.App.1976) 536 S.W.2d 92.

There was no evidence to support judgment that seller had altered or caused odometer of automobile to be altered in violation of this section. Id.

Evidence in consumer's action under this Subchapter, supported finding that seller and servicer of recreational vehicles, who advertised in yellow pages of telephone directory that he was dealer for "Coleman" recreational vehicles at time when he no longer sold such vehicles, violated provisions of subd. (b)(5) of this section, relating to representations that person has sponsorship, approval, status, affiliation, or connection which he does not. Mallory v. Custer (Civ.App.1976) 537 S.W.2d 141.

Where under the pleadings the time of the "occurrence in question" was the date of sale, i. e., November 10, 1972, but only evidence pertaining to fair market value of house with septic tank in its existing condition and with a properly working system was an appraisal made in 1974 and values at that time, no recovery could be had since values at time of sale were not proven and hence, no damage was shown to have arisen out of the sale transaction. Littleton v. Woods (Civ.App.1976) 538 S.W.2d 800, affirmed 554 S.W.2d 662.

Where manufacturer of mobile home made repairs on home after date of effectiveness of this section and stated in letter to buyers that mobile home was "all fixed up," there was some evidence of deceptive trade practice and issue was raised as to manufacturer's liability under Act. Town & Country Mobile Homes, Inc. v. Stiles (Civ.App.1976) 543 S.W.2d 664.

Evidence in action by buyers of mobile home against manufacturer, claiming damages for breach of this section, was insufficient to support jury's finding on damages. Id.

Evidence, in buyer's action alleging car dealer had violated this Subchapter by breaching express new car warranty, supported jury verdict in favor of buyer. Volkswagen of America, Inc. v. Licht (Civ. App.1976) 544 S.W.2d 442.

Evidence, in buyer's action against dealer, et al., for violation of this Subchapter, arising out of alleged breach of express new car warranty, including witness' unobjected to testimony that it was the dashpot in the carburetor which caused the fire in buyer's engine, was sufficient to support jury finding that fire was caused by a manufacturing defect in material or workmanship. Id.

Evidence, in buyer's action under this Subchapter for damages arising from alleged breach of new car warranty, including counsel's testimony as to number of hours expended in preparation of case, and practicing attorney's testimony that he reviewed file of counsel and that in his opinion legal work performed was necessary, was sufficient to support jury award of attorney's fees for services rendered. Id.

Evidence that boat dealer represented to buyer that boat in question was a 1973 model boat built in 1973 when the boat was in fact a 1972 model built in 1972 sufficiently supported judgment for $4,300 in actual and $4,300 in double damages, in suit against the boat dealer under this chapter. Spradling v. Williams (Civ.App.1977) 553 S.W.2d 143.

3.5 Declaratory judgment

After granting judgment for automobile dealer and individual with respect to action initiated by buyer to recover damages for losses allegedly suffered due to fraudulent misrepresentations, trial court had no justiciable controversy before it and properly denied dealer's request for judgment declaring that this Chapter was in violation of constitutional rights of due process and freedom of speech and expression. Byrd v. Fard (Civ.App.1976) 539 S.W.2d 213.

3.6 Attorney fees

Where, although operator of wrecker service was entitled, in his suit against owner of pickup truck, to recover attorney's fees incurred in recovering towing fee and storage charges imposed after he towed truck to his premises at police request, he failed to adduce evidence as to how much of attorney's total time was devoted to that cause of action, as opposed to conducting defense of truck owner's suit for damages under this Subchapter court properly declined to award attorney's fees. Bray v. Curtis (Civ.App.1976) 544 S.W.2d 816.

3.8 Instructions

Any recovery for mental anguish in connection with sale of house having defective septic tank should have been limited to any mental anguish suffered as a direct and proximate result of the act, omission or conduct found to have caused it and the jury, which was given special issue phrased in terms of mental anguish suffered as result of "the occurrence," should not have been left free to speculate as to possible causes and elements of damage; form of the issue was improper and it should not have been submitted. Littleton v. Woods (Civ.App.1976) 538 S.W.2d 800, affirmed 554 S.W.2d 662.

In action under this chapter wherein it was alleged that the defendant boat dealer had represented to plaintiff that a 1972 model boat which was built in 1972 was in fact a 1973 model boat built in 1973, it was error for the trial court to instruct the jury that five specific actions, among which were "representing the boat sold to be a 1973 model boat if it was an older boat" and "representing that the boat sold was built in 1973 if it was built in any year prior to 1973," were instances of "false, misleading, or deceptive acts or practices" within the meaning of this chapter; however, because each of the five acts enumerated was in fact an instance of deceptive trade practices as enumerated by this chapter and because a liberal construction of this chapter was required, the error was harmless. Spradling v. Williams (Civ. App.1977) 553 S.W.2d 143.

In action under this chapter, trial court did not improperly comment on the weight of the evidence by instructing the jury that the term "deceptive trade practice" means an act or a series of acts which has the capacity or tendency to deceive an average or ordinary person, even though that person may have been ignorant, unthinking or credulous. Id.

4. Review

Where purchaser, although not entitled to recover damages for breach of contract or to judgment rescinding sale of property in question in suit against vendors for alleged violations of Deceptive Trade Practices Act (§ 17.41 et seq.) which act was not applicable to such suit, tried her case on wrong theory and, under facts that might be proved if she pleaded and tried her case upon other theories, might be able to justly prevail, judgment awarding purchaser recovery against vendors was reversed and case remanded. Cape Conroe Ltd. v. Specht (Civ.App.1975) 525 S.W.2d 215.

Seller and servicer of recreational vehicles could not complain on appeal from adverse judgment in action brought against it under provisions of this Subchapter, that judgment had been entered that defendant violated provision of subd. (b)(5) of this section, relating to representations as to sponsorship, approval, or characteristics of goods or services while plaintiff's petition pleaded violation of subd. (b)(3) of this section relating to causing confusion or misunderstanding as to person's affiliation, connection, or association with another, where plaintiff pleaded only that defendant violated this section, and where defendant did not specially except to plaintiff's trial petition in effort to require him to set out with more particularity those sections which he claimed were violated. Mallory v. Custer (Civ.App.1976) 537 S.W.2d 141.

§ 17.47. Restraining Orders

(a) Whenever the consumer protection division has reason to believe that any person is engaging in, has engaged in, or is about to engage in any act or practice declared to be unlawful by this subchapter, and that proceedings would be in the public interest, the division may bring an action in the name of the state against the person to restrain by temporary restraining order, temporary injunction, or permanent injunction the use of such method, act, or practice. The consumer protection division may bring any action under this section against a licensed insurer or insurance agent for a violation of this subchapter, Article 21.21, Texas Insurance Code, as amended, or the rules and regulations of the State Board of Insurance issued under Article 21.21, Texas Insurance Code, as amended, only on the written request of the State Board of Insurance or the commissioner of insurance.

Nothing herein shall require the consumer protection division to notify such person that court action is or may be under consideration. Provided, however, the consumer protection division shall, at least seven days prior to instituting such court action, contact such person to inform him in general of the alleged unlawful conduct. Cessation of unlawful conduct after such prior contact shall not render such court action moot under any circumstances, and such injunctive relief shall lie even if such person has ceased such unlawful conduct after such prior contact. Such prior contact shall not be required if, in the opinion of the consumer protection division, there is good cause to believe that such person would evade service of process if prior contact were made or that such person would destroy relevant records if prior contact were made.

(b) An action brought under Subsection (a) of this section which alleges a claim to relief under this section may be commenced in the district court of the county in which the person against whom it is brought resides, has his principal place of business, has done business, or in the district court of the county where the transaction occurred, or, on the consent of the parties, in a district court of Travis County. The court may issue temporary restraining orders, temporary or permanent injunctions to restrain and prevent violations of this subchapter and such injunctive relief shall be issued without bond.

(c) In addition to the request for a temporary restraining order, or permanent injunction in a proceeding brought under Subsection (a) of this section, the consumer protection division may request a civil penalty of not more than $2,000 per violation, not to exceed a total of $10,000, to be paid to the state.

(d) The court may make such additional orders or judgments as are necessary to compensate identifiable persons for actual damages or to restore money or property, real or personal, which may have been acquired by means of any unlawful act or practice. Damages may not include any damages incurred beyond a point two years prior to the institution of the action by the consumer protection division. Orders of the court may also include the appointment of a receiver or a sequestration of assets if a person who has been ordered by a court to make restitution under this section has failed to do so within three months after the order to make restitution has become final and nonappealable.

(e) Any person who violates the terms of an injunction under this section shall forfeit and pay to the state a civil penalty of not more than $10,000 per violation, not to exceed $50,000. In determining whether or not an injunction has been violated the court shall take into consideration the maintenance of procedures reasonably adapted to insure compliance with the injunction. For the purposes of this section, the district court issuing the injunction shall retain jurisdiction, and the cause shall be continued, and in these cases, the consumer protection division, or the district or county attorney with prior notice to the consumer protection division, acting in the name of the state, may petition for recovery of civil penalties under this section.

(f) An order of the court awarding civil penalties under Subsection (e) of this section applies only to violations of the injunction incurred prior to the awarding of the penalty order. Second or subsequent violations of an injunction issued under this section are subject to the same penalties set out in Subsection (e) of this section.

Added by Acts 1973, 63rd Leg., p. 322, ch. 143, § 1, eff. May 21, 1973. Amended by Acts 1977, 65th Leg., p. 602, ch. 216, § 4, eff. May 23, 1977.

1977 Amendment. Subsection (a): In first sentence, inserted "temporary restraining order," and "injunction,".

Subsection (b): In first sentence, inserted "which alleges a claim to relief under this section" and substituted "has done" for "is doing"; in second sentence, inserted "temporary restraining orders," and substituted "such injunctive relief" for "the injunctions".

Subsection (c): Inserted "restraining order," and deleted ", on a finding by the court that the defendant has engaged or is engaging in a practice declared to be unlawful by this subchapter," after "consumer protection division".

Subsection (d): In first sentence, substituted "to restore" for "restoration of", inserted "unlawful" and deleted "restrained" from end thereof.

Derivation:

Acts 1967, 60th Leg., p. 658, ch. 274, § 2.
Acts 1969, 61st Leg., p. 1504, ch. 452, § 1.
Acts 1971, 62nd Leg., p. 2380, ch. 739, § 2.
Vernon's Ann.Civ.St. art. 5069—10.04.

Cross References

Civil investigative demand, applicability to insurers requesting action under this section, see § 17.61(a).

Promotional material, damages or penalties for suit filed under this section, third party action, see § 17.55.

Reports and examinations, applicability to insurers requesting action under this section, see § 17.60.

Index to Notes

In general 1
Evidence 3
Parties 2

1. In general

Where either party, to suit in which Attorney General sought to temporarily enjoin corporation from conducting pyramid sales scheme, could have insisted upon hearing on the merits, and where the corporation would be able at trial on the merits to present all defenses deemed available to prevent State from enforcing Vernon's Ann.Civ.St. art. 5069—10.01 et seq. (repealed) against the corporation's particular business practices without necessity of separate suit or cross action amounting to another suit, effect of temporary injunction was not permanent so as to entitle corporation to supersedeas bond staying effectiveness of the injunction during appeal. Wesware, Inc. v. Blackwell (Civ.App.1972) 486 S.W.2d 599.

Temporary injunction order which was entered in proceeding against alleged operator of pyramid-selling scheme for alleged violation of State Deceptive Trade Practices Act which sufficiently stated the acts prohibited and did not describe them by reference to the petition and which did not go beyond scope of the Act or destroy the status quo complied with requirements of Vernon's Ann.Rules Civ.Proc., rule 683, relating to form and scope of an injunction. Wesware, Inc. v. State (Civ.App.1972) 488 S.W.2d 844.

There was no requirement that prohibitory language of an injunction under the State Deceptive Trade Practices Act had to track any of statutory language of the Act. Id.

Where credit bureau consented to injunction whereby it was restrained from alleged deceptive trade practices, it was immaterial whether its conduct violated Deceptive Trade Practices Act [Vernon's Ann.Civ.St. arts. 5069—10.01 to 5069—10.08 (repealed; see, now, § 17.41 et seq.)] Credit Bureau of Laredo, Inc. v. State (Civ.App.1974) 515 S.W.2d 706, affirmed 530 S.W.2d 288.

Under Deceptive Trade Practices-Consumer Protection Act (this Subchapter), State's right to seek restitution on behalf of identifiable persons was not limited to seeking restitution on behalf of consumers. Bourland v. State (Civ.App.1975) 528 S.W. 2d 350, ref. n. r. e.

2. Parties

Where, at time of filing of suit for injunction for deceptive trade practices against credit bureau and its manager, credit bureau had different corporate name than that stated in complaint, but credit bureau soon thereafter changed its name to that stated in complaint and attorney for credit bureau and manager agreed to judgment against them, the credit bureau participated in injunction proceeding as a real party and was bound by the injunction. Credit Bureau of Laredo, Inc. v. State (Civ. App.1974) 515 S.W.2d 706, affirmed 530 S. W.2d 288.

3. Evidence

Evidence was sufficient to sustain finding that chain-referral or pyramid-selling scheme was in violation of State Deceptive Trade Practices Act and was as such subject to being temporarily enjoined, notwithstanding contention that since the scheme was fully explained there was no deception as to its nature or as to likelihood of market saturation and that the only element of chance involved was that common to any business venture depending on sales of goods. Wesware, Inc. v. State (Civ.App.1972) 488 S.W.2d 844.

In action for civil penalties against credit bureau for alleged violation of injunction prohibiting distribution to debtors of forms which had the appearance of being official documents, evidence that, following injunction order, credit bureau employed attorney, knowledgeable in field of law relating to creditors, to revise such forms and that attorney consulted with Assistant Attorney General regarding the revisions was admissible to show credit bureau's good faith. Credit Bureau of Laredo, Inc. v. State (Civ.App.1974) 515 S.W.2d 706, affirmed 530 S.W.2d 288.

§ 17.48. Duty of District and County Attorney

(a) It is the duty of the district and county attorneys to lend to the consumer protection division any assistance requested in the commencement and prosecutions of action under this subchapter.

(b) A district or county attorney, with prior written notice to the consumer protection division, may institute and prosecute actions seeking injunctive relief under this subchapter, after complying with the prior contact provisions of Subsection (a) of Section 17.47 of this subchapter. On request, the consumer protection division shall assist the district or county attorney in any action taken under this subchapter. If an action is prosecuted by a district or county attorney alone, he shall make a full report to the consumer protection division including the final disposition of the matter. No district or county attorney may bring an action under this section against any licensed insurer or licensed insurance agent transacting business under the authority and jurisdiction of the State Board of Insurance unless first requested in writing to do so by the State Board of Insurance, the commissioner of insurance, or the consumer protection division pursuant to a request by the State Board of Insurance or commissioner of insurance.

Added by Acts 1973, 63rd Leg., p. 322, ch. 143, § 1, eff. May 21, 1973.

Cross References

Promotional material, damages or penalties for suit filed under this section, third party action, see § 17.55.

§ 17.49. Exemptions

(a) Nothing in this subchapter shall apply to the owner or employees of a regularly published newspaper, magazine, or telephone directory, or broadcast station, or billboard, wherein any advertisement in violation of this subchapter is published or disseminated, unless it is established that the owner or employees of the advertising medium have knowledge of the false, deceptive, or misleading acts or practices declared to be unlawful by this subchapter, or had a direct or substantial financial interest in the sale or distribution of the unlawfully advertised good or service. Financial interest as used in this section relates to an expectation which would be the direct result of such advertisement.

(b) Nothing in this subchapter shall apply to acts or practices authorized under specific rules or regulations promulgated by the Federal Trade Commission under Section 5(a)(1) of the Federal Trade Commission Act [15 U.S.C.A. 45(a)(1)]. The provisions of this subchapter do apply to any act or practice prohibited or not specifically authorized by a rule or regulation of the Federal Trade Commission. An act or practice is not specifically authorized if no rule or regulation has been issued on the act or practice.

Added by Acts 1973, 63rd Leg., p. 322, ch. 143, § 1, eff. May 21, 1973.

Derivation:

Acts 1967, 60th Leg., p. 658, ch. 274, § 2.
Acts 1969, 61st Leg., p. 1504, ch. 452, § 1.
Vernon's Ann.Civ.St. art. 5069—10.03.

§ 17.50. Relief for Consumers

(a) A consumer may maintain an action if he has been adversely affected by any of the following:

(1) the use or employment by any person of an act or practice declared to be unlawful by Section 17.46 of this subchapter;

(2) breach of an express or implied warranty;

(3) any unconscionable action or course of action by any person; or

(4) the use or employment by any person of an act or practice in violation of Article 21.21, Texas Insurance Code, as amended, or rules or regulations issued by the State Board of Insurance under Article 21.21, Texas Insurance Code, as amended.

(b) In a suit filed under this section, each consumer who prevails may obtain:

(1) three times the amount of actual damages plus court costs and attorneys' fees reasonable in relation to the amount of work expended;

(2) an order enjoining such acts or failure to act;

(3) orders necessary to restore to any party to the suit any money or property, real or personal, which may have been acquired in violation of this subchapter; and

(4) any other relief which the court deems proper, including the appointment of a receiver or the revocation of a license or certificate authorizing a person to engage in business in this state if the judgment has not been satisfied within three months of the date of the final judgment. The court may not revoke or suspend a license to do business in this state or appoint a receiver to take over the affairs of a person who has failed to satisfy a judgment if the person is a licensee of or regulated by a state agency which has statutory authority to revoke or suspend a license or to appoint a receiver or trustee.

(c) On a finding by the court that an action under this section was groundless and brought in bad faith or for the purpose of harassment,

the court may award to the defendant reasonable attorneys' fees in relation to the amount of work expended, and court costs.

Added by Acts 1973, 63rd Leg., p. 322, ch. 143, § 1, eff. May 21, 1973. Amended by Acts 1977, 65th Leg., p. 603, ch. 216, § 5, eff. May 23, 1977.

1977 Amendment. In subd. (a)(2), substituted "breach of" for "a failure by any person to comply with".

Cross References

Damages and defenses under this section, see § 17.50A.

Promotional material, damages or penalties for suit filed under this section, third party action, see § 17.55.

Venue of actions under this section, see § 17.56.

Law Review Commentaries

A remedy for undermade and oversold products—Texas Deceptive Trade Practices Act. Michael P. Lynn, 7 St. Mary's L.J. 698 (1976).

Emergence of consumer credit protection —Federal and Texas. 8 St. Mary's L.J. 794 (1977).

Preservation of claims and defenses under Texas Business and Commerce Code and under Texas Consumer Credit Code. James G. Boyle, 8 St. Mary's L.J. 679 (1977).

Public and private rights and remedies under Deceptive Trade Practices—Consumer Protection Act. Philip K. Maxwell, 8 St. Mary's L.J. 617 (1977).

Statutory attorney fees in Texas. Ralph H. Brock, 40 Texas Bar J. 139 (1977).

Texas Deceptive Trade Practices—Consumer Protection Act: Application to professional malpractice. 8 St. Mary's L.J. 763 (1977).

Index to Notes

In general 1
Evidence 3
Venue 2

---

1. In general

Legislative classifications of individual actions (this section) and class actions (§ 17.51), including provision that "bona fide error" defense is available in class action suit but not in individual consumer suit (§ 17.54), reasonably promote proper object of public welfare or interest, rest upon real and substantial differences, with reasonable relation to subject of legislation and affect all persons in each classification in same manner, and thus denying automobile dealer defense of bona fide error in suit brought by individual consumer was not in contravention of dealer's right to due process of law. Crawford Chevrolet, Inc. v. McLarty (Civ.App.1975) 519 S.W.2d 656.

In suit by consumer against automobile dealer under Deceptive Trade Practices Act, dealer, who failed to specifically plead setoff by way of counterclaim for affirmative relief for alleged "extra equipment" on vehicle when delivered to consumer, was not in position to avail himself of such claim for setoff. Id.

In action by consumer against automobile dealer under Deceptive Trade Practices Act, court's use of term "contract" when referring to alleged agreement between dealer and consumer for purchase of vehicle for price of $4,000 did not result in rendition of improper judgment where such usage was retracted and special jury issue inquired as to whether "agreement" for purchase price of $4,000 was entered into, not whether "contract" had been entered into. Id.

Purchaser, who brought suit as purchaser of realty, not goods or services, was not "consumer" within purview of Section 17.45 and thus could not bring action against vendors, limited partner of vendor and trustee in deed of trust securing purchase money notes under this section for alleged violations of such section. Cape Conroe Ltd. v. Specht (Civ.App.1975) 525 S.W.2d 215.

Under Deceptive Trade Practices-Consumer Protection Act (this Subchapter), State's right to seek restitution on behalf of identifiable persons was not limited to seeking restitution on behalf of consumers. Bourland v. State (Civ.App.1975) 528 S.W. 2d 350, ref. n. r. e.

Subdivision (b)(1) of this section does not require that prevailing consumer have judgment for treble damages, but merely permits entry of judgment for treble damages to prevailing consumer. Mallory v. Custer (Civ.App.1976) 537 S.W.2d 141.

Court of Civil Appeals would not disturb judgment of county court awarding treble damages to prevailing consumer in his action under this Subchapter since such judgment was allowed by subd. (b)(1) of this section. Id.

General rule requiring plaintiff to plead and prove cause of action to support venue applied to action for damages and attorney's fees under the Deceptive Trade Practices and Consumer Protection Act. Doyle v. Grady (Civ.App.1976) 543 S.W.2d 893.

Where there was no finding of negligence upon part of automobile dealer or importer in cause of action arising under this Subchapter claiming failure to comply with a warranty on a new car, right of indemnity in favor of dealer over and against importer did not exist. Volkswagen of America, Inc. v. Licht (Civ.App.1976) 544 S.W.2d 442.

Subdivision (b)(1) of this section authorizes payment of attorney's fees on appeal. Id.

Where suit for damages under this chapter was not groundless or brought for purpose of harassment, defendant was not entitled to recover attorney's fees for defense of such claim. Bray v. Curtis (Civ. App.1976) 544 S.W.2d 816.

In respect to plaintiffs' "unfair settlement practices" theory of relief against insurance company, predicated on claim that the insurer engaged in false, misleading or deceptive acts or practices in violation of § 17.46 by, inter alia, representing that plaintiffs had unlimited use of a rental car with respect to time and mileage until the insurer obtained a replacement vehicle for them, plaintiffs did not purchase or lease the rental car and therefore were not "consumers" within definition in § 17.45(4) and thus had no cause of action under subsec. (b) of this section. Russell v. Hartford Cas. Ins. Co. (Civ.App.1977) 548 S.W.2d 737, ref. n. r. e.

Award of treble damages is mandatory in suit under this section, treble damages therefore should have been awarded in suit under this section to recover damages for collapse of wrecker bed and boom built for plaintiff by defendant. McDaniel v. Dulworth (Civ.App.1977) 550 S.W.2d 395.

Appellant, only defendant found to have committed deceptive trade practice charged, could not complain of judgment finding him jointly and severally liable with codefendant. Yorfino v. Ferguson (Civ.App.1977) 552 S.W.2d 563.

Word "may" in this section pertaining to relief for consumers which provides that each consumer who prevails in a suit filed under the section "may" obtain treble damages does not express an intent that treble damages are mandatory but rather that the trier of facts "may" award damages up to but not above three times the amount of actual damages, depending on the evidence in each case. Spradling v. Williams (Civ.App.1977) 553 S.W.2d 143.

This subchapter did not permit award of treble damages and attorney's fees to a merchant. Trial v. McCoy (Civ.App.1977) 553 S.W.2d 199.

In action by buyer of antique pistol against seller for treble damages and attorney's fees under this subchapter, issue of material fact existed as to whether buyer was a merchant and was thus precluded from award of treble damages and attorney's fees, precluding summary judgment. Id.

Purchaser, proving deceptive trade practice, has many remedies available against the seller; he can secure an injunction, restoration of money, property, or any other relief which court deems proper, including appointment of receiver or revocation of seller's license to engage in business and he can obtain three times the actual damages, plus attorneys' fees and costs. Cordrey v. Armstrong (Civ.App.1977) 553 S.W. 2d 798.

Under this subchapter, consumer must prevail in his suit in order to obtain attorneys' fees and court costs and consumer plaintiffs must obtain some other relief in order to be considered as prevailing. Id.

Where jury found that construction company failed to install swimming pool in good and workmanlike manner and that this failure was producing cause of damage, trebling of actual damages for breach of warranty of good workmanship was mandatory under this subchapter. Boman v. Woodmansee (Civ.App.1977) 554 S.W.2d 33.

Under this subchapter, trial court does not have discretion to determine whether or not to enter judgment for three times amount of actual damages for breach of warranty of good workmanship. Id.

Absent proof showing that alleged false representation was made after effective date of this subchapter, plaintiff failed to show applicability of this subchapter and, hence, failed to establish cause of action under this subchapter. Burrows v. Texas Kenworth Co. (Civ.App.1977) 554 S.W.2d 300.

2. Venue

In view of fact that provision of Vernon's Ann.Civ.St. art. 2390 for justice courts expressly authorized finance company to institute suit against consumer in distant forum, Vernon's Ann.Civ.St. art. 1995, subd. 5 had to be construed as constituting exception to general law found in this Subchapter and accordingly, consumer was not entitled to injunction restraining finance company from engaging in certain alleged defective trade practices based on its filing of suits against consumer in distant forum; nor was consumer entitled to injunctive relief against distant forum suits which might be filed against him in county or district courts. Vargas v. Allied Finance Co. (Civ.App.1976) 545 S.W.2d 231, ref. n. r. e.

3. Evidence

Evidence, in buyer's action alleging car dealer had violated this Subchapter by breaching express new car warranty, supported jury verdict in favor of buyer. Volkswagen of America, Inc. v. Licht (Civ. App.1976) 544 S.W.2d 442.

Evidence, in buyer's action under this Subchapter for damages arising from alleged breach of new car warranty, including counsel's testimony as to number of hours expended in preparation of case, and practicing attorney's testimony that he reviewed file of counsel and that in his opinion legal work performed was necessary, was sufficient to support jury award of attorney's fees for services rendered. Id.

Evidence, in buyer's action against dealer, et al., for violation of this Subchapter, arising out of alleged breach of express new car warranty, including witness' unobjected to testimony that it was the dashpot in the carburetor which caused the fire in buyer's engine, was sufficient to support jury finding that fire was caused by a manufacturing defect in material or workmanship. Id.

§ 17.50A. Damages: Defenses

In an action brought under Section 17.50 of this subchapter, actual damages only and attorney's fees reasonable in relation to the amount of work expended and court costs may be awarded where the defendant:

(1) proves that the action complained of resulted from a bona fide error notwithstanding the use of reasonable procedures adopted to avoid the error; or

(2) proves that he had no written notice of the consumer's complaint before suit was filed, or that within 30 days after he was given written notice he tendered to the consumer (a) the cash value of the consideration received from the consumer or the cash value of the benefit promised, whichever is greater, and (b) the expenses, including attorney's fees, if any, reasonably incurred by the consumer in asserting his claim against the defendant; or

(3) in the case of a suit under Section 17.50(a)(2) the defendant proves that he was not given a reasonable opportunity to cure the defects or malfunctions before suit was filed.

Added by Acts 1977, 65th Leg., p. 604, ch. 216, § 6, eff. May 23, 1977.

Library References

Trade Regulation ⚷864.
C.J.S. Trade-Marks, Trade-Names and Unfair Competition § 237.

§ 17.51. Repealed by Acts 1977, 65th Leg., p. 605, ch. 216, § 10, eff. May 23, 1977

The repealed section, added by Acts 1973, 63rd Leg., p. 322, ch. 143, § 1, provided:

"§ 17.51. **Class Actions**

"(a) If a consumer has been damaged in an amount in excess of $10 by an unlawful method, act, or practice contained in Subsection (b) of Section 17.46 of this subchapter, an act or practice in violation of Article 21.21, Texas Insurance Code, as amended, or rules or regulations issued by the State Board of Insurance under Article 21.21, Texas Insurance Code, as amended, or by an act or practice or type of act or practice occurring subsequent to the time the act or practice or type of act or practice was declared unlawful or deceptive to the consumer by a final judgment of an appellate court of proper jurisdiction and venue of this state that was reported officially, a consumer may bring an action on behalf of himself and other consumers if the unlawful act or practice has caused damage to the other consumers who are similarly situated, to recover damages and relief as provided in this subchapter.

"(b) A plaintiff who prevails in a class action under this subchapter may recover:

"(1) court costs and attorneys' fees reasonable in relation to the amount of work expended in addition to actual damages;

"(2) an order enjoining the act or failure to act;

"(3) any orders which may be necessary to restore to any party to the suit any money or property, real or personal, which may have been acquired in violation of this subchapter; and

"(4) any other relief which the court deems proper including the appointment of a receiver or revocation of a license or certificate to engage in business in this state if the judgment has not been satisfied within six months of the date of issuance of the final judgment. The court may not revoke or suspend a license to do business in this state or appoint a receiver to take over the affairs of a person who has failed to satisfy a judgment if the person is a licensee of or regulated by a state agency which has statutory authority to revoke or suspend a license or to appoint a receiver or trustee.

"(c) On a finding by the court that an action under this section was brought in bad faith or for purposes of harassment, the court may award to the defendant reasonable attorneys' fees in relation to the work expended, and court costs.

"(d) An action under this section may not be maintained or shall be stayed if proceedings regarding an administrative class action under Section 14, Article 21.21, Texas Insurance Code, as amended, have been initiated regarding the same acts or practices and the same defendant in the action under this section."

§ 17.52. Repealed by Acts 1977, 65th Leg., p. 605, ch. 216, § 11, eff. May 23, 1977

The repealed section, added by Acts 1973, 63rd Leg., p. 322, ch. 143, § 1, provided:

"§ 17.52. **Class Action: Procedure**

"(a) The court shall permit one or more members of a class to sue or be sued as representative parties on behalf of the class only if:

"(1) the class is so numerous that joinder of all members is impracticable;

"(2) there are questions of law or fact common to the class;

"(3) the claims or defenses of the representative parties are typical of the claims or defenses of the class; and

"(4) the representative parties will fairly and adequately protect the interests of the class.

"(b) An action may be maintained as a class action if the prerequisites of Subsection (a) of this section are satisfied and in addition:

"(1) the prosecution of separate actions by or against individual members of the class would create a risk of:

"(A) inconsistent or varying adjudications with respect to individual members of the class which would establish incompatible standards of conduct for the party opposing the class; or

"(B) adjudications with respect to individual members of the class which would as a practical matter be dispositive of the interests of the other members not parties to the adjudications or substantially impair or impede their ability to protect their interests; or

"(2) the party opposing the class has acted or refused to act on grounds generally applicable to the class, thereby making appropriate final injunctive relief or corresponding declaratory relief with respect to the class as a whole; or

"(3) the court finds that the questions of law or fact common to the members of the class predominate over any questions affecting only individual members, and that a class action is superior to other available methods for the fair and efficient adjudication of the controversy. The matters pertinent to the findings include:

"(A) the interest of members of the class in individually controlling the prosecution or defense of separate actions;

"(B) the extent and nature of any litigation concerning the controversy already commenced by or against members of the class;

"(C) the desirability or undesirability of controversy concentrating the litigation of the claims in the particular forum; and

"(D) the difficulties likely to be encountered in the management of a class action.

"(c) In construing this section, the courts of Texas shall be guided by the decisions of the federal courts interpreting Rule 23, Federal Rules of Civil Procedure.

"(d) As soon as practicable after the commencement of an action brought as a class action, the court shall determine by order whether it is to be maintained as a class action. An order under this subsection may be altered or amended before a decision on the merits. An order determining that the action may or may not be brought as a class action is an interlocutory order which is appealable and the procedures provided in Rule 385, Texas Rules of Civil Procedure, apply.

"(e) If the action is permitted as a class action, the court shall direct to the members of the class the best notice practicable under the circumstances, including individual notice to all members who can be identified through reasonable effort.

"(f) The notice shall contain a statement that:

"(1) the court will exclude the member notified from the class if he so requests by a specified date;

"(2) the judgment, whether favorable or not, will include all members who do not request exclusion; and

"(3) any member who does not request exclusion, if he desires, may enter an appearance through counsel.

"(g) A class action may not be dismissed, settled, or compromised without the approval of the court, and notice of the proposed dismissal, settlement, or compromise shall be given to all members of the class in such manner as the court directs.

"(h) When appropriate, an action may be brought or maintained as a class action with respect to particular issues or a class may be divided into subclasses and each subclass treated as a class, and the provisions of this section shall be construed and applied accordingly.

"(i) The judgment in a class action shall describe those to whom the notice was directed and who have not requested exclusion and those the court finds to be members of the class. The court shall direct to the members of the class the best notice practicable under the circumstances, including individual notice to all members who can be identified through reasonable effort.

"(j) In the conduct of a class action the court may make appropriate orders:

"(1) determining the course of proceedings or prescribing measures to prevent undue repetition or complication in the presentation of evidence or argument;

"(2) requiring, for the protection of the members of the class or otherwise for the fair conduct of the action, that notice be given in such manner as the court may direct to some or all of the members or to the attorney general of any step in the action, or of the proposed extent of the judgment, or of the opportunity of members to signify whether they consider the representation fair and adequate, to intervene and present claims or defenses, or otherwise to come into the action;

"(3) imposing conditions on the representative parties or on intervenors;

"(4) requiring that the pleadings be amended to eliminate allegations as to representation of absent persons, and that the action proceed accordingly; or

"(5) dealing with similar procedural matters.

"(k) The filing of a suit under this section tolls the statute of limitations for bringing a suit by an individual under Section 17.50 of this subchapter. An order of the court denying the bringing of a suit as a class action does not affect the ability of an individual to bring the same or a similar suit under Section 17.50 of this subchapter."

§ 17.53. Repealed by Acts 1977, 65th Leg., p. 605, ch. 216, § 12, eff. May 23, 1977

The repealed section, added by Acts 1973, 63rd Leg., p. 322, ch. 143, § 1, provided:

"§ 17.53. **Preliminary Notice**

"(a) At least 30 days prior to the commencement of a suit for damages under Section 17.51 of this subchapter, the consumer must notify the intended defendant of his complaint and make demand that the defendant provide relief to the consumer and others similarly situated.

"(b) The notice must be in writing and sent by certified or registered mail, return receipt requested, to the place where the transaction occurred, the intended defendants' principal place of business in this state, or if neither will effect notice, to the office of the Secretary of State of Texas.

"(c) An action for injunctive relief under Section 17.51 of this subchapter may be commenced without compliance with Subsection (a) of this section. Not less than 30 days after the commencement of an action for injunctive relief, and after compliance with the provisions of Subsection (a) of this section, the consumer may amend his complaint without leave of court to include a request for damages.

"(d) No damages may be awarded to a consumer class under this section if within 30 days of receipt of the notice the intended defendant furnished the consumer, by certified or registered mail, return receipt requested, a written offer of settlement. The offer of settlement must include a statement that:

"(1) all consumers similarly situated have been adequately identified or a reasonable effort to identify such other consumers has been made, and a description of the class so identified and the method employed to identify them;

"(2) all consumers so identified have been notified that upon their request the intended defendant will provide relief to the consumer and all others similarly situated, and a complete explanation of the relief being afforded and a copy of the notice or communication which the intended defendant is providing to the members of the class;

"(3) the relief being afforded the consumer has been, or if said offer is accepted by the consumer, will be given within a stated reasonable period of time; and

"(4) the practice complained of has ceased.

"(e) Attempts to comply with the provisions of this section by a person receiving a demand shall be an offer to compromise and shall be inadmissible as evidence. Attempts to comply with a demand shall not be considered an admission of engaging in an unlawful act or practice. Evidence of compliance or attempts to comply with the provisions of this section may be introduced by a defendant for the purpose of establishing good faith or to show compliance with the provisions of this section."

§ 17.54. Repealed by Acts 1977, 65th Leg., p. 605, ch. 216, § 13, eff. May 23, 1977

The repealed section, added by Acts 1973, 63rd Leg., p. 322, ch. 143, § 1, as amended by Acts 1975, 64th Leg., p. 149, ch. 62, § 2, provided:

"§ 17.54. **Damages: Defense**

"No award of damages may be given in any action filed under Section 17.51 of this subchapter if the defendant:

"(1) proves that the action complained of resulted from a bona fide error notwithstanding the use of reasonable procedures adopted to avoid the error; and

"(2) made restitution of all consideration received from all members of the class, as the court may determine and direct."

See, now, § 17.50A.

§ 17.55. Promotional Material

If damages or civil penalties are assessed against the seller of goods or services for advertisements or promotional material in a suit filed under Section 17.47, 17.48, 17.50, or 17.51 of this subchapter, the seller of the goods or services has a cause of action against a third party for the amount of damages or civil penalties assessed against the seller plus attorneys' fees on a showing that:

(1) the seller received the advertisements or promotional material from the third party;

(2) the seller's only action with regard to the advertisements or promotional material was to disseminate the material; and

(3) the seller has ceased disseminating the material.

Added by Acts 1973, 63rd Leg., p. 322, ch. 143, § 1, eff. May 21, 1973.

§ 17.55A. Indemnity

A person against whom an action has been brought under this subchapter may seek contribution or indemnity from one who, under the statute law or at common law, may have liability for the damaging event of which the consumer complains. A person seeking indemnity as provided by this section may recover all sums that he is required to pay as a result of the action, his attorney's fees reasonable in relation to the amount of work performed in maintaining his action for indemnity, and his costs.

Added by Acts 1977, 65th Leg., p. 604, ch. 216, § 7, eff. May 23, 1977.

§ 17.56. Venue

An action brought which alleges a claim to relief under Section 17.50 of this subchapter may be commenced in the county in which the person against whom the suit is brought resides, has his principal place of business, or has done business.

Added by Acts 1973, 63rd Leg., p. 322, ch. 143, § 1, eff. May 21, 1973. Amended by Acts 1977, 65th Leg., p. 604, ch. 216, § 8, eff. May 23, 1977.

1977 Amendment. Inserted "which alleges a claim to relief", deleted "or 17.51" after "Section 17.50", and substituted "has done" for "is doing."

Cross References

Consumer transactions, venue, see Vernon's Ann.Civ.St. art. 1995, subd. 5(b).

Warranty breach by manufacturer, venue, see Vernon's Ann.Civ.St. art. 1995, subd. 31.

1. In general

In view of evidence that mobile home was sold more than six weeks before it was delivered to site where it was installed and in the absence of evidence as to where the home was stored in the interim and who had access to it, testimony of purchaser, who acknowledged that he was unfamiliar with gas system, was insufficient to support conclusion that there was a defect in the gas system at the time that the mobile home was sold or left the manufacturer's control so that manufacturer's plea of privilege with respect to products liability and negligence action brought against it by the purchaser following explosion should have been sustained. Sundowner Mfg. Co. v. Kinman (Civ.App.1976) 536 S.W.2d 642.

In suit brought under the Deceptive Trade Practices and Consumer Protection Act in Fannin County against pickup truck insurer, Dallas County resident, whose agent referred plaintiff truck owner to adjuster who told plaintiff that necessary repairs to truck could be made by defendant Hunt County resident, wherein defendants filed pleas of privilege, plaintiff failed to demonstrate that faulty or incomplete repair of his truck had been result of deceptive business practices or unconscionable actions covered by the Consumer Protection Act. Doyle v. Grady (Civ.App.1976) 543 S.W.2d 893.

In view of fact that provision of Vernon's Ann.Civ.St. art. 2390 for justice courts expressly authorized finance company to institute suit against consumer in distant forum, Vernon's Ann.Civ.St. art. 1995 subd. 5 had to be construed as constituting exception to general law found in this Subchapter and accordingly, consumer was not entitled to injunction restraining finance company from engaging in certain alleged defective trade practices based on its filing of suits against consumer in distant forum; nor was consumer entitled to injunctive relief against distant forum suits which might be filed against him in county or district courts. Vargas v. Allied Finance Co. (Civ.App.1976) 545 S.W.2d 231, ref. n. r. e.

Under venue provision of this section, plaintiff must follow general rule and both plead and prove a cause of action to support venue. Hudson and Hudson Realtors v. Savage (Civ.App.1977) 545 S.W.2d 863.

§ 17.57. Subpoenas

The clerk of a district court at the request of any party to a suit pending in his court which is brought under this subchapter shall issue a subpoena for any witness or witnesses who may be represented to reside within 100 miles of the courthouse of the county in which the suit is pending or who may be found within such distance at the time of trial. The clerk shall issue a separate subpoena and a copy thereof for each witness subpoenaed. When an action is pending in Travis County on the consent of the parties a subpoena may be issued for any witness or witnesses who may be represented to reside within 100 miles of the courthouse of a county in which the suit could otherwise have been brought or who may be found within such distance at the time of the trial.
Added by Acts 1973, 63rd Leg., p. 322, ch. 143, § 1, eff. May 21, 1973.

§ 17.58. Voluntary Compliance

(a) In the administration of this subchapter the consumer protection division may accept assurance of voluntary compliance with respect to any act or practice which violates this subchapter from any person who is engaging in, has engaged in, or is about to engage in the act or practice. The assurance shall be in writing and shall be filed with and subject to the approval of the district court in the county in which the alleged violator resides or does business or in the district court of Travis County.

(b) The acceptance of an assurance of voluntary compliance may be conditioned on the stipulation that the person in violation of this subchapter restore to any person in interest any money or property, real or personal, which may have been acquired by means of acts or practices which violate this subchapter.

(c) An assurance of voluntary compliance shall not be considered an admission of prior violation of this subchapter. However, unless an assurance has been rescinded by agreement of the parties or voided by a court for good cause, subsequent failure to comply with the terms of an assurance is prima facie evidence of a violation of this subchapter.

(d) Matters closed by the filing of an assurance of voluntary compliance may be reopened at any time. Assurances of voluntary compliance shall in no way affect individual rights of action under this subchapter, except that the rights of individuals with regard to money or property received pursuant to a stipulation in the voluntary compliance under Subsection (b) of this section are governed by the terms of the voluntary compliance.
Added by Acts 1973, 63rd Leg., p. 322, ch. 143, § 1, eff. May 21, 1973.

Derivation:
Acts 1967, 60th Leg., p. 658, ch. 274, § 2.
Acts 1969, 61st Leg., p. 1504, ch. 452, § 1.
Acts 1971, 62nd Leg., p. 2380, ch. 739, § 2.
Vernon's Ann.Civ.St. art. 5069—10.05.

§ 17.59. Post Judgment Relief

(a) If a money judgment entered under this subchapter is unsatisfied 30 days after it becomes final and if the prevailing party has made a good faith attempt to obtain satisfaction of the judgment, the following presumptions exist with respect to the party against whom the judgment was entered:

(1) that the defendant is insolvent or in danger of becoming insolvent; and

(2) that the defendant's property is in danger of being lost, removed, or otherwise exempted from collection on the judgment; and

(3) that the prevailing party will be materially injured unless a receiver is appointed over the defendant's business; and

(4) that there is no adequate remedy other than receivership available to the prevailing party.

(b) Subject to the provisions of Subsection (a) of this section, a prevailing party may move that the defendant show cause why a receiver should not be appointed. Upon adequate notice and hearing, the court shall appoint a receiver over the defendant's business unless the defendant proves that all of the presumptions set forth in Subsection (a) of this section are not applicable.

(c) The order appointing a receiver must clearly state whether the receiver will have general power to manage and operate the defendant's business or have power to manage only a defendant's finances. The order shall limit the duration of the receivership to such time as the judgment or judgments awarded under this subchapter are paid in full. Where there are judgments against a defendant which have been awarded to more than one plaintiff, the court shall have discretion to take any action necessary to efficiently operate a receivership in order to accomplish the purpose of collecting the judgments.

Added by Acts 1973, 63rd Leg., p. 322, ch. 143, § 1, eff. May 21, 1973. Amended by Acts 1977, 65th Leg., p. 604, ch. 216, § 9, eff. May 23, 1977.

1977 Amendment. Rewrote this section, which prior thereto read:

"**§ 17.59. Powers of Receiver**

"(a) When a receiver is appointed by the court under this subchapter, he shall have the power to sue for, collect, receive, and take into his possession all the goods and chattels, rights and credits, money, and effects, lands, tenements, books, records, documents, papers, choses in action, bills, notes, and property of every description, derived by means of any practice declared to be illegal and prohibited by this subchapter, including property with which such porperty has been mingled if it cannot be identified in kind because of the commingling, and to sell, convey, and assign the property and hold and dispose of the proceeds under the direction of the court. Any person who has suffered damages as a result of use or employment of any unlawful practices and submits proof to the satisfaction of the court that he has in fact been damaged, may participate with general creditors in the distribution of the assets to the extent he has sustained out-of-pocket losses. In the case of a partnership or business entity, the receiver shall settle the estate and distribute the assets under the direction of the court. The court shall have jurisdiction of all questions arising in the proceedings and may make any orders or judgments required.

"(b) If the claims of consumers remain unsatisfied after distribution of the assets, the court may order that all persons who knowingly participated in the unlawful enterprise be held jointly and severally liable to the extent of the unsatisfied consumer claims if such person:

"(1) contributed substantial personal services, money, credit, real, personal, or mixed property, or any other thing of substantial value with the expectation of sharing in the profits of the enterprise; and

"(2) had knowledge or should have had knowledge of the unlawful purpose of the enterprise at the time such things of value were contributed, or freely continued in the association or other relationship after gaining knowledge of the unlawful purpose of the enterprise."

Cross References

Receivers, appointment,

Generally, see Vernon's Ann.Civ.St. art. 2293 et seq.

Consumer credit and protection, see Vernon's Ann.Civ.St. art. 5069—2.03.

§ 17.60. Reports and Examinations

Whenever the consumer protection division has reason to believe that a person is engaging in, has engaged in, or is about to engage in any act or practice declared to be unlawful by this subchapter, or when it reasonably believes it to be in the public interest to conduct an investigation to ascertain whether any person is engaging in, has engaged in, or is about to engage in any such act or practice, an authorized member of the division may:

(1) require the person to file on the prescribed forms a statement or report in writing, under oath or otherwise, as to all the facts and cir-

cumstances concerning the alleged violation and such other data and information as the consumer protection division deems necessary;

(2) examine under oath any person in connection with this alleged violation;

(3) examine any merchandise or sample of merchandise deemed necessary and proper; and

(4) pursuant to an order of the appropriate court, impound any sample of merchandise that is produced in accordance with this subchapter and retain it in the possession of the division until the completion of all proceedings in connection with which the merchandise is produced.

This section shall not apply to licensed insurers or licensed insurance agents transacting an insurance business in this state under the authority and jurisdiction of the State Board of Insurance unless the State Board of Insurance or the Insurance Commissioner has requested in writing that the consumer protection division file an action under Section 17.47 of this subchapter.

Added by Acts 1973, 63rd Leg., p. 322, ch. 143, § 1, eff. May 21, 1973.

Derivation:
Acts 1967, 60th Leg., p. 658, ch. 274, § 2.
Acts 1971, 62nd Leg., p. 2380, ch. 739, § 2.
Vernon's Ann.Civ.St. art. 5069—10.06.

Cross References
Penalties for violation of this section, see § 17.62

§ 17.61. Civil Investigative Demand

(a) Whenever the consumer protection division believes that any person may be in possession, custody, or control of the original copy of any documentary material relevant to the subject matter of an investigation of a possible violation of this subchapter, an authorized agent of the division may execute in writing and serve on the person a civil investigative demand requiring the person to produce the documentary material and permit inspection and copying. This section shall not apply to licensed insurers or licensed insurance agents transacting an insurance business in this state under the authority and jurisdiction of the State Board of Insurance unless the State Board of Insurance or the Insurance Commissioner has requested in writing that the consumer protection division file an action under Section 17.47 of this subchapter.

(b) Each demand shall:

(1) state the statute and section under which the alleged violation is being investigated, and the general subject matter of the investigation;

(2) describe the class or classes of documentary material to be produced with reasonable specificity so as to fairly indicate the material demanded;

(3) prescribe a return date within which the documentary material is to be produced; and

(4) identify the members of the consumer protection division to whom the documentary material is to be made available for inspection and copying.

(c) A civil investigative demand may contain a requirement or disclosure of documentary material which would be discoverable under the Texas Rules of Civil Procedure.

(d) Service of any demand may be made by:

(1) delivering a duly executed copy of the demand to the person to be served or to a partner or to any officer or agent authorized by appointment or by law to receive service of process on behalf of that person;

(2) delivering a duly executed copy of the demand to the principal place of business in the state of the person to be served;

(3) mailing by registered mail or certified mail a duly executed copy of the demand addressed to the person to be served at the principal place of business in this state, or if the person has no place of business in this state, to his principal office or place of business.

(e) Documentary material demanded pursuant to this section shall be produced for inspection and copying during normal business hours at the principal office or place of business of the person served, or at other times and places as may be agreed on by the person served and the consumer protection division.

(f) No documentary material produced pursuant to a demand under this section, unless otherwise ordered by a court for good cause shown, shall be produced for inspection or copying by, nor shall its contents be disclosed to any person other than the authorized employee of the consumer protection division without the consent of the person who produced the material. The consumer protection division shall prescribe reasonable terms and conditions allowing the documentary material to be available for inspection and copying by the person who produced the material or any duly authorized representative of that person. The consumer protection division may use the documentary material or copies of it as it determines necessary in the enforcement of this subchapter, including presentation before any court. Any material which contains trade secrets shall not be presented except with the approval of the court in which the action is pending after adequate notice to the person furnishing the material.

(g) At any time before the return date specified in the demand, or within 20 days after the demand has been served, whichever period is shorter, a petition to extend the return date for, or to modify or set aside the demand, stating good cause, may be filed in the district court in the county where the parties reside, or a district court of Travis County.

(h) A person on whom a demand is served under this section shall comply with the terms of the demand unless otherwise provided by a court order.

(i) Personal service of a similar investigative demand under this section may be made on any person outside of this state if the person has engaged in conduct in violation of this subchapter. Such persons shall be deemed to have submitted themselves to the jurisdiction of this state within the meaning of this section.

Added by Acts 1973, 63rd Leg., p. 322, ch. 143, § 1, eff. May 21, 1973.

Derivation:
Acts 1969, 61st Leg., p. 1504, ch. 452, § 1.
Acts 1971, 62nd Leg., p. 2381, ch. 739, § 2.
Vernon's Ann.Civ.St. art. 5069—10.07.

Cross References
Penalties for violation of this section, see § 17.62.

§ 17.62. Penalties

(a) Any person who, with intent to avoid, evade, or prevent compliance, in whole or in part, with Section 17.60 or 17.61 of this subchapter, removes from any place, conceals, withholds, or destroys, mutilates, alters, or by any other means falsifies any documentary material or merchandise or sample of merchandise is guilty of a misdemeanor and on conviction is punishable by a fine of not more than $5,000 or by confinement in the county jail for not more than one year, or both.

(b) If a person fails to comply with a directive of the consumer protection division under Section 17.60 of this subchapter or with a civil investigative demand for documentary material served on him under Section 17.61 of this subchapter, or if satisfactory copying or reproduction of the material cannot be done and the person refuses to surrender the material, the consumer protection division may file in the district court in the county in which the person resides, is found, or transacts business, and serve on the person, a petition for an order of the court for enforcement of Sections 17.60 and 17.61 of this subchapter. If the person transacts business in more than one county, the petition shall be filed in the county in which the person maintains his principal place of business, or in another county agreed on by the parties to the petition.

(c) When a petition is filed in the district court in any county under this section, the court shall have jurisdiction to hear and determine the matter presented and to enter any order required to carry into effect the provisions of Sections 17.60 and 17.61 of this subchapter. Any final order entered is subject to appeal to the Texas Supreme Court. Failure to comply with any final order entered under this section is punishable by contempt.

Added by Acts 1973, 63rd Leg., p. 322, ch. 143, § 1, eff. May 21, 1973.

Derivation:

Acts 1969, 61st Leg., p. 1504, ch. 452, § 1.
Vernon's Ann.Civ.St. art. 5069—10.08.

1. In general

In action for civil penalties against credit bureau in potential amount of $70,000 for alleged violation of injunction against deceptive practices, credit bureau was entitled to jury trial on fact issues relating to whether credit bureau had knowingly violated the injunction and, if so, the amount of penalty to be assessed. Credit Bureau of Laredo, Inc. v. State (Civ.App.1974) 515 S.W.2d 706, affirmed 530 S.W.2d 288.

§ 17.63. Application

The provisions of this subchapter apply only to acts or practices occurring after the effective date of this subchapter, except a right of action or power granted to the attorney general under Chapter 10, Title 79, Revised Civil Statutes of Texas, 1925, as amended,[1] prior to the effective date of this subchapter.

INDEX AND GLOSSARY

Abstract of judgment: a document filed for record pursuant to a judgment by a court of competent jurisdiction which creates a lien on all of the judgment debtor's real estate in that county, 263

Abstract of title: a summary or digest of all recorded documents affecting title to a particular piece of property. Also defined as a history of title as shown by recorded instruments arranged in order of recording, 187

Accelerated depreciation, 334

Acceptance: the act of a person to whom a thing is offered or tendered by another, whereby he receives the thing with the intention of retaining it—such intention being evidenced by a sufficient act, 106

Acknowledgment: a formal declaration before authorized officials by a person who executed an instrument, that it is his free act and deed, 169, 188

Actual notice: a notice expressly and actually given or such as he is presumed to have received personally because of the evidence within his knowledge was sufficient to put him upon inquiry, 186

Ad valorem taxes: real estate taxes levied in an amount determined according to the value of the real estate, 180, 327

Adaptation: the manner in which certain items of personalty are conformed to or made especially for a parcel of real estate, 55

Additional property clause: provision in a mortgage instrument providing for the mortgage to serve as additional security for any additional property to be acquired which will be attached to the real estate, 219

Adjusted basis: the original basis plus the cost of capital improvements less any allowance for depreciation, 339

Administrator: a representative, appointed by a court and not by a will, whose duties are to collect assets of the estate, pay its debts, and distribute residue to those entitled, 177

Adverse possession: an actual and visual appropriation of the land, commencing and continued under a claim of right inconsistent with and hostile to the claim of another, 173

Affidavit: a written or printed declaration or statement of facts, made voluntarily, and confirmed by the oath or affirmation of the party making it, taken before an officer having authority to administer such an oath, 264

After-Acquired Title Doctrine: a doctrine under which title acquired by a grantor who previously attempted to convey title to land which he did not in fact own, inures automatically to the benefit of prior grantees, 149, 169

Agent: One who acts for or in the place of another by authority from the other party, 88, 94

Air rights: the rights of one to that fluid transparent substance which surrounds our globe, 21, 22

Annexation: as applied to fixtures, the manner in which the fixtures are attached to the real estate, 55

Annual percentage rate: a term derived from the Truth-in-Lending Act that represents the relationship of the total finance charge to the amount of loan, expressed as a percentage, 226

Antitrust laws: federal and state laws prohibiting monopolies and restraint of trade, 99

Apartment: in condominium housing, an enclosed space consisting of one or more rooms occupying all or part of a floor in a building of one or more floors or stores regardless of whether it be designed for a residence, or an office, for the operation of any industry, business, or for any type of independent use, provided it has a direct exit to a thoroughfare or to a given space leading to a thoroughfare, 292

Assessed value: the value the assessor and collector of taxes gives to a parcel of real property which may be a percentage of or the same as the fair market value of the property. The tax rate is the amount of dollars per hundred that the landowner must pay in ad valorem taxes as determined by the local taxing authority, 329

Assignee: a person to whom an assignment is made, 285

Assignment: the transfer or making over to another any estate or right in property whether real or personal, 140, 285

Assignment of rentals, 214

Assignor: a person who assigns a right, whether or not he is the original owner thereof, 285

Assumption of mortgage: the taking of title to property by a grantee wherein the grantee assumes primary liability for payment of an existing note secured by a mortgage or deed of trust and would be primarily liable for the amount of any deficiency, 219, 220

Attachment: the act or process of taking, apprehending, or seizing persons or property by virtue of a writ or other judicial order and bringing same into the custody of the court. This is often done to compel an appearance or furnish security for debt or costs to satisfy a judgment which a plaintiff may obtain, 7

Attorney's Title Insurance Company, 237

Bargain and sale deed: a deed purporting to convey real property, but without warranties, 149

Beneficiary: one for whose benefit a trust has been created, 47, 196

Bilateral contract: a contract in which both the contracting parties are bound to fulfill obligations reciprocally towards each other, 86

Bill of sale: instrument by which title to personalty is conveyed, 52

Board of adjustment: a board appointed by a local revenue body allowed to make special exceptions to the terms of the zoning ordinance in harmony with the general purpose and intent and in accordance with the general or specific rules therein contained. The board of adjust-

Board of adjustment (continued)
ment also serves as an appellate board for any person aggrieved by a previous zoning decision or decision of any administrative officer of the municipality, 319

Board of directors: the governing body of a corporation, 42

Borrower: the borrower of money, the mortgagor, 225

Broker (*defined*): *See* pages 75, 76, 77

Business homestead: a place or property used to exercise the calling of a business which is exempt from execution by force creditor by operation of the law, 25

Call clause: a clause often found in mortgages which provides for the secured note to be accelerated to maturity if the property is conveyed, 215

Capital asset: property which is not stock in trade (inventory) used in a trade or business of a kind subject to depreciation, as well as notes in accounts receivable acquired in the course of the trade or business, 339

Capital gains tax treatment: a special tax rate allowed by the Internal Revenue Code for profits on the sale of capital assets, 32, 334, 339

Cemetery lot: a lot in a cemetery, graveyard, or burial ground, 22

Certificate of limited partnership: a certificate which must be filed with the secretary of state that discloses certain facts concerning the limited partnership, 39

Chain of title: successive conveyances, or other forms of alienation, affecting a particular parcel of land, arranged consecutively, from the government or original source of title down to the present holder, 187

Chattel: an article of personal property; any species of property not amounting to a freehold or fee in land, 51, 56

Chattel mortgage: a mortgage on chattels, 56

Charges: in judicial parliaments, the instructions a judge gives to the jury, 8

Circuit court of civil appeals: the appellate court having jurisdiction in the federal court system to which appeals from the district court may be made, 7

Clayton Anti-trust Act: federal statute which specifically prohibits price discrimination, exclusive dealing arrangements, certain corporate acquisitions of stock and interlocking directorates, 99

Clean Air Act, 314

Closing, 140, 249

Coastal Zone Management Commission, 316

Color of title: in adverse possession, a consecutive chain of such transfers down to such person in possession, without being regular, as if one or more of the memorial or muniments be not registered, or not duly registered, or be only in writing, or such like defect as may not extend to or include the want of intrinsic fairness and honesty; or when a party in possession shall hold the same by certificate of head right, land warrant, or land scrip, with a chain of transfer down to him in possession, 173

Commissioner of the General Land Office, 183

Commitment fee: a fee paid to a lender to commit funds which would be advanced at a future date, 228

Common elements: generally includes all parts of the condominium project which are not reserved for a single or private use, 293, 294

Common law marriage: a marriage which becomes operative by operation of law rather than one of formal decree or ceremony, 29

Community property: property owned by husband and wife which is subject to joint management control and disposition, 3, 23, 27

Compensating balances, 230

Component depreciation, 339

Comprehensive plan: a long-term general plan for the physical development of the community, embodying information, judgments, and objectives collected and formulated by experts to serve as both a guiding and predicted force. Such development is the basis of a comprehensive plan from which zoning ordinances are passed in Texas, 318

Compulsory loan retirement, 231

Concurrent jurisdiction: The jurisdiction of several different courts each authorized to deal with the same subject matter, 5

Condemnation, 214

Condominium: the separate ownership of single units or apartments in a multiple unit structure or structures with common elements, 289, 290

Condominium Act, 292

Condominium project: a real estate condominium project; a plan or project whereby four or more apartments, rooms, office spaces, or other units in existing or proposed buildings or structures are offered or proposed to be offered for sale, 292

Consideration: inducement to a contract. The cause, motive, price, or impelling influence which induces a contracting party to enter into a contract, 106, 107

Constitutional liens: those liens which are established by the Constitution in the State of Texas, 269

Constructive notice: information or knowledge of a fact imputed by law to a person because he could have discovered that fact by proper diligence, 176, 186

Consumer: as defined by Texas statute, an individual, partnership, corporation, or governmental entity who seeks or acquires by purchase or lease any goods or services, 101

Contingent remainder: a remainder limited so as to depend upon an event or condition which may never happen or be performed until after termination of the preceding estate, 17

Contract: a promissory agreement between two or more persons that creates, modifies, or destroys a legal relation. An agreement upon sufficient consideration to do or not to do a particular thing, 105

Contract for deed: *see* installment land contract, 142

Contract zoning: an agreement by a governing body to enact a change in land use classification in exchange for certain concessions to be granted by the developer or applicant, 320

Contractual liens: liens which arise as a result from a contract between the parties, 269

Cooperative: a form of apartment ownership. Ownership of shares in a cooperative venture which entitles the owner to use, rent, or sell a specific apartment unit, 291, 303

Co-owner: a person, firm, corporation, partnership, association, trust or other legal entity or any combination thereof, who owns an apartment or apartments within the condominium project, 299

Corporate charter: the official document indicating the existence of the corporation as authorized by the secretary of state, 42

Corporation: an artifical person or legal entity created by or under the authority of the laws of the state in which it is incorporated, 33, 42

Corpus: trust assets, the body of a trust, 47

Council of co-owners: all of the co-owners of a condominium project, 299

County courts: courts whose jurisdiction is in the county in which it is situated but has a ceiling on the dollar amount which can be litigated within its jurisdiction, 7

Courthouse door: a notice given regarding a sale under a deed of trust of a certain property; at any of several entrances to the building provided for holding of district court, 213

Courts of civil appeals: in Texas, the level of courts above the district courts which have only appellate jurisdiction, that is, they can only hear cases which have been previously tried in a district court, 7

Covenant against encumbrances: a covenant in a deed which provides that such estate is at the time of the execution of such conveyance free from encumbrances, 148

Covenant of seizin: a covenant in a deed which provides that previous to the time of execution of said conveyance, the grantor has not conveyed the same estate, or any right, title, or interest therein, to any person other than the grantee, 148

Curtesy: the estate to which a man is entitled upon the death of his wife to the lands which she seised in possession in fee during her marriage. It is a freehold estate for the term of his natural life, 30

Deceptive Trade Practices—Consumer Protection Act, 93, 94, 100, 280, 281

Declaration: *see* master deed, 295

Declining balance method of depreciation, 334, 336

Deed of trust: in Texas, a three party mortgage wherein the mortgagor conveys the property in trust to a trustee as security for a debt owing the beneficiary (lender), 178, 195, 196, 215, 216

Deed restrictions: private covenants affecting the use of real estate which are enforced by the affected property owners or subdivision developer on purely contractual theory, 324

Delivery: the final and absolute transfer of a deed, properly executed, to the grantee, or to some person for his use, in such manner that it cannot be recalled by the grantor, 167, 283

Department of Housing and Urban Development, 311

Department of Justice, 99

Depreciation: a provision in the Internal Revenue Code which allows for a loss of value of an asset for tax purposes, 38, 334

Derivative claimants: a claimant claiming a right or interest in real estate other than the original contracting party. This category includes subcontractor, mechanics and materialmen who perform services for an original contractor who, in turn, performs services for the owner, 264

Determinable fee: *see* fee on condition limitation, 18

District courts: in Texas, state courts whose jurisdiction is within a statutorily defined district which is generally larger than that of the county. Its jurisdiction is for the most part similar to that of county courts, but there is no dollar limit on the amount that can be litigated, 7

Doctrine of merger: a doctrine by which the earnest money contract in a real estate transaction is extinguished by absorption into the deed or other instruments passed at closing, 166

Dominant estate: an estate to which a servitude or easement is attached, 67

Dower: a species of life estate which a woman is by law entitled to claim upon the death of her husband, also the lands of which he was seised and fee issued during the marriage and any that might possibly have been inherited, 30

Dragnet clause: a clause which secures all items of indebtedness of a mortgagor that shall at any time be owing to the mortgagee, 219

Due process of law: law in its regular course of administration through courts of justice, 275

Earnest money: a down payment made by a purchaser of real estate as evidence of good faith, 138

Earnest money contract: a contract for the sale or purchase of real estate in which the purchaser is required to tender earnest money to evidence his good faith in completing contractual obligations, 110

Easement: a privilege, service or convenience which one has in the property of another, 15, 51, 66, 295

Easement appurtenant: an easement which is attached to and belongs to a dominant estate which passes incident to it, being incapable of existence separate and apart from that dominant estate to which it is annexed, 67

Easement by implication: an easement that is imposed by a court in the form of an equitable remedy to provide access to a lanulocked parcel of real estate, 68

Easement in gross: a more personal interest in and right to use the land of another, it is not a pertinent to any estate in land, 67

Eminent domain: the power to take private property for public use, 172, 309

Employee: one who works for an employer who has the right to control and direct the employee as to the details and means by which a result is to be accomplished, 95

Encumbrance: a claim, lien, charge or liability attached to and binding on real property, 15

Entailments: a limitation by which property is different from the course which it would take if the creator of the

Entailments: (continued)
entailment would have allowed the general succession to his heirs in accordance with law. The creator of an entailment normally limits or abridges the fee to certain classes of issue instead of to all his descendents generally, 14

Environmental Protection Agency, 314

Eo instanti: Latin term meaning "immediately", 18

Equal Credit Opportunity Act, 313

Equitable lien: a lien that exists in equity. It is a mere floating and ineffective equity until such time as a judgment or decree is rendered actually subjecting property to the payment of the debt or claim, 261

Equitable maxim: generally accepted statement of equitable rules which are considered to be conclusions of common sense and reason, 6

Equitable title: the beneficial interest of one person in real property although legal title is vested in another, 14, 15

Equity: a doctrine of fairness and honesty between two persons whose rights or claims are in conflict, 5

Equity courts: courts which administer justice according to a system of equity, 5

Equity of redemption: right of the mortgagor of an estate to redeem the same after it has been forfeited, at law, by a breach of the condition of the mortgage, upon paying the amount of debt, interest and costs, 180, 214

Equity participation, 231

Escheat: a reversion of property to the state when the owner dies leaving no heirs and no will providing for the disposition of the real estate, 180, 309

Escrow: the deposit of instruments and/or funds with instruction to a third party to carry out the provisions of an agreement or contract, 249, 250

Estate at sufferance: one that comes into the possession of land by lawful title but holds over by wrong after the termination of his interest, 272

Estate at will: one who holds possession of premises by permission of owner or landlord, but without a fixed term, 272

Estate for years: an estate for one who has a temporary use and possession for lands and tenements not his own, by virtue of a lease or demise granted to him by the owner, for a determinate period of time, as for a year or a fixed number of years, 272

Estate from period to period: a tenancy in which one holds lands or tenements under the demise of another where no certain term has been mentioned but a periodic rental has been reserved, normally a rental from year to year or semi-annually, which may be automatically renewed at the end of the term, 272

Estate in land: the degree, quality, nature and extent of interest that a person has in real property, 13

Estoppel: an inconsistent position, attitude, or course of conduct that may not be adopted to the loss or injury of another, 68, 69

Eviction: the act of depriving a person of a possession of land which he has held pursuant to the judgment of the court of competent jurisdiction, 7, 286

Exceptions, 170

Exclusionary zoning, 321

Exclusive agency to sell listing: a contract giving one agent the right to sell property for a specified time, but reserving the right of the owner to sell the property himself without the payment of the commission, 85

Exclusive right to sepulture: exclusive right of interment of a dead human body, 22

Executed contract: one where nothing remains to be done by either party and where the transaction is completed at the moment when the arrangement is made, as where an article is sold and delivered, and payment therefore is made on the spot, 142

Execution: a legal order directing an official to enforce a judgment against the property of a debtor, normally through a "writ of execution," 157, 212

Executor: a person appointed by a testator to carry out the directions and requests in his will and dispose of the property according to his testamentary provisions after the testator's deceased, 178

Executory contract: a contract where some future act is to be done, 142

Extraterritorial jurisdiction: the unincorporated area, not a part of any other city, that is contiguous to the corporate limits to the city, 321

Fair Credit Reporting Act, 313

Federal Consumer Credit Protection Act, 225

Federal district courts: courts of the United States each having a territorial jurisdiction over a district which may include a whole state or only a part of that state, 7

Federal Home Loan Mortgage Corporation, 312

Federal Housing Administration, 228, 311

Federal Insurance Administration, 312

Federal National Mortgage Association, 312

Federal questions: a case arising under the Constitution of the United States, Acts of Congress, or treaties involving an interpretation and application. The jurisdiction of federal questions is given to the federal courts, 8

Federal Reserve Board, 95

Federal Reserve System, 226

Federal Trade Commission, 99, 313

Federal Truth-in-Lending Act (T-i-L Act): a federal statute which requires disclosure of specific loan information to the borrower before the obligation becomes effective, 95, 225, 256, 313

Fee on condition limitation (determinable fee)**:** an estate created with a special limitation which limits the duration of the estate in land, 18

Fee on condition precedent: an estate which calls for a happening of some event or the performance of some act before the terms of the fee shall vest in the claimant. It differs from the fee on condition subsequent in that the condition subsequent is annexed to an estate already vested, 18

Fee on condition subsequent: a fee estate that is to commence or terminate on some specified condition, 18

Fee simple defeasible: *see* fee on conditional limitation, 18

Fee simple determinable: *see* fee on conditional limitation, 18

Fee simple estate: one in which the owner is entitled to the entire property with unconditional power or disposition during his life time in descending to his heirs and legal representatives upon his death intestate, 15, 295
FHA: *see* Federal Housing Administration
Fiduciary: a person holding the character of a trustee in respect to the trust and confidence involved in his relationship with another, 37, 48
Fifth Circuit Court of Appeals, 8
Finance charge: the total of all costs imposed, directly or indirectly, by the creditor payable either directly or indirectly by the borrower or by another party on behalf of the borrower as an incident to the granting of credit, 225, 226
Financing statement: evidence of indebtedness secured by chattel and filed of record in the county courthouse or secretary of state's office, 57
Fixture: an item of personalty which has been attached to real estate such that it becomes real estate, 51
Fixture filing: financing statement evidencing the fact that the chattel is or is to become fixtures, 57
Flood Disaster Control Act of 1973, 313
Forcible entry and detainer: a proceeding for restoring the possession of the land to one who has been wrongfully deprived of the possession, 7, 271, 286
Foreclosure: the process of taking or selling the property of another to satisfy debt, 213
Four corners doctrine: a doctrine establishing that an instrument is to be examined by reading the whole of it without reference to any one part more than any other, 108
Freehold estate: an estate in land or other real property of certain duration that may be inherited. It is an estate for life or in fee, 13
Future advance clause: *see* dragnet clause, 219
Future interest: interest in land in which the privilege of possession or enjoyment is future and not present, 16

General agency: an agency relationship by which one is empowered to transact all business or principal at any particular time or particular place, a general manager. A general agent does have the power to bind his principal, 88
General common elements: *see* common elements, 293
General Land Office, 316
General partnerships: *see* partnership, 36
General warranty deed: a deed in which the grantor warrants or guarantees the title to real property against defects existing before the grantor acquired title or arising during the grantor's ownership, 148
Government National Mortgage Association, 312
Grantee: one to whom a grant is made, 167
Grantor: the person by whom a grant is made, 167, 196
Gross lease: a lease of property under the terms of which the landlord pays all property charges regularly incurred through ownership. The tenant pays a fixed charge for the term of the lease, 283
Ground lease: lease of land only, sometimes secured by the improvements placed on the land by the user, 285

Habitability, warranty of: guarantee that premises occupied by a tenant are habitable. The definition of habitable is a fact question and is determined by the jury, 281
Holographic will: a will wholly in the writing of the testator, 171
Home Mortgage Disclosure Act, 313
Homestead: a legal estate which is a place of residence for a family or a single adult person which is exempt from sale by creditors except under certain specified conditions, 3, 23
Houston-Galveston Area Council, 316
HUD-1 form, 257

Illinois Land Trust, *see* land trust, 48
Incorporeal hereditaments: anything, the subject of property, which is inheritable and not tangible or visible, 66
Independent contractor: one who exercising independent employment, contracts to do a piece of work according to his own methods and without being subject to the control of his employer except as to the result of the work, 95
Installment land contract: an executory contract for the sale of real estate which usually lasts for a term of years. It is also known as a contract for deed, 142
Installment sale benefits: provision in the Internal Revenue Code by which the profit on the sale of one's capital asset can be spread over a series of years, provided that there is less than 30 percent of the income received during the first year of the sale, 38, 334, 340
Inter vivos trusts: a trust that is established during the lifetime of the trustor, 46, 47
Interest: the compensation allowed by law for the use, forbearance or detention of money, 225, 226
Interlineations: the act of writing between the lines of an instrument; also what is written between lines, 108
Internal Revenue Code: body of laws which codify and delineate the living, collecting and enforcing of federal tax laws, 44, 47
Internal Revenue Service, 41, 45, 97, 218, 334
Interstate: transaction and proceedings that take place between and among the several states, 176
Interstate Land Sales Full Disclosure Act, 311
Interval ownership condominiums: ownership of a condominium by exclusive fee title for a period in which the owner is entitled to possession. Unlike time sharing condominiums, the fee title only vests for a period of time and does not change from year to year, 302
Intestate: one who dies without leaving a will, 3
Intrastate: alludes to procedures and transactions which take place entirely within the boundaries of a particular state, 3
Irreparable harm: harm or injury that exists such that no pecuniary standard exists for the measurement of damages, in forwards, the claimant can receive reasonable recovery in a court of law, 6

Joint adventure: *see* joint venture, 38
Joint tenancy: an estate held by two or more persons hav-

Joint tenancy: (continued)
ing one and the same interest which includes a right of survivorship; the entire tenancy on the decease of any of the joint tenants remains to the survivors and, ultimately, fee will vest in the last survivor, 33

Joint ventures: an association of two or more persons to carry out a single business enterprise for a profit which is limited in its scope and duration, 36

Judge: an officer who presides over the court, 8

Judgment liens: a lien created pursuant to a court judgment, and perfected by filing an abstract of judgment in the appropriate county of records, 262

Jury: a number of people, selected according to the law to inquire of certain matters of fact and declare the truth upon evidence to be laid before them, 8

Justice of the peace court: in Texas, a court administered by the justice of the peace; a judicial officer having a very limited jurisdiction, 7, 287

Landlord: he who being the owner of an estate in land, has leased it for a term of years, on a rent reserve, to another person called the tenant, 271

Land trusts: a trust created solely for the ownership, operation, and management of real estate interests, 46

Lateral severance, 19, 21

Lease: any agreement that gives rise to relationship of landlord and tenant. A contract for the exclusive possession of lands or tenements for a determinative period, 282

Leasehold estate: an estate in realty held under a lease which is an estate for a fixed term of years or shorter duration, 13, 271

Legal description: a description recognized by law which is sufficient to locate and identify property without oral testimony, 111, 168

Legal estates: estates which vest in a person due to statute rather than common law, right, possession or conveyancing instrument, 13

Legal title: one that is complete and perfect in regard to the apparent right of ownership and possession enforceable in a court of law, 14

Lender: the lender of money, the mortgagee, 225

Lessee: *see* tenant, 271

Lessor: *see* landlord, 271

Lien: a claim or charge on a property for the payment of some debt, obligation or duty owed to lien holder, 15, 261

Lien theory, 14

Life estate: an estate whose duration is limited to the life of the party holding it or some other person, 16

Limited common elements: those common elements which are agreed upon by all of the co-owners to be reserved for the use of a certain number of apartments to the exclusion of the other apartments, such as special corridors, stairways and elevators, sanitary services common to the apartments of a particular floor, etc., 293

Limited partners: a different class of partners provided for in a limited partnership which allows for no liability to third parties provided they remain passive investors and never assume the role of general partners, 39

Limited partnership: a partnership formed by two or more persons under the provision of the Uniform Limited Partnership Act and having as members one or more general partners and one or more limited partners, 33, 36, 39

Limited partnership agreement: the agreement which sets forth the details and agreements of the general limited partners to a limited partnership agreement, 39

Liquidated damages: a sum agreed upon by the parties to be full damages if an event of default occurs, 141

Listing agreement: a contract authorizing a broker to sell, buy, or lease, real property on behalf of another, and giving the agent the right to collect a commission if the property is sold through his efforts, 79

Loan brokerage fees: fees paid to a mortgage broker for locating and obtaining funds for a borrower, 228

Loan closing, 250

Massachusetts Business Trust: a business organization where a property is conveyed to trustees and managed for the benefit of holders certificates by corporate stock certificates, 48

Master deed: the deed, lease or declaration establishing the property as a condominium regime, 295

Master lease: *see* master deed, 295

Matured interest: interest which is due and payable, 230

Mechanics or materialmen: individuals or companies who supply labor, services or materials for the construction of improvements on real estate, 263

Mechanics and materialmen's lien: lien provided both by statute and constitution for the protection of one who supplies labor or materials for the improvement of real estate, 3, 262, 263

Mineral interests: an interest in the minerals in land including the right to take minerals or the right to receive a royalty on those minerals, 19

Monopoly: a privilege vested in one or more persons or companies consisting of the exclusive right to carry on a particular business or trade, 14

Mortgage: an instrument by which real property is offered to secure the payment of a debt or obligation, 195, 216

Mortgagee: *see* lender, 225

Mortgagee's title policy, 239

Mortgagor: the person who executes a mortgage, usually pursuant to the borrowing of money, 225

Multiple listing: an agreement among brokers who belong to the Multiple Listing Service that all listings will be placed on a mutually available list, that all brokers may sell any property on the list, and that the commission will be split in a predetermined fashion, 86

Multiple listing service: *see* multiple listing, 99

Municipal court: in Texas, a court whose territorial authority is confined to the city or community in which it is designated. It is one of the courts of lower jurisdiction, 7

Municipal enforcement of deed restrictions, 325

National Flood Insurance Act, 312

National Land Use Planning Act, 315

Negotiable instrument: an instrument signed by a maker or drawer, containing an unconditional promise to pay a certain sum of money, which can be passed freely from one person to another. This is often reflected in a promissory note or bank draft, 215

Net lease: one in which the tenant pays some or all of the operating expenses, giving the owner a net amount of income, 284

Net listing: a listing where the owner receives a net price for the sale of his property; the broker's commission, if any, is the amount that exceeds the net figure, 85

No personal liability, 215

Nonconforming use: a previously existing use which is inconsistent with the current zoning designation, 321

Nonfreehold estate: a leasehold estate, 271

Notary public: an authority appointed by the secretary of state to take acknowledgment or proofs of written instruments, protest instruments permitted by law to be protested, administer oaths, and take depositions, as is now or may hereafter be conferred by law upon County Clerks, 190

Nuncupative will: an oral will declared or dictated by the testator in his last sickness before a sufficient number of witnesses which may pass on only personal property, 171

Offer: a proposal to make a contract, 106

Office of Interstate Land Sales Registration, 311

Official Public Records of Real Property, 187, 188

Old age exemption: an exemption provided in Texas which prohibits the sale of a homestead for taxes if one or more of the occupants is 65 years or older, 333

Open agency listing: an authorization given by a property owner to a real estate agent wherein the agent is given the non-exclusive right to secure a purchaser, 85

Oral earnest money contract, 111

Original basis: the original cost of an asset, 339

Original contractor: a contractor has the direct contractual relationship with the owner of the property or his agent, 263

Original jurisdiction: having jurisdiction to hear the case for the first time, before it is tried in any other court, or appealed, 7

Ostensible authority: such authority as a principal, intentionally or by want of ordinary care, causes or allows a third party to believe that the agent possesses, 94

Owner's title policy, 239

Parol evidence rule: a rule of procedure which provides that parol or extrinsic evidence is not admissible to add to, subtract from, vary or contradict judicial or official records or documents, or written instruments which dispose of property or are contractual in nature, and which are valid, complete, unambiguous and unaffected by accident or mistake, 109, 216

Partial releases, 214

Partial release fees: fee paid to the lender for a partial release of property which is secured by a note, 229

Partition: the dividing of lands held by joint tenants, tenants in common, or other joint ownership to distinct portions so that they may hold them in severalty, 35

Partner (general): a member of a co-partnership who has united with others to form a partnership business, 39

Partnership: an association of two or more persons to carry on as co-owners of a business for profit, 33, 36

Percentage lease: lease on property, the rental for which is determined by the amount of business done by the lessee; usually a percentage of gross receipts from the business with a provision for minimum rental, 283

Permanent Free School Fund, 183

Permanent lender, 219

Perpetual care fund: a fund provided for by statute for maintaining cemeteries which requires the creation of a fund which never ceases and is continuous for the maintenance of the cemetery or graveyard, 22

Perpetuities, 14

Personalty: articles associated with a person or belonging to an individual, being limited to the person, movable property, 20, 51, 56

Points: a point is one percent of the amount of a loan, paid to the lender or his agent at the time the loan is made, if required by the lender or agent, 228

Police power: a right of a government, either federal, state or local to regulate the use of real estate, 309

Power of sale: a provision normally impeded to a deed of trust which provides for a non-judicial foreclosure sale in the event of default by the mortgagor, 178, 196, 212

Prepayment penalty: a clause in a note which provides for a penalty in the event of an early pay-off of the note, 229

Prescription: (easement by) a mode of acquiring the right to use property by long continued enjoyment, at least for ten years, 68, 69

Price fixing: a conspiracy by two or more participants to fix prices, goods, or services, effectively eliminating competition in the marketplace, 100

Primogeniture: the exclusive right possessed by the eldest son of a family to succeed to the estate of his ancestor, exclusive of the rights of the other sons or children, 14

Principal: the employer of an agent, the person who gives authority to the agent or attorney to do some act for him, 88, 94

Privilege: an exceptional or extraordinary power of exemption. A right power, franchise, or immunity held by a person or class, against or beyond the course of the law. In liable or slander, an exemption from liability for the speaking or publishing of defamatory words concerning another, based on the fact that the statement was made in the performance of a duty, political, judicial, social, or personal, 188

Privity of contract: the connection or relationship which exists between two or more contracting parties, 265

Procuring cause: the cause originating a series of events, which, without breaking in their continuity, result in the accomplishment of the prime objective, 87

Promissory note: a promise or engagement, in writing, to pay specified sum at a time therein limited, or on demand, or at site, to a person therein named or to his order or bearer, 195

Proportionate Reduction Clause Formula, 244
Pur autre vie: for or during the life of another, 16

Quantum meruit: an action found at common law founded on the implied promise on the part of the defendant to pay the plaintiff as much as he reasonably deserved to have for his labor, 6
Quasi-contractual recovery: an obligation similar in character to that of a contract, which arises not from an express agreement of the parties, but rather from one that is implied by the court, 6
Quitclaim deed: a deed by which the grantor releases any interest he may have in real property. The deed makes no representation as to ownership or warranty, 160

Railroad Commission, 316
Real estate: a leasehold as well as any other interest or estate in land, whether incorporeal, corporeal, freehold or nonfreehold, and whether the real estate is situated in this state or elsewhere, 77
Real estate investment trusts: a trust set up primarily for the ownership, operation, and management of real estate which normally has many shareholders and is regulated through the Securities and Exchange Commission as well as the Texas Securities Board. It usually involves a very large amount of investors, 46, 49
Real Estate Licensing Act, 79, 138
Real estate lien note: a promissory note evidencing the payment thereof secured by a mortgage on real property, 195
Real Estate Settlement Procedures Act, 255
Realty: real property and anything which partakes of the nature of real property, 20
Recapture, 338
Recording Act, 185, 186
Redemption: a repurchase; a buying back. The process of cancelling and annulling a defeasible title to land such as created by a mortgage or a tax sale by paying the debt or fulfilling other conditions, 269, 331
Regulation X: federal regulations passed establishing guidelines for the Real Estate Settlement Procedures Act, 256
Regulation Z: federal regulations passed establishing guidelines for the federal Truth-in-Lending Act, 95, 226
Relation Back Doctrine, 251, 264
Release deed: an instrument executed by mortgagee or the trustee reconveying to the mortgagor the real estate which secured the mortgage loan after that has been paid in full, 216
Release of lien: an instrument indicating that a previously existing lien has been released and is no longer enforceable, 207
Remainder interest: an estate in land limited to take effect and be enjoyed after another estate has been terminated, 16, 17
Remainderman: one who is entitled to the remainder of the estate after a particular estate has expired, 16
Rescission: the annulling or unmaking of a contract, 6
Restitution: the act of restoring the situation to its status quo, or the equivalent thereof for any loss, damage or injury, 6
Retainage: a fund maintained by the owner, his agent, trustee, or receiver during the progress of construction or labor and service being performed by artisans and mechanics, 265
Reversionary interest: the residue of the estate—usually the fee left to the grantor and his heirs after the termination of a particular state which has been granted, 17
Right of reentry: the right to resume the possession of lands in pursuance of a right which a party reserved to himself when he gave up his former possession or interest, 18
Right of survivorship: right of one party to succeed the right of the other party upon that second party's death, 35
Royalty: a payment to the owner or lessor of property usually involving a share of the product or profit made on that product extracted from the grantor or lessor's property, 20
Rule Against Perpetuities: principle that no interest in property is good unless it must vest, if at all, no later than 18 years plus a period of justation after some life or lives in being at the time of the creation of the interest. This is a constitutional rule in Texas, 14, 47
Rule in Shelley's Case: a doctrine by which an ancestor takes an estate of freehold; in the same conveyance, the estate is limited to his heirs in fee or entail such that the estate is limited to only the heirs of that ancestor, 30
Rural homestead: a homestead which is not in an urban area and can consist more than 200 acres, 25

Sale lease-back: a situation where the owner of a piece of property wishes to sell the property and retain occupancy by leasing it from the buyer, 216, 217
Salesman: (defined, *see* 75), 76
Securities and Exchange Commission: agency of the government which oversees and passes rules and regulations in furtherance of the Securities and Exchange Acts of 1933 and 1934, 2, 41, 49
Security and Exchange Commission: Agency of the government which oversees and passes rules and regulations in furtherance of the Securities and Exchange Acts of 1933 and 1934, 2, 41, 49
Second lien: a lien or encumbrance which ranks second, right behind the first lien, mortgage or encumbrance, 213, 214
Secretary of state: in Texas, an executive officer who performs, in addition to other functions, the maintaining of all official records for the State of Texas and companies doing business in the State of Texas, 39, 41, 43, 57
Security: a bond, note, certificate of indebtedness, or other negotiable or transferable instrument evidencing debt or ownership, 95
Security agreement: a form of chattel mortgage commonly used in Texas, 57
Separate property: in Texas, property acquired before

Separate property: (continued)
marriage or acquired by gift, devise or descent after marriage, 22, 28
Sequestration: a writ authorizing the taking into custody of the law of the real and personal estate of a defendant who is in contempt and holding the same until he shall comply with the order of the court, 7
Servient estate: an estate encumbered by an easement or servitude which is reserved for the use of another, 67
Severable improvements: those improvements which cannot be removed without material injury to the real estate, 267, 268
Severalty: an estate that is held by a person in his own right without any other person being joined or connected with him, 33
Shareholder: one who owns shares in a corporation, 42
Sheriff's deed: typically, a deed executed by a sheriff pursuant to a writ of execution or at a foreclosure sale, 157
Sherman Anti-trust Act: federal law which condemns contracts, culmintion and conspiracies in restraint of trade and monopolizing, attempts to monopolize and combinations and conspiracies to monopolize trade, 99
Shifting executory use: a use which is so limited that it will be made to shift or transfer itself from beneficiary to another upon the occurrence of a certain event after its creation. *See* contingent remainder, 17
Sole control community property: community property which is subject to the sole control, management, disposition, of a single spouse which maintains all of its characteristics of community property, 28
Special agency: an agency relationship by which one is employed to conduct a particular transaction or a piece of business for his principal or authorized to perform a specified act but does not have the power to bind his principal, 88
Special exceptions: a use that is permitted within a certain zoning designation, but subject to control and supervision of the municipal authority, 319
Special warranty deed: a deed in which the grantor warrants or guarantees the title only against defects arising during his ownership of the property and not against defects existing before the time of his ownership, 148
Specific performance: performance of a contract in a specific form in which it was made and according to the precise terms agreed upon, 6, 141
Spot zoning, 320
Springing executory use: a use limited to arise on future event in which no preceding use is limited. It does not take effect in derogation of any interest of the grantor, and remains in the grantor in the meantime. *See* fee on condition precedent, 19
State Bar of Texas, 98, 111
State Board of Insurance, 239
Statement of Principles, 98
Statute of frauds: Texas statute that provides that no suit or action shall be maintained on certain classes of contracts unless there shall be a note or memorandum thereof in writing and signed by the party to be charged or by his authorized agent. Its object is to close the door to the numerous frauds and perjuries, 105, 111, 272
Straight line method of depreciation, 335
Subagent: an agent appointed by one who is himself an agent, or a person employed by an agent to assist him in transacting the affairs of his principal, 88
Subchapter S corporation: a regular Texas corporation which is elected certain tax benefits through Subchapter S of the Internal Revenue Code, 46
Subcontractor: a contractor who has a direct contractual relationship, and works under, an original contractor. He has no direct contractual relationship with the owner of the property or his agent, 263
Subject to: when a grantee takes title to real property "subject to" a mortgage, he is not responsible to the holder of the promissory note for the payment of any portion of the amount due, 219, 220
Sublease: a lease given by a lessee to a sublessee for a part of the premises or for a period of time less then the remaining term of the lessee's original lease, 285
Subrogation: the substitution of one person in the place of another with reference to a lawful claim, demand, or right, 214
Subsurface rights: rights of the owner to use land below the mere surface use, 19
Sum of the years digits method of depreciation, 335
Supreme Court of the United States: the highest court to which any case can be appealed in the United States, 7, 8
Surface rights: the rights of the owner to use the surface estate of his property, 21

"Taking" issue, 320
Tax deferred exchange: provision in tax law that allows for the exchange of "like kind" property, 38, 45, 334
Tax free exchange: *see* tax deferred exchange
Tax rate, 329
Tax sales: sales made pursuant to state law to satisfy a debt created by delinquent taxes, 180
Tenancy: the estate of a tenant whether it be in fee, for life, for years, at will, or otherwise, 271
Tenancy by the entireties: an estate created by the conveyance to husband and wife whereupon each becomes seised and possessed to the entire estate. After the death of one the other survivor takes the whole. It may be terminated only by a joint action of husband and wife during their lives, 35
Tenancy in common: an estate where property is held by several indivisible titles by entity of possession, 33, 34, 36, 294
Tenant: one who has the temporary use and occupation of real property owned by another person, (called the "landlord"). The duration and terms of his tenancy usually are fixed by law or by instrument called a lease, 271
Testator: one who makes a testament or will, 170

Texas Business and Commerce Code: Texas' adaptation of the Uniform Commercial Code, 52, 56, 93, 105
Texas Business Corporation Act: body of Texas law pertaining to corporations generally, 43
Texas Constitution: the most fundamental body of law in the State of Texas. It serves the same function for Texas as the U. S. Constitution serves for the United States, 3, 14, 23, 44
Texas Court of Civil Appeals, 10
Texas Highway Commission, 316
Texas Insurance Code, 101, 237, 255
Texas Miscellaneous Corporation Laws Act: body of laws in Texas which govern certain unique enterprises of corporations, 43
Texas Parks and Wildlife Department, 316
Texas Real Estate Commission: the official agency in Texas for administering rules and regulations that govern real estate licensing, 75, 76, 98, 110
Texas Real Estate Investment Trust Act: body of laws in Texas which govern the operation of real estate investment trusts, 49
Texas Real Estate Licensing Act, 75, 79, 98, 99, 111, 138
Texas Recording Act, 143
Texas State Securities Board: a board established by the State of Texas to monitor and regulate securities being sold within the State of Texas, 41
Texas Supreme Court: the highest court in the State of Texas to which any point of law or case can be appealed, 7, 9, 10, 35, 93, 101, 230, 281
Texas Trust Act: body of laws which govern trusts generally in the State of Texas, 47
Texas Uniform Partnership Act, 36, 37, 38
Texas Water Development Board, 316
Texas Water Rights Commission, 316
Time sharing condominiums: condominiums which are owned among several co-tenants who have the right by contractual agreement with each other, to use the condominium only for a certain time period (usually from two to four weeks). This time period may change from year to year depending upon the arrangement of the co-tenants' contractual agreement, 302
Title: evidence of ownership; or in adverse possession, a regular chain of transfers from or under the sovereignty of the soil, 173
Title insurance: a title indemnifying an owner or mortgage against loss by reason of defects in the title to a parcel of real estate; except for the encumbrances, defects that are specifically excluded by the policy, 238
Torrens system: a method of evidencing title by registration, after a court decree, with a proper public official called the Registrar of Titles, 235
Trade fixtures: such chattels as merchants usually possess and annex to the premises occupied by them to enable them to store, handle, and display their goods, which are generally removable without material injury to the premises, 66
Tri-party agreements: agreements to loan money involving the construction, financing, lender, the permanent lender and the borrower. Each promise to undertake a certain phase of financing a construction project, 219
Trust: a right of property held by one party for the benefit of another, 46
Trustee: a person appointed or required by law to execute a trust. This also includes one in whom an estate and power is invested under an express or written agreement to administer or exercise for the benefit or use of another, 47, 196
Trustee's deed: typically, a deed executed by a trustee at a foreclosure sale, 157
Trustor: individual who establishes the trust, also known as the settlor, 47
Turn around sales, 231

UCC liens: liens which are permitted to be established against real property pursuant to terms of the Uniform Commercial Code or Texas Business and Commerce Code, 56, 57
Unconscionable bargain: a bargain which no man in his right senses would make and which no fair and honest man would accept because of unfairness to the other, 6
Uniform Commercial Code: body of laws which applies to every state with some variations in each state that govern trade and commerce generally, 52
Unilateral contract: one in which one party makes an express arrangement or undertakes a performance without receiving in return any express engagement, or promise or performance from the other, 86
U.S. Code Annotated: volumes which contain the annotated federal statutes, rulings, decisions rendered, and positions taken by governmental agencies, interpreting laws and regulations under their jurisdictions, 4
U.S. Congress, 45
U.S. Constitution, 2, 3
Unity of possession: joint possession of two or more rights by several titles, 34
Unjust enrichment: the doctrine that persons shall not be allowed to profit or enrich themselves inequitably at another's expense, 6
Urban homestead: a homestead in an urban area which can consist of a lot or lots not to exceed $10,000 in value at the time of designation, 26
Usury: the reserving and taking, or contracting to reserve and take, a greater sum for the use of money than Texas statute currently allows, 222, 228

Variance: a use that literally violates the terms of the zoning ordinance but is permitted to stand because an otherwise unnecessary hardship would be created for the owner of a property, 319

Vendor's lien: a lien implied to belong to a vendor for the unpaid purchase price of the land, 262

Venue: at law, a county or jurisdiction in which an actual prosecution is brought for trial, and which is to furnish a panel of jurors. Also, it relates to the territory within which a matter has jurisdiction to be performed or completed, 190

Vernon's Annoted Texas Statutes: the volumes which embody the laws of the State of Texas, 4

Vested remainder: a remainderman whose estate is invariably fixed to remain to that determined person after the prior state has expired, 17

Veterans Administration, 228

Witnessed will: a formal will that is normally prepared by an attorney and properly witnessed according to statute, 170

Wraparound mortgage: a mortgage encompassing previously existing mortgages and is subordinate to them. The existing mortgages remain on the property and the wraparound assumes an inferior position to those mortgages, 220

Writ of execution: a writ to put in force the judgment or decree of a court, 7

Writ of restitution: a writ issued by a court of competent jurisdiction commanding a sheriff to restore the premises to the true owner, 287